Survival of a
Perverse Nation

TAMAR R. SHIRINIAN

Survival of a Perverse Nation

Morality and Queer Possibility in Armenia

DUKE UNIVERSITY PRESS · DURHAM AND LONDON · 2024

© 2024 DUKE UNIVERSITY PRESS
All rights reserved
Printed in the United States of America on acid-free paper ∞
Project Editor: Ihsan Taylor
Designed by Matthew Tauch
Typeset in Portrait Text and Unbounded by
Copperline Book Services

Library of Congress Cataloging-in-Publication Data
Names: Shirinian, Tamar, [date] author.
Title: Survival of a perverse nation : morality and queer possibility
in Armenia / Tamar R. Shirinian.
Description: Durham : Duke University Press, 2024. | Includes
bibliographical references and index.
Identifiers: LCCN 2024003312 (print)
LCCN 2024003313 (ebook)
ISBN 9781478031116 (paperback)
ISBN 9781478026877 (hardcover)
ISBN 9781478060109 (ebook)
Subjects: LCSH: Political culture—Armenia (Republic) | Post-communism—
Economic aspects—Armenia (Republic) | Armenian Genocide, 1915–1923—
Influence. | Homophobia—Political aspects—Armenia (Republic) |
Capitalism—Moral and ethical aspects. | Queer theory. | Armenia
(Republic)—Politics and government—1991- | Armenia (Republic)—
Economic conditions. | BISAC: SOCIAL SCIENCE / Anthropology / General |
PHILOSOPHY / Movements / Critical Theory
Classification: LCC JQ1759.3.A91 S55 2024 (print) | LCC JQ1759.3.A91 (ebook) |
DDC 306.7601094756—dc23/eng/20240802
LC record available at https://lccn.loc.gov/2024003312
LC ebook record available at https://lccn.loc.gov/2024003313

Cover art: lusine talalyan, *փաստաթուղթ (document)*, 2021.
Photo, illustration. Courtesy of the artist.

For Diane

Contents

Acknowledgments

Thinking is a collaborative art, and so too is this book a product of years of thinking and rethinking, layered with various sorts of professional, political, aesthetic, and life-making collaboration. To acknowledge these, I will begin with the obvious collaboration that is clearly visible throughout the book: my work with Lucine Talalyan. Lucine, you became a real partner in this work, always ready to think with me and always willing to invite me to think with you. My thoughts—in their style, aesthetic, and affect—have been deeply shaped by these collaborations. I thank you for embarking with me on much of the research that led to the writing of these pages—literally taking the journeys with me on buses, metros, *marshrutkas*, and by foot—but also for bringing to me the gift of co-creative practice. While many contributed to this book, please know that this is also one of our co-creations.

The research for this ethnographic undertaking would not have been possible without the groups and organizations that invited me to take part in their work, their activities, and their social worlds. These include official nongovernmental organizations at which I interned in order to understand the labor behind transforming social values—Public Information and Need for Knowledge (PINK) and Women's Resource Center (WRC)—as well as the many initiatives and groups that were more organically formed and that invited me to take part in making and remaking worlds—Queering Yerevan Collective, the Redefining March 8 Initiative, and the Armenian Environmental Front. Within and between these groups—the larger rhizomatic formation that I call the grassroots political in Armenia—were many who offered up their time, effort, labor, hospitality, compassion, and joy to make my research, my living, my thinking, and my thriving possible. On no hierarchical scale I express gratitude to Mamikon Hovsepyan, Marine Margaryan, Nvard Margaryan, Kolya Hovhannisyan, Nelli Arakelyan, Lusine Saghumyan, Lara Aharonian, Gohar Shahnazaryan, Elvira Meliksetyan, Shushan Avagyan, Aré Martirossian, Ruzanna Grigoryan, Kara Aghajanyan, Anna Shahnazaryan, Arthur Grigoryan, Arpineh Galfayan, Yuri Manvelyan, Karen Hakobyan, Tigran Amiryan, Ani Baghumyan, and Tsomak Oganezova. Mika Danielyan, who will unfortunately not be able to read these acknowledgments, was always willing to talk, share his perspective, and provide solidarity for which I will always remember him.

Ethnographic research, as I tell my students, requires that one's whole person enter the encounter. For this to be possible, the field site cannot be separated into another domain—an "out there" separate from what constitutes the ethnographer's own personhood. The "field" becomes a part of how the ethnographer is a person in the world and the context in which she lives. It has been friendship that has made my life in the field as I conducted research for this book—as well as my life far beyond the field and into my everyday "here," back "home"—livable. Deep gratitude is owed to those who engaged with me, not just as friends but as comrades. Ani Petrosyan and Hrach Khachatryan became the reasons I felt I could and should return to Yerevan and made it possible that I had a field site, and that this world would become a part of me, and I part of it. Gratitude is also owed to Lusine Mooradian, Edgar Mkrtichyan, Meri Yeranosyan, and Lilia Khachatryan for opening up to me and allowing me to be open with you; and to Harout Simonyan and Qnar Khudoyan, who are always inspiring. Lala Aslikyan, Zara Harutuinian, Lucine Talalyan, and especially Lusine Sargsyan: you all are my home in many respects (here, there, anywhere), and because of you, coming to Armenia feels like a coming home. I hope that you see the moves I make in this book—and especially in any boldness, fierceness, and willingness to take the risks toward the making of new worlds—as borrowed energy from you.

The intellectual spaces in which the thinking and writing of this book took place have been many, and here I have the space to acknowledge only a few of the most critical. The Duke Department of Cultural Anthropology and the Program in Gender, Sexuality, and Feminist Studies nurtured the very beginnings of the framework and articulation of this book. Robin Wesolowski, Louise Meintjes, Charles Piot, Rebecca Stein, Lorien Olive, Samuel Shearer, Can Evren, Jatin Dua, Jennifer Bowles, and Saikat Maitra were parts of crucial reading and writing groups; the Women's Studies Colloquium provided a home for intellectual exchange and growth; and Alyssa Miller, Yektan Türkyilmaz, Jake Silver, Zach Levine, Rachel Greenspan, Leigh Campoamor, Netta Van Vliet, Cheryl Spinner, Sinan Goknur, and Dwayne Dixon formed a larger constellation of intellectual camaraderie. Special gratitude for my cohort, Layla Brown and Yasmin Cho, for being the academic siblings along the beginnings of this path, and especially to Çağrı Yoltar, my cohort sister, without whom those beginnings would have brought far, far less joy. Thank you, also, to Ömer Özcan, a part of this intellectual family. While graduate school is often seen as the space for intellectual growth, I trace my intellectual genealogy to my undergraduate experiences at UC Berkeley's Gender and Women's Studies Program, especially to the mentorship of Mel Y. Chen, Paola Bacchetta, and Roshanak Kheshti, who introduced me to theory and taught me how to love it. Many colleagues at Millsaps College supported my work: George Bey, Louwanda Evans, and Veronique Belisle of the Sociology and Anthropology Department; Anne MacMaster of the English Department and my Codirector of Women's and Gender Studies; and the "Writing-in-Progress" group, led by Liz Egan. Millsaps became a home especially because of Sue Carrie Drummond, Betsy Kohut, and Rahel Fischbach. At the University of Tennessee, the writing of this book has been supported by the encouragement of colleagues: Graciela Cabana, De Ann Pendry, Prashanth Kuganathan, Roger Begrich, and especially the late Rebecca Klenk, whose warm welcome I will always remember and cherish.

Beyond the institutional spaces that nurtured my thinking and writing of this book, there were other spaces that were collectively produced and that held me from time to time. Most of the first drafts of the chapters for this book were written under the support and guidance of the Summer 2020 Writing Group (a recurring Zoom link that lasted far beyond its demarcation). Thank you to Nelli Sargsyan, Jason Woerner, and Sertaç Sehlikoglu for that vital space in uncertain times. Gratitude also for the Thinking/Loving/Writing Group, Jessica Eileen Jones and Lindsay Andrews, who provided love and guidance as this book was just becoming an idea. Dilan Yıldırım, thank you for forming the writing group that was always available for camaraderie, and thanks also to everyone in that group. The Armenian "Infidels" group, organized by Veronica Zablotsky, Deanna Cachoian-Schanz, and David Kazanjian, provided breathing room in the midst of pandemic and war, which also coincided with the time that I was drafting the first version of this manuscript. Thank you, also, to Sara Appel, whose insights into my writing and its many layers allowed me to strengthen my voice and my claims and for which this book is certainly more of what I wanted it to be. Elizabeth Ault, thank you for making it all happen and for teaching me how to write a book.

Much of the writing here was presented in talks along the way. Thanks to those who invited me to speak, share, and receive responses as well as to the institutions that provided the possibility: Kathryn Babayan at the University of Michigan, Ann Arbor Center for Armenian Studies; Caitlin Ostrowski at the Mississippi State University Department of Anthropology and Middle East Cultures; Raja Swamy at the University of Tennessee Department of Anthropology; Lucine Talalyan and Tigran Amiryan of the Queering Yerevan Collective; Houri Berberian, Melissa Bilal, and Lerna Ekmekçioğlu at the University of California, Irvine's Center for Armenian Studies; Svetlana Borodina at the Harriman Institute, Columbia University; Baird Campbell with the American Anthropological Association's Committee for the Anthropology of Science, Technology, and Computing; Kathryn David at the Robert Penn Warren Center for the Humanities, Vanderbilt University; and Eviya Hovhannissyan at the Heinrich Böll Stiftung, Yerevan.

Support comes in many ways, and just one way is financial. The research for this book was made possible by funding support from Duke University, Millsaps College, and the University of Tennessee, Knoxville.

I would like to express deep appreciation to Tomas Matza, Anne Allison, Ara Wilson, Anne-Maria Makhulu, and Frances Hasso, who each, and in very different ways, acted as guides on the journey of writing, publishing, figuring my way around professional spaces and how to be a colleague. I am grateful for how my work continues to bring me into contact with each of you.

I do not know how to thank Diane M. Nelson because I do not have words for what it feels like to see this book to publication knowing that she will not see it. You were the best mentor that I could have wished for, and I hope that you would have seen in this a reflection of your encouragement and your style, your wit, and your care with ideas. Deep gratitude for your guidance and for always being willing to provide shelter and comfort; for the reassurance that brilliance is not necessarily funded, and that funding is never innocent; for the knowledge that being tough is often rooted in fear and anxiety; and for the insight that clarity is sometimes only found in confusion.

Before my first trip to Armenia in 2010, I excitedly called my dad, Moses Shirinian, to tell him the news. "I'm going to Armenia!" I said. "Armenia? Why?" he responded. Later he would tell a friend that he couldn't understand why I would go to a place that he had spent so much energy trying to get out of. A few years later, my dad would come to visit me in Yerevan. He would see old friends and old streets, all of which had been made new by the enormous historical, political, economic, social, and cultural transformations over the decades. I was fascinated by his awe as we walked through neighborhoods that carried only traces of what he remembered. While my dad might not have understood why I wanted to go to Armenia—and in some ways this is still true today—the joyful stories he would tell about his youth, about growing up under socialism, passed on to me a nostalgia that I only realized years later. Thus, I thank my dad and his nostalgia for providing much of the impetus for the curiosity behind this book.

I am indebted to my mother, Aida Shirinian, who gave me music as a way of thinking (who helped me understand the purpose of fugue and thus movement beyond and elsewhere), and to my sister, Sose Shirinian, who loves and supports me unconditionally, and who might "look up" to me but for which I certainly look up to her.

Raja Swamy, my life comrade and accomplice, this book and so much more would have never been possible without your support, your celebration, and your unrelenting encouragement. Thank you, every day and forever.

And, finally, Mher, whom I made and birthed as I was also making and birthing this book: you cannot read *yet*, but one day maybe you will read this, and you will see in writing that you gave new perspective, new objective, and new foundation to *why* it is that I write and why futurity matters.

Yerkire yerkir chi. (The country is not a country.)

APHORISM OF YEREVAN CAB DRIVERS

INTRODUCTION

Survival of a Perverse Nation

On the very early morning of May 8, 2012, two young men fire-bombed DIY Pub, a small basement-level bar in central Yerevan, the capital city of post-Soviet Armenia. According to the firebombers, the act was done to protect their nation against homosexuals and Turks, both of whom they considered national enemies. For weeks following the fire-bombing, mainstream news outlets—in print, on television, and online—as well as social media and popular blogs discussed the event and its implications for the Armenian nation. What did it mean that there was a "gay bar" in Yerevan? What did it mean that there were homosexuals in Yerevan? On May 21, just two weeks after the firebombing, when national attention was still fixated on this new public figure of the homosexual, members of the newly founded nationalist organization Hayazn attacked a march called the Diversity March, which had been planned by a coalition of nongovernmental organizations. The organizers of the march saw it as a celebration of ethnic, religious, cultural, and subcultural differences in the city. Members of Hayazn and others who joined the counterprotest claimed it was a "gay parade" whose "faggots" (*gomikner*) had to be stopped. The Diversity March led to hours of clashes between participants and counterprotesters. While it was mediated by the police, who eventually provided the march's organizers safe harbor in the building of the Yerevan Writer's Union, it was also clear to those participating that most of the police officers sympathized with the counterprotesters. These two events became prominent subjects of discussion. Like the firebombing of DIY, the Diversity March incited its most public discussions *not* around what it meant that these were targeted attacks against a certain group, and *not* around what it meant that these were attacks on difference itself, but rather around the question of what it meant that there was a gay bar, a gay parade, and gay people at all in Armenia's capital city.

By the time I arrived in Yerevan in August 2012, Tsomak Oganezova, one of the owners of DIY Pub, had left the country after she and her sister had received a frightening number of death threats. They were given asylum in Sweden and returned to Armenia only in 2020. The grassroots political world—from which LGBT, feminist, environmental, liberal, progressive, democracy, and leftist as well as right-wing nationalist activists had emerged—had been split in two: those who could tolerate LGBT persons and those who could not. This split had consequences for activism in areas that had seemingly little to do with gender or sexuality: struggles around urban public space, against mining, against European or Russian neo-imperialism, and centered on contentious economic and human rights policies. Mainstream media made homosexuality into a hypervisible mark of Armenia's entry into the postsocialist spatiotemporal landscapes that included the European Union and its "neighborhood," Russia's Eurasian Economic Union, industry's privatization, and the monopolization of critical goods and services by a handful of men. Armenia was changing; it was becoming something other than what it had been—not necessarily since the times of state socialism, but since its very inception as a nation. The figure of the homosexual was placed front and center among these crises and became the cause, the sign, the point of a visible identification of these changes. While these ideas regarding homosexuality as a crisis were largely right-wing concerns, they were also frequently utilized by some members of government and publicized through popular media.

Homosexuality around the world is often framed within traditionalist discourses as a threat to national values.[1] There was something particular in the case of Armenia, however. Often presented not *just* as a threat to national values, homosexuality was claimed to be a threat to the very possibility of the nation's survival. For many right-wing activists, public officials, and members of the Armenian Apostolic Church, homosexuality threatened to annihilate the Armenian nation. This threat of annihilation is a part of a wider national narrative. If non-Armenian readers of this book know one thing about Armenia, it is probably the Genocide carried out by the Ottoman Empire in the early twentieth century. While the politics surrounding this event in the post-Soviet Republic of Armenia are complex—and not to be equated with its centrality in political and social discourse in the Armenian Diaspora—it plays a significant role in this ongoing sense that the nation and its survival are constantly under threat. Indeed, the term *survival* has its place in the titles of several monographs about Armenia.[2] Further, there are many articles, exhibitions, short films, and other accounts of Armenia framed through the prism of survival. Armenia, a *pokr azg* (small nation), has reason to harbor not only a "fear of small numbers" (Appadurai 2006) that fuels revanchist discourses of war but a fear of total annihilation. Armenia's history is a history of survival.

The 2012 DIY Pub firebombing and the attack on the Diversity March started a sex panic that continued for years, punctuating post-socialist temporality with heightened emotions centered on threats to the nation's survival. In October 2012, the German Embassy and an EU delegation attempted to screen (in Armenia) the Serbian film *Parada* (Dragojevic 2011), which explores the struggles surrounding the first Gay Pride parade in Belgrade. Right-wing protesters, claiming the film threatened children, were successful in stopping the screenings. In 2013, Armenia's National Assembly passed Law No. 57, "Protection of Equal Rights and Equal Opportunities for Women and Men," which controversially used the term *gender*, transliterated but not translated into Armenian, leading to protests that this was a European attempt to make all Armenians transgender. In 2018, a mob in the village of Shurnukh went after a group of queer youth gathering at a local farm. A few youths were beaten, but it seemed as if the mob had come for a lynching. These events brought the figure of the homosexual into the public eye and produced a powerful rhetoric that circulated widely within popular media: that of sexual perversion, or *aylaserutyun*, which identified sexual and gender transgressions as threats against the nation's survival.

Postsocialism as Constant Crisis

While this sex panic consumed both mainstream and social media, there was another major rhetoric in wide circulation: that of the moral perversion, *aylandakutyun*, of the nation. Within this rhetoric of moral perversion, it was the political-economic elite—the post-Soviet oligarchs and their government henchmen—who had destroyed the possibilities of the nation's everyday life and its reproduction. The oligarchy's greed, corruption, and general immorality, I heard very frequently, was leading to the destruction of the nation. While this narrative homed in on the question of the *moral*—something to which I dedicate much discussion in this book—this framework was undergirded by various political-economic realities. Following the collapse of the Soviet Union, through prescription from the World Bank as well as from a whole host of Western capitalist institutions (Wedel 2001), often referred to as the "Washington Consensus," the Armenian government set out to privatize public industry and state assets, leading to deindustrialization and mass liquidation and, as a result, mass unemployment and emigration. Primitive accumulation and accumulation by dispossession (Harvey 2003), state capture by the elite, corruption, poverty, unemployment, and other forms of economic violence and crisis had drawn the nation's survival into question. These economic crises also came with political challenges—shootings, terrorist plots, attempted coups, state violence against citizens, and mass uprisings.

Quick privatization was conceived as an economic necessity by the World Bank (Roth-Alexandrowicz 1997) to fix the problems of distribution that came about not only as a result of the breakup of Soviet allocative systems but also as a result of Armenia's war with neighboring Azerbaijan in the midst of the Soviet Union's collapse, which led to a blockade on Armenia for some essential goods, especially petroleum. The war over the territory of Nagorno-Karabakh had been an ongoing crisis—a "frozen conflict"—for the Republic, even before independence. The Nagorno-Karabakh Autonomous Oblast (NKAO), predominantly populated by Armenians, was originally created in 1923 from land that had been under dispute between the Armenian and Azerbaijani Republics prior to their Sovietization. While the region was autonomous in its status and led by the First Secretary of NKAO from the capital city of Stepanakert, it was kept within the Azerbaijani Soviet Socialist Republic (SSR) nonetheless. Major political upheaval surrounding the status of the territory did not begin until the 1980s. However, throughout the decades of the Soviet era, Armenians made demands to Moscow to unify the region with the Armenian SSR. Following Mikhail Gorbachev's implementation of glasnost—or openness, meant to democratize the USSR—citizens of the Armenian SSR as well as Armenians in NKAO responded by demanding the unification of NKAO with Armenia. In February 1988, hundreds of thousands of Armenians in NKAO protested. Later that month, they submitted a formal petition to the Supreme Council of the Soviet Union. These demands, established originally on claims for Armenian self-determination, became charged with nationalist sentiment and led to violent clashes between Armenians and Azerbaijanis. Most notable was the pogrom against Armenians in the Azerbaijani town of Sumgait, which left more than two hundred Armenians dead in late February 1988 and was followed by an almost total population exchange. After the dismantling of the Soviet Union in 1991, the conflict became a full-fledged war with episodes of mass violence, such as the massacre in the town of Khojaly in 1992, during which more than two hundred Azerbaijanis were killed by Armenian military forces. While Armenia was able to gain control of the NKAO territory—including seven key regions of Azerbaijan—at the time of an official ceasefire in 1994, the reemergence of the armed conflict in 2020 resulted in Azerbaijan taking much of this territory back, leaving Armenian and Russian peacekeeping troops in control of north-central areas and Stepanakert, the capital of Nagorno-Karabakh. In September 2023, after a nine-month blockade and military attack by Azerbaijan, an estimated one hundred thousand Armenians fled the region and the Armenian Nagorno-Karabakh Republic—self-declared as the Republic of Artsakh—was dissolved. For Armenians, this conflict—especially as it started with pogroms—was a continuation of the Genocide, or as Harutyun Marutyan (2007) has noted, its "sequel." It also meant a consistent militarization of everyday life and politics.

Heavy emphasis on militarization, justified by an external enemy's territorial threat, allowed the elite to maintain power and halted the processes of democratization for decades. The protracted war between Armenia and Azerbaijan produced a status quo that pitted democratization against national security (Ghaplanyan 2018), creating an "entrenched authoritarianism" resistant to social change (Ohanyan 2020, 231). Social scientists attuned to questions of gender and sexuality in Armenia, however, point out that along with the lack of resolution to the Nagorno-Karabakh conflict, the political use of homophobia has also been a major obstacle to social transformation, marking change from the status quo as something dangerous to the nation's survival, and manipulating this fear to foster attachment to the political-economic elite in the country (Shahnazaryan, Aslanova, Badasyan 2016; Anna Nikoghosyan 2016; Beukian 2018). Feelings of national, cultural, and traditional survival as being under threat have been the foundations of an exploitative and violent political-economic status quo.

Survival of a Perverse Nation interrogates the moral discourse of these political-economic crises. I show how systemic, structural, political, and economic problems were taken up as issues of morality—of disintegrating values, a lack of respect for tradition, a declining investment in care for Armenians and Armenia—and as consequences of a missing Father figure for the nation. Here, I should distinguish what I mean by the *moral* so as to not confuse it with the ethical or the political. In this book, my use of the moral refers to tautological authority—what Jacques Lacan has called the "Master's discourse" (Fink 1995). Unlike political or ethical claims, moral claims are not based in reason concerning justice, material benefit for the collective, or struggle toward the betterment of conditions through systemic considerations. In a tautological fashion, moral claims are based in how things are *supposed* to be because that is how they are supposed to be. In Armenia, the focus on morality displaced political-economic discussions—discussions of historical mechanisms—onto questions of an ahistorical, continuous, proper Armenian Symbolic order. Because of the emphasis on morality rather than on political critique when it came to the crises with which the Republic was faced, feelings about the corruption and indecency of the oligarchy were easily manipulated to become feelings about homosexuality's perversion of the nation. While the oligarchy's violations are based in capitalist exploitation, its psychic and discursive uptake as a moral issue (rather than as a political-economic one) allows its violations to collapse into generalized anxieties about social reproduction and thus conflate these anxieties with homosexuality as another kind of violation of proper familial expectations.

I examine what we might call *homophobia* through its very sites and nodes of production, although following various critiques of its common usage and the assumptions that undergird it, I most often refrain from using the term. Gregory Herek (2004), for instance, argues that homophobia is often treated as an individual complex about fear while it is actually a prejudice supported by a larger heterosexual society that fuels anger, hostility, and disgust toward nonheterosexual persons. Maya Mikdashi and Jasbir K. Puar (2016) have also maintained that homophobia is an inadequate way of expressing a full political picture when there are larger forms of violence present in which sexual intolerance exists (see also Atshan 2020 for a critique of this position). What might be called *homophobia* in Armenia is an incited and inciting rhetoric, part of a concerted effort by right-wing actors to produce a deep fear and anxiety about homosexuality. Some of this anxiety-production is fueled by actual fears of homosexuality—a phenomenon seen as a threat to the family, the nation, and life as it should be governed by proper Armenianness. Much of this anxiety-production, however, as I show in this book, is also fueled by other concerns, some that right-wing nationalists are conscious of and are intentional about and others that are driven by unconscious displacements and condensations.

What does it mean to survive? In what ways is survival dependent on continuity? And what kinds of continuities count if we are naming something (a nation) as the thing that has survived or should survive? How far off can something (a nation) veer from its path of continuity with the past—that time before an event or some phenomenon threatened its survival—for it to still be identified as the same thing as that which came before? What allows for *survival*, and who decides? Is survival—the pull toward continuing and remaining—always conservative? To what degree is the continuing remnant—that which survives—the same as the thing that existed before? Does survival always entail a before and an after; is it, in other words, always marked by an event that splits time? Or can survival be threatened through small, incremental, changes of the everyday, slippage into the unrecognizability of the thing that can now be said not to have survived? These questions are about ontology—fueled by ontological angst regarding a core way of life that is *supposed to be*. Armenia is *supposed to be* proper and is defined by a history of miraculous existence and survival based on its moral strength. Armenia especially owes this survival to a genealogy of valorous national Fathers. I refer to this ontology, based on moral propriety, as Armenia's Symbolic order. In recent years, many Armenians have felt that this moral strength is waning. In the face of visibilized homosexuality, public discourse has placed Armenianness and its survival at an ontological crossroads: if Armenia veers in these sexually perverse (*aylaservatz*) directions, it will no longer be Armenia. The oligarchy, however, has also been implicated in these threats against national survival. Their moral perversion (*aylandakutyun*) has oriented everyday life away from its proper paths, and Armenia, if it follows these improper paths, will also no longer be that which once existed; it will no longer have the strengths of morality, tradition, and familial values with which it has always withstood attempts at its annihilation. This book investigates the entanglements of these threats against the nation's survival. It also, however, speculates on the possibilities and potentials of nonsurvival. Intense focus on the need for the nation to survive has constrained various forms of life, including queer life. *Survival of a Perverse Nation*, thus, investigates the present from which other—perhaps nonnational, or improper— forms of life and world might take flight.

Queering Political Economy and Spatiotemporality

Survival of a Perverse Nation makes two central propositions. The first of these is *perversion as a queer theory of political economy*. I maintain that discourses around national threats having to do with social and cultural deterioration, deviation, or perversion—whether these are sexual or of a larger moral concern affecting the social and biological reproduction of the body politic—have their roots in political and economic crises whether or not these crises are apparent or named. The claim that life-as-we-know-it is turning into something else, becoming other than that which sustains a nation, is a claim about governance, labor, production, consumption, distribution, allocation, exchange, geopolitics, geo-economics, and other factors that we might call *political economy* and see as the basis of *real* material social relations. Political economy, however, for the purposes of this book, should not be taken as strictly economic and political operations and mechanisms. In other words, I do not take political economy as a space detachable from everyday life, as a space limited to formal production, ownership, and distribution. Rather, I hone the intimate, affective, and "feelings" side of how political economy is a site of everyday world-making and take seriously the politics of how production and ownership are *felt* as moral questions and, importantly, how *reproduction*—both social and biological—are at the heart of political economy.

Toward a queer theory of political economy, I am interested in providing analysis that traces social and moral anxieties regarding national survival and fears of a radically deteriorated future to political-economic realities. By this I mean that queer theory can also become a framework through which to understand political-economic processes. I see the rhetoric of perversion as a social, political, and economic phenomenon, and I make use of it here toward a social theory. This theory of the social, drawing on psychoanalytic conceptualizations of the Symbolic realm (which I discuss below), remains Marxian in its insistence on understanding social relations as intricately and inseparably tied to material production, consumption, distribution, and exchange as well as to *feelings, attachments,* and the *Symbolic meanings* of those processes. Following my interlocutors and their use of the rhetoric(s) of perversion, I suggest that beyond individual psychic pathology and even social pathology, perversion may be an apt way through which to describe capitalism's spatiotemporal processes and its cuts, disturbances, interventions, and violations of and on the social psyche. I read discourses of *aylaserutyun* (sexual perversion) and *aylandakutyun* (moral perversion) as symptomatic of real forms of the perversion of the social, political, and economic material world and, as such, as real threats against survival (of the nation and of life itself) while also, simultaneously, critically interrogating the meanings of sexuality and morality claimed within these rhetorics.

Through ethnographic introspection as well as (at times) through speculation, I refuse the language and discourse of transition and insist on the language of political-economic *transformation*, which remains open-ended. Postsocialist studies hotly debated this question in the late 1980s and into the 1990s. Caroline Humphrey (1991) offered the view that the seeming chaos of the postsocialist world in this period, often taken as an inevitable stage toward market reforms, was rather an indication of the making of feudal structures, as various big men in Russia formed their own suzerainties and took the matter of maintaining order as well as the distribution of necessary goods within provincial locales into their own hands. Where these personal kingdoms ruled, state law did not seem to be operating (and was sometimes not even known by those who occupied seats of authority within governments). Katherine Verdery (1996) extended this line of questioning around whether the end of state socialism was bringing about free market economies and capitalist states. She highlighted the ways in which privatization was often uneven in order to facilitate state control, how agents of privatization also felt compelled to continue forms of allocation that were once the responsibility of the state, and how "destatizing" and "restatizing" (209) mechanisms—what can also be called "state capture" (Visser and Kalb 2010)—often meant horizontal forms of reciprocity in regard to power, what we might understand as Mafia control. These arguments fed into a larger debate around the language of postsocialism. The use of the term "transition" highlighted the change from socialist institutions to free market institutions and ideologies, often pointing to the violence of "shock therapy" (Verdery 1996; Burawoy and Verdery 1999; Wedel 2001) instituted by Western agencies, but at times also falling into the traps of a teleological "transitology" that assumed that 1989 (for Eastern Europe) was when "market reform" began (as opposed to earlier), and that what was taking place in the 1990s was, indeed, market reform rather than a multifaceted transformation with various and varying phases (for a critique of this work, see Kirn 2017). For these reasons, some scholars chose, instead, to use the term *transformation*—to highlight multiplicity and to critique teleological assumptions about "transition" from socialism to capitalism (Stark and Bruszt 1998; Hörschelmann and Stenning 2008). Ethnography played a key role in these analyses in challenging top-down (Western) perspectives of "rescue"—either through "shock therapy" in which the West saw itself as healer or through "big bang" theories of institutions and history in this part of the world starting anew (the beginning of history) in which the West could see itself as God (Verdery 1996, 205).

I take up *postsocialism* not as a temporal descriptor nor as a region but rather as a naming of a processual worlding that insists on bringing political-economic realities to the forefront. In this sense, the "post" might refer to a time after but not necessarily as a probationary period. As Shannon Woodcock (2011, 65) has argued, taking "post-socialism" as a strictly temporal category marks Central and Eastern Europe, and we might say other postsocialist contexts such as Cuba and China, as waiting for Europe and the United States to bestow upon these regions a recognition of civilization for having finally arrived formally to capitalism. Postsocialism (without the hyphen), critically, can have liberatory potential (Zhang 2008) as an insistence on naming the socialist past, because a part of the contemporary world recalls that other worlds, innovations, values, and ways of life were real and are thus always possible. In this sense, *postsocialism* here should not be taken to mean that socialism is of the past and not part of the future. Indeed, I am committed to studying the fissures, ruptures, and breaks of the political-economic world of socialism into what came after, and especially its intimate realities, toward the possibilities of reimagining socialisms as futures. Furthermore, I use postsocialism and its conceptual embeddedness in political-economic realities not as a statement about the centrality of particular institutions or about the institutional qualities of socialism and what came after—what Tatjana Thelen (2011) has critiqued as the "neo-institutionalism" of Western socialist and postsocialist studies that constructed a form of "area studies" with an exotic other in mind—but as forms of worlding, ideas, possibilities, and potentials. I am interested in desire, subjectivity, intimacy, and political possibility and see these as intricately caught up in the affective realms of political economy—not as a set of institutions but as a set of conditions that make life. A *postsocialist* queer theory calls on us to think about gender, sexuality, and worlding in general as always already entangled with political economy.

By using the language of transformation, I also emphasize that a *transition* to the capitalist mode of production was not and is not inevitable. Regarding Armenia's particular mode of production within this transformation, we might reference capitalism as well as neoliberalization ("capitalism on steroids"). We certainly witness the commodification of labor (Wolf 1982), which comes with the general enclosure of the commons and thus capital's command of labor—the simplest way of defining the capitalist mode of production, in which most Armenians depend on the sale of their labor power for their livelihood. However, much of the wealth being produced among the elite of the nation-state is not produced through the buying and exploiting of labor but through various other forms of exploitation, especially mercantile forms of wealth production like the monopolization of imports (sugar, butter, gasoline, cigarettes, etc.) and selling off what had been looted from the socialist state and from the properties taken after the resettlement of lands during and following the Nagorno-Karabakh war. Neoliberal economic policies have certainly had effects on life in Armenia—with the privatization of once-public services like education and transportation and the stripping away of social services like pensions and the state provision of housing. However, neoliberalization[3] itself has been an incomplete process because of the social demands that have come from post-Soviet citizens used to having economic rights, such as in housing markets (Zavisca 2012), in already-built infrastructures that are communal (Collier 2011), in reproductive healthcare (Rivkin-Fish 2013), and in various other social protections (Petryna 2002). Thus, while I use *capitalism* and *neoliberalization* in this book, I will often also employ the language of *oligar-*

chic capitalism or *oligarchy* to point to these variances and the importance they have in the meanings produced in their everyday effects.

Many of those with whom I spoke while conducting the research leading up to this book did not necessarily find capitalism at fault; rather, the cause they identified as the root of their contemporary life conditions was the particularly aggressive and immoral forms of economic exploitation, especially at the levels of expensive consumption (as a result of monopolies on imports) and unemployment they were experiencing at the hands of and under the reign of the post-Soviet oligarchy. In other words, the colloquial concept of *oligarchy* had somehow become separated from the capitalist mechanisms that made this oligarchy's emergence possible. Underneath these moral complaints, however, I often found sharp critiques of capitalist processes. Thus, while I make use of the colloquial and moral usage here as it was articulated throughout my research, my analysis adds historical and political weight to the category of the oligarchy. The oligarchy was on a continuum with what are today the more acceptable "large businessmen" (*khoshor biznesmen*)— a term that is sometimes even used for the slightly more morally acceptable oligarchs—and the bourgeoisie; in other words, they made up a part of the owner class. While the oligarchy vulgarly showcased their wealth, begotten through exploitation and theft (sometimes also flaunted), the more "respectable" bourgeoisie maintained and continues today to maintain a more humble demeanor. It is critical to point out that the term *oligarchy* in widespread usage in the postsocialist world is also applicable to Western and Euro-American modes of wealth production. In other words, while the billionaires of the West, like Jeff Bezos and Bill Gates, certainly do depend on the surplus value produced by workers to make their wealth, they also very much depend on state capture to provide a hospitable environment for this exploitation, marking them and their affiliates within the state also as an oligarchy. In these ways, while I find it necessary to specify a particular oligarchic mode of capitalism, it might also be fair to say that late capitalism itself functions as an oligarchy, by which I understand political rule by the economic elite and, in the case of Armenia, an elite fraternal horde—a brotherhood of oligarchs and other bosses. As I will discuss throughout this book, this fraternal horde had a psychic and affective force beyond its position as political-economic elite: as brethren to and within the nation, they marked political-economic realities with the personal and intimate feeling of betrayal.

As this work is an ethnography in the postsocialist context, a note on Armenia's geopolitical positioning between East and West is critical. Scholarly discussions about the effects on Central and Eastern Europe and Central Asia of this in-betweenness have focused on the effects of being a part of Europe but at its margins (Buelow 2012; Butterfield 2013; Suchland 2018; Shirinian 2017, 2021c); a desire to "return to Europe" (Suchland 2011); and national(ist) self-representations of whiteness (Imre 2015). Some threads of this discussion have centered colonialism and imperialism, claiming that the postsocialist region's alliance is with the "postcolonial" world rather than with the West or Europe. The "colonial" in these readings, however, does not necessarily reference either European powers or the United States as a major imperialist global force (Wood 2003); rather, (Soviet) Russia becomes the imperial metropole (Zhurzhenko 2001). If the West is taken up as an imperial power at all, it is only in abstraction and usually in reference to epistemology rather than to political economy. Madina Tlostanova, Suruchi Thapar-Bjorkert, and Redi Koobak (2019) for instance, argue that postsocialist feminists have become the "missing other" of transnational and postcolonial feminism—a result of these critical frameworks' overreliance on Western categories of colonialism and race. While the authors take Russia as the imperial metropole, their claims center postcolonial theory, emanating from the West, rather than the political-economic power of Russia or the United States and Europe. In a retort to this line of reasoning regarding a "missing other" as well as to what constitutes the "Western," Chiara Bonfiglioli and Kristen Ghodsee (2020) point out that the real "missing other" is global socialist feminism, which is erased not only within Western epistemology but also in postsocialist feminisms. Bonfiglioli and Ghodsee argue that the silencing of socialist feminist global solidarity movements is a continuation of Western liberal feminist political agendas, aligned with US hegemony, and not necessarily just their epistemological perspectives. As a result, it is toward this very same agenda that postsocialist feminists reduce the possibilities of socialism to coloniality. In a somewhat similar critical vein Maria Mayerchyk and Olga Plakhotnik (2021) argue that contemporary Ukrainian queer and feminist movements have focused their critiques of colonialism on Russia, creating a nationalism and an uncritical Eurocentrism at the heart of mainstream feminism.

The specters of Russia, Europe, and the United States and claims of colonialism and imperialism are present throughout my ethnography.

These were major components of the politics of sex, gender, and sexuality. As I show, however, these claims were most frequently moral and cultural in nature—established on anxieties about a disintegrating Armenian ontological propriety. The quasi-political sentiment of being an indigenous nation struggling for sovereignty produced an insistence on ontological purity, policing those regarded as transgressors. In this way, claims of "colonialism" (including that of Russia) were not only anti-queer and anti-feminist; but they were also not necessarily anti-colonial in that they provided no critique of actual *material* forms of colonialism, imperialism, or oppression.[4] It is also important to note that the Soviet Union is rarely seen as having been an imperial force in Armenia. Even those who are today pro-Western who might consider Russia's military, economic, political, social, or cultural presence in Armenia (and in Nagorno-Karabakh until September 2023) as imperial or colonial, rarely extend this to the history of the Soviet Union.

Popular media and most of my interlocutors claimed that Armenia was a perverse nation—deviating from family, the Church, and other national values—either because of new, dangerous ideologies like homosexuality or feminism or because of the oligarchy that ruled over Armenians through threats but did not provide the care for the people that is obligatory for proper Armenian leadership (for good Armenian Fathers). I point out, however, that underneath these depoliticized claims are the actual political-economic realities of contemporary oligarchic, capitalist, and neoliberal structures, which Armenia shares with many other nations and political-economic contexts throughout the world. Because of heightened anxieties concerning national survival and an attunement to these anxieties in public discourse through a rhetoric of perversion, readers of this book might find Armenia an ideal case study through which to understand capitalist global free market mechanisms' perversions of life and sociality. In this sense, *Survival of a Perverse Nation* is a queer ethnography that takes as its object of study a perverse political-economic context that highlights the ways in which *social and biological reproduction* and feelings about them are inseparable from *governance and material production* and feelings about them. Furthermore, in dwelling on the ways in which production and reproduction are described as perverse processes in the postsocialist era, I bring sexuality to the center of an analysis of political economy. Material structures of production are affective, emotional, and moral structures. Importantly, they are also structured through sexuality.

While invested in sexuality as a site of social and biological reproduction, *Survival of a Perverse Nation* is less interested in LGBT identity,
life, and practice. Some chapters here (especially chapters 1 and 4) will
draw on ethnographic fieldwork among queer Armenians. For the most
part, however, this queer ethnography takes what David L. Eng, Jack
Halberstam, and Jose Muñoz (2005) describe as a "subjectless" approach
to critique. Queer studies has, for a long while already (see, for instance,
Cohen 1997), become a field that "disallows any positing of a proper subject *of* or object *for* the field by insisting that queer has no fixed political referent" (Eng, Halberstam, and Muñoz 2005, 3). Subjectless critique
unsettles any proper subject or object of queer analysis, especially as
subjects that crop up tend to be based on a white Euro-American middle class understanding of "nonnormative" sexual and gender identity.
As such, queer theory has effectively, in Eng and Jasbir K. Puar's words
(2020, 4), "provincialized" itself within the global South, taking interest
in the geopolitics of sexuality that involves a wide scope for the mechanisms, crises, possibilities, and politics of what count as subjects and
objects of queer analysis (Eng, Halberstam, and Muñoz 2005; Rosenberg
and Villarejo 2011; Mikdashi and Puar 2016; Eng and Puar 2020).

Central to these theoretical formations has been the question
of political economy, especially as neoliberalism (Duggan 2002) and its
ends (Amar 2013), capitalism and global crises (Rosenberg and Villarejo
2011), and convergences between queer and Marxist theory (Floyd 2009;
Hennessey 2006) have become principal sites of inquiry to the deploy-
ment of *queer* as a concept and conceptual framework. These shifts are
also visible in some lines of investigation within postsocialist studies,
such as examinations of the intimate effects of privatization and the
commodification of life (Stout 2014), and inquiries into the geopolitical and geo-economic entanglements of LGBT politics (Butterfield 2013;
Rexhepi 2016, 2017; Ye 2021b). More marginal to these framings, but of
critical insight, are the contributions of Marxist theory from the existing socialist and communist worlds, and its interventions in sexuality and the human within liberal society (Liu 2012; Popa 2021). *Survival
of a Perverse Nation* extends these queer theoretical forays into political
economy. I provide a materialist queer analysis from the former Second
World—a world that, while currently making up a part of the Global
South, has seen modernity in its capitalist as well as socialist forms. I investigate these political-economic realities and histories *queerly*, which
is to say that I look for their potentials for rupture and the making of

difference. I also look at them as *queer* in themselves, as deviating from proper moral orders.

Readers may be surprised that this queer ethnography largely avoids the frameworks of normativity and antinormativity and employs, instead, the concept of the proper. In the introduction to a special issue of *differences*, Robyn Wiegman and Elizabeth A. Wilson (2015) take apart the notion of the norm, making the case that while normativity and its undoing have been at the heart of queer theory since its inception as a field, the actual relationship between *queer* and *norm* has not been well articulated. While the norm is average and fungible, within queer theory's imaginary it also becomes an unchangeable space, filled with whatever is imagined to be restrictive and exclusive (heterosexuality, cisgender identity, whiteness, etc.). Wiegman and Wilson suggest that the norm might also be thought of as capacious, as it already holds within it the possibilities of difference and opposition and, as an average, is liable to change. The norm, as an average, in postsocialist Armenia is widely felt to be perversion, as the conditions for morality have disintegrated. The notion of the *proper*, thus, allows me to reflect on these feelings of deviation. The proper is an imaginary ontology of an ancient, surviving Armenianness. Improprieties of the present lead the nation (too) far away from this ontological status.

Drawing on and contributing to ongoing discussions about social reproduction within Marxist, feminist, and queer theory (Hennessey 2006; Bhattacharya 2017; Fraser 2016; Sears 2016; Ye 2021a) as part and parcel of production, this book demonstrates the intricate relationship between the production of capital/wealth and the reproduction of children/a next generation and how this relationship is felt deeply within everyday life. How possibilities of production and reproduction *feel* has consequences on the political legitimacy of the ruling elite, especially as this elite, within the context of what I describe as a "nation-family," are taken as intimates. Capitalist oligarchy and the conditions it produces in everyday life are understood as constituting the end of a nation that has survived for millennia, pointing to the antilife and antisocial currents of our current hegemonic global political-economic structures. The rhetoric of perversion is an indictment against global capitalism, expressed in the feelings and affects of local and intimate Armenian everyday life and experience.

The second central argument of this book concerns *the radical spatiotemporal possibilities of moral rupture*. Rather than lamenting the end of the nation's survival with many of my interlocutors, *Survival of a Perverse Nation* locates radical potential for world-making at these very ends. If many Armenians in the Republic of Armenia in 2012–13 were struck by hopelessness in the face of decades of entrenched social, political, and economic violence—which they articulated as the *aylandakutyun* (moral perversion) of the nation—I argue that this also created a context for the possibilities of radically transforming moral worlds. If the nation could not and would not survive—or, by some estimates, had already not survived—because it was becoming or had become something so different from what made its survival possible, this very set of conditions make conceivable new forms of social relation. One of the main claims within the rhetorics of perversion in popular circulation was that Armenia lacked proper kin relations—and especially a proper Father for the nation (as a proper leader) and proper fathers within households (as men had either become too improper to be fathers or were actually absent—gone off as migrant laborers). I maintain that while these circumstances were mourned as having brought about an end to the nation, they also brought about other possibilities for life and sociality, and especially (as I investigate in chapter 6) potentials for a world without political Fatherhood or patriarchy: a world without Daddy. The perversion of the nation, which threatens its survival, is also a site of great queer spatiotemporal potential.

I offer the conceptual framework of perversion, thus, as a new means of understanding the queer political. V. Spike Peterson (2014) has provocatively suggested that queerness can be an unintended consequence of the global inequality that has created mass migrations, led to the breaking up of households, and challenged familial normalcy. Capitalism's constant disruption of intimate relations and politics of care undo norms, "queering" the family and intimate relations. Here, "queer" is read as nonnormative forms of intimacy and kinship. Natalie Oswin (2019) similarly offers a spatial analysis of how the global city of Singapore, which only very marginally tolerates LGBT persons, also "queers" migrant workers and foreign workers through their non-belonging and the limitations placed on their rights to the city. "Queer" becomes marginalization. My investigation of perverse temporality and spatiality, however, reveals that it might not necessarily be productive to read all deviation or marginalization as queer. Deviation might result from attempts at propriety and even from intense desires for a good, proper, normal life. The undoing of social norms and threats against "the good life" do not always come from queer imaginaries. The moral ruptures that paved these perverse paths resulted from capitalist and oligarchic modernity's failures, producing spatiotemporal mutations that resulted in (real and imagined) perverse figures like the homosexual or the oligarch. Perversion moves *away* from the *should be* and the *supposed to be*—those sensibilities of time and space that are the basis of the expectations for propriety and national survival—but not necessarily in a way that emancipates.

There is a necessary step between perversion and queerness: the transformational, translational, and affirmational work that activists do. New norms might emerge from mutated political-economic realities and social infrastructures, and thus we might see in capitalism a potential toward queer possibility. If, however, these forms of transformation continue to be seen either as purely negative consequences of moral failure or as depoliticized formations, then new realities, values, and norms remain *resignifications* rather than *asignifying ruptures* (Deleuze and Guattari 1987, 9) of the proper and thus do not change systems but requalify them. Here, I draw on Gilles Deleuze and Felix Guattari's insistence on maintaining an undercurrent of constant disruption to discipline and regimes of order rather than resignifying one regime into another. I thus refuse readings of capitalism's perversion of life as queerness, reserving queerness and queer potential as affective signifiers for active projects that seek to transform worlds rather than as passive mutations and condemnations of political-economic failure. Perversion is the rupture on which queerness may emerge, much like how capitalist contradiction is the rupture on which revolution is made.

The transformational work required to seek the queer potentials of political-economic crisis requires politicization, eschewing tendencies toward the moralization of social or economic issues. In this way, I posit queerness not just as a liberatory sensibility, but—and toward this liberation—as a critical impulse against the moral, the proper, and other forms that insist on the conservation, on the survival, of the status quo that is embedded in violent political, economic, and social mechanisms. Politicization demands affirmational work: not just to negate the world as it is—as an improper life making way for an impossible future and the end of the nation—but to *affirm* desire for what can and may come. It is critical to note, however, that this work of affirmation also requires negativity.[5] It is the end of a social world—the nonsurvival of the nation— that makes possible the queer affirmations of the *otherwise* and the *else-*

where (Povinelli 2012). For queer potential to capitalize on perversion, it must embrace both negativity and affirmation, both the deterioration of worlds and the production of new, possibly radically different worlds.

A Journey through Perversion(s)

This framework of perversion—the entanglements of fears and anxieties regarding sexuality and political economy—emerges from research I conducted in Yerevan from 2012 to 2013. I began this research as an intern at Public Information and Need for Knowledge (PINK), an LGBT advocacy organization, and at the Women's Resource Center (WRC), a feminist organization, both located in Yerevan. There, I worked closely with the staff on ongoing projects, organized workshops with their larger communities, conducted social scientific studies for the organizations, wrote pieces for PINK's e-magazine, and offered my translation skills when needed. PINK and WRC each had their own networks that expanded out into wider social and political worlds. Through my work with these organizations I also met environmental activists, human rights activists, advocates against militarization, and members of organizations working toward governmental transparency and democratization. And I had the opportunity to meet members of the Queering Yerevan Collective (QYC), a group of queer and feminist artists, writers, and translators. I collaborated with QYC on translations and other writings for their blog, on video installation projects with founding member Lucine Talalyan, and in conceptualizing and organizing art exhibits and other "happenings."

In my process of immersion in these spaces, I saw the ways in which the firebombing of DIY Pub and the attack on the Diversity March in May 2012 had complicated the everyday workings of what the policing of gender and sexual propriety looked like. The firebombing was a political and politicized act, which meant that LGBT and feminist activists were no longer just in everyday social negotiation with national sensibilities of what was properly Armenian and what was not; they were now a group directly targeted by fringe organizations, taken up within the popular media through a new rhetoric of sexual perversion that had the figure of the homosexual (that sometimes also included "the feminist") at its center. Prior to these events, which hypervisibly pushed the figure of the homosexual into public consciousness, much of the activities of PINK, WRC, Society Without Violence (which had also participated in the organization of the Diversity March), and independent activists (who had been outspoken during these events) had gone unnoticed. They had operated largely with the privilege of anonymity that had allowed them to build community and produce queer and feminist discourse and knowledge. Following the May 2012 events, the widespread rhetoric of sexual perversion circulating within everyday discourse and across popular media and social networking sites had jeopardized this anonymity and forced activists to have to think about the ways in which their work would be taken up by this multiplicity of new actors.

There were various contradictions and debates among LGBT advocates and feminists. When, for instance, PINK staff felt the need to "include" lesbians within their campaigns, lesbian feminists felt excluded by the vary narrow frameworks of those campaigns that foreclosed questions of desire and thus were not feminist in their orientations. When, in another instance, some WRC staff members claimed that they were not responsible for standing up for gay rights because they were a women's rights organization, the director had to remind the whole staff that some women were lesbians (Shirinian 2022a). In other moments of conflict and debate, leftist feminist queers disapproved of the consumerist orientation that PINK video campaigns—which featured fancy cars, fancy clothes, and new parking structures that had displaced residents in the city—were taking. Rather than as divergences between LGBT and feminist struggles, we might read these conflicts as between liberalism and more leftist political leanings. Liberal-leaning activists, who tended to be in the mainstream of NGO staff, aimed toward cultural acceptance and tolerance of LGBT people and women's rights, public education, policy change, and the provision of services to affected communities. Leftist-leaning organizers, however, were invested in more radical shifts in political, economic, and cultural structures (Nikoghosyan 2019). Left-leaning queers and feminists insisted on radical structural changes grounded in political economy as well as on imaginaries that would break with cultural demands and expectations firmly rooted in ontological claims of Armenianness. In this way, they were inspired both by socialist-era women driven by an insistence on class-based analyses critical of "bourgeois feminism" (Ghodsee 2018a) and by more recent calls for reimagining sexual liberation and critiques of heteronormativity. Left-leaning queers and feminists were also invested in cultural transformation, bringing to light feminist writers of the past like Shushanik Kurghinyan and Zabel Yesayan. These cultural politics, however, were not "merely cultural"[6]; they were attempts to draw attention to other ways of being Armenian and to other histories of Armenianness—to the transformation of contemporary life, which also included the redistribution of resources and rights to women.

Public attention focused on homosexuality through the rhetoric of sexual perversion, however, targeted anyone who deviated from the proper, no matter what their political leanings, especially because homosexuality, feminism, and a whole array of related concepts (such as gender and human rights) were perceived as foreign and dangerous movements with the capacity to destroy the nation. We cannot, however, take for granted the fact that these claims of foreignness were based in some actual facts: prominent women's NGOs (the Women's Resource Center, Society Without Violence, the Women's Fund Armenia, and the Armenian Young Women's Association) and LGBT organizations (PINK and the more recently established Right Side NGO) were funded through external granting agencies and foundations. Because they worked on issues that were not only intimate but central to political questions of social reproduction, right-wing nationalists articulated the mission of these organizations as the spread of sexual perversion by Europeans hoping to destroy Armenia from the inside out.

How was this rhetoric of sexual perversion being configured, and what were its precise logics? To explore these questions, I spent time in some spaces frequented by right-wing nationalists and conducted focused interviews with people who identified as *azgaynakan* (nationalist) or *hayrenaser* (patriotic). Because of the role of national liberation discourse in Armenia, especially as a result of nationalist political ideology coming from the Armenian Revolutionary Federation (ARF), a democratic socialist party founded in the late nineteenth century, it is difficult to place the ideologies of nationalism on the same left-to-right spectrum that came out of French revolutionary politics and that continues to make sense today in the context of liberalism. There are various forms of nationalism in Armenia: some liberal, some illiberal, some pro-Europe, some pro-Russia. In this book "right-wing nationalism" will refer to illiberal ideologies opposed to European political orientations in the country (although with more diversity in regard to their positions toward Russia) that are also socially conservative regarding feminism and queerness.

Spending time with right-wing nationalists was a risky endeavor. I— as a queer, pierced, and tattooed feminist—was one of their targets. This research, however, was valuable to activists at PINK and at WRC who were well-known by right-wing nationalists and who thus had little access to them. My identity as a conspirator with LGBT and feminist groups would also become apparent to right-wing nationalists over time, jeopardizing the possibilities of my continuing this work. For instance, my appearance at the DIY trial almost a year after the firebombing—showing up with well-known human rights activists and advocates of DIY Pub—served to "out" me as on the side of queers and feminists. Furthermore, as I began to publish portions of my research, and as my articles made their rounds among right-wing nationalists, I realized that my name had become too well-known to garner their trust and openness. This work was risky in another way, as it also jeopardized my trust among some leftist and progressive activists, something I had to negotiate. One friend found it disturbing that I was going to nationalist bars and pubs. That I was willing to hear them out meant, for her, that I believed they had "legitimate" opinions and that I was justifying their ideas as ideas. This research, however, gave some depth to my understandings of "sexual perversion" as a discourse and how it was tied up in various other political, economic, social, and (mytho-)historical concerns.

Another question that arose as I was conducting this research was how Yerevantsis, or residents of Yerevan, the largest condensed population in Armenia (at the time officially 1.5 million people out of 2.8 million),[7] felt about the nation. Did Armenians see homosexuality as *the* crisis of the times the way in which right-wing nationalists claimed it was, or how popular media, following this rhetoric, constantly reported it? What were the various assemblages of thought, feeling, and affect surrounding these concerns within the body politic? I began to work with Lucine Talalyan—a visual artist and founding member of QYC, with whom I was already collaborating on a number of different projects—as my research collaborator for a series of household survey interviews. Together, Talalyan and I conducted 150 survey interviews[8] with people in ten different neighborhoods of the city. We chose different neighborhoods for their particular histories, such as when they were built, and the class, education, and employment differences of their residents in accordance with Soviet urban planning schemes. We chose neighborhoods that had been industrial hubs in the Soviet era—such as Shengavit, Gortzaranayin (Factory District), and Yerord Mas—in which people might still live but now with vastly different (or no) opportunities for work in industrial production. We chose neighborhoods that were close to the city's center—such as Komitas or Sasuntsi David—in which members of the intelligentsia had once lived or might still live. We also chose neighborhoods far from the center—such as Charbakh, Erebuni, and Masiv 7—because those neighborhoods would have housed those more marginal to privilege during the Soviet era.[9]

As a rule, we did not directly ask about homosexuality during these interviews. Talalyan and I discussed this strategy before beginning our surveys. We went into these interviews assuming that most Yerevantsis would not be welcoming to newly visible nonheterosexual identities. Not asking allowed us to gauge how common the notion had become that "sexual perversion" was threatening Armenia's national survival. During these interviews we asked about gender and sexuality, family and nation, and concerns the households faced about their present and future. Only *three* of our 150 interviewees mentioned homosexuality at all. To be clear, this does not mean that everyone else with whom we spoke was entirely open and welcoming toward gendered and sexual practices and identities that strayed from national expectations. It also does not mean that feminism was an accepted political ideology, however defined. It does mean, however, that Yerevantsis writ large did not regard homosexuality or feminism as the major crises facing the nation. The rhetoric of sexual perversion (*aylaserutyun*) emerged only once during this survey. However, it was during these interviews that I discovered the rhetoric of *aylandakutyun*, or the *moral* perversion of the political-economic elite, which was something almost never brought up within popular media.

The massive disparity between what mattered to the people and what mattered to media led me to take media production more seriously, and as the final leg of this research project, I conducted interviews with journalists who worked across varying platforms of information dissemination. I wanted to understand how the rhetoric of sexual perversion and the figure of the homosexual had come to loom so large in public discourse. What were the routes of this language? What were the reasons for its invention? I interviewed ten journalists and other representatives of the media to get at these questions. Two of these journalists worked for mainstream circulations—sites of information that were not necessarily committed to anti-homosexual activism but that had nonetheless contributed to the publicizing of homosexuality as a national concern. These included *168 News* and the ARF-sponsored *Yerkir Media*. I also spoke to representatives of circulations that were highly committed to anti-homosexual activism or that were very welcoming of publishing inciting rhetoric around it. These included the editor-in-chief of *Iravunk* newspaper and one of the editors of *BlogNews.am*. And, finally, I spoke to journalists at *Epress, CivilNet*, and *Hetq*, three (less popular) progressive news sites that had not published inciting pieces on homosexuality at all and were more aligned with progressive politics (whether liberal or leftist), including taking LGBT rights seriously.

In talking to right-wing nationalists and other conservative individuals—such as my language instructor Knar or most of my household interviewees—I learned to be a trickster. I did not lie, because that would be a violation of ethical standards in ethnographic research. However, I did often euphemize my interests and topics of study in a way that would be more palatable to some subjects. With right-wing nationalists as well as with interviewees in the household surveys, I often said I was doing research on the role of the family in contemporary Armenian life. While this was true, it also omitted mentioning the role that (homo)sexuality played in my research interests. At times, especially among younger people I would meet, I would reveal what I *was* actually studying and often, following their reaction, realized I should never bring it up again if I wanted to maintain a relationship with them. This was also the case with Knar, who provided me language instruction for two summers and with whom I maintained ties for years following. Only once after my initial disclosure to her did my research interests ever come up again. I also often manipulated my appearance. For the household interviews, I made sure to remove my nose ring before knocking on anyone's door. I conducted these interviews when the weather was cold, and thus wearing a coat or jacket and pants allowed me to cover up my tattoos. In interviewing right-wing activists and journalists (in June and July), however, this was less possible. I tried to cover up, but I was still outed as a *different*. In this book I will use the term *different*, as a noun, to capture the ways in which the "We" of the nation, the "self," came undone by various improper modes of looking, behaving, practicing, and existing. A singular sense of a proper Armenia, in other words, was threatened by those who might belong (were not national Others) but existed improperly. Unlike the term *Other*, my use of *different* as a noun gets at the anxieties regarding the makeup of the self. My being a different—because of my tattoos, my nose piercing, my queerness, my feminism—had an impact on how my interviewees responded to me. In not avoiding those people who might see me, as a queer feminist, as lacking humanity, or as being a scourge on society, I also learned to listen, humanize, and analyze in new ways. Freud (1989a, 319) referred to psychoanalysis as a process of translation that could locate the "sense" of symptoms that seemed entirely irrational or unreasonable. Similarly, I began this research having an inkling that there was a sense behind right-wing claims that seemed entirely unhinged, and that conservative attachments to proper Armenian "tradition" could be mined for their larger claims and their political possibilities. I found that sense in the links between sexual and moral perversion.

Ethnographic research also led me to the social analyses of particular texts. Talalyan's and my interviews with members of households across Yerevan also included discussions of favorite films. In chapter 1, I provide a reading of one of the films that was commonly brought up as a family or personal favorite: *Hayrik* [Father] (Malyan 1972). Other texts—such as songs, a myth, an epic poem, and a fairytale—emerged from everyday conversations, happenstance, and political events. I discuss these texts within the contexts in which they became ethnographically relevant. It is the particular context that gives each of these texts their importance. Some are very common and well-known (like the myth of the giant Hayk, the first Armenian). Some are very rare and likely unheard of for most (such as the satirical Tale of Little Gender-Boycott that circulated through a blog post). Some are directly named in political events (such as the epic poem of *Sasna Tzrer* during a hostage crisis in 2016). And some are used here by me as hermeneutical devices, such as the film *Hayrik* or the origin myth of Armenia about the giant Hayk. Each of these is relevant because it speaks to a set of affects, emotions, and conditions from which its discussion or indirect indexing arose. In this sense, my reading of these texts should also be taken to be specific to the particular context of my ethnographic analysis—that is, in relation to the structure of perversion.

Perversion(s)

The terms *aylaserutyun* (այլասերություն) and *aylandakutyun* (այլանդակություն) and their relations to the ways in which I use the term *perversion* in this book are complex and deserve some attention. *Aylaserutyun* is composed of the prefix *ayl*, which means "other than" or "different," and *ser*, rooted in the term meaning to generate, *seril*. The word thus literally means degeneration. I translate *aylaserutyun* as "perversion" in English because of resonances with the English meanings and connotations of the term. "Perversion" in English can be defined as "the action of turning aside from what is true or right; the diversion of something from its original and proper course, state, or meaning; corruption, distortion." But it is most often used to refer to "sexual behavior or preference that is different from the norm; *spec.* that which is considered to be unacceptable or socially threatening, or to constitute mental illness" ("perversion" (n.), *Oxford English Dictionary*), meanings popularized especially through psychoanalysis and sexology in the nineteenth and twentieth centuries. While *aylaserutyun* might refer to any kind of moral, physical, or biological degeneration or degeneracy, in its contemporary colloquial use in Armenia, it almost always smuggles in attention to sexuality and connotations of the sexual. To refer to an act or behavior as *aylaserutyun*, or in its expression as an adjective (as *aylaservatz*), is to condemn it as sexually immoral. It is important, however, to note the particular differences in meanings within English and Armenian to get at some of the other connotations within the language of *aylaserutyun*. The *Armenian Language New Dictionary* (Der Khachadourian 1992b), a Western Armenian dictionary, defines *aylaserutyun* as "alienation from national (*azgayin*) features; removal from the resilience of national morality's strengthening; weakening." Furthermore, the *Explanatory Dictionary of Modern Armenian* defines *aylaserel*, the verb form of the noun *aylaserutyun*, as "to distort morality, to make ugly, to corrupt" and to "move toward a decline in morality, to make immoral" (Aghayan 1976). *Aylaserum*, a noun that refers to the thing that happens in *aylaserutyun*, is also defined by the same dictionary (Aghayan 1976) in biological terms, as "degeneration" or "existence in unfavorable conditions that have consequences on an animal or plant organism's properties, passed from generation to generation." The term, in all these uses, connotes or denotes something gone awry, something not what or where it is supposed to be, something distorted, corrupted, made improper—especially in regard to social and biological life and reproduction, including that of the nation.

The term *aylandakutyun* also carries connotations of the sexual but remains firmly grounded in divergence from what is good and proper. The *Armenian Language New Dictionary* (Der Khachadourian 1992s) defines *aylandakutyun* as "ugliness, clumsiness/grotesqueness, out of the ordinary," and the adjective *aylandakoren*, perversely, as "with ugliness, monstrously, absurdly, out of the ordinary." Colloquially in Armenia during the time I conducted research, the use of the term was often derogatory and connoted not just strangeness but impropriety; in other words, not just difference, but difference that was wrong, immoral, and dangerous to the body politic. Differences and eccentricities in behaviors and practices were commonly construed as dangerous. As I will discuss in chapter 2, this would include not only LGBT people but also feminists, those belonging to an emo subculture, punks, and religious minorities. Difference from what is proper Armenianness in Armenia is a dangerous path, for it opens up possibilities for Armenia to no longer be Armenia, threatening the nation's future survival.

Thus, while *aylandakutyun* has a less direct connection to the notion of perversion in the English language, I translate it here as "perversion" for three main reasons. First, the eccentricities and difference implied by the notion of *aylandakutyun* bring to the forefront the emphasis that Armenianness places on propriety and the dangers of swerving or deviating from what is expected, from what is proper, which maps on to the ways in which sexual perversion threatens the intactness of the Armenian family, the nation, the Church, and the institutions that are believed to allow the nation to survive. Both *aylaserutyun* and *aylandakutyun*, thus, imply dangerous deviations. Second, *aylandakutyun* is intimately connected to *aylaserutyun* in that the terms are sometimes used interchangeably when referring to the political-economic elite's sexual improprieties, especially as these improprieties are tied to their *excesses* and thus what I read as *surplus jouissance* in chapter 3. The excessive appetites of the political-economic elite for power, wealth, violence, brutality, food, and ostentatious display as well as for (perverse) sex makes them perverse, and largely morally improper. In other words, their excesses—which include sexual excess and extend beyond it—are akin to the excesses of what I call the figure of the homosexual, the imaginary character who threatens to put the nation on a perverse path through his (usually a male figuration) excess pleasure and lack of reproduction. And, finally, *aylandakutyun* (moral corruption) of the body politic itself (as a result of the elite's perversions, in a trickle-down effect, as I will discuss in chapter 5), is akin to sexual perversion. Improper forms of life and living—young men and women remaining unmarried because of a lack of jobs and the ability to sustain families; children being raised without fathers who are abroad, working as migrant laborers; men becoming alcoholics; families experiencing domestic violence and abuse, and so on—lead to the corrupt social reproduction of the body politic.

These meanings of perversion share facets of how "perversion" is defined within psychoanalytic thought, even as this differs greatly within psychoanalytic literature, especially between the meanings given to the idea by Freud and those given to the idea by Lacan. While the meanings of perversion that I develop in this book are not entirely dependent on either of these frameworks explicitly, they share with them some threads. For Freud, perversion was the movement of the subject away from proper object choice or "normal sexual aim." Perversions are either "(a) anatomical transgressions of the bodily regions destined for the sexual union, or (b) a lingering at the intermediary relations to the sexual object which should normally be rapidly passed on the way to the definite sexual aim" (Freud 1910, 14). Included within this notion of perversion is also sexual inversion, in which the whole of the object (belonging to the same sex) deviates from a normal sexual aim.[10] In my use here, perverse sexualities, desires, and behaviors are those that deviate from what is held to be proper social and biological reproduction: homosexuality; feminism; gay, lesbian, bisexual, or transgender identity; being an LGBT activist or in solidarity with LGBT activism; women smoking or drinking in public; any form of dress or aesthetic that differs from expectations of proper femininity and masculinity, including dressing emo or punk; women with tattoos; men with long hair; young unmarried persons, especially but not only women, moving out of their father's home; and so on.

Lacan's conceptualization of perversion, unlike Freud's, homes in not on the sexual aim of the subject but rather on a structure of the psyche in which there is an inverted effect of fantasy (Lacan 1998, 185).[11] My discussion of perversion in this book draws partially on Lacanian understandings of the perverse psychic structure, especially on its primary aspect having to do with the inadequacy of the paternal function. Without the paternal function in play, the subject does not undergo (symbolic) castration, and thus he expresses excess enjoyment (Swales 2012). *Survival of a Perverse Nation* traces two perverse figures: the homosexual and the oligarch. Both of these figures are marked by excess—the oligarch's excessive wealth, power, and enjoyment, and the homosexual's excessive (and unreproductive) pleasure. Furthermore, both of these figures are perverse—whether *aylaservatz* (sexually perverse) or *aylandakvatz* (more generally morally perverse)—because of their deviance and violation of

Armenian Symbolic authority. These figures do not abide by the Symbolic authority's Law of the Father, a moral order put in place within the very mythological beginnings of Armenianness (as I take up in chapter 1) and, as such, they undermine the survival of the nation. Thus, there are overlaps between what I describe as *aylaserutyun* and *aylandakutyun* as structures and as processes of Symbolic transgression and the Lacanian perverse. It is important to note, however, that while my discussion of perversion in this book maps fairly well onto Freudian and Lacanian readings of perversion, it is largely invested in tracing the colloquial feelings about *aylaserutyun* and *aylandakutyun* in Armenia.

The Ends of Symbolic Authority and Imaginary Potential

In 2010, during my first visit to Armenia, I was enrolled in a language course to learn to read and write (as well as to speak, considering that I had not spoken the Armenian language since I was about six and that when I did speak, it was the Western dialect, a bit different from the Eastern dialect spoken in the modern Republic). My language instructor, Knar (who also comes up from time to time in this book as someone from whom I learned a lot more about the context of the nation-state than its verbal language), had me do an assignment in which I had to write a paragraph about the family. In response to the prompt, I had written about radical feminist theories of marriage as the site of women's oppression. This upset Knar greatly. "Armenians have survived Genocide. They have survived the rule of many empires. They have survived without their own government. They have survived as a Christian nation amongst Muslims. And how has all of this been possible?" she asked. At this, I decided there was no convincing her to get on board with radical feminist theory, so I just looked back at her and asked, "How?" "With the family. With our Armenian traditions. With our language. Because we have had strong fathers who have protected these traditions. With our morality. Armenia would have been annihilated centuries ago if it were not for the strength of our family and our traditions," Knar insisted. She was not alone. During the rest of my visit that summer, I heard these narratives many times over by others, and I would continue to learn about the family's centrality in Armenianness.

Family is not just an important facet of daily life practice but also an ideological container of the nation's very possibility of survival. The question of the political in the various iterations of Armenia since the Genocide have centered questions of national survival and, importantly, the family as the repository of that survival. A look at the history of Armenian feminism is instructive here. A feminist movement has rarely existed within Armenia's modern history and does not currently exist within the Republic of Armenia. As Armine Ishkanian (2008) has argued, feminism is seen as standing against the traditional family, and Armenian women have historically held onto that family as critical for national survival. Unique in this history is the women's movement following the Genocide and World War I in Allied-occupied Constantinople. As Lerna Ekmekçioğlu (2016) argues, there were a combination of factors that made this feminist movement possible, and yet, the family was central. A National Revival movement in the immediate aftermath of the Genocide placed emphasis on women's work to rebirth and nurture back into existence a nation. While much of this feminine work was domestic, much of it also extended into public work in nursing, lobbying, teaching, and gathering financial contributions. This, Ekmekçioğlu maintains, emboldened women to demand various public and political rights while maintaining the importance of women's domestic duties. Thus, while inspired by the French liberal tradition, Armenian feminists made clear that they did not stand against a woman's role in the family through domestic work, although they believed that too much of this for women was wasteful to the nation. Furthermore, these Armenian feminists were more committed to national revival and survival than to the woman's cause when these two concerns were in contradiction. Threats to social reproduction—whether through genocide or neoliberalization—bolstered protective feelings around the institution of family and "traditional" gender relations.

Because feelings about kinship and the moral orders on which they are established are so central to understanding anxieties about the nation's survival and threats posed against it, Jacques Lacan's notion of the Symbolic order (1997, 2013) becomes an apt framework through which to understand the particular configuration of sovereignty,[12] intimacy, and political legitimacy I explore in this book. There are two notions of family that are critical to conceptualizations of Armenianness, and a principal agent in both is the Father. The Father is the leader of the household (*endanik*, those who live under one roof) as well as of what I call the nation-family[13] (*azg*, the extended family or tribe), the practice of the Armenian nation as an extended family in which private expectations seep into public demands. The concepts of Symbolic order, and Symbolic authority to which it is fastened, allow me to get at the personal, intimate, and affective dimensions of this power and authority.[14] Lacan's framework of Symbolic authority, which I find within the position of the Father as it stands in the context of Armenianness as Symbolic order, allows me to analyze moral assertions and axioms (especially those of survival), anxieties, fears, and identifications with power, with attention to the ambiguities and psychic tensions that define relations to the Father as sovereign power. While the Church—and especially the Armenian Apostolic Church—also holds a privileged position within the narrative of the nation's survival (as well as within the post-Soviet state, which I discuss in chapter 5), this position still functions within the Symbolic order and makes up one iteration of the Father. Though the Name-of-the-Father is a function of Lacan's Symbolic order, it is always also plural: the Names-of-the-Father. The Father is not a person, nor any one particular feeling, but the function of the superego (Lacan 2013)—what I am here calling the proper.

Psychoanalytic theory has long been used to understand the workings of sovereign power and its ideology (Freud 1961; Žižek 1989; Kaganovsky 2008; Borneman 2004; Shirinian 2020a). "What is the psychic form that power takes?" asks Judith Butler (1997b, 2), highlighting the necessity of understanding not only power but its relation to the psychic dimension that subjection forms. Power's psychic form, I suggest, is what we might call legitimacy. To be subjected, in other words, is to legitimate power by becoming its subject, by internalizing (or, in Foucauldian conceptualizations, externalizing, on the body) its validity. But, just as importantly, the psychic form that power takes can also produce power as illegitimate. Within psychoanalytic parlance, we might call these senses of legitimacy "identification," which Freud described as making possible an intimate link between the "suppressed classes with the class who rules and exploits them," which is also coupled with an emotional attachment to "masters" (Freud 1961). Psychic life and intimate connections are essential to the maintenance of sovereign power. and it is also—through the Symbolic order as the Name- and the No-of-the-Father in Lacanian thought—where I locate fissures in political legitimacy. The Father's Name, as such, is the site of Symbolic identification; it is always coupled with the No, the authority and power that upholds that identification with castrating power and potential. As their practices, behavior, and lack of care for the Armenian people violates Armenianness (as the Symbolic order), however, the oligarchic horde's position within Armenia's Symbolic order only precariously wields the Name while maintaining the authority of the No. This has, I argue, led to a fragmentation of their ability to maintain hegemony and a sense of "law and order" in Armenia, seen as the very epitome of violators of the Father's Law (the Name- and the No-of-the-Father).

Symbolic order and its authority are not the whole of the self, of consciousness, or of the possibilities of imagination, creativity, and action. There is always a gap of representation—something within the subject, some reality, some knowledge that is not entirely symbolized (Moore 2007). As Henrietta Moore (2007) has provocatively suggested, a psychoanalytic anthropology can make sense of how agency, imagination, and resistance might be limited and constrained by the "social imaginary" but are not closed off by this imaginary, which we might otherwise understand as the Symbolic order. Fantasy, which constitutes the outside of this order, offers anthropological investigations of political intervention tools with which to understand how new worlds and new world orders are actively desired, imagined, and brought into being. *Survival of a Perverse Nation* is interested in, but also politically committed to, locating the cracks and fissures from which new sexual, gendered, intimate, political, and economic realities might take flight. Each chapter locates how dimensions of the rhetorics of perversion point to and highlight these spaces and sites—how, in other words, anxieties concerning the breakdown of Armenianness as Symbolic order make room for imagining and fantasizing outside the constraints of that order, toward more liberatory, queer, and, perhaps, fantastic worlds.

What Is to Come

Each of the following chapters of this book takes up a different aspect, site, or figure of perversion. While some chapters focus more exclusively on one or the other form (*aylaserutyun* or *aylandakutyun*), each chapter articulates the relationship that these two forms have with one another. In tracing perversion throughout these chapters, I also trace the ways in which queer possibility and potential bubble up at these various sites. In chapter 1, "From National Survival to National Perversion," I trace the history of the 2012 sex panic through popular histories and mythologies of Armenianness, demonstrating the ways in which the proper social and biological reproduction of the nation was felt to have been located in strong, heroic father figures and their moral leadership. I draw links between contemporary notions of propriety surrounding Armenianness and the mythical first Armenian, the giant warrior Hayk. Providing a mytho-poetic reading of the nation's and Republic's history, which combines elements of myth with speculative readings of historical developments, I show how the 1991 independence of the Republic from the Soviet Union produced a new ruling elite with an uncanny resemblance to the mythical Father Hayk, but in morally deviant form, threatening the nation's proper social reproduction. The chapter sets the scene for how the postsocialist period became a rupture in the nation's millennia-long survival, paving the path toward perversion and, thus, national annihilation.

The two chapters that follow each take up one of the figures of perversion that inform the book's central argument. In chapter 2, "The Figure of the Homosexual," I explore the production and cultivation of the rhetoric of *aylaserutyun* (sexual perversion). I draw on a 2013 sex panic about *gender* and perverse futures imagined by the right wing that the figure of the homosexual threatened to make real. Through interview material with journalists and right-wing nationalists as well as with the three (of 150) members of households surveyed across Yerevan who pointed to concerns about homosexuality as a problem for the nation, I also show how this figure of sexual perversion (the homosexual) emerged as a displacement for other political-economic crises. As a figure imagined to be unproductive and unreproductive, the homosexual stood as the subject/object of the felt impossibilities of national reproduction—a conflation of widespread concerns about labor migration, mass emigration, and low fertility rates. This investigation highlights how political-economic perversions, deviations, and violations are cast as sexual in nature and that feelings about sexuality and sexual morality are inextricable from material conditions and demands.

In chapter 3, "The Names-of-the-Fathers," the oligarch becomes my main figure of analysis. I trace popular feelings about the political-economic elite through their nicknames. I examine these nicknames, which often combine a shortened diminutive version of their first names (marking them as intimate figures) with another name that points to their brutality and criminality (marking them as brutal sovereigns to be feared), through speculatively narrating the material and intimate connections these elite figures claim over localized spaces and neighborhoods. These "nicks"—cuts in the name of local sovereigns whom we might understand as political Fathers—bifurcate these figures, producing them as the Name-and the No-of-the-Father, but one in which their brutality (their wielding of the Father's No) is separated from identification (the Name). This bifurcation through nicknames produces oligarchs and other members of the governing elite as both rulers and as illegitimates, making them the illegitimate Fathers of the nation. The chapter continues to weave together the threads between sexual perversion and moral perversion by exploring the ways in which the figure of the oligarch is imagined as a sexual degenerate. I also explore the possibilities of queer futures that might emerge through the perversity of present conditions.

Although space and time are never separable, chapters 3 and 4 each take up space and time, respectively, and somewhat separately (although still in relation to one another), in order to home in on the workings of perversion within each. Chapter 4, "Wandering Yerevan," is primarily concerned with the question of postsocialism's perverse spatiality. I show how the transformations brought on by the end of state socialism changed the spatial configurations of the city of Yerevan, creating fragmentations (through privatization and organized abandonment to capital's speculation) formed around private wealth rather than centered on public human needs. Exploring the discontinuities in the construction plans that disorient and reorient leisurely strolls (wandering) through the city, the scenes of abandonment in residential and factory zones, and the changing landscapes and meanings of parks and other public spaces, I reflect on the feelings and experiences of perverse space that bring the contexts of sexual perversions (*aylaserutyun*) and larger moral deviations (*aylandakutyun*) into conversation with one another. I examine public parks that are made proper (and governed by the Law of the Father) through the investment of capital as well as spaces abandoned by state and private capital that leave spaces of wild growth amenable to queer life. My analysis of postsocialist space highlights how, against the backdrop of socialist centralized plans, capitalism can be understood as lacking in coherent or intelligible ideology, pointing to the emptiness in promises of capitalist development and official nationalist narratives of state and Church. Capitalist development, in other words, is a mechanism that perverts life and its possibilities.

Following these reflections on postsocialist space, chapter 5, "An Improper Present," focuses on postsocialist temporality by analyzing various common negations of life and existence: "There is no Armenia," "There are no Armenian families," "There is no government," and others. I situate these negations within larger discussions of the present in which dilapidated residential buildings and homes, as well as the conditions of families residing in them, are described as "ruins." I show how a time-space of negation points to a feeling that the present is too improper—too unintelligible within ontological understandings of Armenianness, its time, and its movement—to be considered a present, producing a feeling that the present is not a livable time but a time in which nothing feels possible. I produce an ethnographically informed theory of postsocialist spatiotemporality as deviation from the proper reproduction of life and its conditions. Within this context of feeling the present as having perverted temporal propriety, however, there also emerge possibilities of radical change and radical hope, figuring new gendered and sexual possibilities for a future-in-the-making that we might understand as queer desires cropping up from unexpected places.

Postsocialist time and space—felt as ruins of the present and as a time of impossibility leading to no future—were a difficult construction from which to activate the political. Negations of the present and the future, based in dire material conditions and reigned over by an illegitimate horde, had left many Armenians feeling hopeless and thus unwilling to act. This hopelessness, as a negative and negating affect, however, could at times be translated and transformed into affirmations of the present and of radically different futures. Chapter 6, "The Politics of 'No!'" follows grassroots activists and the movements that they cultivated from 2012 to 2013. The politics of "No!" that were expressed through these movements affirm worlds to come through the negation of the world as it is. I also show how the politics of "No!" transformed larger political feelings in the country, especially through the 2013 post-presidential elections, which wavered and then eventually fractured—splits brought on by ambiguous feelings about replacing one political Father, a Daddy, with another. The politics of "No!"—a response to the illegitimate Father's No—imaginatively make future worlds in a liminal present, opening up new future horizons. Most importantly in Armenia, the politics of "No!" have been making way for a future without a political Daddy, a radical alternative to a millennia-long surviving nation with a strong Father to lead it.

I hope readers find in these pages glimpses of hope, thresholds to new material and affective orders, and portals that may lead to radically different life-worlds, even if these are tucked in places that seem hopelessly driven toward the making of the unlivable. I hope that readers speculate with me.

CHAPTER ONE

From National Survival to National Perversion

It was the summer of the year 4503. I had just arrived in Yerevan, and Alis and Albert, two friends whom I had not seen since the previous year, brought me to the apartment they had arranged for me in the central district of the city; they then left me to take a nap after twenty-four hours of traveling from Durham, North Carolina, to Warsaw to Moscow and finally to Yerevan. Now, it was II p.m. and Alis had just gotten off work and was calling to tell me that she was on her way over with wine and a video that I had to see. After some catching up in general and pouring some wine, I finally asked her, "So, what is this video you have to show me?" It was a YouTube video—a live recording of a song performed by Arthur Meschian during a concert in 4501.[1] That is, 4501 in the *bun Hayots* (actual Armenian) calendar, used by the official circulation of the Republican Party of Armenia until 1997 (Panossian 2002, 130). The calendar, following the timeline of historian Mikayel Chamchian, dates year I to 2492 BC, the year of the battle in which the giant Hayk defeated the tyrant Bel and established what is now known as Armenia. By the Gregorian calendar, it was 2011, and Meschian—a dissident Armenian singer-songwriter (as well as an artist and architect) who had been popular among the intelligentsia in the late socialist period and who continued to be an important icon of dissidence in post-Soviet times—had performed the song in 2009. Alis and I had bonded over our love of his music when we first met in the summer of 4502 (2010, in Gregorian calendric years). She was impressed that I knew of Meschian's work; that, for her, made me Armenian even if I was way more American than Armenian. And now she was excited to watch me react to this song that was new to us.

The song, "Aha ev Verch" (That's It), retells the story of the battle of Hayk and Bel. In Meschian's version, however, Hayk is no longer the valiant hero. It is Hayk who is defeated by the tyrant Bel. And Bel, it turns out, might not be an external Other but an enemy within. In the song, the battle between Hayk and Bel is no longer the inauguration of Armenia but its end. We played the video on Alis's smartphone over and over again, discussing the lyrics and their implication.

> And the pages turn, this tired myth.
> A hardened statue, a story forgotten.
> There is no beginning or end to this eternal struggle.
> All of you, who have turned, have been defeated by Bel
> That's it. Hayk was defeated by the warrior Bel.

After this last line, during the one brief moment of silence between guitar strums and drumbeats, a woman from the crowd in the live performance shouts out "No!" (*Voch!*), audible to the whole auditorium. Alis and I were stuck on this performative refusal. We played the song over and over again, each time waiting for that one second in the recording. This was our *punctum*, the "sting, peck, cut, little hole" that was also a "cast of the dice" (Barthes 1981, 27) in the song's performativity. This "No!" was the accident that penetrated our aural attention. And this moment of refusal and negation was not lost on Meschian himself, who addressed it after he finished the song: "That 'No' was very good. I don't know who it was but it was completely 'of us' [*meronqakan er*]," he said as he gave a thumbs up. This "No!" as defining an "us" became the topic of many discussions that Alis, Albert, and I would have that summer and beyond. What kind of "No!" was it, and who constituted the "us"? What did the song imply about Armenia's origins myth and its history as it was retold through the crises of its present?

Armenia's "national time" (Panossian 2002; Platz 2000) is most often produced in relation to three critical events that may have happened and/or that have been said to have happened: the battle between Hayk and Bel, the adoption of Christianity in the fourth century, and the Genocide of the late nineteenth and early twentieth centuries (often dated to events in 1915). Each of these critical moments, in different ways, can be understood as a history defined as "traumatic departure" (Caruth 2016), an "accident" that leads toward the making of culture and tradition while also shocking a collective unconscious toward fragmentations of its history and the possibilities of remembering and forgetting, knowing and unknowing, avowal and disavowal. While Hayk as a figure is mythical and predates the main Christian history of Armenia as told today, he embodies the particular values of heroism, valiance, bravery, and the determination to survive against all odds that have become tropes in narrating Armenia as a nation, a people, and a special (chosen) ethno-nation. The myth of how Armenia became a Christian kingdom follows this structure of bravery and survival, combining with these tropes a miraculousness that threads myth to known and studied histories. The Genocide is often cast as *aghed* (catastrophe), following early twentieth-century witness writings, marking the event as senseless and unimaginable (Nichanian 2003) and thus, in some ways, ungraspable as an event. While the Genocide is not myth at all, it has been continuously denied by its perpetrator (the Ottoman Empire, now Turkey), producing gaps in knowing and remembering within a national (un)conscious. These aspects put the Genocide in a mythological position in collective consciousness. Together, these three event-myths narrate Armenianness as extraordinary. Importantly, also, and as I will discuss below, while the Genocide is a recent and modern event, it acts as a retrospective precursor to the other events, giving the narrative of the nation a structure of survival.

But these three critical moments of mytho-historical time, so important to the understandings of an Armenian national identity within the Diaspora, do not fully encompass and undergird the temporalities that are lived and experienced within the Republic today, which take on instead different temporal dimensions: sovereign time, perverse time, and queer time. A mytho-historical understanding of feelings surrounding Armenianness within the Republic also needs to take into account the massive protests that marked the years of glasnost toward the end of the Soviet Union's existence; the devastating earthquake on December 7, 1988, that turned Leninakan (now Gyumri), the second largest city in the Republic, into ruins; the pogroms in Azerbaijan, followed by war during the first years of independence; the popular "democratic" elections of Armenia's first President, Levon Ter-Petrosyan, followed by his unpopular and "fraudulent" second election a few years later, partly because of his closeness to a rising oligarchy (Astourian 2000); the emergence of a visibility surrounding homosexuality and LGBT identity and the fissures it brought to a collective sense of national belonging; the constant political tumult that included terrorist plots, militant hostage situations, mass social movements, and the eventual *My Step* movement that ousted the ruling Republican Party from power in 2018; and the resurgence of the Nagorno-Karabakh war in 2020 that produced yet another political crisis in the nation when Armenia lost many more lives and territories. In the post-Soviet Republic, sovereign time, which *should have been* a time of real collective Armenian expressions of national identity, collided with perverse time and queer time, which fissured the possibilities of what should have been that singularity and instead left unfulfilled the long-held dream of a proper nation-state that would ensure survival. As a result of these fissures—which interrupted and disoriented Armenia's Symbolic order—the nation's survival has come into question.

"History" is experienced both through participation and narration: it is not just the realm of "what happened" but also "what is said to have happened," which sets an ambiguous tone to what we mean when we imply or state a history of something (Trouillot 1995).[2] History and the past—whether the past as it happened, as what is said to have happened, and as all that has happened and was said about it in between—are also realms of public and political feelings. Rather than a one-way movement of the political as shaping feelings and emotions, feelings and emotion influence the political and the forms and possibilities of social belonging (Cvetkovich 2012; Berlant 2008).[3] In this chapter, I look for nation, myth, and history at the level of feelings, sometimes reading between the lines to get at attachments and associations that are not always easily and directly detectable in discourse, speech, and action. These are attachments that are driven by desire rather than by facts and rational justification. Myths and a history based on mythological forms structure feelings about the political, even if they are not usually directly stated.

I provide a mytho-history of Armenia's narrative of survival and brave determination, which in the postsocialist era under consideration —from the 2010s until the so-called Velvet Revolution of 2018—was felt to be deviating in directions that were deemed perverse, immoral, and anti-Armenian, raising the question whether today's Armenia is in continuity with the origins it claims. Was impropriety always there? Was the myth itself misremembered? "Nation" here is, of course, contested. It is not an object that is purely and singularly defined by all members of society who may (or in some cases may not) identify with it. The very questions that I produce here—about origins, time, and propriety—point to the object's contestability. My mytho-historical narrative and analysis also makes use of poesis and poetics. I speculate on the connections between Armenia's past and its postsocialist present. I use language and other constellations of signs (such as the Chamchian calendar) in order to home in on emotional worlds and capture the spatiotemporal disorientations that have resulted from postsocialist experience.

I begin with the myth of Hayk and Bel, which holds a particular power within the Symbolic order of Armenianness. Hayk's name is the Name-of-the-Father. Armenia, Hayasdan in Armenian, traces its naming to Hayk. If the unconscious is structured like a language and the Symbolic order is made up of various signifiers in precise relation to one another, as in Lacanian understandings (Laplanche and Pontalis 1973, 440), then the name of Hayk, the Father of Armenians, is the master signifier within an Armenian national unconscious. As a word, or signifier, within Armenia's Symbolic order as well as the very Name of Symbolic authority, it structures ontological propriety via a particular set of values traceable to the role of Hayk: survival at all costs, continuity, care for the Armenian people to ensure that survival and continuity, and heroic masculinity (a particular kind of Father) in the seat of authority. I investigate other myths—structured and figured around a Symbolic world already apparent in the story of Hayk and Bel—and how these myths resonate within political events as well as in everyday life. These mytho-histories of survival are suddenly ruptured in the postsocialist era with the emergence of *aylandakutyun* (moral perversion) and *aylaserutyun* (sexual perversion) as both discourse (anxiety articulated at the level of language) and reality (with the emergence of the oligarchy as well as of sexual difference in public life). I explore these ruptures and what they mean for Armenia's Symbolic order and the survival of the nation.

Heroes and Survivors

Who are the Armenians? Moses Khorenatsi, the fifth-century historian,[4] had a lot to say on the subject. Khorenatsi wrote one of the most comprehensive histories of Armenian people prior to the introduction of Christianity in the fourth century (Khorenatsi 1978). Khorenatsi's *History* begins with a criticism of Armenian kings who had the bad habit of not keeping archives of their own history. Because of this, when King Vagharshak came to reign over Armenia in the second century, he did not know the history of the throne. "Had he succeeded to the throne of valiant men or of cowards?" (82) Khorenatsi asks, as he begins telling the history of history. King Vagharshak sent Mar Abas Catina, a Syrian and "a diligent man versed in Chaldean and Greek" (82) to the royal archives of Arshak the Great, the King of Persia. There he found, written in Greek, a book that considers "the authentic account of the ancients and ancestors" (83). Vagharshak was, according to Khorenatsi, "personable and valiant . . . expert at the bow, eloquent, and intelligent," (84) and, from the recordings of the archives brought to him by Mar Abas Catina, he sees that his ancestors came from similar stock.

According to Khorenatsi, the history of Armenia extends far back to the most ancient of times, to the times when gods and giants roamed the earth—"monstrous and enormous in force and size" (84)—to the time immediately after the great flood and the destruction of the Tower of Babel. The history tells of the first Armenian, Hayk, a giant who settled the lands that belong to the territory known today as Greater Armenia, also known as Mets Hayk, or Larger Hayk, which spanned Armenian kingdoms from the second century BC through the classical, late antique, and medieval periods. Noah had three sons after the great flood. Khorenatsi argues that scripture has generally dedicated itself to narrating the stories of the descendants of Sem, who begot Abraham, leaving the histories brought forth by the descendants of Ham and Yapheth, Noah's two other sons, with very few traces. The battle that begot Armenia was fought between the descendants of Noah's two other two sons: Bel, the descendant of Ham; and Hayk, the descendant of Yapheth. Hayk refused to let Bel, the warrior who had been "impos[ing] his tyranny on the whole land" (85), rule over the land on which he lived with his own clan, "his sons and daughters and sons' sons, martial men about three hundred in number, and other domestic servants and outsiders who had joined his service and all his effects" (85). Hayk created an army ready to fight. When Bel and his army arrived, Bel was not pleased by Hayk's maneuver but was still determined to expel him from the land. After all, he had already been successful in defeating many other armies and in creating a much larger army than Hayk's. But Hayk was such a magnificent warrior with his bow that he was able to defeat Bel and his whole army, thus allowing his people to settle on his land with no imposition from the now-defeated Bel. The location of this battle is placed near Lake Van but also under the mountain of the northern regions—or Mount Ararat, the site at which Noah's Ark is said to have finally washed up after the floods: "He came and dwelt at the foot of a mountain in a plain where had lingered and dwelt a few of the human race who had previously scattered. These Hayk subjected to himself, and he built there a residence . . . and gave it in inheritance to Cadmos, the son of Aramaneak" (85). Aramaneak was the son of Hayk and would be the forefather of Aram and finally Ara the Handsome, the courageous warriors who were known to have increased the borders of Armenia.

Hayk left a legacy of miraculous heroism. As a mythic hero, he may have been the first, but he was not the last. There have since been other men of larger-than-life valor like Hayk in Armenia's mythohistory. One of these was the man who was able to convert the entire kingdom of Armenia to Christianity in the fourth century. As the story goes, in the early fourth century, King Trdat of Armenia, a sinful king who persecuted Christians, punished his former assistant Gregory for his Christianity by throwing him into a dungeon pit known as Khor Virap. For this sin, God punished the king by turning him into a wild boar. Gregory miraculously survived his incarceration in the pit, which is said to have been the home of snakes and other dangerous elements. It was after years of Gregory's incarceration that the king's sister had a vision that Gregory was still alive in the pit and could cure the king of his curse. After Gregory was released from the pit, he miraculously cured Trdat, who then converted Armenia to Christianity and, along with Gregory, founded the first Church of Armenia and named it after his healer—St. Gregory the Illuminator, Grigor Lusavorich.

In 2016, another mythical horde came into play within the Armenian political imaginary. The *Sasna Tzrer*, or the *Daredevils of Sassoun*, an epic poem that had circulated through oral storytelling since approximately the ninth century and that was recorded for the first time in 1873 by Bishop Srvandzatyan, was reanimated when a group of armed men entered a police station in the Yerevan neighborhood of Erebuni, taking the station hostage for fourteen days. The group—which called itself Sasna Tzrer and was a part of the larger group, Founding Parliament, that had been calling for the resignation of President Serzh Sargsyan since 2012—demanded the resignation of the president as well as the release of political prisoner and opposition leader Jirair Sefilian, who had been arrested in June 2016 for an alleged plot to take over communication facilities in Yerevan. Aside from the hostage situation within the police station that led to the death of three policemen as well as to the destruction by arson of at least three police vehicles, the siege also led to protests outside of the police station in support of the Sasna Tzrer. On July 31, after shooting down one officer in a stand-off, the Sasna Tzrer surrendered.

The epic tale after which the group named themselves tells the story of four generations of heroes who protected the Armenian village of Sassoun from Muslim rule: Sanasar and Balthazar, David of Sassoun, Great Mher, and Little Mher. The epic is a popular one in Armenia, narrating the stunts of great, fearless warriors who protect their Armenian compatriots and save Armenia from the enemy. In this sense, it follows the origin myth of Hayk and is, thus, "associated with the very spirit of the Armenian people and its historical destiny" (Zolyan 2014, 55).[5] The Sasna Tzrer in the epic poem were not just heroes, they were also somewhat mad and willing to go to any means to protect their people, especially women, children, and the elderly. As such, Armine Ishkanian asked during the hostage crisis in 2016, "While Armenians have taken to Facebook to debate whether the Sasna Dzrer are heroes or terrorists, if we take a step back, can we not say that these men appear to personify the stereotype of the ideal or real man in Armenian society?" (Ishkanian 2016). In this sense, the 2016 Sasna Tzrer, who in some ways could arguably have been inciting revolution in the sense of undoing the order of oligarchic power, might instead have been participating in an older notion of *revolution*: the restoration of power (Arendt 1990); or, in this case, the restoration of a properly operating patriarchy that was withering away in the postsocialist era due to the immoralities of those in power and the illegitimacy of those who materially as well as, in some ways, symbolically, governed the Armenian nation-state; or, the restoration of a political and properly patriarchal power that would allow Armenians to continue to survive.

While some saw the historical reality of 2016 as repeating the myth of the same structure (that of mad but heroic men who fight and win against all odds [Zolyan 2016], as was the case of the Sasna Tzrer in general and of Hayk in particular) others had different interpretations of the relationship between the tale and the historical event. Lusine Kharatyan (2016) draws attention to the very meaning of finding myth in the historical event and the historical event in myth. She explains:

> Many in modern-day Armenia seek the realities of the present and the future in the past. At every opportunity, we remember Khorenatsi's *Lament* and, once again, confirm that nothing has changed and nothing will change.... What is remarkable [here]? The fact that we think that there is a code of Armenian identity that was once and for all recorded somewhere in the Middle Ages and is repeated forever.

Kharatyan's critique points to the problems of reading historical reality as structured by myth. We might extend this critique to reading the "moral" of a historical event (as one would read the "moral" of a myth or fable) as tied to an Armenian Symbolic order that has ontological reverberations—a way in which Armenianness always has been and will be (lest it cease to exist entirely). The trope of survival within Armenian mytho-history has produced a forceful continuity—a repetition of the drama of survival in which contemporary historical events become sites for the rearticulation, reenactment, and analysis of Armenia's struggle with survival from time immemorial.

Survival and National Reproduction

Myths and history involving Armenianness are structured through the narrative of survival, summoning a question: Who are we who survived? As Cathy Caruth has argued, survival produces a "peculiar incomprehensibility," a "nonexperience" of remaining unharmed and "*being chosen for* a future that remains, in its promise, yet to be understood" (Caruth 2016, 60–73). Collective survival, however, can also come to mean tragedy, as survival may lead to fragmentation beyond the recognizability of an "ethnical unit" (Oushakine 2009, 81). This "ethnotrauma"[6] is a site of uncertainty regarding the objective and purpose of a future that must be fulfilled, which marks it as a site of discipline, surveillance, and policing. Survival in the past mandates a collective psychic survival into the future, which demands strict control of boundaries of a "We" (that which has/those who have survived). The constitution of the "We" has to be ontologically preserved at all costs.

The theme of survival within these myths and histories—especially as they have contemporary resonances—is produced as a result of the history of Genocide/catastrophe. Although the myth of Hayk and other mytho-histories predate the nineteenth- and twentieth-century pogroms, massacres, and deportations by the Ottoman Empire, they are retold and remembered today as a projection of those later historical events. Furthermore, historical events after the Genocide—for instance, the 1988 earthquake in the Spitak region that was seen as one more tragedy in a long line of tragedies that the Armenian people had to overcome (Fassin and Rechtman 2009) or the Nagorno-Karabakh war that was seen as the Genocide's "sequel" (Marutyan 2007)—are also read through the theme of great and impossible survival.

The relation between Armenianness and an assemblage of danger, threat, incursion, and historical (and future impending) catastrophe is not quite a mourning but a holding on—an incorporation (Abraham and Torok 1994)—with the hope that through memory a solid, singular, identity will allow for the continuation of survival. In this sense, Armenia becomes "a community of sufferers" (Panossian 2002, 137) who, in spite of it all and against all odds, continue to survive. Sebouh Aslanian has suggested that as a result of this sensibility there has been an overreliance on the nation-form within Armenian studies and history—projecting into the past contemporary sociopolitical realities—as well as a narrative that, if not nationalist, remains "nationist" with the assumption that "there has always been an Armenian 'spirit' or 'soul' characterizing all Armenians and acting as the master subject of their national history" (Aslanian 2018, 96). Genocide, thus, as a structuring mytho-history of Armenianness, calls forth an ontology that informs Armenianness not only as it is experienced but also as it is studied. On the one hand, we may read this ontology of survival as a "wound culture" that makes claims on and forms the political basis of identity (Ahmed 2004). On the other hand, it is a conservative impulse that surveils, polices, and extricates any form of existence that deviates from that defined as the "We" that has survived. This community and its survival, however, comes at the cost of—with the sacrifice of—those who pose contradictions to the singularity of the "We" (as those who have survived).

Survival is a critical (masculine) characteristic that is celebrated as both a part of Armenian ethnic *nature* as well as the labor of centuries of *nurture*. The national reproduction of Armenia, like that of other nations (Delaney 1991; Ozyurek 2006; Woodcock 2007; Schoeberlin

2004), is a masculine endeavor; it is based not on a mothering but on a fathering that ensures the transmission of critical masculine values from one generation to the next; it is often traced back to an original Father who embodied these values. Thus, genealogy—including mythical genealogy—which has become an essential component of Armenian nationalism, not only traces biological reproduction but also places great emphasis on a social reproduction of a proper Armenianness that will remain recognizably Armenian in its values, in its "traditions," and in its respect for older generations of men who protect and have protected Armenia from dissolution from within and tyranny from without. To "multiply" Armenia, that with which Hayk was credited, is not just a matter of reproducing bodies. It is about reproducing a particular kind of social world made of a courageous stock of men, who are devoted to their nation and willing to fight to keep Armenia safe and free from the tyrannical sorts, or those like Bel. Critical to this survival is the transmission of morals from father(s) to son(s).

The Genealogy of (Im)morality

Paternal social reproduction and its dependency on proper values and traditions is poignantly captured in the 1972 Soviet-era film *Hayrik* (Father) directed by Henrik Malyan. The film was often listed as a favorite by interviewees my research collaborator, Lucine Talalyan, and I surveyed. It tells the story of one family—a carpenter, his wife, and their six children—through its fathers. It begins with a call for father: a little boy yells "*Hayriiiiiiiiiiiiik*" (Father) to a carpenter, who is working on a rooftop as part of Armenia's immense urban development projects in the 1960s–70s. The boy is calling his father because his grandfather—his father's father—has come from the village to visit. The family gathers in the home—all of them except the eldest son who is doing his duty. *Papik* (Grandfather) shows his family a photograph taken of his grandfather who was a freedom fighter against the Turks during Armenia's First Republic period in 1918. The teenage sons make fun of the picture, teasing the pathetic look of the fighters: "They look a little thin to be fighters," one of the young men claims. The new fighters of their time are strong with weaponry and a mighty army. How could these small men, wearing ordinary village clothes, be respected as strong and mighty fighters if they look so weak?

The film captures the juxtaposition of the thriving energy of the Soviet heyday—the 1960–70s when the middle class grew and the union became politically and economically stable—and the decline of an old way of life. The importance of the figure of *Hayrik* (an endearing and yet formal term for Father) seems to be on the decline. The young men do not respect their forefathers—neither their grandfather nor these fighters who are his forefathers. In them, they see an outdated world. They actively tease their grandfather and laugh at him. In doing so, they threaten to break away from an Armenianness that places the highest importance on father-right. When Talalyan's and my household interviewees explained Armenianness, or particular values that needed to be honored, we often heard "Paperits a galis," or "It comes from the grandfathers [forefathers]." The phrase was also sometimes used to explain some negative manifestations of Armenianness, such as domestic violence or the disregard for the value of women as people. In its proper form, Armenianness is passed down from father to father. The young men in the film will not get their Armenianness from their fathers, because they see their fathers as unnecessarily stuck in the past and with little to offer. From where will they get their Armenianness, then? How will they become fathers, and what kinds of fathers will they become? Hayrik (played by the beloved actor Frunzik Mkrtichian), living between the old world of his father and the new world of his children, feels unable to be the good son his father wanted as well as to act as a proper father to his own sons in a modern world.

With massive global changes, captured by television scenes of the tumultuous 1960s with its mass-protest movements in the United States and Western Europe and its shifts from a village life of duties and obligations to individualized homes with room for leisure (and perversion), the film seemed to be suggesting that fatherhood was deteriorating by way of new forms of *aylaserutyun* (sexual perversion) and *aylandakutyun* (moral perversion), leading to new dangers transgressing Armenian propriety. These two forms of perversion are evinced in the film through its two main plot lines. In the first, one of Hayrik's unmarried sons impregnates a young woman and does not marry her. For Hayrik's father, the pregnancy must be fixed through marriage. Papik denounces Hayrik, first, for raising a son who could do such a thing and, second, for not forcing him to marry the girl or at least go to her himself and bring her to the patrilocal home. For Papik, a village man, the state-granted marriage license (known still by the Russian acronym ZAKS) is of less importance than bringing the girl home. Hayrik goes to visit the girl, who refuses to come home with him. At the end of the film, when she gives birth, it is Hayrik, and not his son, who is the only one from the family to visit and see the baby. Hayrik's son fails to fulfill his moral obligations, and thus we might read Hayrik's taking up of these obligations himself as a mournful capture of Armenia's Soviet-era modern perversion and a last grasp on the proper. However, we might also read this scene not as showing a discontinuity with a moral past but as underscoring instead an insistence on its social and biological reproduction as continuity and survival. Regardless of his son's improprieties, Armenianness survives through Hayrik, who looks after and claims his blood kin. No matter what perverse roads loom out ahead, the proper path—Armenian propriety—continues to reproduce itself and survive.

In a second plot line, another one of Hayrik's sons does poorly in school, leading Hayrik's wife to talk her husband into giving a bribe so that their son will be admitted into university. "Do something" she tells him, knowing how uncomfortable he is with the prospect of corrupt behavior. After much urging, he finally agrees apprehensively. He meets a man to whom he is to give a sum of money, who tells him, "You already know the conditions," meaning he knows how much money to give and for what. Now it is time to complete the transaction by transferring the money, which Hayrik has in an envelope in his coat pocket. After hours—from midday to sunset—of wandering the city of Yerevan to find a spot in which he can feel comfortable enough to commit bribery, the man finally gives up and walks away from Hayrik and never receives the bribe. Hayrik's son, however, finds his own way toward corruption. He hires a few classmates to take his exams for him. When they receive the news about the boy's success on the exams, father and mother sit at the dining table with their son. The mother, thinking Hayrik gave the bribe, is proud of her husband who transcended his own fears and "did something" for his son; the son knows how he was able to achieve his success through his own perverse ways. Hayrik is the only remaining moral agent (seemingly in all of Yerevan). He smiles, thinking that his son passed based of his own hard work.

Hayrik's youngest son (about eight years old) is representative of the open possibilities of the future. In other words, sons may still have something to learn from their fathers and might become proper fathers themselves, even in the face of perverse social trends. Toward the end of the film, Papik has passed away. As the film closes, father and son walk around the streets of Yerevan, Hayrik supporting his son on his shoulders while having a hopeful conversation as his son asks him how to be a father and if he will have a family of his own one day. But while the film offers this bit of hope, father-right continues to disintegrate: Hayrik was unable to raise his three other sons in a proper way, where morality comes from their father's ability to know best and where family obligations are prioritized over all else in life. If in 1972, when the film was produced, Hayrik was cast as a rare kind of man, by 2012 when I began my fieldwork, he, much like Hayk in Arthur Meschian's song, was being mourned as a heroic figure now defeated.

The Battle of Hayk and Bel, Cast in the Fifth Millennium

Arthur Meschian's retelling of the battle of Hayk and Bel opens various new dimensions of Armenia's origin myth, providing an allegorical foundation for what was taking place in the postsocialist era. If Hayk was the Father of Armenians, fulfilling the Symbolic positions of both pater and genitor—both as an identificatory paternal symbol as well as the one who biologically reproduced the nation (Borneman 2004)—there were large resounding dissonances between him and those who occupied this position within the Armenian national imaginary in the 2010s. Armenia has been a configuration of territory—or the dream of and demand for such a territory—only since the late nineteenth century. The modern formation of national political parties—in Western Armenia (Ottoman Empire) and in the Russian Empire—transformed the nation, which had been based on cultural-religious heritage, into the politicization of culture and nation capable of demanding territorialized sovereignty. As Gerard Libaridian (2007) has put it, "By grounding nationalism in a historically well-defined territory, love of fatherland gave the emancipation movement a political legitimacy denied to those whose love was for the abstracted cultural-religious heritage of the Armenians" (52). A century after dreaming for independence, with the exception of the short-lived First Republic of Armenia (1918–20), which Richard Hovannisian refers to as an "unfinished symphony" (2018), in 1991 Armenians finally had their own sovereign territory, an *azat, ankakh Hayasdan* (free, independent Armenia), as the national anthem of the new Republic would express it. By the mid-1990s, however, this euphoric sense of national unity was being undone by a number of political and economic processes.

The first years of the new postsocialist Republic are known in Armenia as the "cold and dark years" (*tsurt u mut tariner*), marked by a war with neighboring Azerbaijan and the continuous shortage of electricity, gas, water, and food. The war would be catastrophic in various ways. Along with the conditions of scarcity that led to massive emigration from the country, 20,000 Armenian soldiers perished, including 8,000 from the territory of Karabakh. Additionally, the ethnic violence against Armenians in Azerbaijan and Karabakh led to the deaths of 6,000 (de Waal 2013, 285), wounded 20,000 (Bertsch 1999, 297) and, coupled with the war, would lead to hundreds of Armenians gone missing (Hakobyan 2010). Concurrently—as the Karabakh movement that would lead to this war was taking shape in almost daily protests in the streets of Yerevan and in Nagorno-Karabakh—on December 7, 1988, Armenia experienced a devastating earthquake that, by some estimates, killed 50,000 people (Brand 1988).

Aside from the daily experience of horror, the war also created massive political-economic upheaval and made possible aggressive forms of privatization. Azerbaijan's blockade against Armenia cut its means of accessing petroleum and other critical resources. During the 1980s, Armenia received 80 percent of its fuel from the USSR, 82 percent of which went through Azerbaijan (Astourian 2000). Needing to quickly develop its own economic processes because of the geopolitical restrictions brought on by the collapse of the USSR and the war, the government of the new Republic began to rely on privatization based on demand—through the "pro rata" system advised by the World Bank (Roth-Alexandrowicz 1997). In this system, the number of shares that enterprises were divided into would rapidly grow so that each share would cost less and less. This was done to ensure the sale of all shares and so the number of shares would increase until all shares were sold. Eventually, however, the majority of these shares would end up in the hands of the few (Astourian 2000, 7). By 1997, only 7 percent of the population participated in privatization. By 1998, 2.5 percent of these shareholders controlled 60 percent of the shares of 713 companies that were privatized as a part of open share subscription (Astourian 2000, 13). A few came to power by privatizing Armenian enterprise, and rather than investing in and building these infrastructures, mass privatization was followed by mass liquidation. The new owner class, once the managers of industry in the socialist era, literally dismantled industry, selling parts of machinery, scraps of glass, and metal for a quick profit and leaving landscapes of industrial ruins all across Armenia (Khatchadourian 2022). State revenues from the eventual liquidation of these industrial assets amounted to one thousandth of the projections of their worth (approximately $700,000 of $700,000,000) (Astourian 2000, 13–14). As a result of these processes of privatization and liquidation, unemployment rates in Armenia have soared since independence in 1991—officially (by World Bank statistics) at a high of 19 percent in 2010 until it peaked again, in 2020 (at 21 percent), as a result of the COVID-19 pandemic (World Bank, 2022). Many argue that it has, in reality, been much higher, especially if accounting for *under*employment.

Armenians popularly call the few who profiteered during mass privatization and liquidation—those who came into large sums of money—the oligarchs (*oligarkhner*). This is not just because they are an economic elite, but also because they were able to capture state power by cultivating close ties with government officials or, in some cases, by using economic power and coercion to take government seats themselves. This new class of owners became rich through these privatization schemes, by looting during the Nagorno-Karabakh war (Özkan 2008) and exploiting the gray market in the liminal years of Soviet-era economic collapse (Astourian 2000; Ghaplanyan 2018), and in the creation of monopolies ("commodity-based cartels"; Giragosian 2009) on necessary goods (like food, gas, and electricity). The unemployment and the massive increases in the cost of living that these activities wrought have impoverished many in the country.

The government of the newly independent Republic of Armenia in 1991 was led by the Armenian Pan-National Movement (APNM) that arose out of the Karabakh and independence movements and that widely made use of intense nationalist and racialist (*tseghakron*) notions of an Armenian racial supremacy and unique calling made popular by the mid-twentieth-century (counter)revolutionary Garegin Nzhdeh (Panossian 2002). By 1998, however, this government became one of oligarchs and their close friends. Razmik Panossian (2006) has referred to this transition as "postnationalist governance" in "which elites are preoccupied with issues of power and economic gain and the main issues in the political sphere relate to socioeconomic policies and day-to-day concerns" (225) rather than the fate of the nation. Unification in the name of national ideology, Panossian argues, died with the 1996 elections, when the first president of the Republic, Levon Ter-Petrosian, became the object of massive protests that eventually led to his resignation in 1998. Earlier forms of mass protest, based on "a primordialist ethnonationalism" (Suny 2006, 287) and "euphoric" senses of national unity (Abrahamian 1990, 72) waned as economic struggle that swept the country placed national identity on the backburner; the focus moved toward everyday survival.

In 1998, Robert Kocharyan came into power as president, beginning the reign of what is today popularly known as the "Karabakh clan"—the rule of Armenia by those who came into wealth and power through the war and who originated from the Nagorno-Karabakh oblast. The leadership of Kocharyan and later, Serzh Sargsyan, the head of the Republican Party, produced the uncanny (Freud 2003). While the dream of a sovereign national government was now fulfilled, it seemed more like a nightmare. The postsocialist political-economic elite of Armenia might have been the official leadership and might have, thus, occupied the Symbolic position of Hayk, but their immoralities and lack of concern for Armenians' well-being had a not unfamiliar resemblance to Bel, producing a narrative of perversion of Armenia's origin myth. In conducting our household interviews in 2013, Talalyan and I heard a litany of sentiments that pointed to this uncanniness. "Armenia was one of the mightiest nations. As a people, we have survived anything and everything. But what is left?" asked Mihran, a man in his seventies in the neighborhood of Masiv 2. "Mihran dear," his wife Yevgine chimed in, "what are you mourning? It's not the Armenian people. It's that we don't have a government. Why are you blaming our people?" Talalyan and I sensed that this was something that had already been discussed within the household—something that had already formed into oppositional positions. "But it's our government, right? It's our authority. It's our people." Mihran's insistence was that the Armenian government could not be separated from the Armenian people. For him, having the kind of government that Armenians had said something meaningful about the kind of people Armenians were—that they were now the kind of people who would allow a government like this to be in the position of authority. Furthermore, those within the government were themselves Armenian. Yevgine, however, represented another popular opinion: those within the government were not actually Armenians; they were traitors of the Armenian people.

Aside from pointing to these uncanny resemblances between Hayk and Bel, Meschian's retelling of the myth, with which I began this chapter, interrogates the temporality of the nation and its myths. When is the time of the myth? Where does it begin, and where does it end? Two years into Armenia's independence in the early 1990s, as Stephanie Platz (2000, 114) has shown, the nation was popularly discussed as coming to its dark ends. If Gregory the Illumintaor had delivered Armenia to Christianity, Levon Ter-Petrosian was joked about as "Levon the Terminator" (Levon *Anjatich*), whose leadership led to mass shortages in electricity and light as well as to other forms of darkness. Postsocialist Armenia, in other words, was not moving forward in time, but backward into nonexistence. Similarly, Meschian's song offers up a sequel to the myth, one that does not end with the battle in the year 0 of the Chamchian calendar (2492 BC), but that continues over millennia and finally comes to an end in the fifth millennium, when Hayk is defeated.

By the 2010s, when I began conducting research in Armenia, an atmosphere of the uncanny, produced by various violent events, had intensified around seats of authority. On October 27, 1999, five armed men led by Nairi Hunanyan—a journalist and member of the Armenian Revolutionary Federation (ARF), a nationalist (social democratic) political party—broke into the Republic's Parliament building in Yerevan, killing eight people, including then prime minister Vazgen Sargsyan and National Assembly speaker Karen Demirchyan. Hunanyan referred to Armenia's government as "bloodsuckers" (Suny 2006, 288), and the group claimed their action as a patriotic coup to save the country from a "catastrophic situation" in which people were hungry and the government was not offering a way out (Mulvey 1999). On March 1, 2008, after postpresidential elections, protesters widely claimed that the election of Serzh Sargsyan had been fraudulent and, in opposition, occupied Liberty Square in central Yerevan. To squash the protest, President Kocharyan's administration called in the military, which killed ten people and wounded many more. Throughout the postsocialist years, Armenia became more militarized—passing various laws to tax income to support the military budget and placing further obstacles in place so young (non-elite) men could not escape obligatory military duty. The government continuously decreased social assistance budgets, cut pensions for the elderly, and attempted to increase the cost of transportation (which, it ultimately failed to do due to protests). Various monopolies formed, increasing the prices of necessary goods and services. Privatization severely decreased public amenities, leading to the transformation of more and more land that was once the commons into spaces of privatized consumption—parks became boutiques and cafés; sites of subsistence became poisonous mines.

If Bel was once the foreign tyrant, this tyrant was now the uncanny resemblance of those who occupied the Presidential Palace on Baghramyan Avenue and the seats of the National Assembly, reaping various political and economic benefits from the suffering of Armenians. In the continuous battle between Hayk and Bel, the Bel of the modern Armenian era is most often cast as the "Turk," who was not only the perpetrator of Genocide in the early twentieth century but also the Azerbaijanis who committed pogroms and waged war on Armenians. Within affective economies (Ahmed 2004), it was the "Turk" who was most frequently the object of the hatred through which love of the nation emerged. However, the "Turk," much like Bel, was appearing in new and perhaps more familiar spaces closer to home. Some of my interlocutors found the perpetrators of genocide not necessarily in any foreign enemy or state but within their own government and its structures. One of our interlocutors accused the political-economic elite of "economic genocide" (which I discuss in chapter 3). Furthermore, right-wing nationalists also positioned the Armenian government not as the longed-for dream of national governance but as foreign occupiers who were in Armenia only to pillage and exploit until there was nothing left (which I also discuss in further detail in chapter 3). Many, like Yevgine above, believed that those in Armenia's government were not Armenian because they did not protect the Armenian people and Armenia's national sovereignty. A genealogy of survival based on proper morality—according to Armenia's Symbolic order—had, following state sovereignty, devolved and become perverted.

The Year 4504, or the Year of the Nation's Sexual Perversion

In 2012, the perverse figure of the oligarch (with its uncanny resemblance to Bel and the Turk) congealed with an emergent figure—the homosexual—signaling another rupture in the mytho-history of the nation, this time toward its *sexual* perversion. This came with the firebombing of DIY Pub and the attack on the Diversity March, birthing the figure of the homosexual in public consciousness.

DIY Pub, which opened in 2011, was a venue for alternative imaginaries. It was a space for punk shows and art exhibits, and a meeting place for grassroots activists and organizers. Unless you were immersed in the worlds of leftist thought, punk music, and experimental art, or were in with the queer scene, it is unlikely that you would have known about DIY Pub—that is, until one of the owners of the bar, Tsomak Oganezova, and her punk band Pincet, were invited to participate in Istanbul's Pride March (in Turkey). At the Pride March through Istiklal Street, near Taksim Square, Tsomak and the other members of the band had waved a tiny Armenian flag to show Armenian LGBT solidarity with Turkish LGBT people. When my friend Alis introduced Tsomak and me to one another at DIY Pub in 2011, Tsomak had just returned from this trip. Interested in queer spaces, I was curious about how Tsomak conceptualized DIY Pub. Was it a gay bar? Was it a punk bar? Did it matter to her? As the bar was very crowded and noisy during this first encounter, Tsomak invited me to come back the following day before the bar opened to hang out and to chat some more. When I arrived the next day, Tsomak was irritated. All day she had been fielding phone calls from journalists and news outlets who had been requesting interviews about her presence at Istanbul Pride. We talked about other things, but the phone calls kept interrupting. By the time I left a couple of hours later, Tsomak had answered at least ten phone calls, all while chain smoking out of angst; and she had finally agreed to give an interview to *Yerkir Media*, a TV station associated with the ARF. This interview turned out to be a disaster for Tsomak as well as for DIY Pub. *Yerkir Media* asked that the interview take place at the pub, to which Tsomak agreed, and its televised and online publication of the interview would clearly show the address of the bar. During the interview, Tsomak spoke about how much she liked Turkey. She spoke about the freedom that she saw there, especially in sexuality, and told the interviewer that she wanted Armenia to be more like Turkey in this way. The harassment began not long after this televised interview.

Tsomak later told me that from then on, there was at least one incident a week. "Every other night some group would try to enter and cause a spectacle [*shukhur anel*]," she said. But there was one group in particular that continuously harassed the owners and patrons of the pub:

> They called themselves the Dark Ravens, like patriotic soldiers or something. They were young boys—some of them looked like they were 15. In the beginning they started coming into the pub, but after they started trouble a number of times we stopped letting them in. Then they started hanging out outside the pub, smoking ciga-

rettes, throwing things at the door, spitting at the walls of the building and the door. Sometimes we would find vomit right outside with
Nazi swastikas on the wall and we knew it was probably them. We
would clean it up and they would do it again. That morning [on May
8, about 11 months after her return from Istanbul]—it was like 5 in
the morning—I received a phone call from the fire department saying
that my bar had burned. I thought, "What?! What do you mean my
bar has burned?!" I panicked. I was just there a few hours before that. I
had left at around 1 in the morning and left the bartender to close up.
When I showed up, the whole place was charred. At first, I thought
that maybe someone had not fully put out a cigarette or something. It
was devastating, but you know, accidents happen. Then, a few hours
later, we looked at some video footage from a security camera of the
store next door. And I couldn't believe it. These assholes had broken
through the door and thrown bombs inside. The video shows all of it.
They approach the bar, they get through the door, they throw their
bombs [Molotov cocktails made in beer bottles] inside. There were
two of them in the video, but their friends were likely waiting on the
street. The bombs started a fire that eventually spread and burned the
whole place down.

The two boys Tsomak had seen in the video were Hampig and Mgrdich
Khapazian, eighteen and twenty-one years old, respectively.

While the Khapazian brothers were arrested a couple of days after the firebombing, they were quickly bailed out by ARF members in
the National Assembly, Artsvik Minasyan and Hrayr Karapetyan, who
posted the bail of 1 million dram (approximately $2,500 USD at the time).
Additionally, Artsvik Minasyan made a statement about the attack and
his reasons for bailing out the young men, claiming that he knew they
were good, normal boys and that they did not deserve to be detained. He
also claimed that the attack was in "accordance with national ideology,"
stating that he "consider[ed] [Tsomak's] types destructive to Armenian
society." Even though he didn't want to "sound offensive," he explained,
the firebombing was a "practical step." Other members of government
made similar statements. Eduard Sharmazanov of the Republican Party,
for example, was reported to having claimed that the firebombing was a
"rebellion" and that it was "right and justified."[7]

About a week following the firebombing, after Tsomak (rather
than the firebombers) was continuously represented by the media as a

threat to national security, Tsomak agreed to give another interview on the popular political talk show *Urvagitz* on the television network *Kentron TV*. The firebombing, according to Petros Ghazaryan, the host of the show, was a unique situation because "in the 22 years of this Republic, there has never been a bombing based on ideology that has targeted a particular place—be that a restaurant, a bar or any other institution. This bombing occurred, if we want to be correct, let's put it this way, because in this bar there was so-called 'cultural diversity' propaganda being spread." Ghazaryan also highlighted another important dimension of leftist claims—the emergence of a kind of "fascism"—when he argued that "because, well, us Armenians are fixated on all remaining the same and to not change and thus it is really important to think about how we will have to change . . . the owners of the pub and the customers of the pub describe this event as a moment of classic fascism." Ghazaryan pushed Tsomak to answer for "two deadly sins": "You didn't just go to Turkey. You participated in a gay rally. You are promoting both Turk[s] and gay[s]. Those, for Armenians, are the two most deadly sins, do you understand?"[8]

Tsomak's response would heighten her visibility as threat to the nation:

> Our nation has to be cured. We need to cure and free it from these kinds of stereotypes, from these kinds of nationalist ideas. To be honest, I think our nation is a bit sick. It has a sickness in it—this nationalist sickness. The more it goes, this sickness is growing and it is growing in everybody. The more we continue like this, one day it will blow up and this will be the annihilation of the nation. This is if people do not start working on themselves.

Adding insult to an already self-injurious speech, Tsomak named this "sickness" as "fascism":

> You know what? *Hay, Hay, Hay* [Armenian, Armenian, Armenian], we're tired of it already. We're already a tiny nation and we give nothing to the world and think of ourselves as *yes im inch* [I don't know what]. I am in solidarity with everyone. I do not recognize borders. I am an artist, I am a person. I will go wherever I want, relate to whoever I want, and say whatever I want to say. I have never hurt anybody. But those people who have invaded my personal life, that's a terrible thing. And it's not enough that they have invaded my personal life,

but they have threatened me . . . saying that this isn't enough, that I must be murdered, they've put up my picture [online] and said "Remember this face. This person must be burned." In 1941 when World War II started, 300,000 Armenians died fighting against fascism and now we have these ants, these pathetic little bugs, who are trying to propagate their rotten fascist ideas?

While Tsomak's claim that the "nation" was "sick" came out of an intense political and emotional situation, right-wing nationalists took it not only as insult but as the politicizing of homosexuality. While it was right-wing nationalist ideas that had led to the firebombing of DIY Pub, and while it was also right-wing nationalists who insisted that Tsomak and other homosexuals be "burned," it was Tsomak who was now represented as the one propagating a politicized discourse around homosexuality. The right-wing nationalists with whom I spoke, as well as others who made their rhetoric easily available on public interviews and blog posts, argued that they had no problem with homosexuality as a personal affair but that they found it dangerous when it began to enter public speech. This was the difference between homosexuality and homosexual propaganda. Popular nationalist blogger Tigran Kocharyan—who is also rumored to have been working for the KGB, which I will discuss in more detail in the following chapter—defined "homosexual propaganda" as spreading information "that homosexuality is a really good thing. That there shouldn't be a difference between mother and father. That those who are against homosexuality are homophobic and fascist."[9] In other words, by virtue of discussing publicly the terror and horror—the destruction of her means of living, the death threats, and the harassment—that she was experiencing, Tsomak became a propagator of homosexuality.

The *Urvagic* interview was followed by a media onslaught, in which social media, blogs, and official news outlets debated Tsomak's claims and furthered the question of what it meant that there was a gay bar in Yerevan and how to make sense of the insult against the nation posed by the very woman who had opened that bar. In other words, these discussions veered even further away from the question of terrorism and centered instead on Tsomak herself as the danger to the nation. In July of 2012, Tsomak, along with her girlfriend and her sister who were also being threatened, left Armenia to claim political asylum in Sweden. Tsomak gained citizenship in Sweden in 2020. When I interviewed her on Skype a few months after her departure from Armenia in 2012, she insisted that Armenia had become a fascist nation with no freedom for individuals.[10]

The DIY Pub firebombing was an event. It created fissures within the well-rehearsed narrative of a nation that has continuously been threatened and endured nonetheless, bringing into the open not only possibilities of difference, but those of improper difference, within the nation: the feeling that something was wrong with Armenia and that it was something internal. Journalists, right-wing nationalists, bloggers, and other voices in the country, following this event, began regularly to deploy the notion of sexual perversion (*aylaserutyun*) as this something that was wrong. Advocates of DIY PUB, including Tsomak—in her insistence on Armenia's nationalist "sickness"—refused the singularity of Armenianness, throwing into question Armenian propriety and revealing the possibilities of multiplicity long ordered into singular submission to the myth-narrative of the nation's survival. With tensions centered on proper Armenianness already tangible within public discourse— brought on by the uncanny oligarchic horde in the seat of Symbolic authority—the now hypervisible figure of the homosexual added a new dimension to a narrative of national failure: that of Hayk losing to Bel. Hayk, it now became possible to say, was weakened by sinful predilections and lost to Bel. This occurred not in battle, but through perversion, as Hayk became something other than the valiant hero on which the nation's survival depended. "The idea of homosexuality is inherently dangerous to our nation," argued Konstantin Ter-Nakalyan, one of the editors of *BlogNews.am*, when I interviewed him. Homosexuality, he claimed, has radically transformed our nation whose survival depended on moral (including sexual and familial) propriety.

In July 2011, a year prior to the DIY firebombing and around the time when the harassment of Tsomak about her appearance at Gay Pride Istanbul was only just beginning, I first met with Lara Aharonian, the director of the Women's Resource Center (WRC), in her office. In addition to an introduction to the organization, its mission, and its activities, Aharonian also told me about an event that would take place the following year to raise awareness of diversity. "We hope to change things in the culture so that people are not afraid of differences," she said. "This is a big problem in Armenia. People see it as a threat and not as a strength. So we are planning a big event, next spring or summer maybe, to show the diversity of Armenia. It will include all kinds of people. Religious minorities, ethnic minorities, people who are part of subcultures like punks and emos maybe. You know, to show the people that being different can be beautiful."

This event did take place. It was called the Diversity March (*Bazmazanutyan yert*). But in 2011 and the early part of 2012, when WRC and other organizations and activists were busy preparing for it, they could not foresee the social and political climate of the city in the aftermath of the DIY firebombing. The Diversity March was planned mostly in response to then recent police attacks on an emo subculture, when police were detaining groups of youth seen walking the streets dressed in black and pink clothing, with dyed hair and dark eye make-up. There was a moral panic unfurling—one made worse when a young man known to belong to the emo subculture committed suicide in November 2010. The Diversity March was also imagined as a response to hate speech and intolerance toward religious minorities, like Jevovah's Witnesses and Mormons, who were very few in number but who had become a target of right-wing nationalists as well as mainstream media for being anti-Armenian and threatening Armenia's Apostolic Christian legacy and future. The panic over homosexuality, in other words, had some precedents, contextualized within difference itself as a threat to the moral and affective economies of Armenian values. The organizations planning the Diversity March had invited a number of community members to represent Jehovah's Witnesses, Yezidis, Iranians, and others, which would mark the *Other* Armenia—the 5 to 10 percent of the nation-state's population that was not ethnically Armenian and not Apostolic Christian.

On the afternoon on which the Diversity March was to take place, the organizers went to the meeting point, at the Cascade in the northern part of the central district of the city, with all the posters they had prepared. "We were a few blocks away when we heard shouting and chanting, people singing songs in large groups, and we were confused. We didn't know we had so many supporters!" Hripsime, a staff member at PINK, explained. It was five months after the event, but she, along with other members of the organizations who had planned the march, became emotional and viscerally upset every time they talked about the event. During an interview I conducted with Hripsime and Armen, another PINK staff member, both teared up, hugging each other, as they narrated the events of the day. They explain that only when they had reached the Cascade did they realized that all the sounds they had heard a few blocks down the street were not their supporters, and that all those people were not there to participate in their march. Rather, they were "ultranationalists," mostly young men. Hripsime continued her account: "We couldn't get through to our people when we arrived. Everyone started marching down the street and there was so much yelling and fighting that some of us got caught up with them [the counterprotesters]. At one point, I realized that I was alone among them and they were all yelling at me, calling me a faggot. The same thing happened to poor Lala [Aslikyan, a leftist activist who was very vocal after the DIY firebombing]. They started spitting on her." There were about two hundred counterprotesters, a number much larger than those participating in the Diversity March. While the organizers were expecting about fifty people for the march, including representatives of minority groups to whom they had reached out, they estimated that in the end, during the clamor, only about thirty were able to make it. Some watched from the sidelines, unable to join, surrounded by both policemen and right-wing nationalists. Others saw what was taking place and decided to leave. Even with the absence of rainbow flags and any mention of homosexuality, right-wing nationalists and popular media following their rhetoric depicted the Diversity March as a "gay parade." The public discussions around the Diversity March further heightened the problem of "homosexuality" and sustained its public hypervisibility, articulated as sexual perversion (*aylaserutyun*).

The main organizer of the counterprotest was the group Hayazn. The organization existed prior to this moment, mostly rallying against Russian and English private schools and demanding that education in Armenia be in Armenian. But the Diversity March would be their shining moment, and anti-homosexuality would become the main platform through which they increased their numbers, especially among young men and some young women. Other right-wing nationalists present at the Diversity March's counterprotest were the popular blogger Tigran Kocharyan and Hovhannes Galajyan, the editor-in-chief of the newspaper *Right* (*Iravunk*).

There were differences among these actors. Hayazn imagined an Armenia with a national government that worked for the Armenian people and that pushed forward decisions that would benefit the enrichment of Armenian culture. As such, the organization stood against Westernization as well as against Russification. They seemed to have much in common with another right-wing organization, Mek Azg Miyutyun (One Nation Union), led by Gor Tamazyan, who had an army capable of plastering flyers and posters all around Yerevan and other cities with slogans against "Western-minded" and "Russian-minded" officials as well as against *hamaseramolutyun*, which refers to homosexuality as a disease of same-sex addiction. In 2013 when Talalyan and I walked the city to conduct our household surveys, we found these flyers and posters in the stairways, elevators, entrances, and hallways of nearly every residential building of the city. They were also easily spotted on bus stop benches and kiosks, telephone poles, and on the sides of building exteriors. While we sometimes tore them down, at other times there were so many that we eventually gave up. These flyers also appeared in other cities and towns across the country. In 2012–13, I spotted them in Gyumri and Dilijan. Tigran Kocharyan, however, who often spoke adamantly against Western influence and homosexuality as a Western value that threatened the nation, never spoke about the role of Russia in Armenia's political, economic, or social landscapes. Kocharyan also rarely, if ever, criticized the ruling oligarchic regime. Galajyan was a bit more eccentric in his views. He traced a more radical genealogy to Hayk and practiced paganism rather than the more recent (fourth century in the Gregorian calendar) Apostolic Christianity. Thus, while the questions of geopolitics, political economy, or what exactly constituted a proper Armenian culture were contested among various right-wing nationalist organizations and actors, they all agreed on homosexuality's threat to the nation. *Aylaserutyun* (sexual perversion) was becoming a threat of convenience, something more palpable as a defeatable enemy—a new Bel—in the name of Armenia's continuity with its heroic past than the *aylandakutyun* (moral perversion) that had already begun its paving of dangerous paths toward un-Armenian futures.

The Myth's Order Word and Its Refusals

As in the film *Hayrik*, cast in the Soviet Socialist Republic of Armenia in the 1970s (or the 4460s in Hayk's temporal framework), the Republic of Armenia in the 2010s (or the 4500s) was a venue for the collision of multiple temporalities. There was mythic time, as the battle of Hayk and Bel, or Bel and Hayk, was still ongoing. There was national state time, as Armenia continued to build a sovereign nation-state and was confronted by its own immoralities and discontents. And there was also queer time—the making way for desire's fragmentation of wholeness through the introduction of difference not just in the social reproduction of the nation's present but in its future pathways and unexpected (yet possible) extranational connections. The myth of Hayk and Bel and other myths of the nation's heroic survival, so dependent on the proper and singular movement of time, had splintered into multiplicities.

In this space-time of multiplicity, we might return to the "No!"—the call of refusal shouted by a member of Arthur Meschian's audience during the 2009 (or 4501) performance—as I have done many times throughout the years, sometimes joined by others like Alis, Albert, my father, my language instructor Knar, and so on. What was this "No!" a refusal of? When (in which temporal landscape) did it present itself? If we read Meschian's retelling of the myth of the battle as a redefining of the Armenian nation not as a nation that survives but as a nation that is defeated, the "No!" might be a recuperation of Armenia in the Name-of-the-Father Hayk. In this sense, the "No!" refuses this retelling, insisting instead on reproducing Hayk's heroism. But, this same refusal in the 4500s—when those who were seated in the Symbolic position of Hayk had strayed so far from the values for which Hayk is remembered—could also be read as a refusal of those who now claimed that seat: a refusal that postsocialist Armenia was really the Armenia for which Armenians had survived, the refusal of the uncanny nightmare that had not been a dream after all. It was not that Bel, the external enemy, finally defeated Hayk but perhaps that Hayk had, for the last two decades, not been Hayk at all but Bel playing as if he were Hayk. We might, however, also hear this "No!" as a refusal of the myth itself, a refusal that there was any singular path for Armenia and thus a reclamation of what multiplicities, even if perverse, could bring. This last "No!" is the one I take up in the final chapter of this book.

The anxieties regarding *aylaserutyun* and *aylandakutyun* that I explore throughout this book interrogate the nation's future and its possibilities. Whatever futures may come from the present will depend, also, on how the past is cast. While these particular tropes of narrating national failure take mytho-histories, especially in the genealogy of Hayk, as templates—as Symbolic order—there are ways in which myth might make and remake worlds. Meschian offers one: retelling the story of the myth as defeat, and thus as the end of what it is that Armenia celebrates about itself. We might say, then, that this is also the end of Armenia. Lusine Kharatyan, however, offers another way. Kharatyan argues that we might see Little Mher of the *Sasna Tzrer* myth as ever-present in Armenian historical reality. Little Mher is known for hiding in a cave until the world is free of injustices, when it will be safe for him to come out again. Like Little Mher, Kharatyan argues, the Armenian people have closed in on themselves, not attempting to change the injustices of this world but hiding and waiting for the world to be better. The point, she tells us, should be to break this mytho-poetic cycle—to become historically something other than Little Mher and to actively work toward changing and transforming the world and the myth. The nation's perversion—as sexual deviation or larger moral digression—signals the end of the nation's survival, but it might also be a moment to seize upon and transform. Whether Armenia concedes the battle to Bel or refuses to hide like Little Mher, in other words, the 2010s in Armenia brought about serious questions regarding the future, which necessitated further examination and reflection of its mythic and historical pasts.

In the following chapter, I present yet another (satire-)myth—this time of a perverse little figure named Little Gender-Boycott imagined by a right-wing nationalist playwright—that demonstrates the dangers of transforming the world. Through an unraveling of the various meanings invested in the figure of the homosexual, I show how the nation's annihilation is imagined through its sexual perversion and the ways in which this imaginary works to displace and condense various dangers having to do with the production and reproduction of life and living.

CHAPTER TWO

The Figure of
the Homosexual

In the summer of 2011, my language instructor, Knar, suggested that we take a field trip to a museum in Yerevan commemorating the life and work of the poet Yeghishe Charents.[1] We had, at the time, been reading his poetry together, and the trip was meant to acquaint me with Charents's life and the circumstances in which he wrote. The museum trip was also to be a history lesson in Armenia's Stalinist experience. The curator at the museum explained to Knar and me that Charents was a hero in his time. And that he was a true socialist. But his love of Armenia had made him a threat to the Soviet Union, and it was for his patriotism that he was murdered. "You see," she explained,

> back then, Armenians were not allowed to freely show love for their country. For this they were deported, exiled, put in prisons and executed. Now we are independent and so we are free. And how do these people choose to express this freedom? By becoming homos [*gomikner*] and screaming that they want homosexual marriages? It's a pity what they have done with the freedom for which they had longed for so many years.

I reflected, and continue often to reflect, on why Armenian independence or the Great Purge should have recalled homosexuality for the curator at this museum. A recent intellectual scandal was, perhaps, responsible for this conflation of Charents, homosexuality, and national crisis. In 2008, some of Charents's lost poems were published for the first time in *Inknagir* magazine. During the Great Purge of 1937, these poems were hidden away with other documents, and had only recently been brought to the attention of Harvard professor of Armenian Studies James Russell, who was given copies of these papers by a man who had known Charents in his youth.[2] Some of these poems had a homoerotic character to them. One of them discussed the poet's love for drugs and the beautiful high he felt from morphine, alcohol, and hashish. But the greatest and most beautiful thing in the world, Charents declares in poetic form, more beautiful than gold or the prettiest woman, was a young boy aged fourteen or fifteen. This poem set into motion debates across prominent online presses about whether or not Charents was a homosexual. Vahan Ishkhanyan, writing for *Tert.am*'s blog at the time, expressed frustration around the hypocrisy of Armenia's literary circles. Writers and literary critics, Ishkhanyan wrote, often deny the realities of the artists, writers, and filmmakers whom they consider national icons. Ishkhanyan claimed that Armenians celebrate artists like Sergei Parajanov, the Soviet-Armenian filmmaker best known for his film *Color of Pomegranates*, "rais[ing] him to the sky" all the while suppressing the fact that many of these artists were homosexual.[3]

While the museum curator's labor of linking Charents to contemporary crises involving homosexuality might have been brought on by this scandalous discovery, it may have also been the precursor of a hermeneutics that was just emerging at the time and would become a popular mode through which to understand political worlds after the firebombing of DIY Pub in 2012. This new hermeneutics would take up the figure of the homosexual (and other kinds of differents, like feminists), as a hypervisible sign of crisis, and would become a primary means through which homosexuality as well as other moral crises would be popularly analyzed. Sexual, gendered, and intimate forms of difference from—or deviations or perversions of—what was considered proper, and on which national survival was said to depend, became dangerous forms of freedom. These freedoms also came to stand in for how independence and the foundation of a sovereign nation-state had gone wrong.

There were some other such precursors to the events of 2012. One Nation Union (Mek Azg Dashink), founded by Gor Tamazyan and Ruben Gevorgyan, a collective of various right-wing organizations, had been plastering anti-homosexual posters and flyers all over the country since 2008. They had also held a few rallies to contest the existence of *aghandner*, religious sects (different denominations of Christianity), that were separate from the Armenian Apostolic Church. In 2009, a collective of feminists—organized by the Women's Resource Center (WRC)—staged a march that culminated in a mock burial of "the red apple." The Red Apple tradition, which is still practiced in various forms throughout Armenia, requires that the women on the groom's side of the family deliver a basket of red apples to the bride after inspecting the bedsheets for a blood stain from the wedding night. WRC's burial of the red apple was intended to represent symbolically the end of this patriarchal practice. Right-wing protesters attempted to disrupt the event of the mock burial and continued, afterward, to speak of the event as dangerous to Armenian culture. One right-wing blogger, who at the time was writing under the pseudonym Pigh (the elephant) and has since been identified as Tigran Kocharyan, a major player in the 2012 sex panic, claimed that such marches and other acts should be illegal because, "next thing you know, narcotics addicts will want to stage their own demonstrations too."[4] In 2009–10, a moral panic surrounding emo subculture, a form of punk, emerged. During this panic, schools in Yerevan conducted wardrobe checks for torn jeans, body piercings, black gloves, and the pink and black colors emblematic of the subculture. Following the suicide of a fifteen-year-old boy who belonged to the subculture, the police began rounding up teenagers who seemed to fit the "emo" bill and questioning them at police stations. The Yerevan chief of police at the time, Alik Sargsyan, claimed that this crackdown was reasonable because "emos are dangerous" and that they can "distort our gene pool."[5]

These earlier moments of right-wing protest and panic set the stage for what was to come in 2012 and already carried within them the seeds of a coalescence of various national anxieties about social and biological reproduction into some kind of a depoliticized figure that would come to stand in for a difference in—or a perversion of—national propriety. The feminist, the Protestant, the drug user, the emo, and eventually the homosexual were all parts of the same amorphous bugaboo. In this chapter, I explore the rhetoric of the homosexual's sexual perversion. How did this figure emerge as a major object of discussion in popular media? How did it condense national anxieties? The figure of the homosexual must be differentiated from queer life as it actually existed. It is a *figure*, an abstraction that made up a part of an imaginary world in which there were other caricatured, yet threatening, figures such as the Turk, "sexless" beings that threaten to dismantle the holy union between man and woman, European spies, religious minorities that are slowly undoing the fabric of Armenianness, and other differents and Others. These figurations of difference challenged national propriety by figuring cultural, social, political, and desiring difference within. In other words, Armenianness as a coherent, singular ontological whole that must survive at all costs was fissured by differences from the proper. The figure of the homosexual, like these other shadowy forms, was strongly linked to a sense of dangerous difference that disrupted and (dis)oriented the nation, setting it onto perverse paths. The figure of the homosexual, however, was unique in its (un)productive and (un)reproductive capacities. This figure opened up pathways for desire, for freedom, and for radically different configurations of the future. I have so far defined the Armenian Symbolic order and authority as a collective feeling regarding an ontological purity that structured social expectations in the Name-of-the-Father Hayk and that defined Armenianness as necessitating a strong Father to maintain continuity with a past and a timeless surviving nation. As an aberration of—a deviation from—this Armenian Symbolic order and authority, the figure of the homosexual threatened national survival from the inside out: from within the critical depths of the most intimate unit of the family.

A Dangerously (Un)productive and (Un)reproductive Being

In May 2013, the National Assembly of the Republic of Armenia passed Law No. 57, regarding the "Protection of Equal Rights and Equal Opportunities for Women and Men."[6] Law No. 57 had existed in draft form since 2009, but only soon before its passing did it acquire the new language of *gender*. Article III of the legislation defines *gender*, transliterated in Armenian and pronounced with a hard *g*, as "the acquired [*dzerkberovi*], socially fixed behavior of the different sexes," and the term is used throughout the rest of the articles in the law. For this reason, the law became popularly known as the "Gender Equality Law." This use of the term *gender* would become the focus of intense right-wing nationalist dissent. Right-wing anxieties about *gender* and perversion were part of the larger international right-wing populist anti-gender movement (Graff and Korolczuk 2022). As Agniezska Graff and Elzbieta Korolczuk (2022) argue, the movement had much to do with the economic upheavals caused by neoliberalization. Focusing in on the social reproductive anxieties heightened by the term *gender* reveals the intricate dimensions of the dangers the concept posed, the perverse futures to which it was feared it might lead, and its ties to political-economic realities. In 2013, *gender* as a word was new within public discourse—except for its use in the word *transgender*, which LGBT activists had themselves implemented through advocacy, as a replacement for the common *transeksual* in problematic television exposés. The idea, however, that biological and "natural" sex was not necessarily always the basis of socialized behavior was not entirely new. This had been a disturbing thought for right-wing nationalists since the 2012 sex panic following the firebombing of DIY Pub and the attack on the Diversity March. For instance, in November 2012, the European Delegation held an event in Yerevan's Ani Hotel to discuss human rights and European integration in Armenia. PINK was invited to speak on LGBT rights. Marine Margaryan, a staff member at PINK, spoke about the rights violations experienced by LGBT Armenians in their families, schools, and places of work as well as by the military and the public. She was followed by Armen Aghayan, one of the founders of Hayazn, the organization largely responsible for the counterprotest against the Diversity March. Aghayan was not invited to participate in the conference, but he stood up and insisted that he receive time at the podium, arguing that Hayazn's invitation had been withheld because Europe discriminated against anyone struggling for national rights. Once at the podium, Aghayan explained that Ms. Margaryan's statements posed a danger to the nation.

> Ms. Margaryan argues that educational institutions in Armenia violate the rights of faggots [*hamaseramolner*]. But I wonder why she thinks it is a good idea to educate children to become gay. Why does she think it is moral to spread perversion [*aylaserutyun*] among them so that they go home and are confused about who their mothers are, who their fathers are, and what restroom they should use as boys or girls? Doesn't this homosexual propaganda violate the rights of children? Of the family? Our nation?

For Aghayan, sexuality was not only intimately linked to gender but could have deeply transformative effects on it. If homosexuality were allowed to exist in schools, he imagined, not only would many children (if not all children) become homosexual, they would no longer be boys and girls or be able to differentiate their mothers from their fathers or women from men. These were the preexisting vocabularies and grammars for "homosexuality as sexual perversion" when the right wing read the Gender Equality Law as the state's insistence, through European coercion, that all Armenians become transgender. *Gender* threatened the family because it would threaten the proper roles of men and women, change their routes of desire for one another, and disrupt the biological reproduction within the family and the nation. Gender was, thus, unsettling to both biological and social reproduction. Titles of blogs and news posts—such as "Under the Name of Gender Equality, NA Secretly Accepts a Law to Spread Perversion"—articulate the conspiratorial logic by which the fabric of Armenian society was being slowly and quietly undone.

After various protests, debates, blog posts, and speeches by popular media personalities, members of the Armenian Apostolic Church, and members of government (including the National Assembly), the government finally decided, by the end of August, to amend the law by removing the term *gender*. Instead, it kept the basic premise, replacing the term with "men and women." At this point, however, the protests and dissent did not stop. Rather, the fight against the Gender Equality Law became a fight against *gender* itself, framed as the protection of Armenia and the Armenian family from homosexuality and defined by Komitas Hovnanyan—a prominent priest within the Armenian Apostolic Church who, on October 15, 2013, led a March through central Yerevan against "gender perversion"—as "the ruins of our nation, because if a man marries a man, he cannot ensure a next generation. This is what we are saying 'no' to. What the law is saying, what it had said, does not matter." This statement, like many of the other speeches and acts against the legislation, was broadcast on national news networks. Discussions of *gender* as perversion also produced various meanings of the term in everyday talk—as a verb, noun, and adjective. I encountered phrases like "I will *gender* you," meaning something like "Fuck you," and the adjectivization of the word into *genderot* (gender-like) both online and on the streets of Yerevan.

Blogger Tigran Kocharyan, famous for his active role in publicizing the dangers of sexual perversion, also spoke on the matter. In a *Tert.am* article he was quoted as saying "We [now] have a law giving power to sex's reproduction: man, woman, transgender, non-gender, bi-gender, etc. So, man now decides for himself what social sex he has. This is a topic that needs to be seriously considered."[7] *Gender* was, thus, presented as having the potential to multiply in form. With each newly produced and reproduced form, proper ways of the nation's reproduction were undermined and thwarted. Freeing possibilities of sexual expression from the constraints of "nature" (assumptions about biological/physical sex), would give freedom to particular, perverse, and dangerous beings. Nelli Sarukhanyan, a journalist for the prominent news site *Zham.am*, asked why the government had given a "green light to perversion," arguing that the law had nothing to do with equality between men and women but rather "the rights of randomly sexed or unsexed persons, so that they may work and act freely in all domains of society."[8] Here again, like in Kocharyan's anxieties around "choosing" social sex, it is the reproduction of the possibilities of meaning one can give their sex that is perceived as both perverse and dangerous. One can now choose to be any one of a "random" set of social sexes, not just man or woman, but even unsexed. *Gender*'s potential dangers lay in its productive and reproductive capacities.

Gender's danger was also tied to already existing anxieties about social reproduction in Armenia—the consequences of ongoing political-economic upheavals in the country since independence. Kocharyan argues that *gender* would eventually lead to a "sexless"—as in without the male/female form—and "familyless" society. But, as I explore in chapter 5, many in Armenia already believed that there were no more (proper) families in Armenia and that ongoing strife had made it impossible for men and women to be proper men and women. Sarukhanyan makes these linked anxieties—between sexual perversion (*aylaserutyun*) and moral perversion (*aylandakutyun*)—even clearer by discussing the danger of *gender* in an Armenia already plagued by other familial issues:

> It is not enough that because of forced migration, especially of men who have to leave for work abroad, that many young boys and girls are forced to have a relationship with their father through the "Skype" screen in families half-broken by emigration. But now there is a new, and much more dangerous, blow to the understanding of family. And

let no one tell you that the ruin of traditional families cannot spread in this way.[9]

Gender and homosexuality writ large did not necessarily bear full responsibility for the destruction of Armenianness but would certainly ensure a quicker and fateful end.

"The Tale of Little Gender Boycott,"[10] a satire by Christ Manaryan, a right-wing nationalist playwright and musician, was written in the context of this panic and, in its bizarre narrative, lays out the anxieties cathected onto *gender* and onto the figure of the homosexual. The tale begins with "Once upon a time" (*linum e, chi linum*) and describes a grandma and grandpa of "the traditional sexual orientation."

> So, they are normal people. While they have for a long time forgotten what is sexual everything, in the depths of their soul, it doesn't matter, they are traditional from head to foot. But come and see, the European God of Democracy watches their peaceful life and, dying of jealousy, sends the grandpa and grandma a half-baked being, Genderik Boykotik [Little Gender Boycott]. And Little Gender Boycott is also unsure of what exactly they are—not a transvestite, not a hermaphrodite, not a pederast. In any case, they are an unsexed, no-headed little being. The grandma and grandpa worry a lot, constantly trying to understand why the European God of Democracy has punished them in such a cruel way, but because they do not have a necessary and trendy imagination, they cannot approach their nontraditional grandchild with any understanding.

No gender is ascribed to Little Gender Boycott within the tale, an aspect made possible by the Armenian gender-neutral pronoun *na*. There are a number of remarkable moments in just the opening of this story. The European God of Democracy, Manaryan tells us, is jealous of the traditional way of life in Armenia. The narrative, thus, forms a part of a right-wing nationalist discourse that sees Europe as having destroyed itself with its dangerous concepts—like democracy, homosexuality, feminism, gender, and so on. One of my interlocutors, for instance, who identified as a *hyrenaser* (patriot), told me that Europe was finally beginning to see the trouble they were in because their own citizens had all become gay and had stopped reproducing, and only Muslim immigrants were now reproducing. "Soon, Europe will belong to the Muslims. I will not let that same danger come to my country," he said. The tale, importantly, has the

European God drop the perverse figure not in a home with a young couple, but in a home with an elderly couple, to further cement the notion of an old, surviving, traditional Armenia. This millennia-long survival was now threatened by the "half-baked being." The traditional grandma and grandpa, the narrator also tells us, have forgotten anything having to do with sex long ago, positioning them as good and moral Armenians whose emotional investment is in being traditional—in the survival of the nation—rather than in personal desire and pleasure.

Little Gender Boycott refuses to go to school, join the military, pay taxes, obey Armenian law, and cut wood in the forest for the grandma so that she may cook a "traditional dolma." They refuse, in other words, to be productive for their nation. With "the appropriate law" on their side—a reference to the Gender Equality Law and perhaps also other laws that Europe has "coerced" Armenia into adopting—Little Gender Boycott can violate Armenianness. Little Gender Boycott has no interest in any of the institutions necessary for the survival of the nation. This includes proper reproduction. Little Gender Boycott is described throughout the story as failed masculinity. They wear earrings, mascara, and a "Kurd-like skirt"; speak in a "blatantly arrogant" as well as "disgusting" voice; "smile femininely"; and stretch their words when they speak (a reference to a feminine tonality). The only thing that is on Little Gender Boycott's mind is going to a gay parade. The grandpa's disappointment, anger, and exhaustion from serving this un(re)productive being eventually leads him to have four heart attacks, going into diabetic shock eight times, and ending up bedridden.

As Little Gender Boycott eventually abandons the grandma and the bedridden grandpa—showing that they have no sense of duty, responsibility, or obligation and are concerned only with their own desires and pleasures—they go in search of a gay parade as they sing a song:

> I am Little Gender, I am Little Boycott.
> I am the little bastard of an unknown whore.
> I have run away from grandpa,
> I have run away from grandma,
> I have run away from school,
> I have run away from the army,
> I have even run away from manliness.
> Let me go and turn, from our village,
> A participant in a gay parade . . .

On their way through Armenia, in search of a gay parade, Little Gender Boycott runs into a European spy.

"Armenian!" calls the spy, "*Hav ar you?*" ["How are you?" transliterated into Armenian], Little Gender? No one insults you?"

"No way," Little Gender Boycott says, proudly. "Who can insult me? The appropriate law is with me."

"*Very good* [transliterated from English]." The spy is very happy. "So where are you going?"

"I am going to a gay parade."

"Even more *very good.*" The spy is delighted. "Do you need money or anything?"

"Why not?" responds Little Gender Boycott. "I have to buy lipstick and such, transvestite bras . . . and all of that is exceptionally expensive."

"*O key* [transliterated from English]," says the spy, "Go and do a good, noisy gay parade, stir the whole city up, incite everything, boycott things, the money is no problem. I'll put the amount on your card."

"It's done, *kyank* [a colloquialism associated with femininity, literally meaning life]." Little Gender Boycott is very happy. "But aren't you going to come to our gay parade?"

"I will be in the sado-masochist leather underwear," responds the spy, "and on top will be many feathers and glitter . . ."

"Oooo," responds Little Gender Boycott, "That makes me feel good in all kinds of ways! So, look, don't be late, cutie! See you!"

"See you, too!"

The European spy's perversions—their sadomasochism and its accompanying outfit, their flirtatiousness, and their excitement about a gay parade—reference Europe as a site of general perversion, much like the discourse of "Gayropa" in Russia, which fixes Europe as the site where LGBT rights and the permissive cultures that accompany them are affirmed (Suchland 2018).

The tale of Little Gender Boycott ends tragically. Before they can organize their gay pride parade with the European spy's money, the sexless little being is attacked by a group of *kyartus*, a derogatory term for macho street thugs who are often talked about as having a "backward" (*hedamnatz*) outlook, especially on questions of gender and sexuality. While Little Gender Boycott fears the *kyartus*, they do still attempt to protect themselves with the "appropriate law." But the law no longer seems to offer any protection. The *kyartus* do not seem very receptive:

> "Who?!" ask the Kyartus. "This one is completely crazy. Listen, you fruit, you will fold that appropriate law of yours in four ways and bury it in your appropriate place, okay? Good. Get the hell out of here. Or else we'll break your shaved legs, you understand? And you'll tell your sisters too, theirs too. And that law of yours, that law's—the writers' mothers, too . . . got it?" . . .
>
> There is no meaning in continuing to tell this story, because from that day on, Little Gender Boycott spends the next four months laid up in the recovery ward, until they somewhat relearn how to drag around their shaved legs and never again do they go out into the light of day in the city. Only when the dark falls, do they wander into the streets and, with other Little Gender Boycotts, create trouble, remembering those good old days when the appropriate law was still in force; and every time this memory comes to them, in their mind they damn the liar spy, who never once visited in the hospital and never paid a cent.
>
> Three kumquats fall from the sky . . . at the end of the tale of Little Gender Boycott, of course it would have been something stupid like that. . . .

The ending of the tale produces an interesting take on national resilience. Although little *genders* and homosexuals—and perhaps other differents who produce complexities in the singular ontology of Armenianness— threaten the nation, the nation also has its safeguards. These safeguards might be problematic elements of society themselves, but they can also offer protection. The "appropriate law" does not have the effect that the European spy or the European Gods of Democracy had wanted it to have. The ideas in that law are so foreign to the national body politic that resistance against them will always organically emerge. Manaryan also conveys another position of right-wing nationalists when it comes to foreign funding. The European spy never comes to visit Little Gender Boycott in the hospital. In other words, although European organizations will fund Armenians to cause chaos in their own country, "stir the whole city up," they do not actually care about these Armenians and will not help when their own funded activists are in trouble. Europeans, I was often told, lack any sense of duty, responsibility, and care as they are too caught up in individual desire, will, and freedom.

In Manaryan's tale, Little Gender Boycott was a condemnable being—one who had to be stopped by the nation's macho men. This was not just because they were themselves immoral but because their immorality was (paradoxically) reproductive, spawning more immorality, a viral contagion that could sabotage many of Armenia's most sacred institutions: the family (and, as an extension of this, the nation), the military, and tradition writ large. While Little Gender Boycott's immorality was reproductive, it was reproductive of values that were unproductive and unreproductive for the nation. "I will do whatever I want" is perhaps the most representative line for how Little Gender Boycott threatens the nation. Their individual will, desire, and difference from national propriety weakens the nation. Freedom, in other words, is a dangerous thing.

The Sacralization and Familialization of Armenianness

Preoccupation with freedom is tied into the postsocialist national collective (un)conscious to national independence and the fulfillment of the longed-for dream of national sovereignty that, by many accounts, has also been a failure. Armenia is now an independent nation-state—what early twentieth-century Armenian intellectuals and political parties had dreamed of and toward which they had struggled. But independence has taken Armenia on unwanted paths; it has deviated from its course of millennia-long survival. As the curator at the Charents museum lamented, freedom and independence were now used to demand perverse forms of life (such as homosexual marriages [although at the time there was no such articulated political demand]). This discomfort—and sometimes anger—regarding freedom was heard often in discussions about DIY Pub. In 2011, in the lead-up to the firebombing of DIY Pub, public dissent against Tsomak Oganezova, one of the pub's owners, began not *just* because of her attendance of a gay pride parade in Istanbul. When Tsomak returned, she was interviewed by *Yerkir Media*, the television news network funded by the Armenian Revolutionary Federation (ARF, or Dashnakstutyun); in that interview she stated that she enjoyed spending time in Turkey and had been there a few times because she found that there, people—and especially gay people and women—had much more freedom than in Armenia to express themselves in their bodies and sexualities. The broadcast of the interview also included an interview with journalist Arpi Beglaryan, herself a (punk) rocker, who was very unhappy about how Tsomak had represented Turkey. "It is really unappealing to me that an Armenian rocker goes to Turkey and further, says that Turkey is more free than Armenia. . . . In the end, freedom, let's be clear, is not about gays taking over the streets, you understand?"[11] That notions of freedom were caught up in fears and anxieties about homosexuality was not coincidental, because social and biological re-production were at the forefront of national anxiety. This assemblage of feelings regarding freedom, fear, and perversion were also displacements of feelings having to do with the new national elite who had made an un-canny mockery of Armenian Symbolic authority and sovereignty.

The difficult road to independence—through pogroms in Azerbai-jan and through a protracted war in Nagorno-Karabakh, both of which were reactions to struggles for the self-determination of the Armenian people—also culminated in a paradoxical reality: Armenians saw them-selves as both having an independent nation-state while simultaneously being an oppressed indigenous people struggling for sovereignty. This fixed in place a particular—static, singular, unmovable—sense of a na-tion. Importantly here, those very calls for national self-determination and the framing of Armenia as an oppressed nation were based on un-derstandings of what had happened to Armenians in Nagorno-Karabakh as a "sequel" (Marutyan 2007) to the 1915 Genocide by the Ottoman Em-pire. In this sense, popular notions of history framed the nation as now and eternally oppressed by Others. Sebouh David Aslanian (2018) refers to this as the "lachrymose" narrative of Armenian national and nation-alist history: Armenia as always and forever persecuted.

Karen Hakobyan, an activist and DIY Pub advocate, argued that whatever nationalist and protectionist energy was directed outward to-ward the enemy (the Turk, the Azerbaijani) during the war was even-tually turned inward because, even after a "victory" following the 1994 ceasefire, Armenians continued to see themselves as an oppressed in-digenous people. While justified by the logics of the threat of national annihilation (at the hands of an external enemy) and the need to sur-vive, the enemy, an Other, of the nationalist gaze became an internal different. For Hakobyan, as well as for Lala Aslikyan—who was perhaps the most outspoken advocate for DIY Pub—Armenian nationalism in-sisted on a singular way of being properly Armenian and on the need to rid the nation of any forms of life that violated that singularity. "We have a picture of this oppressed Armenia . . . Armenia as a victim. You become this oppressed nation with old roots, old culture that is oppressed for so many centuries by everyone," Hakobyan explained. Since the national independence movement in the late 1980s, during which Armenians were responding to pogroms in Azerbaijan as well as demanding self-determination for Nagorno-Karabakh, "independent thinking" or "thinking alternatively" had been formed through national identity, such that a sense of individual identity had either been scrapped as a necessary part of life or, worse, made to seem dangerous to the vision of national identity on which the nation's survival depended. This, according to Hakobyan and Aslikyan, obscured the "human."

> HAKOBYAN: The human being doesn't exist. . . . The human is not there. When we are thinking about blood, territory, language, etc., the human being is not there. No individual. No one is asking you, "Do you want to be Armenian?" You are born Armenian and then you have to do this and this and this and this.
> ASLIKYAN: And if you don't do that you are betraying your nation and you are an enemy. If you are a man, your job is to be a soldier and fight for your nation. If you are a woman, your job is to make soldiers. You are not human, you have no desires, you have no humanity.

Like Little Gender Boycott, the Armenian subject who actively desires rather than properly implements the national will is a national enemy.

During my interview with Hakobyan and Aslikyan, I also remembered an interview I had conducted with Yevgine, the photographer who had gone to the Diversity March to document it and who had been harassed by the counterprotesters. When she was surrounded and accosted by a group of men yelling at her, "Faggot, get away from here!" she explained to them that she was not gay and that even if she were, she had every right to be there in the streets of her city. "It was then that they asked me if I had any children and I said yes. One of them then asked me if I had a son and when I told them that yes, I have a son, he turned around to the others and told them 'Okay, leave her alone, she has given us a son.' Do you understand?" Yevgine asked me, "I gave them a soldier."

Hakobyan dubbed these forms of reproductive and nationalist surveillance "fascism" as well as "the sacralization of Armenianness." I would also like to think about these intimate expectations of propriety within public space as the familialization of Armenianness. The necessity of serving the nation with one's life, body, and reproductive capacity was perceived as a burden by many with whom I spoke during my fieldwork. For some, this was the unbearable burden of belonging to the nation-family in which one was subject not just to the pressure from one's own immediate kin and intimates to conform to expectations of national propriety, but in which the public became an extension of those intimate familial expectations. For many young people in Armenia who did not look and behave "properly" in public—men, for instance, who wanted to grow their hair long, or women who wanted to have pink hair or smoke in public or who did not have heterosexual marriages and did not reproduce a future generation (of soldiers and reproducers of soldiers)—Armenia was an unbearable site of kinship and its intimate demands (Shirinian 2018c). Within the mainstream media and its rhetoric of national survival (prompted by right-wing nationalists), the figure of the homosexual—because of its difference, its reproductivity of perversion but its unreproductivity of the proper nation, its propensity to be moved vis-à-vis individual will and desire rather than by national survival, and its freedom from the constraints of propriety—became a perfect figuration of the internal enemy and the threat against the Armenian family as well as against Armenia as a family.

Kolya, a journalist for the alternative news site *Epress.am*, reflected on the absurdities of this burden of the nation-family. From everywhere in Armenian society—from one's parents to grandparents, aunts and uncles, friends and acquaintances, colleagues and strangers, politicians and talk show hosts—there was that demand to have children. He pointed out that this imperative for increasing the nation's population, always discussed as being in crisis, implied that the decision to reproduce belonged to the nation. "What does this mean? Like if I have a child, I'm having it for you? So that your numbers can increase? If I'm deciding to have a child, I need to call the people and ask them, 'People, should I have a child or not?' This is an absurd situation!" The homosexual was consistently presented as the cause of the demographic crisis. Kolya pointed out that within this rhetoric, not contributing to the increase in the nation's population, or having fewer than three children, was also often equated with homosexuality because "you are not giving anything to the nation."

While complaints about the imperative to reproduce and the association of a decreasing population with homosexuality were commonplace, especially among feminist and LGBT activists, Kolya added an interesting dimension to how he interpreted these phenomena:

During many of these discussions [around homosexuality] I began to understand that there is, what seems to me ... a deep jealousy. A deep jealousy because in peoples' consciousness this gets tied to their own lack of freedom ... when a boy comes back from the military he must get married right away, we must find him a girl, and it doesn't matter with whom—whether he has a home or not—just so they have children and then the child becomes this precious doll. This situation in which there is no pleasure, there is only necessity, responsibility. And then there are people who are not expected, don't have to, who have made a deep and difficult decision. ... It seems to me that there is a jealousy ... precisely because of that freedom. His sexuality doesn't belong to the state, doesn't belong to the family, doesn't belong to anyone. He decides. And it seems to me even if this is not jealousy there is a feeling like, "Go away, so that I won't see you, a free person. Because I'm not free. I want to get pleasure too in my life. I talk about pleasure, but I'm not free enough to be able to be open with another person. So, my not receiving pleasure is justified by the necessity that I will have children."

In this sense, the homosexual is a figure who threatens the nation because of the freedom the figure represents—the freedom from the constraints and boundaries of propriety and singularity. This freedom, however—as threatening as some perceived it to be—is also presented by Kolya as an object of intense desire. The figure of the homosexual elicits disgust, anger, and hatred but also represents a surplus enjoyment and pleasure that is coveted.

Freedom and Its (Dis)contents

While the family, biological reproduction, and proper social reproduction were sacralized, this was certainly not without its contradictions, perhaps best captured by Kolya when he described the attempt at blaming homosexuals for population declines as well as for immorality in the country as a "huge fraud." If that were actually the case, he explained, Armenians might be concerned with actual children. "Are children in Armenia happy? What do they dream about? Or let them go see the level of violence toward children in Armenia, those people who are so worried about children. Children are one of the most vulnerable classes of our society—and they claim to be thinking so much about the children." Kolya's statement problematizes what Lee Edelman has called "reproduc-tive futurism," an embrace of a future strongly committed to the figure of the Child. Edelman argues that this future and all politics (because politics are always based on this reproductive futurism) are inherently conservative. The proper queer response, for Edelman (2004), should be: "Fuck the social order and the Child in whose name we're terrorized . . . ; fuck the whole network of Symbolic relations and the future that serves as its prop" (29). Kolya takes the child not as a figure—not as Edelman's Child—but as an actual population who have nothing to do with the op-pression of homosexuals. In other words, he calls the bluff of right-wing nationalists both in Armenia and elsewhere, who speak in the name of "the Child," but who do not turn their attention to real children. If we were to follow the actual, material, conditions of the child in Armenia (and beyond), we see that children are not necessarily the epitome of fas-cist expectation, as Edelman argues, but are instead themselves subject to the horrors committed in the name of the Child. The child is central to the real, material crises of social reproduction under neoliberalization and oligarchic capitalism. Kolya also points to the ways in which the conservative imperative—to preserve the Symbolic order by any means necessary (for the Child)—is a displacement of other concerns, anxiet-ies, and fears, which underscores the political-economic motivations of these appeals that are missing in Edelman's discussions of the role of the Child. For Edelman, the future fantasized around the Child excludes from view the nonreproductive queer whose enjoyment comes at the expense of the (reproduction of the) social order. Edelman thus argues that a queer position is an antisocial position, as pleas regarding social order are always tied to the reproduction of the status quo.[12] We might think with Kolya further about the relationship between sexual politics and the larger field of the political to counter these assumptions about the social. This is, of course, not to say that sexuality is not political. Rather, it is to suggest that if sexuality is political, which it is, then it must in some way be in relation to other political and economic condi-tions, claims, and structures.

The "huge fraud" that Kolya spoke about during my interview with him in June 2013 was much larger than the nation's condemnation of the homosexual's lack of capacity for reproduction and its simultane-ous ignoring of the conditions of children's lives. The fraud was also the displacement onto the homosexual of the political-economic issues that stemmed from privatization, monopolies, and other problems for which the political-economic elite were responsible. This fraud involved the quasi-, perhaps even faux-, politicization of events and phenomena in order to avoid the hard work of raising real political questions. For instance, when I asked Kolya why he thought there was so much public attention paid to homosexuality—something about which he had spoken passionately during a press conference in May 2013 to commemorate the one-year anniversary of the DIY Pub firebombing—he began answering by laying out the workings of the press in Armenia. The journalist in Armenia, Kolya explained, wants to be a hero, wants to be brave and to report on the hard-hitting facts of the day. But at the same time, this journalist cannot necessarily go after the real bad guys—the oligarchs, the generals of the military, the state officials. Doing so would not only drown his career, as he would likely lose his job in the big mainstream press for which he works, it might also endanger him physically. So, instead, the hero journalist takes up an "oppressor" who is easier to target (precisely because this oppressor is not an oppressor at all) and who has already been identified by the public as an enemy. This "oppressor" can be the homosexual, the feminist, the Jehovah's Witness and members of other "sects" (*aghandner*), the Azerbaijani, the Turk, and so on. "He hasn't been oppressed by the homosexual, right?" Kolya asks me. "His [actual] oppressors are Nemets Rubo, Samvel Aleksanyan, and so on," naming two prominent oligarchs whom I discuss in the next chapter. "But, with them," Kolya continues, "you should see how they act! Yelling at the podium about homosexuals and the next day going to a press conference where these big men are talking and sitting quietly in the corner. These are the owners. The ones who dictate the country."

Araksi, Kolya's colleague at *Epress.am*, elaborated on these politics when I interviewed her a few weeks later. Araksi and Kolya had worked at another press a few years prior, and both had left to come over to *Epress.am* when it was founded because they preferred to be at an "alternative" press. Much of what happens in the press, according to Araksi, is driven by editors. Some editors are put under direct pressure by the owner of the press, who himself might be under direct pressure by someone who has political or economic power. In these cases, the editor will not allow certain kinds of ideas or perspectives to be published because he has been given boundaries. In these cases, it is also often the editors who decide to pick up sensationalist stories. These stories are good for increasing "clicks" on their site, and they do the work of distracting attention from whoever is putting pressure on the website to stay silent or positive about particular political or economic issues. Sometimes, however, there is no direct threat to the editor, but he decides to be careful anyway, to avoid garnering too much attention from those in power. Araksi's last straw at her previous place of employment, for instance, was when a piece she had written criticizing Russia's role in Armenian and Georgian relations was pulled because the editor, explaining that the Armenian government was close to Russia, did not think it was appropriate to publish. Most journalists in Armenia, Araksi argued, did not see news from the perspective of human rights but rather from the perspective of the nation. And from the perspective of the nation, homosexuality was the best topic on which to publish because you already knew that everyone would agree, and you did not have to be afraid that anyone in power would come after you or your press.

For nationalist journalists, the constant discussion of homosexuality in the mainstream media was not a result of some kind of manipulation on the part of the right in conjunction with the press (as most left-leaning journalists would explain to me); it was the result of too much (and the wrong kind of) freedom. When I asked Vazgen, a journalist who worked for *Yerkir Media*, why homosexuality was the object of so much discussion in Armenia, he explained that the recent spike in the circulation of homosexuality as a topic was a direct result of the attempt by some organizations to launch a gay parade in Armenia (here Vazgen was referring to the Diversity March). Vazgen, like other right-leaning journalists and activists with whom I spoke, insisted that the Diversity March was a gay parade, even after I pointed out that this is not how its organizers characterized it. Vazgen also blamed the structure of digital media. Because of the importance of increasing "clicks," he argued, "online news media received a big incentive for everyone to talk about *everything*. As a result, there came a very serious danger: everyone started talking about suicides, sexual minorities, and other such issues that spread further the more they are discussed. By talking about it, you guarantee that the issue will spread further." Like suicide, homosexuality was a contagious topic, according to Vazgen; it was dangerous to the individual and the body politic, something that one might begin to desire as one realized its possibility. For him, some things should not be publicly discussed in order to protect public safety. Though Vazgen took tolerance to be an important practice in a modern state, he asserted that "when I say that I am tolerant toward sexual minorities, that does not mean that I will be tolerant if one of my children was kissing someone of the same sex, for instance. Tolerance is based on freedom. I recognize that experiences are diverse and everyone has the right to do what they want to do. But, when that freedom is upsetting to me and my life, I cannot be tolerant of that." Vazgen was enrolled in a human rights and communications program at the time of the interview and likely felt compelled to be slightly more "tolerant" than those leaning more to the right.

Vazgen's comments on tolerance accentuated the problem of freedom that the figure of the homosexual elicits. That freedom, he warned, needed to be curtailed. The homosexual, however, did not have a monopoly on dangerous freedoms; the threat of freedom extended into a larger assemblage of concepts and ideas that, while associated with the figure of the homosexual, were seen as direct imports from Europe. For instance, for most of those within the right-wing or nationalist circles with whom I conducted interviews, "human rights" were a problem precisely because of the freedom they implied. This was especially true when "rights" did not recognize duties, responsibilities, and obligations. Armen Mkrtichyan, for instance, one of the founders of Hayazn, the organization mostly responsible for the counterprotest to the Diversity March, argued that while human rights were important, equally important were responsibilities toward the nation. "It's not just the nation that owes the individual something, correct? Every individual also has responsibilities to their nation. And if an individual's expression of their rights tramples on the rights of the nation, then that should not be their right." Mkrtichyan, like Vazgen, described himself as "tolerant" of everybody, but he also argued that some phenomena—like homosexuality—should be a private matter and not be made public. "It's not something that children should see, for instance. I believe I am not saying anything wrong. Do you agree?" he asked me. I left it at "Our opinions differ on this."

Hovhannes Galajyan, the editor-in-chief of the right-wing newspaper *Iravunk*, expressed similar disquietudes about "freedom" and "human rights," but from a much less "tolerant" place. Ironically, *Iravunk*—which means "Right," as in protected entitlement, and which is also the official publication of the Constitutional Rights Party—was devoted not to *human* rights but to the rights of the nation, which Galajyan believed the Constitution had the obligation to protect. "So what kind of a thing is 'human rights?'" he asked. "It's incomprehensible. And under these so-called human rights, what is being pushed forward is not rights of the healthy majority, but the rights of sick sexual minorities." For Galajyan and others, rights have more to do with responsibilities and duties than with freedom and desire. It was the "freedom" of the new immoral postsocialist era, Galajyan told me, that allowed television networks to broadcast whatever people wanted to watch, whatever gave them pleasure: murder, violence, sex, and homosexuality. Television networks should have obligations to show patriotic stories about Armenian heroes, Armenian history, and Armenian tradition, Galajyan maintained. Also ironic was that it was *Iravunk* newspaper and other right-wing nationalist news sites and spokespersons that were the most vocal about homosexuality in print, in the digital world, and on television in Armenia.

Stories on homosexuality, sexual perversion, *gender*, a sexless society, and laws mandated by Europe that were threatening to force all Armenians into becoming transgender were available every day on *BlogNews.am*, *Tert.am*, and *Zham.am*, on *Yerkir Media* television network and various talk shows and news on other television networks, as well as all over social media. Belief in the narrative that homosexuality was the primary threat to the Armenian nation, however, remained limited to a particular niche. It was right-wing nationalists who spoke in the language of standing against "sexual perversion" (*aylaserutyun*) as the ultimate form of saving the nation. While popular and mainstream media would give these particularly positioned actors a voice—much more so than they would give voice to LGBT activists or feminists—the feeling of homosexuality's imminent danger had not seemed to penetrate the body politic.

The Moral Perversion of Sexual Perversion

When my research collaborator, Lucine Talalyan, and I surveyed households across Yerevan, only three out of 150 individuals or families with whom we spoke made any mention of homosexuality at all. Lidiya, a middle-aged woman who worked as a desk clerk in a hospital, responded to our question about the role of the family in Armenia today by stating that it was the duty of all Armenians to protect this sacred institution, otherwise "they will ruin it [*kkanden*]." Talalyan asked Lidiya who would ruin it and how would they ruin it, and Lidiya listed the usual suspects: feminists, homosexuals, and non–Apostolic Christian sects. "This is our tribe [*tsegh*]," Lidiya proclaimed, "and we need to protect it, our traditions. There are so many who are now trying to destroy our tribe." The term *tsegh* has racialized connotations; it is tied to breeding, bloodline, and species. For Lidiya, Armenian traditions were ingrained in the blood. She argued that there were too many women now who were having sex before marriage and ruining the nation's future. She cited a "famous" case that I had heard of a few other times about an Armenian woman who had, many years prior to being married, lost her virginity to a Black man. When her first child was born, in a marriage with an Armenian man, he was born Black. This "case" proved to Lidiya and some others that a woman carries the genes of every man with whom she has sex. Such "scientific" stories populate anxious imaginaries regarding sexuality. Lidiya used this "scientific" reasoning to explain why it was necessary for her to protest the 2010 burial of the Red Apple, and why she found such perversions of Armenian traditions a danger to the survival of the nation.

At this point, Talalyan asked her to comment on what else she thought was threatening to the nation, which led to a long discussion of homosexuality, the existence of gay bars in Yerevan (DIY Pub), and the spread of "homosexual propaganda" (*hamaseramolutyan karoz*) through gay pride parades (the Diversity March). Lidiya was clearly a follower of the right-wing media and right-wing organizations. Her language was recognizable. I had been reading it and hearing it in all the probing I had done into right-wing nationalist movements. For Lidiya, the Armenian tribe was threatened by new, European ideas like feminism and homosexuality, which would eventually distort Armenian traditions and pervert the bloodline to such an extent that Armenia would cease to exist. "I will not let that happen, my girls," she told us proudly.

Lidiya was the only true follower of right-wing narratives and theories we came across during our interviews. The two others who mentioned homosexuality at all made only passing mention and had little else to offer when we followed up. Both were middle-aged men, Gevorg and Nshan, and they used the term *gomik* (a pejorative meaning "homo," from the Russian word for homosexual, *gomoseksual*) to refer to the moral and at times sexual deviances of Armenia's governmental elite. Gevorg had had a hard time getting a job in the post-Soviet era. He had held a government job in construction during the Soviet era. More recently, he told us, he had had multiple experiences with employers who refused to pay him for the jobs that he had done. Furthermore, when he complained to the local government, trying to sue for compensation, he had been accused of harassment, and his license to work was stripped from him. "Gomikner en ara, saghe. Satana, gomik," Gevorg ranted. "They are homos, man, all of them. Satan, homos." When Talalyan asked him what this had to do with their sexual orientation—a kind of provocation, considering she knew quite well that he was not using *gomik* to indicate sexual behavior or identity—Gevorg just seemed confused and got upset. "What are you talking about?" he asked, defensively. We moved on. Similarly, when Nshan began ranting about the *gomiks* in Armenia's government, he was using the term to indicate a larger (moral) depravity.

Moral deviations, however, are always intimately caught up with the sexual, including within the terms for perversion (*aylaserutyun* and *aylandakutyun*) that I discussed in the introduction. When we asked Nshan why he was calling corrupt government officials *gomik*, he responded: "Well, aren't they *gomik*? Why do you think all of those transvestites walk around there all day and all night, in front of their building? They are built wrong, in their minds and bodies." Nshan was referring to Komaygi Children's Park across the street from the government building that had more recently become a popular spot for the solicitation of sex work—sometimes pejoratively referred to as *Gom-aygi* (faggot park). There were popular rumors in Yerevan that government officials regularly visited the park to solicit transgender sex workers—a rumor confirmed by some transgender sex workers. Whether or not these rumors were true, however, Nshan was psychically and discursively linking politically and economically corrupt behavior to sexual "deviance." If government officials were morally bankrupt, they were also sexual perverts. Moral perversion (*aylandakutyun*) and sexual perversion (*aylaserutyun*)—both as deviations from proper Armenianness and as a threat on Symbolic order—shared an intimacy.

The sexual and moral pervert also shared propensities for freedom. While the homosexual declared himself free from the constraints of the family and proper production and reproduction, the political-economic elite also behaved as if they were free from national moral expectations, from law, and from expectations and obligations to care for the Armenian people. While the freedom of the oligarchs—to do what they pleased no matter what the consequences on the body politic—had real, everyday, and often devastating effects on the people, the anger and fear surrounding them was at times conflated with notions of sexual perversion and feelings of animosity directed toward the figure of the homosexual.

Distractions, Displacements, and Condensations

As an archive, Talalyan's and my interviews made clear that the right-wing nationalist anxiety around the nation's sexual perversion was a minority concern. Our interlocutors, as I will discuss in subsequent chapters, were far more concerned about the oligarchy's and other elites' deviations, which had direct effects on their own lives, than with "sexual perversion." However, mainstream press loudly expressed right-wing nationalist fears geared against the figure of the homosexual within the public sphere, making use of events like the DIY firebombing, the Diversity March, the Gender Equality Law, and others. LGBT and feminist activists saw this as distraction, and many were convinced that these anti-gay positions, for the most part, were not authentic. They had been manufactured, I was told a few times, to distract the left, as well as the prospective left, away from real concerns. The homosexual was a convenient figure. While in content he was unproductive and unreproductive, as an object of hate and blame, he was very politically productive.

Right-wing activists, many of my progressive interlocutors frequently argued, used the figure of the homosexual as the object onto which to directly displace attention from where it should have been—on the political-economic elite's actions. Many of the staff at PINK and WRC were convinced that right-wing organizations and popular figures were working for the government—either directly or indirectly. There were rumors, for instance, that popular blogger Tigran Kocharyan worked for the KGB (technically, the National Security Service, or NSS, in the post-Soviet era, but still called by its Soviet-era name). He was frequently spotted coming and going from the Yerevan headquarters on the corner of Nalbandyan and Moskovyan Streets, which also happened to be across the street from the PINK office at the time. I was often told that Kocharyan always had information before anyone else and thus was seen as a kind of epicenter of the moral and sex panic. "He posts something and then you see everyone posts after him. Check it, the dates on all of his posts are before anyone else starts talking," explained Hripsime to me at PINK. She was right. When it came to the DIY firebombing, the Diversity March, the Gender Equality Law, and various other events that had stoked sex panic, Kocharyan seemed to have been the first to cast a stone. Some believed that Armenian government officials had been trained in tactics of distraction and suppression by Russia's Putin regime, which had nurtured the right-wing skinhead movement to suppress journalists and leftists. "They use fascist organizations to take care of opposition, and then say 'Organizations are fighting against each other, what can we do?'" explained Karen Hakobyan. There were many rumors that the right-wing organization Hayots Artsivner (Armenian Eagles) was a government front to foment unrest. The fact that the nongovernmental organization had an office in a government building and that the head of the organization, Khachik Asryan, also held the office of Deputy Minister of Sports and Youth, provided more fuel to these rumors.

Progressive activists rarely ever engaged right-wing nationalists because they were seen not as the main opposition but rather as decoys and state tools. During a Human Rights House Network meeting in November 2012, for instance, when conversation moved to new anti-homosexual protests and members of the network wanted to know what could be done to respond to these protests, Zabel, the representative of WRC, spoke up: "Honestly, I think we should do nothing. I'm sick of this. Look, there are presidential elections coming up, and there are other very serious problems in this country. Every day I hear from another woman who has been beaten by her husband, and I have to deal with these problems. I don't have time to be drawn into some stupid game that they are playing. The best thing to do is to ignore them. They will get tired after a while." Anna, from PINK, agreed: "That is exactly what they want. For us to be scrambling to deal with their new made-up problem so that we get nothing done. We have better things to do." If we follow these suspicions, then, the objective of the sex panics was not to incite the *public* about sexual perversion but rather to incite fighting between right-wing nationalists and progressives in the hope that the right wing would eventually stymie the progressives.

Politicizing the Figure of the Homosexual

The convenience of homosexuality as a productive, fabricated political target—a scapegoat on which to displace the attention and politicized energy that should rightfully have been focused on the political-economic elite—is not arbitrary. The figure of the homosexual was a productive figure because of the meanings of the nation's reproduction (both biological and social) that were invested in it. That is, it was social reproduction that was felt to be under threat. Using the figure of the homosexual, social reproductive concerns—which are economic in nature, having to do with the means of social reproduction—were instead displaced onto questions of propriety, or the proper reproduction of the nation. And what better object is there, so clearly and obviously outside of this frame of proper reproduction, than the homosexual? While it may not work entirely—neither to sway the public nor to fuel wars between the right and the left—public panic about homosexuality makes a particular kind of sense. It is rarely, if ever, questioned—except by LGBT and feminist activists. The *aylaserutyun* (sexual perversion) of the homosexual, the feminist, and other improperly reproductive figures and the *aylandakutyun* (moral perversion) of the political-economic elite are psychically attached by way of their connection to social reproduction, and together they constitute an assemblage of threat to Armenia's Symbolic order. In the public collective unconscious, the homosexual and the oligarch have an affinity and can be interchangeable.

The displacement and conflation of the elite's immorality—and the general moral decline of the postsocialist world in general—onto the figure of the homosexual is possible because of an already existing perception of homosexual life as a perverse, improper, mode of life and living. This also makes possible the condensation of the figure of the homosexual and the figure of the oligarch. And when social reproduction is already at risk, threatening life and the survival of worlds, the appearance of perversion within public discourse—whether it is believable or not—comes to make sense. In this way, right-wing populism—including anti-gender activism, anti-homosexuality, and anti-feminism—might be seen as forms of resistance against the crises of democracy and the chaos of modern life caused by neoliberalization, as Graff and Korolczuk (2022) have shown. Importantly, Graff and Korolczuk point out that while feminist analysis has assumed a symbiosis between neoliberalism and conservatism, this is not necessarily the case. Conservative sections of the Armenian public, while not necessarily directly calling attention to privatization and free market logics, respond to these processes nonetheless—sometimes through seemingly unrelated claims, such as sexual perversion—making a reactionary cultural critique of a political-economic phenomenon. What explorations of the sex panic in this light reveal is that when intense emotions around sexuality and other forms of moral deviance crop up, they are not a product of ignorance. They are the displacements and condensations of anxieties stemming from political-economic and, especially, social reproductive perversions.

Queer theory cannot take for granted the intimate linking between sexual, private, familial, personal, cultural, subcultural, or gendered worlds and political economy. Critically, this needs to go much farther than understanding the public life of sexuality or "sex in public" (Warner and Berlant 1998). The sexual is always a concern around reproduction, both biological and social. Thus, it is always about production, exploitation, and subsistence; about power; and about the making of future worlds. These conditions vary across geopolitical boundaries, and it is in the nuances of expectations regarding production and reproduction that we find the particular resonances of how feelings and practices regarding sexuality emerge. Neoliberalism, capitalism, feudalism, oligarchy, economies of favors, urban development projects, socialism, Communist Party rule, and so on are not just *contexts* in which queer theory must situate itself but sites and objects of queer investigation in and of themselves.

Keeping the figure of the homosexual in mind, I now move—in the following chapter—to the perversions of the elite. Exploring the surplus enjoyment of the oligarch—another figure within the constellation of the Republic's perversion—one discovers echoes of the same anxieties around social reproduction that the figure of the homosexual raises. Following the end of the Soviet Union, Armenians experienced capitalism, oligarchy, and neoliberalization as rule by the morally perverse. But critically, the moral depravity of the elite is not completely disentangled from sexual perversion, neither in the assumptions nor feelings about the elite's sexual or social deviations. Afterall, political economy involves social reproduction and, thus, sexual politics.

This is your street, the school of life
Where they remember you, they still haven't forgotten

RUBEN HAKHVERDYAN, FROM "THIS IS YEREVAN"
("SA YEREVANN E")

Better to lose your eye than your good name.

ARMENIAN PROVERB

CHAPTER THREE

The Names-of-the-Fathers

Many of Yerevan's residential buildings share a yard with surrounding buildings on the block. These yards (*bak* in the singular, *baker*
in the plural) are squared in by the buildings. The *bak* is often also home
to one or more small grocery shops for fresh fruits and vegetables, a bak-
ery, and a convenience store that serve mainly the residents of those
buildings. The popular film *Mer Bake* (*Our Yard*) and the comedy TV show
by the same name tell similar stories capturing how these small yards are
intimate settings. They are places in which one can witness and experience the same dramas, comedies, and tragedies—characterized by the
caring and agonistic kin relations—as those that typically take place in
the home. The *bak* is an extension of the homes that surround it. These
shared communal spaces become the sites at which these relations take
place, involving members of various households who are bound by living
in the surrounds of the same yard and by making use of the commons
of that yard. Interactions often involve consuming the food brought to
the neighborhood by the same vendors and sold by the same local shop-
keepers as well as the run-ins within these local shops. The experience
also involves shared time. Individuals of a *bak* spend time together. This
might be intentional time. It might also be unintentional time, as when

neighbors overhear conversations through windows, walls, and doors. The *bak* is a space of making intimacy.

An important part of *bak* intimacy is the boy child, whose play involves the making of fraternal hordes that in some ways might be regarded a form of taking ownership of the yard. It did not take long for me to learn the names of the children, especially the boys, who lived in the building in which I rented an apartment during my year-long fieldwork in Yerevan. The eight-story building in which I lived had three apartments on each floor. I lived on the sixth floor. There were twenty-four units in the building, including mine. In the afternoons, when school let out, I heard young boys calling out "Haykoooooooooo!" from below. Hayko was one of the boys—about ten years of age—who lived in my building, one floor below me. His friends lived in the ten buildings that made up the square of the yard, and they would often approach the building and call out his name so that Hayko could come out and play. The name Hayko is diminutive for Hayk, which was the boy's proper name. Sometimes I would hear Hayko's mother, grandmother, or aunt respond, "Hayko can't come out now," and the boys would scurry away. Often, when they yelled for him, Hayko would come to the balcony, which had a view of the yard, and yell back at them, "Galis em!" (I'm coming!). In the evenings, I would hear someone else, his mother or grandmother, calling "Haykoooooooooooo!" for him to come back home.

Walking out of my building, or around the other buildings in the yard, I would often see the (nick)names of these boys tagged on the bricks or cement of walls: "Hayko," "Arto" (a diminutive of Artavazd), "Sako" (a diminutive of Sargis), and others. This was their neighborhood; this was their yard. And their names carried some weight. What might happen when these boys got older, came into some money through the very connections they had made growing up in these neighborhoods or through connections made in other intimate networks? To better understand the neighborhood intimacies of which the oligarchy is a part, we might speculate about what would happen if Hayko were to grow up and become an oligarch (however unlikely that might be). He might become Hayko with an added flair; he might gain an additional name having to do with the way in which he came into his power or wealth, or one having to do with a negative characteristic with which he or his family is associated. This name would be tagged onto the diminutive of his proper name. He might also remain Hayko but be known by people all over the country as *that* Hayko, that child who has become a sovereign, the boy we raised who now wields power over us. Or perhaps he would not become a powerful sovereign at all and grow up to be Hayk, or be called Hayko, without any social cachet outside of his most intimate circles. Hayko was likely not the son of Soviet-era *apparatchiks*, low-level bureaucrats or managers in industry, or the son of military personnel who came into power through the war in the 1990s. Considering this—that he would not inherit his father's wealth, acquired through the stripping of Soviet industry that he sold for parts, or through the privatization of a once-public factory or land, or by selling off war-looted property—it is most likely that he will grow up to be just Hayk, or just Hayko. His name will not give rise to hatred, fear, or resentment. Still, this name will carry meaning for him. While many in Armenia are embedded within intimate networks through their nicknames (usually in the form of diminutives), nicknames given to the political-economic elite carry critical significance. From childhood antics to adult business, nicknames produce household and neighborhood intimacies but can also circulate beyond that neighborhood to interpellate their carriers as intimately known and ambivalently hated by the nation.

This chapter is concerned with the political-economic elite, popularly called the oligarchy (*oligarkhnere*). The term refers to the wealthy who rule over Armenia. However, some who are often lumped into this notion of the *oligarkhner*—like Serzh Sargsyan, Armenia's former president —are not themselves among the wealthiest in the country but are nonetheless at times characterized as being part of the same group of elite because they aid in the oligarchy's procurement of wealth and power. Sargsyan himself is intimately connected with two well-known oligarchs—Alexander (Sashik) Sargsyan, his younger brother, and Mikayel Minasyan (Mishik), his son-in-law. It is hard to say how many oligarchs there are in Armenia, considering the political influence of those who may not themselves have direct seats in government; but a 2013 Finance Ministry report found that at least one-third of big companies (of which there were 941 at the time) did not pass an external audit because their owners were high-rank functionaries (Yernjakyan 2013). Here I focus on the most well-known and talked about among this horde.

I am particularly interested in the moral perversion (*aylandakutyun*) of these political-economic elites. Who are these authority figures, and what makes them perverse? And how might their perversion be tied into the forms of sexual perversion as embodied by the figure of the homosexual? It is critical to note that this elite is not the intellectual elite and usually not even the elite that made up the Soviet-era *nomenklatura*, or Communist Party appointees in positions of power. Many of the oligarchs in Armenia come from rural or peasant backgrounds and, thus, their status as "elites" is, in itself, ambiguous (Antonyan 2016). While they are elite in the sense that they have access to wealth and political power, they are the antithesis of elitism with regard to their education, backgrounds, families, and culture. This new elite—or what Irina Ghaplanyan (2018) has called the "counter-elite"—came into power via the strategic positions they held in the military or industry during a period of massive political and economic upheaval. These positions gave them access to great power through post-Soviet marketization schemes and war, allowing them to usurp the power of the Soviet-era elite, including that of first president Levon Ter-Petrosyan, forcing him to resign in 1998.

I take up the intimate connections and relations between the nation's sovereigns and those over whom they rule through the nicknames the ruled often use for their rulers. Armenians commonly give diminutive names—similar to those one would call a child, for example, by adding the suffix *-ik* (signaling the diminutive) or *-o* (attributing intimacy and innocence) to the end of the shortened first name—to those high up on the political and economic ladders of the nation-state, but especially to those who are characterized by the negative attributes of corruption, thievery, violence, brutality, and other *aylandak* (morally perverse) qualities. The nicknames for the political-economic elite, as such, call attention to the elite's *illegitimacy* as sovereigns because of their perversions of Armenianness.

These elite are the intimates of the people with whom and by whom they were raised. And the intimates are aware of the authority figure's background—his lack of "culturedness" and education, his everyday activities, and the ways in which he acquired the wealth and power through which he now rules. He is, or once was, one of them. But now, having become a sovereign through less-than-moral means—having performed various acts of impropriety outside of the bounds of the moral values of Armenianness—he has been rendered something different. He is no longer one of the people from the neighborhood in which he was raised. But the oligarch is still known to them as the once-troublesome child who became a member of an "unsavory band."[1]

Intimacy, "a narrative about something shared" (Berlant 2000, 1), expects. Intimacy is a story of the expectations of others that might be, and often are, unmet. The nickname for the political-economic elite points to intimacy by way of failed expectations. It highlights a violation of that very intimacy: a betrayal of Armenianness. The "nicking" of the name "cuts" the figure of authority—splitting the Name-of-the-Father and the No-of-the-Father from one another as a kind of castration of his authority. With little power over the sovereign who emerged from their yards, those with whom the oligarch is intimately connected and over whom he now rules use the nickname (a marker of their shared intimacy) as a symbolic rejection of this power.

Intimacy and authority are deeply intertwined. In the anthropological category of the "kin-ordered mode of production," kinship is defined as the site of control over the reproductive powers of women, granting rights over the social labor of women as well as over their offspring and their relatives (affines). Kinship is also a site of parental power, defining not only descent but differential access to resources and social labor that come with a law of descent (Wolf 1982). The very category of "kin-ordered societies" implicitly suggests that state-based societies making use of tributary or capitalist modes of production are less reliant on kinship. Feminist anthropologists, however, have found kinship to be tied to various "modern" institutions. Susan McKinnon and Fanella Cannell (2013), for instance, argue that while "'modern,' state-based societies are seen as organized by reference to territory and market, relations between individuals, and rationalized, secular contract laws" (4), modern institutions continue to be structured by the vitality of kinship, even if these have been made invisible within anthropological discourse. Lauren Berlant (2000) makes a similar point when she argues that intimacy spreads and that liberal (read: modern) society was founded on the spread of intimate expectations from the domestic to the public. The move to relinquish kinship from theory and analysis is often credited to David Schneider, whose *A Critique of the Study of Kinship* (1984) provides a deep-cutting critique of anthropology's use of kinship, arguing that kinship as an analytic came out of anthropologists' and ethnographers' own conceptualizations of relation (embedded in American and European forms) rather than from actual realities observed elsewhere in the world. Kinship as an analytic began to disappear from anthropological theory and came to be replaced by other categories of analysis—such as personhood, gender, and nation (Carsten 2004). More recently, scholars have pointed to actual as well as metaphorical kin relations—paternal bonds (Ozyurek 2006; K. Phillips 2010), the continued fetishization of past

Father-leaders (Hubbert 2006), and expectations of feminized hospitality in the context of masculinized gerontocracies (Riley 2019)—that continue to structure kin-based obligations between rulers and the ruled. My analysis here of a modern society's moral reliance on intimacy with public and powerful figures extends these claims by showing how modern state legitimacy may also be kin-ordered.

The familiarizing and intimate-making mechanism of using nicknames for the political-economic elite is embedded in a sense of governance based on a moral Symbolic order and authority. The expectations on which a (nick)name is founded are based not in liberal democratic sensibilities of law and order, but rather within a moral economy. The elite are *aylandak* (perverse), corrupt, and illegitimate not because they have violated state law. Their criminality is not brought to judgment within the domain of that law. Rather, their corruption is based on violations of the Symbolic authority that I have been referring to in this book as "proper Armenianness" and that we might also understand as the *Law of the Father*—a social (collective) unconscious sense of proper and improper, a kind of collective superego governed by moral power. This Law of the Father is a realm beyond worldly governance and transcends (and precedes) state law, having emerged from a mytho-history of Armenian survival. This difference points to a further bifurcation, beyond that of the Name and the No. It points to the split between the Imaginary and the Symbolic that produces law as incongruent with Law. In other words, the realm of (state) law to which individuals are subjected is in tension with "idealized social relations" (Butler 2000, 3), what I call the Law of the Father, with which we might define the Lacanian Symbolic order.

The proper Law (of the Father), in line with the Name-of-the-Father Hayk (the mythical first Armenian), is established based on values embedded in proper kinship, proper Armenian traditions, and care for the Armenian people to ensure the survival of the nation in continuity with the nation's past. The proper Law (of the Father) is the Symbolic order. My interlocutors, however, saw the political-economic elite as deeply in violation of this Symbolic order and authority. These elite—whom I will refer to as the nation's sovereigns, those who have given themselves the power to rule—have usurped the power that originally belonged to Hayk. They include the president, the prime minister, members of Parliament, mayors, the chief of police, military elite, and so on. My analysis of my interlocutors' claims and feelings points to how these usurpers have replaced the Name-of-the-Father Hayk, severely undercutting the possibilities of national survival. In this way, they can be likened to Freud's fraternal horde, who kill the primal Father and eat his flesh in order to share the power that once belonged solely to him. So, although the new sovereigns ruled over Armenians, they did not follow the Law of the Father Hayk, especially not in its most critical expression, which is to ensure the survival of the nation. These figures, and their names, are perversions of the Name-of-the-Father Hayk via a violation of his Law.

"Nicking" the Name

There is a wide variety of intimate meanings—such as love, faith, respect, or mockery—conveyed in nicknames given to powerful figures.[2] Nicknames for oligarchs and other elites in postsocialist Armenia index intimacy, but only in relation to violations of that intimacy. During my fieldwork in Armenia, I would most often hear discussions about political and economic practices with reference to actors whose names were "nicked." Prime Minister (from 2014 to 2016) Hovik Abrahamyan, was known as the *Muk*, the mouse, because, as many people told me, he was known even during the Soviet era to steal slowly, small pieces at a time, like a mouse. The mayor of Yerevan (from 2011 to 2018), Taron Margaryan, was most often referred to as Taron, marking him an intimate figure to the city but also as an illegitimate ruler. These names, as they floated around conversations and discussions in Yerevan, seemed somewhat out of place to me at the beginning of my fieldwork. Taron's last name and the actual full names of other political-economic elite were frequently dropped in everyday conversation, and so I often found myself having to ask, or later Google, the nickname to find out who the discussion was about. For some of these figures, the nickname was used more frequently than the proper name itself. A common joke about Samvel Aleksanyan (nicknamed Lfik Samo) highlights the commonality of these nicknames. As the joke goes, Aleksanyan wants to open a supermarket and asks an elderly woman's opinion about it. She responds to him that while it may be a good idea to open a supermarket, Lfik will not let him. Aleksanyan becomes annoyed and tells her "My name is Samvel Aleksanyan" to which the woman replies that she does not care what his name is because, in any case, Lfik will not let him open a supermarket (Antonyan 2016, 137). As the joke makes apparent, "Lfik" as a nickname is better known than the proper name of its holder and signifies a figure that might very well be more than the man himself.

At times, everyday conversation made such intimate references to major oligarchs or members of government, that I often confused conversations as being about friends or other intimates. For instance, one morning, Lucine Talalyan (the friend and visual artist who became my research collaborator) came to join me at a café near our respective homes. As she was preparing to sit down, removing the earbuds attached to her phone, she asked, "Did you see what Manvel said?" I quickly generated a cognitive map of the mutual friends and acquaintances Talalyan and I shared and tried to recall the "Manvel" in question. Talalyan did not wait for a response from me and continued telling me about how Manvel had told the National Assembly that Armenians are all, first of all, "brothers and sisters" belonging to the same nation and that instead of in-fighting they should wed their daughters and sons to continue the fate of the nation. In a month or so, Manvel had argued, the government—president, prime minister, speaker of Parliament—could change (causing outcry), but Armenia would remain Armenia, a family. It was in this context that I realized Talalyan was referring to General Manvel Grigoryan, a higher-up in Armenia's military apparatus. Even though I had seen the video to which she was referring circulating on social media that morning,[3] the ability to place the intimate naming of "Manvel" within a constellation of political and economic power was something that I would have to learn to do more quickly as I became more aware of these "nicks" in the Names-of-the-Fathers.

If one were to discuss the political-economic elite of Armenia, Ruben Hayrapetyan's name would surely come up. But he might not come up as Ruben Hayrapetyan, but rather as Nemets Rubo, his nickname. Nemets Rubo was one of the major oligarchs of Armenia. Like many of these wealthy men, he was elected to office in 2003 as a member of the National Assembly in the Yerevan district of Avan, where he had grown up. He was the president of the Armenian Football Federation, from which he was asked to resign, time and again (and which he finally did in 2018), for reasons most would describe as criminal behavior. He is the co-owner of Grand Tobacco (part of the larger Grand Group, that includes the very popular Grand Candy stores and confections company) and the owner of Aragats textile production plant, several gas stations, the Bijni mineral water company (the object of various calls for boycott in the first decade of the twenty-first century), and the high-end Harsnakar hotel and restaurant in Yerevan and Sevan.

Nemets Rubo is also associated with several violent events. On June 17, 2012, during a party at the Harsnakar restaurant, Vahe Avetyan, a surgeon for the Armenian military, was beaten to death by a group of men who also severely injured other military doctors. Police arrested four suspects—two security guards, a restaurant manager, and a waiter—and charged them for the murder and the assaults. Many, however, suspected that Nemets Rubo had ordered the beatings himself. Following this incident, protestors demanded that the state bring criminal charges against Hayrapetyan in connection to the violence at Harsnakar. The charges were never brought forth, although pressure through petitions and protests forced him to resign as member of the National Assembly in July of that year. The violence at Harsnakar was not the last time Nemets would be implicated in assault. In August 2015, he physically assaulted Arsen Avetisyan, a major shareholder of Air Armenia (the biggest Armenian airline), sending Avetisyan to the hospital with a broken nose and other injuries. Nemets Rubo admitted to his act of violence, claiming that he had been sent to Avetisyan to collect a debt owed to a third party. The Prosecutor General's office did not press charges against Nemets Rubo, and Avetisyan decided to take a reconciliation deal outside of the courts in order to "take into account every detail concerning the future of the airline when making decisions."[4] In May 2020, the Investigative Committee of the Republic of Armenia reported that there was evidence that Nemets, his son, and his son's friends had violently kept the head of the executive body of Harsnakar hotel hostage at the Sevan hotel complex.[5]

The nickname Nemets Rubo is a combination of the descriptor "German" (*Nemets*) that, in Armenia, is often connotatively synonymous with fascism and betrayal, and the shortened, diminutive version of his first name, Ruben. The name was in circulation even prior to the violent events described above. Nemets Rubo was known as a brute with a propensity to harass and threaten journalists. He was also commonly known for his openness about his role in election frauds and the aggressive usurpation of power. Nemets Rubo maintained that he should *not* be prosecuted for the murder of Vahe Avetyan and the assault against Arsen Avetisyan, but he also never specifically denied his role in the violence. He made it clear that beyond demanding that those over whom he rules recognize his power, he had little concern for what they thought of him.

In 2013, during a press conference held for the Armenian Football Federation, a year after the murder at Harsnakar restaurant, Nemets Rubo announced that he would not be resigning from his position as president of the Federation. He also declared that he did not understand any of the claims made against him. He stated,

> And who has demanded of me a resignation for me to give it to them? You have to understand one thing well: if the people and those in charge want me to go, then I will go. It is not nice that people, sitting in front of social networking sites, are discussing a bunch of nonsense. Let all of them who have suggestions and thoughts come forth. I am ready to talk with them for hours.[6]

Of course, those asking for his resignation and for charges of murder to be brought against him were not just "sitting in front of social networking sites." They had been organizing protests and demonstrations in front of public buildings for months.

Nemets Rubo's expression of interest in "talking" with people "for hours" came across as a threat, especially in the context of an earlier admission, during a 2011 press conference, to "beatings" he carried out as an acceptable form of punishment, in his home district of Avan. When asked about how he deals with crime in his district, Hayrapetyan had responded, "Go to Avan and ask them, 'How does he deal with drug addicts? How does he treat someone who is a drug dealer? A hashish dealer?' Everyone knows how I treat these kinds of people." When asked, further, to explain *how* he deals with "these people," he responded, with a smirk: "I call him and talk to him and say 'You have done a very bad thing.'" The audience laughed along with Nemets. Still laughing, he said, "Don't you know what I am going to do? I am going to punish them, beat them up." As the audience continued to laugh uncomfortably, Nemets held himself erect, smiling pridefully. Perhaps made more comfortable by this bit of uneasy comic relief, he continued, "Or you think that I am going to avoid doing so [sarcastically]. . . . If someone tells you that I have played violin, then at that time you can be surprised. That's when you should be surprised, my dear people." Nemets was managing his own violent image. While he did not name himself Nemets Rubo, he seemed to find it suited him. The name recalled his violent excesses but also indicated that he was in a position of authority.

Nicknames, and especially the criminality that they imply, are sometimes managed by way of revisionist narratives that are applied to their etymologies (Abrahamian and Shagoyan 2012), efforts to give the nicknames more honorable roots. Khachatur Sukyasyan, for instance, a deputy to the National Assembly, elected three times and a major oligarch in Armenia, was known also as Grzo. Many I spoke to did not have a concrete sense of what this name meant, but they knew that it was vulgar. The name most likely comes from the word *grzod*, meaning dirty or messy, that is used in a colloquial dialect in the town of Gavar in the Gegharkunik region. Grzo might have gotten this name because his father was known to have been dirty and untidy.[7] Sukyasyan, in an attempt to disassociate himself from the dark criminal background signaled by this nickname, released a TV documentary in which he ties this name, which previously did not have any specific widely known etymology, to his humble peasant ancestry (Abrahamian and Shagoyan 2012, 23).[8] Nemets Rubo attempted something similar by claiming in a 2012 interview with a French journalist that his nickname, Nemets, derived from his uncle's courageous acts in World War II.[9] His uncle, he claimed, had been injured by the Germans, leaving metal fragments in his body. When he returned from the war, he worked as a driver. Working on the vehicles he drove caused the fragments in his body to shift. Each time he experienced pain from these fragments he cursed the Germans, and thus he and his whole family were referred to as "Nemets." This explanation, even if it were accurate, does little to do away with the negative connotations of *Nemets*.

Attempts at distancing a nickname from a criminal context usually fail. Oligarchic authorities, with or without a nickname, are associated with a social backwardness and ineptness at governance that cannot be undone even with the relinquishment of the nickname. As Levon Abrahamian and Gayane Shagoyan (2012) have pointed out, even after Sukyasyan's (Grzo's) documentary about himself, a "joke arose that the parliamentary seats were going to be reshaped so that the newly elected deputies could squat—another pejorative reference to their lower-class descent" (23). Squatting in public spaces is often associated with lower-class street culture or rural life. It also connotes the act of defecation in rural outhouses. Here, the joke about squatting in parliament places these oligarchs, these men in power who hold seats in National Assembly, as made up by a class of men who are unfit to rule over others since they are uneducated or uncultured (a common reference in Armenia is the phrase *cultura chunen* [they have no culture]), which also explains their criminality and corruption.

The imagery of criminality or unculturedness signified by nick-names is sometimes managed by their carriers in other ways. Samvel Aleksanyan (Lfik Samo), also a former member of the National Assembly, was widely known for his monopoly on sugar. This monopoly caused major political and economic concern during the 2007 "sugar crisis," when no sugar was available for purchase except in grocery stores owned by Aleksanyan. This placed a spotlight on the monopoly problem among oligarchs in Armenia. Aleksanyan also held a monopoly on cooking oil and butter. His nickname takes a diminutive of his first name—Samvel becomes "Samo"—and adds to it *Lfik*, from the Russian term for brassiere. When I asked about the etymology of this name, I was told that it had something to do with his involvement in the bra-importing industry and that his brother owned a bra shop in the Soviet era. While most people knew Lfik Samo as the oligarch who had a monopoly on importing sugar and who acted out aggressively to protect this and other monopolies, he claimed that he was not an oligarch at all but rather "just a poor man who happens to be a member of Parliament."[10]

Aleksanyan was a widely disliked figure who added another accomplishment to his résumé of betrayals when he shut down the Pak Shuka (Closed Market), which was an indoor venue in central Yerevan at which farmers and small vendors sold their produce. Aside from the pragmatic values of the Pak Shuka, the building had historical importance to the city and its people. But, as with many other public sites of old Yerevan—like the Afrikyan House or the outdoor theater of Kino Moskva—privatization led to demolition. In 2013, Lfik Samo hired bodyguards and paid off residents of the neighboring buildings to disallow anyone inside while daily protests in front of the not-yet-demolished Pak Shuka were taking place. He responded to complaints about his shutting down of the Closed Market by stating that it was his personal property. In 2013, *Hetq*, a left-of-center online press, published a video displaying a discussion between journalists and one of Lfik Samo's guards at the Pak Shuka. When journalists approached the guard to ask questions about the Market, he assaulted them verbally and physically, shoving one of them aside and attempting to grab the camera away from the cameraman, all while denying any of the suspected plans for the Market.[11] When I expressed shock at the behavior of the guard, who seemed to personally identify with Lfik and his reputation, a journalist friend of mine in Yerevan pointed out that he was being paid to care for and identify with Lfik. "If he's on Lfik's side now, he probably wants to stay there, for his own good," she added, pointing to the possibilities of the guard facing violence himself if he did not work effectively for Lfik. Identification with the Father (here, Lfik) is strongly based on the function of the No (his threats), while the function of the Name (identification) remains weak.

Gagik Tzarukyan, also known as Dodi Gago, was the wealthiest of all the oligarchs in Armenia. Tzarukyan had perhaps one of the better reputations of those within the Father, or fraternal, horde as he was also considered a philanthropist, donating millions to various charities. Aside from his philanthropist reputation, Dodi Gago displayed the epitome of oligarchic aesthetics, owning gaudy mansions and flaunting a gold-plated phone.[12] He is also well-known for his expression of authority within Armenia by building churches, as I will discuss in the following chapter. As good friends with the elite of Karabakh as well as with Belarussian president Alexander Lukashenko, Dodi Gago had amassed his wealth through access to state contracts in Armenia and key investments abroad. Rumors circulated in Yerevan, especially among leftists, that much of the money that was funneled into the Armenian military came from his personal funds, enabling Armenia to develop its military without making use of public funds and thus staying off the radar of international observers and limits or sanctions on military development. While associated with the militarized goals of the nation—for the protection of Armenia—many were also aware that this mechanism allowed him to evade paying taxes. His philanthropy was suspect, in other words; many of my interlocutors pointed out that he talked big about development but did little beyond some production within Armenia to provide a few jobs here and there.

Dodi Gago was, until March 2015, the head of the Prosperous Armenia Party (Bargavach Hayasdan), which he founded in 2004. The Prosperous Armenia Party was popularly known as a clan of oligarchs,[13] one of the *akhberutyuns* (brotherhoods) of Yerevan. While Prosperous Armenia was separate from the ruling Republican Party, for all intents and purposes, the alliance between these two parties had been effective at not only propping up the rule of the Republican Party but also ensuring the maintenance of power for an oligarchic brotherhood (a class solidarity that closely resembled Mafia rule). Until very recently, these two parties had never actively—or in any apparent way—worked against one another, and in 2012–14, many of my interlocutors claimed, "they're the same thing." This claim referred to the ways in which most state actors in Armenia were seen as involved in the accumulation of wealth through their positions of state power. In the case of the Prosperous Armenia and the Republican Parties, both worked to ensure a shared interest in their respective wealth holdings. Having different political parties devoted to the same cause produced democracy as a spectacle and worked as a strategy for the Republican Party to maintain political dominance in the National Assembly and the executive branch of government. This executive branch, under the system of what Stephen Astourian (2000) has called "hyperpresidentialism," had nearly full control over the legislative and judicial branches.

In February 2013, talk began of a possible constitutional change. This change, initiated by the Republican Party, called for transforming Armenia from a presidential government to a parliamentary one. Most opponents of this change argued that it was meant to allow Serzh Sargsyan, whose presidency was limited to the two terms that he had already served, additional terms without limit as head of office, this time as prime minister. Serzhik—as he is commonly called—had "stolen" the presidency in 2008, his opponents claimed, through fraudulent elections and the violent repression of postelection protestors, and now he was seeking a lifetime of power. Although Serzhik denied these claims, promising that he would not allow himself to be nominated by the National Assembly as prime minister, he lacked the legitimacy to make such promises. A constitutional referendum in December 2015, made the change in government (via changes to the constitution) official (through fraudulent elections). Put into effect in 2018, when Sargsyan was elected as prime minister by the National Assembly, many of my activist as well as my not-necessarily-activist friends and acquaintances in Armenia saw this as the last nail in the coffin of his rule and the event that would ultimately ignite the 2018 "Velvet Revolution" (Shirinian 2020, 2021a).

Before talks of a constitutional referendum began, the next most likely candidate for the theft of the presidential seat would have been Dodi Gago. Thus, he was infuriated—perhaps even rightfully so within the moral economy of the oligarchy. Dodi Gago saw the referendum as a declaration of war on "opposition" parties. He called on Prosperous Armenia, the Armenian National Congress (ANC), and the Heritage Party to form a unified opposition against Serzhik and the ruling Republican

Party in October 2014. The notion of Prosperous Armenia as an "opposition" party was laughable to most activists. Joining forces with more legitimately oppositional parties like the ANC, President Ter-Petrosyan's party, and the Heritage Party, which was the major opposition in the 2013 presidential election, was also seen by many progressives as ridiculous. The "troika,"[14] however, did come together, and these allied parties were able to gather 10,000 opposition supporters in Yerevan's Liberty Square to protest the government and the referendum on October 24, 2014, bringing together various political actors. Ultimately, however, Dodi Gago did not have the legitimacy to be trusted in his claims that he was committed to changing the political situation in Armenia. Most saw his forms of public outcry as a vie for power—he was seen as a "political heavyweight"[15] attempting to poach the fraternal horde of the elite from Serzhik the Father. Dodi Gago had graduated from the Armenian Institute of Physical Culture in 1989, and in 1998 he won the title of World Champion in arm wrestling. Strong-arming, literally, was his game of choice.

The nickname Dodi Gago was, to me, the most absurd and insulting of the nicknames given to members of the illegitimate horde. The name combines a diminutive of his first name—Gagik becomes "Gago"—with *Dodi*, which literally means "belonging to the idiot." Thus, Dodi Gago is the idiot's Gago, or the idiot's son, Gago. Most people I asked attributed the name to his father, Nikolay Tzarukyan, who had been an electrical engineer in the Soviet era and was often called an idiot. Nicknames for the political-economic elite in Armenia—while not necessarily or always recalling images of defecation, digestion, or phallic body parts common among names for the sovereign elites in postcolonial contexts (Mbembe 1992)—are obscene nonetheless. They insult those in power as a way of calling attention to knowledge of the true, intimate origins of the sovereign but in ways that those in power, at times, ambivalently enjoy. Within the genre of the nickname and the jokes that follow it, those in power are usually described as "stupid," *aylandak* (morally perverse), *geghtsi* (a derogatory term for a villager that implies a lack of education and uncultredness), and inadequate to govern in various other ways. Dodi Gago, like many of the others within this horde, was often derided for being uneducated—perhaps because he graduated school in Arinj village rather than a city school, or because he did not speak the language of the educated elite. Nicknames mock their carriers, signaling both intimacy with the larger social world as well as the bearer's less-than-averageness within it. Dodi Gago and his ilk were below par on the properties and proprieties of Armenianness.

Nicknames that were already in circulation needed to be managed; but the production of a new nickname might also come as a threat—as an insult to the legitimacy and respectability of a public figure, or as an attempt at dishonoring him. During and after the 2018 "Velvet Revolution," the opposition leader who would become prime minister, Nikol Pashinyan, was popularly referred to as Nikol. This name, however, had a different connotation.[16] Nikol Pashinyan had never been an oligarch. His role in governance had always come through legitimate means—campaigning, being elected, leading an opposition movement, and becoming a kind of voice for the people. Pashinyan, however, suffered some disrepute after his handling of the 2020 "44-Day War" with Azerbaijan, in which Armenia lost many of the territories it had gained in the 1990s war, including key areas of Nagorno-Karabakh. As calls for his resignation poured in and the oligarchic regime that the opposition movement had ousted from parliamentary authority reemerged—once again seeking that authority—snap elections were held in June 2021. The campaign for this election would be a dirty one, perhaps dirtier than any other in the Republic's history. In early June 2021, as Azerbaijan still held onto hundreds of Armenian prisoners of war, calls began to come in from the illegitimate Fathers of the past for Pashinyan to send his son, Ashot, to Azerbaijan in exchange for Armenian prisoners of war. The uncanny feudalist tones of these demands aside, Pashinyan did not contest this demand. After his son posted on Facebook that he was ready to go to Azerbaijan "as a prisoner or in any other status to help Armenian prisoners,"[17] Pashinyan agreed and publicly declared that he was open to his son's exchange for other Armenian prisoners. He did, however, contest the nicknaming of his son.

> Today, Serzh Sargsyan is making a so-called declaration. He is telling me to send "Ashotik" to bring back the prisoners. First of all, "Serzhik," *ay tgha* [roughly translatable as "dude," a reference to the street language from which such nicknames emerge], you don't have enough to call my soldier son *Ashotik*, you irrelevant upstart [*dus prtzuk*].[18] It is *you* all who are "Serzhik," "Mishik,"[19] "Armenchik." Next time do not say "Ashotik" or I will pull your tongue out and stick it back into another side of you.[20]

The remaking of Ashot Pashinyan as "Ashotik" was a graver sentence, a more serious punishment, than being sent to Azerbaijan as a prisoner. For Ashot to have become Ashotik would have meant relinquishing the possibility of becoming a national hero, conceding any claims to have acted on behalf of Armenians, and confining himself to the realm of criminal within Armenia's Symbolic order. The nickname, after all, affirms power and authority through intimacy, but this intimacy also relegates its bearer to the realm outside national propriety.

The Illegitimate Horde's Betrayal of Symbolic Authority

The Names-of-the-(Illegitimate)-Fathers were recurrent signifiers Lucine Talalyan and I encountered during our household survey interviews in 2013—sometimes in their "nicked" iterations and sometimes not. Names were brought into discussion as if their holders were intimate members of the family themselves. Most often, however, they emerged in the context of betrayal. The violence they had done to Armenia was taken as violence against the (nation-)family. As authorities (Fathers) of the nation, they were metonymically members of the household (as one part of a whole nation-family). In this role, however, they were also violators of that very family through their failures to provide the care and leadership expected of them as occupiers of the seats of authority.

Astghik was a seventy-one-year-old woman who lived in the neighborhood of Sasuntsi David. She was on a pension and lived with her son, his wife, and their two daughters. For Astghik, those in power—for whom she interchangeably used the terms *karavarutyun* (government) and *ishkhanutyunner* (the authorities)—were "strangling" the people with high taxes, all while not providing the people with what they needed to pay these taxes and to get by. In reflection on these issues, however, Astghik relied on a rhetoric of care: "The government doesn't care about families. They don't care what people need"; and "They do what they are going to do without even thinking of asking the people first." Falling back on a language of proper morality to express her discontent with those in power, Astghik did not eschew questions of political economy but rather couched political economy within a framework of propriety, care, and kinship. When she explained that those in power were illegitimate rulers, it was not because they had not been democratically elected but rather because they did not act in the best interests of Armenians. The authorities were not good, proper, moral leaders of the nation. Astghik explained the unhappiness of her home and the homes of others in Armenia as connected to "all of the violence that those brutes [*tavarner*] do out there, you know the *Tzarukyanner* [referring to Dodi Gago in the plural, to indicate that there are many like him], *yes im inchner* [and all the rest of them]. . . . That violence comes home. Where else is it going to go?" Expanding the context of intimacy beyond the boundaries of the familial home, Astghik talked about major oligarchs as actors within the realm of the intimate. Here, Tzarukyan and the rest of his horde were intimately associated with the family, but their intimate association with the family was also a problem, not only in the household but in the nation-family. Through their metonymic intimate ties, the perversions of the authorities had seeped into the everyday life of her household.

Astghik's son, Vahan, was present during our conversation, though he was watching television over a meal of cigarettes and coffee at the dining table that shared a room with the sofa and the armchairs at which Talalyan, Astghik, and I sat. He did not seem to be paying much attention to our discussion until Astghik made mention of the failing family business:

> We keep thinking that maybe things are going to get better, but they don't. And they get worse. We used to run a small shop, and then Star Supermarket came and bought the building and they threw us all out. That's why now we work a small stand at the market. What else are we to do? All we can do is keep working and hope things get better. But I don't have any hope. The director of the market is a nice man, but if we can't pay our dues he will have to throw us out.

Star Supermarket was one of the first supermarket chains in Armenia. Ironically, as Astghik complained about Star's usurpation of their own shop, the company was also facing bankruptcy and accusing Samvel Aleksanyan (Lfik Samo) and his supermarket chain, City Market, of threatening Star's survival through Lfik's use of his government connections (especially in the Customs Committee, a government body) to maintain de facto monopolies. Vahan had owned a small shop selling baked goods, jams, and other foodstuffs; the shop had been located within a larger building that was bought out by Star. At the time of our interview, Vahan and Astghik were renting a small kiosk within the Star Supermarket, where they continued to sell their wares; but they were having a hard time selling enough to be able to pay the rent on the kiosk and to turn a profit as well. As Astghik explained this to us, Vahan chimed in. He did not look directly at us; he continued to stare at the television, which was playing an advertisement. As if talking to his own ghosts, he declared, "Aylandakner en, ara. Hay chen srank" (They are moral perverts, man. They are not Armenian). Astghik ignored her son—she did not even turn to look at him as he uttered these words, as if this were a regular outburst.

The national intimacy[21] that is shared by the rulers and the ruled marks the violation of Armenian propriety not just as a violation but as deep betrayal. Instead of being "one of us," the political-economic elite's lack of investment in the survival of the nation— their behavior constituting de facto active threats to the nation's survival—marks them as unfaithful to their national kinfolk. Vahan's declaration that oligarchs are "not Armenian" belongs to a hermeneutics of postsocialist Armenian national ontology, which interrogates the Armenianness of those who have betrayed the nation.

In our interviews, many of our interlocutors discussed Armenia's political-economic elite with a fierce, often extreme, anger. "They need to be hanged. I am very serious, all of them, in a row, they need to be hanged," Daniel lashed out. Daniel was in his fifties and lived in Shengavit. He had worked at a rubber plant until it closed in the early 2000s, and he had since had a difficult time making ends meet. Realizing it would be too difficult to start his own business—in light of the many hindrances placed on small business owners in Armenia—he used his networks of friends, relatives, and acquaintances to get work as an electrician. He told us that the horde (of oligarchs) had done so many terrible things to the people of Armenia that one day the people's rage would reach a critical mass and there would be a violent uprising. "That day is coming. Listen to me. These people are going to burn them one day." Daniel, however, also theorized that those in power had some safeguards in place:

> Really, I think about it and I don't understand. Okay. . . . let's say they become really rich. They raise the prices, they hold monopolies. Flour, butter, sugar, apricots, I don't know what. Right now they are getting by this way because there are people still living in the country. People who have money, to survive, to live, they will buy what they need. They will pay those prices. And these *aylandakner* [moral per-

verts] will get richer and richer. But if they keep price gouging, then of course there will come a time when the people cannot afford to pay anymore. They will not buy anymore. They will either starve and die here or they will leave the country. Where will [the oligarchs'] money come from then? But, see, they don't think about this. Because by then they will have their money and maybe they will just sell the land. When people leave, that rage also leaves with them. And like that they secure their . . . thick stomachs.

Daniel reasoned that the endgame of the oligarchy was to make money now, even if it led to Armenians suffering. Realizing that suffering Armenians might at some point resist, they were content with creating conditions of starvation for profit that might eventually lead all Armenians to flee the country (or die). This might, in other words, not only save the elite from enraged resistance—which could otherwise lead to them getting hanged or being burned at the stake—but would also leave land behind that could be sold to make further profit.

Daniel was not alone in his reasoning that the oligarchy's main goal was to eventually do away with the Armenian people altogether. Mkrtich, another of our interlocutors and to whom I return in chapter 5, summarized the actions of Armenia's oligarchy class as "economic genocide":

> If this government had the sense to give people jobs that paid let's say 200,000 [dram] or so [a month] and said here, take this money and take care of your family, the man would take care of his family here. They pay 200,000 just for one *sheesh* of barbecue to eat. But you are left to work all day and night for 100,000 with which you can't even survive. . . . It's just a fact. That if today the average person cannot live on the average income, this is not a country. As in, this path will only take the country toward annihilation. They want to bring up genocide all the time, only when it benefits them. This is genocide. This is *their* genocide. This is economic genocide.

The naming of the political-economic elite's perverse violence as drawing a path toward national annihilation—as "genocide"—was palimpsestic. If the Ottoman state had, in the early twentieth century, massacred over a million Armenians and then driven hundreds of thousands of others out of its territory, taking their land and wealth for its own elite, Mkrtich writes over this history as if it had been left incomplete by the

Turks and was now being completed by Armenia's own elite, internal, intimate enemies. Armen Mkrtichyan, one of the founding members of the right-wing nationalist organization Hayazn, also described Armenia's rulers in a similar vein during an interview I conducted with him. Mkrtichyan saw Armenia's elite as alien colonizers: those who ruled over Armenia, he maintained, were "like aliens, from somewhere else, who have come to take as much as they can get. . . . they have no regard for the land and the people of Armenia. . . . They are not Armenian. This is not an Armenian government."

The use of nicknames for the political-economic elite in Armenia recognized the intimacy of these figures to the Armenian nation while also consigning them to an in-between space in which their perversion of Armenianness constituted a criminal act of betrayal. The elite did not just hurt the Armenian people with their actions—their corruption and greed; they did so as *Armenians*. They were Armenian themselves but occupied a space far beyond the propriety of Armenianness. They perverted Armenianness from the inside out. In this way, some understood them as colonizers—as external thieves. Others understood them as fulfilling the historical role of the enemy par excellence—the Turk. When Mkrtichyan claims that those who sit in seats of Armenian governance are not Armenian, he does not mean that they are of another ethnicity or nationality. He means that their betrayal of the Armenian nation places them outside of the bounds of what counts as proper Armenianness.[22]

State Authority outside Moral Authority

If those in power were illegitimate, a fact that both the left and the right accepted—progressives, including LGBT and feminist activists, and right-wing anti-homosexual activists—then what would legitimate governance look like? This question produced a space of great debate within Armenian grassroots politics, and one that I will take up here by exploring a prank and the discussions it initiated. In 2013, a group of progressive activists staged a mock protest in front of the Italian Embassy in Yerevan. As parody, they stood outside of the embassy and condemned Armenia's recent loss of the FIFA Club World Cup to Italy, shouting claims such as, "There was a shoe found in Areni that was made and used by our ancestors, a shoe that they used to play football! Where were the Italians then?!" This was a reference to Armenians' jubilant celebrations centered on the oldest leather shoe discovered by archaeologists in a cave dwelling outside the village of Areni. For many Armenians, this shoe was taken as proof that Armenia was an important ancient civilization. The pranksters also shouted, "We do not accept the defeat of Armenia! We believe in the moral triumph of Armenia!" The protest was a mockery of the nationalist organization Hayazn and their genre of protest that relied on a sensibility of the political based on questions of morality and cultural propriety.

A member of Hayazn was present for the mock protest and, upset at the realization that he and his organization were being targeted, he had asked for a spar, or to have a physical fight, which only elicited further ridicule. That evening, after Shant, one of the pranksters, posted a Facebook status about the mock protest and Hayazn's proposal for a spar, creating an opportunity for another member of Hayazn to contact him to say that Hayazn wanted to discuss this issue for "constructive" purposes. Anna, a staff member at PINK who relayed this story to me the next day, found this hilarious, laughing at the thought that a discussion of what was "traditional" Armenianness and what was improper to it could ever be "constructive" of anything, especially in political debate.

The pranksters and members of Hayazn thus planned to meet at 80s Pub, a bar in central Yerevan that was known to be a hub for many Armenian Revolutionary Federation (ARF), or Dashnagtsutyun, supporters, including many who came to Armenia as "repatriates" from Syria and Lebanon but some locals as well. There, Shant parodied the nationalist position through overidentification with it (Yurchak 2005), articulating the importance of recognizing Armenia's moral triumphs over a perverse nation like Italy. Italy, it was known, had many homosexuals, Shant explained to them, and thus had no right to win the football match. As Anna gave me detailed minutes of this encounter the following morning, she explained that besides mocking Hayazn by speaking in their discourse, Shant had also used "big philosophical words" that were supposedly lost on Hayazn members and intended to confuse them and point to the absurdity of their rhetoric. Hrant, another of the pranksters, simultaneously translated these big philosophical words into *kyartu*—a Yerevan slang that is associated with a machismo street subculture that is often connected with hypertraditional forms, especially regarding gender and sexuality. Anna could not contain her laughter; she stopped, hunched over every few seconds to catch her breath while narrating the events. This "translation" into *kyartu* was, of course, even more infuriating to members of Hayazn, who saw themselves as politically educated and quite separate from "backward" street culture. But for progressives and liberals like Shant and Hrant, there was very little difference between Hayazn's politics, based on national morality, and street culture's vulgar tradition.

Shant asked a member of Hayazn why they wanted to "spar" instead of just suing them. In Anna's words, Grigor, a member of Hayazn responded: "It's better to deal with things morally rather than through a trial." This led to a more serious conversation—a couple of hours of debate over "morality" and its place in politics. Anna explained, "For them, law isn't the realm of enforcing morals. Law is immoral . . . It's pointless trying to talk to them, you understand? It's a waste of time." She continued to laugh about the absurdity of Hayazn's desire to have a "constructive" discussion.

Both groups found Armenia's current situation intolerable. However, progressive activists (like Shant, Hrant, and Anna) saw shifts in law (or its enforcement) as necessary, while right-wing nationalists as well as many other Yerevantsis referred instead to the domain of morality based on sensibilities of Armenian propriety and national values (such as Astghik's reliance on a rhetoric of care). During my interview with Hovhannes Galajyan, the editor-in-chief of the right-wing newspaper *Iravunk*, for instance, Galajyan expressed discontent with the kinds of ideas and images disseminated in mainstream media. He held the owners of private networks, as well as the Republican Party in power, responsible for public broadcasting. "They sell. They only sell. They worry about what will be popular and not about what is best for the nation." Galajyan's disaffection was not centered on the selling per se. He was not necessarily concerned with private capital and investment in images that benefited the elite. His apprehension lay in the morally improper content of what was on television. Galajyan also explained that although his newspaper was formed as the media outlet for the Constitutional Rights Union, a political party that emphasized the rule of constitutional law in Armenia, constitutional law was, in fact, no longer legitimate because it had abandoned "Armenian values." For Galajyan, the constitution was a dead document that did not serve a proper *national* law and order.

Other right-wing political parties similarly emphasized morality over law. Armen Mkrtichyan (who earlier described the political-economic elite as "aliens") argued that the government's illegitimacy stemmed from its undignified treatment of citizens. Armenians *should* care for other Armenians, but the authorities in contemporary Armenia were uncouth toward their own people. They had betrayed the Armenian people and, thus, the very foundations of the nation. For this reason, those in power were not fit to rule. Mkrtichyan told me that the mission of Hayazn was to form a "national government" based on "national values." When I asked him what he meant by "national government" he explained:

> A government of which control is founded by citizens and not extra-governmental institutions like the European Union or European this or that, and so on. Or Russian dominance through oligarchs and so on. As in an independent government and a government in which citizens find themselves safe, which, unfortunately, does not exist today in Armenia.[23]

Mkrtichyan argued that Armenian citizens were living undignified lives. Taxi drivers and other workers were putting in twenty hours a day just to barely make ends meet "and are even happy for this because they have a job"; they were forcefully displaced from their "fatherland" (hayrenik), becoming migrant laborers; and their government was waging a "class war" on them. While there are hints of a postcolonial liberatory nationalist ideology in Mkrtichyan's discourse,[24] and while, at first, it might seem that he is speaking in a politicized language of self-determination, his framework relies almost entirely on moral sentiments of national propriety based in tradition and family values rather than in class struggle and national sovereignty. He insisted on a "national government" that would not be made up of a class of overlords that resembled a foreign force; what would be "national" would be based on sensibilities of what is properly Armenian, and not necessarily on that which would bring justice for the people of Armenia. The ruling elite, Mkrtichyan maintained, should be kind to the Armenian people—not because this is what justice looks like but because they are Armenian and because national survival and familial love and care are proper Armenian values. Critically, Mkrtichyan's notion of a "national government" is not necessarily democratic. How authority is formed and organized matters less than the values with which this authority rules. For him, if Armenia were to be run democratically, it would not incorporate "European" values and ideologies such as feminism, gay liberation, and so on. As conditions for entry into the European neighborhood and ascension into the Council of Europe, the Armenian state had ratified a number of laws protecting LGBT persons' rights.[25] While these legal protections have done very little to provide safety for LGBT people in Armenia, for right-wing nationalists, they have further delegitimized the state. These kinds of laws, as I have shown in the previous chapter as well as elsewhere,[26] were taken as proof that the Armenian state does not constitute proper national governance and has sold out to the imperialism of the West.

Liberals and progressives in Armenia contested right-wing nationalists not only in the social and the cultural realms—on issues having to do with gender and sexuality, for instance. They also took great issue with a political imaginary that centered questions of morality: the notion of Armenia as a familial site where members of the nation should care for one another. Liberals and progressives were invested in a decidedly political and legal apparatus in which each individual would be given full rights regardless of family, networks, or Armenian nationality. The point of the prank protest of the football match, in this sense, was to underscore that winning and losing are based on the rules of the game and not on the morality or national values of the opposing teams. Winning and losing should be based on individual merit within established legal structures (the game's rules). The prank called out what its performers found to be the absurdity with which right-wing nationalists approach the question of right and wrong in the world. Like the football game, which has nothing to do with morality, the political world should also not have anything to do with morality. While the realm of the law within liberal democratic ideology regards (or should regard) each individual as equal and prohibits particular actions across the board no matter what the personal connections of any individual or group of persons may be, the Law of the Father is a structure that is personal and affective. Based on expectations of propriety, it is inherently relational and, as such, its prohibitions depend on intimacy.

Reflection on the negotiations of meanings attached to criminality and corruption might make these disparities clearer. The improprieties of the political-economic elite are named as improprieties only when they do not benefit oneself. In other words, those who are positioned—through personal connections or networks—to benefit from the actions of the political-economic elite do not regard the elites' behavior as corrupt or as illegitimate. During our household survey interviews, we saw this in a number of ways. Sometimes, it was a refusal to use a nickname that articulated a personal or institutional connection to an oligarch or another member of the elite. For instance, although not often, we heard Serzh Sargsyan referred to as *Paron* Sargsyan (Mister Sargsyan) or as *mer Nakhagan* (our President)—names that legitimated his authority. Some explained to us that the Republican Party was doing an excellent job and thanked God that the nation had such a strong leadership. These were often people who, whether through their places of work or through some philanthropic activity, had benefited from the elite. Whether or not Sargsyan had acted legally—for instance, in his role in the state violence that occurred during the 2008 postelection protests, or by possibly losing 70 million Euros of Armenian public funds while gambling in Europe[27]—was not pertinent. What mattered was that for these particular individuals, Sargsyan and his party were legitimate because they had acted to benefit their own personal interests.

An oligarch might go from being a great man and legitimate leader to criminal and corrupt depending on an individual's personal interaction with him. A street vendor, for instance, might be allowed by the local officials to sell his product on the street as long as he paid a certain amount from all his sales to a local oligarch. If the amount he is asked to pay is one he can afford and still turn a profit, the oligarch remains a great man, even if this activity violates state law. However, once the amount the vendor is asked to pay exceeds his ability to turn a profit, he condemns the oligarch for his corruption. In this way, the violation is not that of state law, but of an affective and personal Law—a Law that is established based on moral concerns of interpersonal care and the well-being of the Armenian people.

The role of the proper sovereign as a paternal figure—as a good Father who looks after his people and who ensures their survival through the Law in the Name-of-the-Father Hayk—can smuggle in further ambiguous contradictions between legality and morality, love and hate, and fear and respect. Authority figures who are disliked, and thus delegitimized, for their ruthlessness might also be seen as caring and loving in other ways that legitimize their brutal actions. Two polls conducted in Armenia make these ambivalent feelings toward the Father apparent. The first, conducted in 2013 by the Carnegie Foundation and published in a report called *The Stalin Puzzle* (de Waal 2013), found that a substantial number of citizens in post-Soviet Republics (Russia, Armenia, Georgia, and Azerbaijan), regarded Stalin as both a wise leader and a brutal authoritarian. In the poll conducted in Armenia, while 49 percent completely agreed and 20 percent mostly agreed with the statement that

"Stalin was a cruel inhuman tyrant, responsible for the deaths of millions of innocent people"; 27 percent also completely agreed and 28 percent mostly agreed that "Stalin was a wise leader who brought the Soviet Union to might and prosperity"; and 39 percent completely agreed and 30 percent mostly agreed that "For all Stalin's mistakes and misdeeds, the most important thing is that under his leadership the Soviet people won the Great Patriotic War." Furthermore, in Armenia, 38 percent of polltakers completely agreed or mostly agreed that "Our people will always have need of a leader like Stalin, who will come and restore order" (de Waal 2013, 8–10). Stalin's inhumanity, in other words, did not necessarily make him a bad leader. His paternalistic deeds of protection and securitization of the Soviet Union made him a good leader regardless of his cruelty.

The second poll, this one conducted by the Armenian Election Study in 2021 (published by EVN *Report*; see Oganesyan and Kopalyan 2021), prior to the snap elections that were called following the demands that Prime Minister Pashinyan resign, found that 43 percent of polltakers agreed with the statement that "Armenia needs to prioritize security over democracy," while only 3 percent agreed that "Armenia needs to prioritize democracy over security." While the majority of polltakers rejected the dichotomy between "democracy" and "security," with 54 percent agreeing that "Armenia needs to prioritize both," these numbers suggest that many Armenians foreground security over democracy. In this sense, a good leader may not be elected democratically but he might do well in providing security to the nation-state. It is important to note that this poll was taken in the aftermath of a devastating war and at a time when questions of territorial sovereignty and protection from foreign militaries were on the minds of most Armenians. It was precisely these kinds of concerns that made possible Robik and Serzhik's return to the realm of official politics. Even though they had both been deemed illegitimate to rule—as was made evident in the 2018 popular movement that ousted them from power and demanded that criminal charges be brought against them—widespread concerns regarding national security allowed their return—at least among some voters and polltakers. Although their parties did not make great gains in the elections, these feelings of the need to prioritize paternal might over democratic process highlight another kind of authority puzzle: an illegitimate father can gain legitimacy if he can be seen to bring protection and might to his people.

Surplus Enjoyment

While a number of oligarchs and other political-economic elites in Armenia show their strength through their brutal behavior, and thus might be legitimated as good strong Fathers for the nation, this legitimacy is often stymied by another of their behaviors: their violation and betrayal of Symbolic authority via excess enjoyment. The "nick" in the Names-of-the-(Illegitimate)-Fathers often signifies more than brutality, violence, might, and strength. These are not necessarily always negative characteristics within Armenia's moral economy, as I have shown above. The "nick," however, also calls attention to a surplus in enjoyment, an excessive flaunting of wealth and power.[28] Within this moral economy, the political-economic elite are *aylandak* (morally perverse) not only because they are uncouth and cruel but because they are excessive in their enjoyment. The violations of Dodi Gago, Serzhik, General Manvel, Lfik Samo, Shinanyuti Sergo (the nickname of Sergey Manukyan, best known for his monopoly on building materials through his company Evropa), and so on are marked by this excess. These men do not just live well and they do not just have power; they live in perverse excess. They *enjoy* power and thus their claims on power are marked as sadistic.

In April 2021, a few months after Armenia's devastating loss of the 2020 war, when at least one thousand prisoners of war were still being held captive in Azerbaijan, Dodi Gago hosted a wedding for his son. With 2,100 attendees (at the cost of $350 USD per person) who were flown in for the wedding in private jets, and with fireworks, chaperones costumed as statues, a whole slew of well-known musical artists to perform at the reception, and a waitstaff of 800, the wedding is estimated to have cost $4 million USD.[29] These excesses, and especially at a time of national crisis, were judged to be criminal. Following *Mamul.am*'s publication of the breakdown of these numbers, online commentators referred to Dodi Gago as a "pillager" and characterized this performance of wealth and power as "the limit of shamelessness." One commenter noted, "Such a pillager of the people we have, unlike the world has ever seen," playing on the trope of Armenia as the most civilized nation in the world (for, say, having had the first shoe ever recorded in history), turning a superlative on its head. While the amount spent on the wedding and its unfortunate timing were indeed shocking to many, in the larger scheme of Dodi Gago's excesses, this was to be expected. Dodi Gago's mansion sits atop a hill on the outskirts of Yerevan and includes not only a church on the property but also a zoo in which he keeps his pet lions. In an interview given to the press, when asked about what he has to say about Azerbaijan's press criticizing him for his pet lions, fed meat on a daily basis while Armenia's population is starving, Dodi Gago commented that if Azerbaijanis keep dogs and cats as pets in their homes, then Tzarukyan (referring to himself in the third person) deserves to keep lions.[30]

Dodi Gago was not the only oligarch in Armenia with a private zoo. When the National Security Service entered General Manvel Grigoryan's country estate in Armavir in 2018, following the "Velvet Revolution's" criminal charges against him for theft from the public, they found a zoo that housed lions, tigers, and bears as well as a whole warehouse of military foodstuff that he had taken into his personal possession and with which he was feeding his animals. Aside from mansions with zoos, there are various other well-known mansions flaunting excess in the area surrounding Yerevan. The most opulent of these is Shinanyuti Sergo's house, which ostentatiously displays hundreds of statues, baroque style neo-Hellenic architecture, fountains, and gazebos all surrounded by an ornate rococo fence.

The violence of the oligarchy is frequently articulated by the comparison of how they live with how "ordinary" Armenians live. This is how Mkrtich above, for instance, represented the authorities' violence. While people do not have enough food to eat, Mkrtich maintained, the elite are spending absurd amounts on a single feast. This money spent—money available for flaunting—is, of course, a product of surplus value. The oligarchs exploit Armenian land, labor, and obligatory consumption (especially in regard to monopolized commodities) in order to produce a surplus. This surplus thus constitutes theft from Armenia and Armenians. This fact, one that Marx pointed out centuries past, is not in some way concealed from Armenians. It is made very apparent, especially in the massive disparity between the haves and the have-nots (the rulers and the ruled). Surplus value as theft formed a major part of the discourse about the oligarchy, as when the oligarchs were commonly referred to as *gogher* (thieves); *orenqov gogher* (thieves-at-law) (Antonyan 2016, 121), who are reminiscent of Mafia but who have managed to legalize their trade by manipulating personal connections with governance (and often through taking governmental positions themselves); or *talanner* (pillagers). The fact that their power and wealth come through illegal means or through "lawfare"—the strategy of using or abusing law to achieve operational objectives beyond violent or militarized means (Dunlap 2008)—and that it involves theft, is no secret. Here, again, however, it is necessary to highlight that the violation experienced by many of my interlocutors was not in the realm of law but in the realm of Law. That Lfik Samo held a monopoly on sugar and butter, a monopoly that might go against state law, was not necessarily seen as the problem. Rather, the oligarchy's violation was that it operated financially in a way that devastated the abilities of regular Armenians to survive or live with dignity. Lfik Samo's monopoly on sugar and butter was immoral because it left many Armenians struggling to be able to buy these necessary commodities. It was uncouth. Its immorality, however, was not necessarily tied to the manipulation of law or the ethics of "free" markets.

Karine was a middle-aged woman who lived in Yerord Mas. Talalyan and I interviewed her while her neighbor Gayane, an older woman, was visiting her home. Gayane also chimed in. At one point in our discussion with Karine and Gayane, Gayane expressed disgust with Lfik Samo's wealth. "We know, right, where he lives and what kind of life he enjoys [referring to another well-known mansion in Armenia on a massive plot of land, rumored to be owned by Lfik]? We also know how much we have to pay when we go to the market. It's wrong, there's no other way of looking at it." At this, Talalyan asked the two women if it was wrong to be rich. Karine stepped in and explained that it was not wrong to be rich but that there should be limits to how a man becomes rich.

> To be rich, what bad is there in that? If a man is rich, let him be rich. But when that man is rich and he is seeing the suffering of his nation [azg] and he continues to get richer while those around him get poorer, with no shame, that is unforgivable . . . [he] should also have responsibility toward his azgagitsnerin [referring to fellow nationals, as in Armenians, but also to relatives, those who share common ancestry].

What stands out as the violation for Karine, thus, is not just wealth or surplus in and of itself, nor the prohibition of the law, but the flaunting of excess wealth while fellow Armenians were suffering. The surplus enjoyment by the oligarchy was an offense to national propriety because it showed lack of care and responsibility toward the Armenian people.

This form of surplus might best be captured as surplus jouissance —an excessive, and perhaps sadistic, pleasure.[31] The surplus enjoyment that the political-economic elite flaunt is unnecessary—for their own lives and livelihoods, for their maintenance of power, as well as for the social reproduction of the nation. Indeed, it is *unproductive*, or we might say *de-productive*, of the nation. Within liberal economic theory, the maintenance of monopolies in Armenia has been deemed the number one cause of the nation-state's lack of economic development (Hrayr Maroukhian Foundation 2013). The oligarchy's excessive enjoyment of wealth did not contribute to the nation and, further, worked against its (economic) survival. The perverse excesses of this minority have had repercussions in the perversion of the nation. It is not just that they enjoyed excessive wealth and the power they derived from it. Their wealth impeded the proper development and possibilities of life for the people of the nation.

If the oligarchy's *aylandakutyun* through surplus enjoyment of wealth was unproductive (or de-productive, setting back the growth of productive mechanisms) for the nation, there are spaces in which we might read these excesses as conflated with those of the homosexual. As I discussed in the previous chapter, right-wing nationalists targeted the homosexual for his lack of reproductive sex—his refusal to reproduce the nation. The homosexual (like the oligarch) did not just fail or refuse to reproduce the nation but produced dangerous desires and forms of life that were destructive to the nation. In this sense, the homosexual, like the oligarch, is also a *de-reproductive* figure, a figure who sets back the nation's reproductive forces—toward annihilation. As I also noted in the previous chapter, there was little mention of homosexuality among our household survey interviews. The few times that homosexuality was brought up, however, it was in regard to the political-economic elite. The surplus jouissance that marked both the nation's *aylaserutyun* and *aylandakutyun* condensed sexual improprieties with other forms of impropriety, producing an assemblage of national threat. Through this assemblage, the oligarchy might be deemed homosexual, but more critically, the homosexual is deemed a traitor to the nation because his behavior threatens the nation's future.

In the previous chapter, I drew on an interview with Kolya, a journalist with a progressive online press, who argued that the homosexual was hated because of a "deep jealousy"—because he represented a way of life that was free and that many others could not permit themselves to have. This freedom was an object of both jealousy and hatred, Kolya explained. Talalyan and I found in our interviews that there was a similar affective desire held for the oligarchy. A moral framework, rather than a political-economic analysis, enabled some to intensely hate the oligarchy for their excesses but also to desire that way of life for themselves. A moral framework, however, also made possible claims that one could and wanted to also be rich—but not through violent means and in a more caring manner. Daniel, for instance, who expressed deep resentment toward the oligarchy above, also told us that he, too, would like to be rich and live in a house with many swimming pools. "One, two swimming pools. A house in the city and a dacha in the country. It's good, it's not a bad thing. But is it necessary to strangle your people, your *own nation*, to have more?" In this way, while Daniel admitted that he, too, would not mind enjoying some excesses, excessive excesses are immoral and a betrayal of the nation. Like in the case of homosexuality, as argued by Hovhannes Galajyan, where individual freedoms should be limited by moral responsibilities toward one's family and the nation, Daniel (and some others) maintained that the enjoyment of the oligarch should be limited by his responsibility toward his people.

The Name and the Limits of Law

While the use of nicknames and other forms of recognition of the political-economic elite as illegitimate do not necessarily function as acts of resistance, they do place limits on the elites' authority; the names place them outside of Armenianness altogether, labeling them thus as illegitimate to rule over Armenia and Armenians. It was precisely this illegitimacy of the Fathers of the nation that led, in 2018, to the mass social movement now known as the "Velvet Revolution" that would oust Serzhik and some others within his fraternal horde from their official seats of authority. One of the most common slogans of this movement was "Serzhik, heratsir!" (Serzhik, go away!). As I have shown in this chapter, however, while illegitimacy stems from the criminal and corrupt behavior of those in seats of authority, criminality and corruption must be seen as operating within a moral economy that is based on personal, intimate, and affective relations to rulers—a collective Symbolic order that governs Armenian propriety—rather than on the basis of a violation of state law. The Law, in the Name-of-the-Father Hayk, transcends the meanings and values placed on the law, and it comes with intimate expectations on those who govern. The oligarchs and their government associates were in violation of this Symbolic authority because of their failure to meet these intimate demands and expectations.

In violation of the Law and the Name-of-the-Father, the oligarchy's moral perversions are conflated into the sexual perversions that mark the improprieties of the figure of the homosexual. The homosexual becomes an easily targetable object of national anxiety—for right-wing nationalists as well as for mainstream media—because his violations constitute an assemblage together with those who have placed Armenian political-economic survival in precarity. The homosexual is not just a scapegoat like any other scapegoat. His enjoyment, his excesses, and the dangers he poses against proper morality are exchangeable and interchangeable with the excesses of those who wield political-economic power. Both the homosexual and the political-economic elite—through their perversions—work toward the disintegration of what Armenians know and understand of Armenia itself: the annihilation of Armenianness, or mutations of Armenianness toward its unrecognizability. The homosexual's nonreproductive futurities, assaults on the gendered and sexual proprieties necessary for the family, and new freedoms that might mean freedoms from the family and Armenianness all endanger the institutions that have preserved Armenian morality and guaranteed its survival for millennia (or so say right-wing nationalists). Having usurped not only state power but the seat of Armenian authority that once belonged to the rightful Father Hayk, the oligarchy also endangers Armenian propriety. The oligarchs rupture the continuity of proper leadership that is essential to the ontology of national imaginaries.

What I have been describing in this chapter has been the subject of much discussion in postsocialist studies; it is sometimes called "clientelism" or "the economy of favors," in which informal exchanges, agreements, and orders based on personal relations (rather than formalized and impersonal bureaucratic processes) dominate the political and economic world in post-Soviet (Ledeneva 2009) and other postsocialist (Bian 2019) worlds. Alena Ledeneva (2009), for instance, argues that these informal tactics within political worlds "undermine the fundamental principles of the rule of law, separation of powers, and secure property rights; ultimately, they compromise the chance of reaching strategic goals of modernization" (281). Ledeneva argues that *blat*, the use of personal networks for obtaining goods and services and for getting around formal processes, emerged in the Soviet system to get around a "corrupt regime"—effectively corrupting a corrupt regime. According to Ledeneva, *blat* was not necessarily corruption in the Soviet era (as it worked against a corrupt system) (259), but it is corruption in the post-Soviet era when free markets can resolve all problems of access and are not established on corruption. Carna Brkovic (2017), however, has shown how the use of informal networks in postsocialist and post-war Bosnia-Herzegovina is not a result of the past socialist system and its corruption but rather the result of neoliberalization and the privatization of social protection mechanisms. Using personal networks to obtain goods and services is not a characteristic of a premodern and predemocratic social and moral world; it is produced by ambiguity in who or what is responsible for the provision of social services and by difficulty in obtaining those services. Fabio Mattioli (2018) similarly argues that the practice of *kompenzacija*, or exchange in kind rather than money, was a benign practice in state socialist Macedonia. In the postsocialist context, however, this has become a pernicious mechanism for the elite among the ruling party to accumulate wealth in money while forcing others to receive goods (such as apartments, cars, etc.) that lack liquidity. The difference, Mattioli argues, is that while money was used largely for the purposes of accounting in the socialist era (and thus exchange in kind did not severely impact any party), within free market systems money is used to accumulate profit. Free markets, in other words, did not solve problems of informal exchange. Rather, they provided opportunities for the accumulation of wealth, creating new and pernicious uses for informal practices.

Global capitalism does not function as a system of exchange through impersonal means under the rule of law—as bourgeois political economists would have us believe (Weber 1968). As many have pointed out, the use of personal networks, "playing in the gray" (Hoang 2022), forms of trickery like maintaining invisibility from the public (Christophers 2023), and plundering (Harvey 2003) are not only endemic to capitalism but necessary for its growth. While there were informal exchanges in goods, services, appointments, and positions in state socialist systems, the very logic of the systems themselves—driven toward allocation and distribution rather than by extraction and accumulation—did not allow for the kinds of disparate levels of wealth that capitalism has made possible. This massive disparity in wealth is a global condition of late-stage capitalism—or what Fred Magdoff and John Bellamy Foster (2023) describe as "grand theft capital," distinguishable from the usual robbery inherent in capitalism by its enormity of scale—and it is perhaps most true in the postsocialist world, as postsocialist transformation acted as one of the "boldest experiments with neoliberal ideas in the world" (Stenning et al., 2010, 2, as cited in Brkovic 2017, 12).

The criminality with which the political-economic elite in post-Soviet Armenia are associated is one derived from limitless possibilities of wealth accumulation under the post-Soviet privatization and marketization regimes. While the oligarchy as well as their government henchmen operate informally, it is not their informality that is taken as cause for concern. Rather, it is the lack of care toward the Armenian people—their use of informality to do violence, including the hording of surplus wealth. Critically, many of those with whom Talalyan and I spoke marked distinctions between the Soviet past and the postsocialist present and labeled the present as irredeemably perverse. In the following chapter I take up these feelings of perversion by examining the complaints about postsocialist urban development—perceptive critiques of neoliberalization.

The streets have emptied of your intimate faces,
Walking around are merely the shadows of the past
It is the same city, the same sun, the café on the corner,
but they are other, foreign eyes, unfamiliar foreign faces,
in the steps that follow behind you.

ARTHUR MESCHIAN, FROM "SAME CITY"
("NUYN KAGHAK")

I remember this city of mine, where people lived like people.

RUBEN HAKHVERDYAN, FROM "I REMEMBER"
("HISHUM EM YES")

CHAPTER FOUR

Wandering Yerevan

One hot Saturday afternoon in the summer of 2011, Arthur and I sat on a bench on Yerevan's Northern Avenue. Arthur had just given me a tour of queer Yerevan. The journey had taken us from the Hrazdan *dzor* (canyon) at the southern end of Mashtots Avenue, a cruising spot for men's illicit and anonymous sexual encounters, to the tunnels nearby that were a favorite hangout of emo kids and tagged with their graffiti. We then made our way out from the tunnels and wandered into Komaygi Children's Park, which had become a source of major right-wing nationalist complaints and was sometimes referred to as "Gom Aygi," or "faggot park." Surrounded by government buildings and foreign embassies, the park was known as a hotspot for solicitation by sex workers (often trans women). After having wandered the queer city for a couple of hours, Arthur and I sat down at Central Spot. Central Spot was an *alternativ* space in Yerevan. The diner was not necessarily a gay space, but it was queer in that it made possible forms of life and being that were outside national propriety. It was a space that belonged to a map of queerness in Yerevan, (in)visibly disturbing proper social reproduction (Shirinian 2018b). Central Spot was owned by two Armenian American brothers and styled as an American diner, including in service. As Alis, who bartended at Central Spot for many years, complained to me many times, her coworkers were constantly confused about how to provide service with the logic that the customer-is-always-right. Alis believed that if you wanted to cultivate a clientele that could afford to dine or drink at Central Spot (which was significantly more expensive than other Yerevan spots), then the workers needed to understand that they had to treat the customers well. "They are paying for the service as much as the food, but the workers here don't understand this like they do in America," Alis explained. Its Americanness also had other connotations—of sexual permissiveness and liberalism.

I had met Arthur for the first time at Central Spot a few weeks prior to this queer tour, when he told me the story of how he had been forced to come out because he was seen at the very table at which we now sat. A member of the Protestant church where Arthur was a junior director of the choir had seen him sitting there, assumed that his appearance there meant that he was gay, and had informed the church pastor, who then called Arthur's mother. These events had undone the life that Arthur once knew in Yerevan. He was no longer living with his family. Arthur had been informed by his brother (who had found out about the pastor's phone call) that he was no longer welcome. A couple of months later, Arthur would leave Armenia and settle in Moscow, only to return in 2022 during the Russian invasion of Ukraine to escape conditions wrought by international sanctions. Space is of great consequence to life.

Arthur and I left Central Spot as the sun was making its descent, creating cool shadows under the tall buildings of Northern Avenue, and we took a seat on a bench across from the Armani Exchange to wait for some friends. "Where are they going? Where are they coming from? What are they searching for?" Arthur sang, looking out at the people slowly passing by in all directions. "It's a Saturday evening," I offered naively, implying that they might not be going anywhere in particular, that they might be exactly where they wanted to be, leisurely wandering along one of the city's promenades. "What difference does that make?" Arthur asked, rhetorically. "They spend all their time wandering about. What else are they going to do? They have no joy in their lives. All they can do is wander about the city [*kaghakum man gal*], looking at people."

As we sat there watching, people wandered, watched, and sometimes also took a seat on a bench like we had; the shops up and down Northern Avenue saw less action. A child walking with her parents waddled into the Armani Exchange and enjoyed the air conditioning for a few moments before her parents went in and carried her out. A group of teenage boys walked into another Italian designer shop and then, perhaps made to feel as if they did not belong, walked back out, snickering. Free market ideology in postsocialist spaces promised to bring in new goods and new opportunities to buy and sell these goods. On Northern Avenue in 2011, however, these promises were proven empty by the very emptiness of these sites of consumption. The reconstructed Northern Avenue had officially opened in November 2007, commemorated by a walk-through by then president Robert Kocharyan, who had also given a speech celebrating the space as a new center for business, a "business card for contemporary Yerevan" (Ter-Ghazaryan 2013, 580). But for many Yerevantsis there was little to celebrate. The street quickly became known for the displacement it had caused. For many years, the street's previous residents, who had been displaced by the reconstruction, forced to abandon their living spaces, waged a bitter struggle through an NGO called Victims of State Needs along with others who advocated against new construction projects (Ter-Ghazaryan 2013). Northern Avenue's 2007 redevelopment transformed it from a residential street lined with trees (a space of life) to a walled structure of stone and cement (see figure 4.1). In 2014, the city added lights and banners to bring some color, which accompanied the construction of an underground mall beneath the avenue. However, it is still sometimes described by Yerevantsis as a space devoid of life. As Susanne Fehlings (2016) documents, her interlocutors often took offense to Northern Avenue's very conception, one describing it as if "someone set off a neutron bomb there and all life was snuffed out" (199).

As Arthur and I sat on a bench on Northern Avenue and watched others who were also sometimes watching us, I remembered a time during the previous summer, when a taxi driver had found out that it was my first time in the country and decided to give me a tour of the "real" Yerevan, not the "fake touristic places" he imagined I was likely to see. At the red light of the intersection formed by Isahakyan and Abovyan Streets, he had pointed out a woman standing alone at a bus stop. "She is in her twenties and still waiting to get married. *Man a galis* [she is searching], but she won't find a husband. All the men are gone or cannot afford to keep a family." As he continued to describe the "real" Armenia—where people didn't have jobs or had to spend their entire lives working, he said, adding that he also never even saw his family because he worked eighteen hours a day—we came to Northern Ave-

4.1 Northern Avenue in 2010. Photo by Anya Semeniouk.

nue. "You see those buildings?" he asked, referring to the high-rises that lined the street, "They are empty. They have built them for no one." He turned around to look directly at me as he repeated, "For no one." As I remembered this, Arthur was formulating his own contemplations. Watching a group of men arguing from across the promenade of Northern Avenue, he quietly muttered, mostly to himself: "They don't have bread to eat, so they eat each other." New developments, construction projects, and spatial reconfigurations in Yerevan were made not in the interest of life and joy but in the interest of something else entirely.

In this chapter, I explore the meanings of *man gal* in Yerevan. *Man gal* means to wander, to stroll. It is a term often used to convey leisurely walking about, roaming, taking pleasure in swaying to the rhythms of the city. *Gnum enq man galu* (We are going for a stroll) implies intent, collective or individual, over how time and space will be experienced—a structured use of unstructured time, or an organic and unstructured use of a structured space. It is a colloquial term, a less official and less formal way of expressing *zbosnel*, going for a walk. *Man gal*, however, might also mean searching for something. While the intentions of wandering might be purposeful—to get fresh air, to have a conversation, to enjoy time, and to spend time (perhaps frivolously)—the other notion of *man gal* is purposeless. *Inch es man galis?* (For what are you searching?) points to a loss of purpose in time and space. Unlike the term *voronel*, a more active verb for searching, the use of the informal *man gal* conveys a certain melancholic experience of space, a searching that might not be aware of its object, that might not have any particular goal. Although the two—*man gal* as wandering and *man gal* as searching—are not the same words, but homonyms, both imply spatiotemporal ambivalence.

Once a favorite pastime in the Soviet era, a leisurely use of space for pleasurable ambulation, *man gal*, had become something else in postsocialist times. The centralized grid of the Soviet-era city plan was being undone, changing the landscapes that had shaped leisurely wandering in public spaces and in everyday life. This undoing marked the new postsocialist free market logics as perversion—not as organization, but as the perversion of organization; not as ideologically produced, but as created through failed moral promises. Postsocialism was certainly a transformation, but what it had transformed Yerevan or Armenia into was not entirely clear. The uncertainties of life that constituted experiences of postsocialism in Yerevan could be felt in the space of the city, and especially through a leisurely wandering that had become an aimless searching, merging these two practices of *man gal*. Wandering had become an ontological formation.

As capitalist and oligarchic logics transformed life—pushing plans (planned economies, planned ideologies, and lives that could be planned based on these) to the margins—space was also transformed. Space was no longer organized as pathed "gardens" (Abrahamian 2006) that materialized a coherent ideology and coherent identity. Yerevan was no longer discernible as a planned city—the "garden city" of architect Alexander Tamanyan's 1936 master plan.[1] Rather, it was (dis)organized through the logics of pathless cruising, a phenomenon that was only at times gay, but that was ontologically perverse and with queer potential. Here, I borrow from David Harvey's (2006, 397) notion of "organized abandonment," or the processes through which space is forced into abandonment only to be appropriated by capital for speculation (and then left abandoned again as capital seizes state abandoned territory elsewhere and speculates on that). By using the term *(dis)organized abandonment*, however, I seek to highlight the ways in which organized abandonment leaves a palpable sense of a disorganized space, especially in the postsocialist city, once rigidly planned and organized, as it develops new and uneven layers that do not seem to have a plan or a logic. The disorganization of space appears as spatial disconfiguration. Many of my interlocutors expressed feelings about contemporary life as disorder, often as a response to the discontinuities in ideology and meanings that emerged from the unevenness of Yerevan's built environment. Life had become pathless. Postsocialism's spatial and temporal (dis)order was patterned on *mangal*, wandering with no goal and also no longer as leisure. As I show below and in the following chapter, many of my interlocutors felt that life was no longer life and that it no longer had purpose. *Sa kyank a?* (Is this life?) This was a question Lucine Talalyan, my research collaborator, and I heard frequently as we conducted our household survey interviews.

This chapter and the next are concerned with the radical spatiotemporal possibilities of perversion. Through an examination of capitalism's perversion of space and everyday life—and the various roles that the perverse figures of the oligarch and the homosexual play therein—this chapter moves into an analysis of how moral deviance might pave the way for different (queer) forms of life. These different forms of life, however, might deviate too far from the expectations of propriety to be considered Armenian, and thus are seen as spaces and times in which the nation has no longer survived. My interlocutors overwhelmingly felt that the privatization of space that resulted from the political-economic elite's greed and corruption had led to a lack of concern for the public and care for the body politic and thus to the proliferation of immorality. This postsocialist spatial perversion, however, had also opened up new places for sexually queer uses—such as the queer destinations on the map of Arthur's tour that were abandoned public spaces now put to private uses and moralized by many Yerevantsis as signs of the degeneration of space. Beyond these moral rheortics, however, we might also read a profoundly politicized critique of the destruction that capital wreaks. I start here with the queer city, extensions of the spaces to which Arthur first introduced me in 2011 that I would discover throughout my later excursions through Yerevan. I then move into the less affirmative feelings of spatial perversion, perceived as capitalist encroachment and disorientation. It is this disoriented and disconfigured savage space that queer creativity has made into spaces with wild potential.

The Public (Private) Law of the Father

The spaces to which Arthur took me on our tour were *queer* spaces not because of what they, in themselves, provided but because of how they sheltered possibilities for life, desire, and practice away from the harsh expectations of the Law of the Father, or the Father's No—private and intimate understandings of propriety, uprightness, and tradition that also operated in much of Yerevan's and Armenia's public space. To understand queer spaces in Yerevan, thus, it might help to deviate from our tour and to step instead into a space lacking this shelter. In April 2013, on the first weekend when the weather had finally warmed and it was not raining, inspiring a springtime urge to be outside rather than enclosed between walls, Adrine and I decided to walk over to Lovers' Park on Baghramyan Avenue. As we made our way to the park, Adrine, who was also from the United States, had said, "I can't wait to feel the grass between my toes!" We imagined that we would spend the day lying in the grass, feeling the sunshine.

Lovers' Park, named for having been a popular rendezvous point for young lovers, was in the late Soviet era known as Barekamutyan Aygi (Friendship Park), to commemorate the friendly internationalist alliance between all members of the Soviet Union; it shared its name with the metro station located about a mile away. In the post-Soviet era, the park was entirely renovated and then reopened in 2008. The undertaking was funded by the Boghosian Foundation. It remains a public park, although it is now surrounded by gates that are closed at night and reopened again in the morning. At the entrance of the park on its Baghramyan Avenue side, there is a placard that lists rules of conduct: no smoking; no pets; no littering; no climbing trees, waterfalls, and stone structures; and no damaging and defacing park property, and so on (figure 4.2). The park is lined with pathways to accommodate strolls and leisurely wandering. Grassy areas are roped off, and benches line the roped-off areas throughout the park (figure 4.3). On one side of the park—facing the entrance from Baghramyan Avenue—there is a private café that serves sandwiches and drinks.

When Adrine and I arrived, we found a grassy patch away from others, laid our bags down, and sat . Within two minutes, just as I was taking a book out of my bag and Adrine was removing her socks and shoes, a park worker—a middle-aged woman wearing the customary green apron of public green-space keepers—approached us. "Girls, you cannot sit on the grass. Do you see anyone else here sitting on the grass? We keep our parks clean. Sit on a bench." We asked her if that was a rule. I pointed out that I had not seen that written anywhere on the list of rules, which I had made sure to look at when we entered (to satisfy my ethnographic curiosity). She told us that whether it was listed on the

4.2   Rules of Lovers' Park. Photo by author.

4.3   The tamed gardens and pathways of Lovers' Park. Photo by author.

rules or not, it was a rule. We were not to sit on the grass. "Have a little bit of grace [*shnork*]," she said as she began walking away from us. When she left, Adrine and I discussed whether we should get up or if we should stay, considering first that it was not a rule that we had seen listed and also that the woman had already walked away. We then caught a glimpse of her turning back to check on our progress, and we began gearing up to leave our spot. This encounter in Lovers' Park highlights the problematic nature of public space as a privatized spatial configuration. Lovers' Park is a public park, but it is also tacitly and morally privatized to keep the zone safe from "perversion."

These aspects of the city and its spatiality were critical topics of social and political discussion. In 2018, for instance, activists and scholars organized a conference around the imaginaries of public space in Yerevan. Drawing on old plans for the city—some that had eventually been realized and others that had yet to be realized—Ruzanna Grigoryan, a feminist environmentalist who was one of the speakers at the conference, argued that at some point the main logic of city planning in Yerevan had been to create so many walkways that a pedestrian could continuously move through the city via its green spaces. According to this ideology and these plans, a person should be able to walk from one side of the city to the other, from one neighborhood to the next, without being interrupted by scenes of brick and mortar and thus experience the city as a space connected to life. And so, in this way, the city's original plan included various bridges and boundaryless parks that created possibilities for traveling through space that was green and that connected the city's space to a centralized ideology (of life and vitality). Now, Grigoryan argued, space was discontinuous. Paths were frequently broken, sometimes interrupted by construction sites for buildings that had nothing to do with the larger city space, like cafés, restaurants, and shops. This ruptured a connection to life as well as to a collective sensibility. Grigoryan pointed out that parks in the Soviet era were not necessarily named and were not seen as entities separate from city space; rather, they were envisioned by planners as linked to the city and to one another, composing an imaginary of the city as a park. Postsocialist marketized realities have interrupted these connections to life. Buildings line both sides of most streets and are sometimes so high that one cannot even feel oneself in space and in time; one has only a scant glimpse of the sky above (rather than all around), or has little experience of the breeze (except when one passes by an alleyway where wind funnels through at higher speeds). Postsocialist space, Grigoryan argued, was imagined as opportunity for constant commercialized "image spamming" through advertisements and other signs. This development, Grigoryan maintained, was not new to the administration of Taron Margaryan, Yerevan's mayor from 2011 to 2018, but had been a part of a larger global imagination since the 1980s.

Grigoryan argued that much of what was happening to the configuration of public space in Yerevan could be understood by looking at the way in which London was organized. As urban planning began transforming the city of London, "green spaces" became a part of these plans. These green spaces, however, were not organized as open spaces that connected parts of the city to other parts; they were instead closed off zones of green space that were both intimate and private. They were often gated parks, open during the day and closed at night, and while they were technically public space, they also had different rules of conduct, sometimes actually written out on placards near their entrances. Public parks, in other words, were privatized public zones.

Unlike the notion of the city as a park—or the city as a public space with interconnected green zones that allow the wanderer to be in connection to the social life-worlds and life-as-world-beyond-the-human—the imagination of a park as an enclosed, protected public space operates under the logic of privatization. Susan Gal and Gail Kligman (2000) problematize clear-cut notions of public/private binaries in postsocialist contexts, pointing out that these are often imagined not as separate spaces but as fractalizations of one another, where private spaces do not exist in domains of their own but within larger domains that are considered public but that are in themselves, in this way, made up of smaller privates and publics . In Yerevan, "public" parks kept up by private foundations or by the city become otherwise private spaces within a public space—as enclosed domains. As a private public space, parks and other such enclosed public spaces become zones temporarily protected from the possibilities of economic abandonment that might also produce moral and sexual perversion (*aylaserutyun* and *aylandakutyun*). Kept clean and cared for, the "common space" of the park in the postsocialist era is attended to as private space. Unlike the public commons, such as alleyways or common spaces of residential buildings (hallways, staircases, etc.), in the postsocialist world (Boym 1995), these privatized public spaces are not abandoned.

In this way, private public space becomes more policeable and zonable as a space in which to enforce not only public law but the Law of the Father. The lovers of Lovers' Park—who can be witnessed on any given day—are proper lovers. They are lovers who are properly (heterosexually) courting one another with the consent of their parents and relatives, who are engaged to be married, who are married, who are taking wedding photos, who are with their children. Their displays of affection in the park are sanctioned by law (during the park's open hours) as well as by the Law of the Father. The open spaces and gardened paths of Lovers' Park make possible the constant and consistent surveillance of gendered and sexual behavior. Lovers' Park, in this way, is a tamed garden. The green lawn and the carefully curated trees and flowers do not grow wild but, like their visitors, are kept in their place—proper and not perverse.

Capital, however, is also liminally tamed in such a place: it is not barred from existing inside the public park—as the privatized café makes clear—but it becomes less visibly savage. While the spaces outside of the gates of Lovers' Park are for the wild and savage roaming of capital—investing, building, destroying, divesting—wreaking havoc and leaving unevenness in its wake (symptoms of postsocialism's moral perversion of life), Lovers' Park is a public site that *feels* like a place of refuge. While it remains open to the possibility of abandonment itself, like many of Yerevan's and other cities' parks, Lovers' Park as it existed at the time of my fieldwork for this book felt worlds away from the world right outside its gates. In the tunnel of the Barekamutyun metro stop beneath Lovers' Park, for instance, is a stone and concrete world abandoned by the state and capital and left open to the untamed work of graffiti artists. On hot days, the Republic Square metro less than a mile away smells of urine. There, one might find the occasional unofficial retailer—an older woman selling apricots, an older man selling an assortment of knick-knacks. This used to be the case at the underground crosswalk at Abovyan Street at Isahakyan, which led to the Yeridasardakan metro stop a block away and was known for its working-class booksellers. It is where Knar once took me and bought for me my first volume of Charents's poetry in 2010. It is where one used to go to look for various genres of literature. In 2013 the booksellers were dispersed, forced to abandon their posts, as capital discovered the public space and privatized it, creating the Metronome shopping center. Capital colonizes and then abandons. It is fickle, uncommitted, without purpose or objective (other than profit, of course). Capital is savage; it devours and leaves to waste; it uses up then tosses aside, having destroyed what was once there and making its reemergence impossible. The spaces on which capital is currently feeding shine; they are clean and proper and abide by the Law of the Father. Capital's savagery is tamed as it feeds. These same places, someday, will be abandoned and left as ruins, and capital's monstrous, vampiric (Marx 1976, 342) ravenousness will be visible again.

Despite its shiny greenness, Adrine and I quickly learned that day that Lovers' Park was no space of queer refuge.

Queer Refuge in a Wild Place

Parks, however, can still be sites of designated and gated wildness—where wildlife, queer life, and new forms of human and nonhuman relation are sheltered from the taming impetus of the Law of the Father as well as from capital's savagery. In Yerevan, the Busabanakan Aygi (the Botanical Garden) is such a space, where not only plants and brush go untamed and thrive, but where they have created spaces of unexpected seclusion in which other forms of life (human) might let go of their own tameness and propriety. While the Botanical Garden is a planned space, with a large, vined archway that covers its main path from the park's entrance into the garden, and a greenhouse in the center of the park, the lack of municipal funding in the postsocialist era has led to its untamed growth (and thus, to its possibilities). As of this writing, trees and bushes growing in the greenhouse plunge beyond the structured ceiling and outgrow their containment. Fehlings (2016) poignantly describes her visit to the garden like a scene from Stanislaw Lem's *Solaris*, "as if in a forgotten outpost of humanity inhabited by bewildered remains of the species: the windows of the huge glasshouse were broken; nature had won back the territory; and some elderly women wearing white coats seemed to be living an absurd life in the ruins of their former workplace" (197). While the paths of the garden are still visible, many of them have been narrowed by native species that have outgrown their plots and intermingled with one another. There are also various spaces, off the beaten paths of the park, that are ideal spaces in which to set up for a day of queer fun. This was what PINK did in June 2013 for one of its community events. When we arrived at the park in taxis, we carried our bags of sandwiches, snacks, drinks, and games (a deck of Uno, a Twister mat, and some other props) through the park's gated entry, attended to by a security guard, and looked for a spot off the main path that would be secluded enough to provide us privacy and security. In that private and secure space, a clearing left by the brush and tall grass otherwise growing all around us, we could take comfort in knowing that the jokes and improper (nonheterosexual) displays of affection shared among the group would go unsurveilled. Except for a few occasions on which we heard footsteps or voices nearby and quieted down to make sure no one approached us, the untamed park provided shelter not only from capital's "image spamming" but also from the Law of the Father and its disapproving gaze. Sexual perversions were not gated out from this wild public space.

The Botanical Garden had a curious relation to development and abandonment. Its ambivalently secluded landscape had been made possible by the state's abandonment as well as by capital's disinterest in keeping up with the development of this public space in the postsocialist era. The organized abandonment in this place had made queer spatiality and queer wanderings possible: a kind of disorganization that allowed for reorganization. It is through similar logics of abandonment and disinterest that we can locate the spaces of improper public sex. There were various garden spaces of the city that had been left to overgrow and that became sites of improper midnight make-out sessions for young non-heteronormative (not engaged, not married) persons. The parts of the Hrazdan Canyon at the end of Mashtots Avenue that were not visible from the high-end Monte Cristo restaurant (that sits atop its far end) became sites of cruising. Beyond Yerevan, the far side of Lake Sevan's coast, became the site for queer vacationing, especially in its cheap *dormikner* (trailers).

The moral abandonment of Yerevan—left to a perverse oligarchic horde that produced spatial disconfigurations and (dis)organized abandonment (which I will discuss further on in this chapter)—paved the way for queer possibilities. But these were not always affirming possibilities. They were forms of emergence that were still in-the-making. As Arthur walked me along some of the pathways and through tucked-away tunnels near the Hrazdan *dzor* as part of our queer tour, he explained to me that men who cruise this site looking for other men with whom to engage in anonymous sex had not yet been able to come to terms with their own sexual desires. "I know what this feels like and I know how hard it is, so I understand them. But, it has to change. It's not good for their families and it's not good for them either," Arthur explained. A more visible queer Yerevan needed to emerge from this (in)visible city. For Arthur, the illicit emergent forms of sexual desire made possible by these abandoned spaces in the city needed to affirm themselves and become grounded in a social politics. A queer right to the city, thus meant coming out from the wild shadows of abandonment and seclusion to make visible demands on the public: to claim a right to the developed city rather than to the abandoned one.

José Esteban Muñoz (2009, 48) teaches us that there is a "primary linkage between queer desire and queer politics" that can be found not in the ideality of public, anonymous, promiscuous, and unprotected sex nor in its dangerous actuality, but in exceeding both. The queer political's transformative potential is located in excess, in utopian longing (47), in a "will that is different" (Adorno, as quoted in Bloch and Adorno 1988, 12, cited in Muñoz 2009, 39). While Arthur's and others' political aspirations seemed to be located at the inclusion of a gay world into propriety, within these aspirations were also always traces of different queer pasts. Mamikon Hovsepyan, for instance, the president of PINK Armenia, gave me an oral history of the various bars and pubs in which gay nightlife was located in the years prior to the emergence of LGBT politics proper (vis-à-vis NGOs, public campaigns, and the emergence of the figure of the homosexual in 2012).[2] As *alternativ* spaces, these were not necessarily demarcated LGBT places but rather places in which queer life could exist with slightly more safety than in other spaces. In his oral history, Hovsepyan celebrated the emergence of more proper LGBT spaces, such as NGO offices, community groups, and a gay bar where one could simply be gay without being overly sexually excessive as a mark of queerness. He also lamented the loss of this liminality—in which gay identity was not yet cemented in Armenian public life and queer performances through excess were fun and frivolous opportunities to be openly *different*, to refuse propriety. While bars—and even gay bars—constituted a public (albeit privatized public), in which proper behavior mattered for perceptions of gay identity and practice, the Botanical Garden remained a space that was private enough to offer possibilities for unleashing the campy, flirty, excessive behaviors and practices of a queer past in the present without the risk of becoming "the homosexual" and, like Little Gender Boycott, being cast into the shadows.

As Arthur gave me his perspective on how Armenian culture needed to be changed through queer visibility, I remembered the first time I had heard about "the *dzor*," the canyon. It was about a month before my queer tour of the city, when my language instructor, Knar, with whom I met every morning that summer in her home, had opened her door for me looking entirely disheveled. Eleven in the morning, when I usually arrived, was a time of domestic chaos cooling down, as she was usually just cleaning up breakfast from her two kids and preparing another pot of tea for us to share on her balcony while she guided me in reading passages and writing reflections in Armenian. This time, however, she was home alone. She had clearly been crying and when I asked her what was wrong, she broke into tears again. I made some tea and gave her a cigarette, which she said might calm her nerves, and she told me about what had happened the night before.

It had started off as a typical night. At 2 a.m. her husband was still not home. Knar had told me before that he was an alcoholic, who frequently stayed up all night drinking with his friends. He was often unemployed, and she had complained about how he used the money that she earned, which was meant for the benefit of the family, on his drinking habit. When she called him, she would often hear him in the company of many other men. She had told me before that she suspected he slept with other women. "That's how men are," was a common refrain with which Knar explained her husband's behavior—including the few times that she had hinted that he was physically abusive toward her.

"But, Tamar, this time I realized it's different. He was not with a group of men. He was with one man. I heard one other man when he picked up the phone. I asked him who he was with. He refused to tell me. I was angry so I said that he was probably at the *dzor* and he said, 'So what if I am? What business is that of yours?'" Her husband had hung up the phone on her and had not picked up any other calls from her throughout the night. He had still not come home. That morning, Knar had put her kids into a taxi and sent them to stay with their grandmother in a nearby village.

I had not quite put the pieces together, because I didn't know what it meant that he could have been at the *dzor*. The previous summer, when I had first met Knar, I had told her that I needed to be fluent in Armenian as I was planning on conducting research in Armenia. When she asked what I would be researching, I had told her that I was interested in the experiences of lesbian, gay, bisexual, and transgender Armenians (as this was my initial research agenda). "Are there such people in Armenia? Are you convinced? I have not heard of such a thing," Knar had commented. My reply, "Yes, there are," ended the conversation. Knar had never again asked me about my research. Now, noticing my confusion about why it was such a shocking revelation that her husband might have been at the *dzor*, she said, "You must know what the *dzor* is as you are observing the kinds of immoralities that happen in places like that." That is when I realized the significance of what she had just told me. Knar, who believed that Armenia's perversions were tied to a lack of collective sensibility, that the lack of work in Armenia had made people lose their moral footing in relation to others and in relation to the nation now explained, "this is what this country has become." Men, in Knar's assessment, no longer understood their proper role within the social sphere; they no longer took care of their families because in many cases—including her husband's—they could not make money to care for their families. For Knar, spaces of degenerate behavior, like the *dzor*, were made possible by the lacunae left by moral abandonment, which itself was a product of postsocialist political economy and (dis)organized abandonment. The destruction of the social collective that was Armenian and Soviet society, destruction made possible by the emergence of the oligarchs, had led directly to the emergence of the homosexual. To put it in the rhetoric of perversion, the *aylandakutyun* of the nation by the oligarch had produced the conditions for the sexual perversion (*aylaserutyun*) of the nation by the homosexual. Knar never allowed us to revisit this conversation during subsequent encounters. Her husband returned home and a few weeks later was employed again, which Knar announced to me one morning, celebrating not just the needed income but the moral equilibrium his employment would restore.

A month after this incident I was at the *dzor* myself, on Arthur's queer tour. I sympathized with Arthur's desire to make homosexuality a respectable part of life, something that could come out to the light of day (what Little Gender Boycott was barred from doing). I wondered, however, what this would mean for feelings of sexual and moral perversion writ large. Would well-respected gay-identified men and women in cafés, restaurants, bars, promenades, and parks—if included within the Law of the Father's propriety and allowed to participate in the good, privatized public life—dispel anxieties of perversion? I couldn't help but think that if these newly proper sexual minorities entered the good life, someone would nonetheless continue to bear the brunt of the feeling that postsocialist life had gone astray. Someone (else) would continue to be the one who was forced to bear the responsibility for what had gone wrong. Because what had gone wrong would continue to go wrong. Because meaning would still be replaced by simulacra, political possibility would still be displaced onto moral attachments, and social life would still be organized around private wealth (and its empty promises) rather than centered on life and its needs. These realities have effects on feelings about love, sex, desire, and social reproduction—all of which had been twisted into sites of impropriety as a result of the spaces in which they were practiced and experienced. It is these forms of spatial perversion to which I now turn. The Botanical Gardens and the *dzor* might be wild, untamed places, but they remained attuned to life and provided (queer) refuge for human and nonhuman species. The rest of Yerevan, however—as tamed and developed as it was and despite how much attention went into it—was becoming a place of savagery that no longer abided by the needs of life, neither by logic or rationale.

Feeling Spatial (Dis)configuration

In April 2013, Talalyan and I began our interviews in the neighborhood of Yerord Mas, whose name refers to the Third District of the larger Shengavit District. Visible from the metro when traveling southbound toward Shengavit were the ruins of Yerevan's Factory District (Gortzaranayin), what was once the most industrialized zone in the city: a

4.4   An abandoned and hollowed-out factory in Gortzaranayin District, now property of the Yerkimshin Trust. Photo by Lucine Talalyan.

space of activity that had come to a halt (see figure 4.4). Even as passengers sped by, the district's missing windows and broken machinery were visible. But much as the scene from the moving train elicited feelings of loss, melancholy, destruction, and abandonment, these feelings were also rooted deeply within the intimate life-worlds and experiences of those who continued to inhabit that district and its surrounding neighborhoods.

After witnessing the ruins of the Factory District fly by as we rode on the metro, a scene we had already witnessed multiple times—sometimes marveling at the beauty of its abandonment, sometimes wondering what it might take to turn some of those spaces into galleries, music venues, or squats—Talalyan and I got off at the Garegin Njdeh stop. Yerord Mas had been built in the 1930s as a center for industry, particularly for the production of chemicals. The district is the object of the most popularly circulated stories, jokes, rumors, and reputations—perhaps second only to the "Bangladesh" neighborhood, the unofficial name given to the district of Malatia-Sebastia after the 1971 independence of Bangladesh from Pakistan, but often colloquially traced, instead, to the fact of its poverty. Many described Yerord Mas as the home of *kyartu*s, a derogatory term for a macho subculture characterized as backward. Some described Yerord Mas as a dangerous place—as a place of people without "culture," a reference to its residents' lack of "class." Yerord Mas, a few of my interlocutors in Yerevan told me, was the site of a recording studio that produced *rabiz* music for a mass audience in the Soviet era. Thus, it is known as the home of *rabiz* music—a popular "low culture" and unofficial genre that amalgamated various Eastern styles into a "national" sound and became associated with "uncultured," "unprofessional," and unofficial worlds during the Soviet era.

Getting off the metro, Talalyan and I walked a few blocks on Garegin Nzhdeh Street until we found ourselves in a quiet neighborhood, away from the crowds, the traffic, and the noise. At a seven-story building, we took the elevator up to the highest floor and began knocking on doors. On the sixth floor of the building, Ayda, a woman in her fifties, answered. Ayda lived alone in a three-room apartment. Her husband had died two years earlier, and her son had emigrated to Russia. "The opportunities for feeling loneliness and meaninglessness are everywhere," she told us when we asked about the artwork that populated the living room of her apartment. "That room, over there," she said, pointing to a sunny room that had a balcony facing out onto Garegin Nzhdeh Street, "that is where I paint and make my sculptures. These here," she continued, gesturing toward the works of art that surrounded us, "are the ones that I take with me to the market every week to sell." She had not sold many works. There were some tourists who had been interested and had bought some items, but "we Armenians are not so interested in art anymore. I suppose we have different things that occupy our minds," she explained. Ayda worked as a seamstress at a local shop throughout the week and spent her spare time working on her art and her weekends at the Vernissage Market in central Yerevan. She explained that she did not make the work to sell it, but rather to give her life purpose, because it gave her a sense that she was still making something with her life. "The most painful thing that has happened in this country over the last twenty years is the feeling of meaninglessness [*animastutyan zgatsoghutyune*]," she said. She described the lives of everyone she knew—friends, family, neighbors—as being "eaten up by meaningless activity": "They want to make money, somehow, by doing anything they can, so they can buy things. But for what? I occupy myself with art because it gives my life meaning. And I hope that maybe it can give someone else meaning, too."

In Ayda's apartment, Talalyan and I looked around us at the paintings—vibrant yellows and reds and oranges, deep blues and greens and purples. Some of the paintings were figural, but none were realist—grasping for meaning, perhaps, to be somewhere outside of the real world. There were sculptures, too—painted with acrylic. Some had a more-than-aesthetic use-value (ashtrays, bowls, cups). Some were not made for anything other than to be seen.

"Did you study art at an institute?" Talalyan asked Ayda. It was an innocent question, inspired perhaps by her own curiosity (as Talalyan was herself an artist), or maybe as a way to break the quiet in the room that was, by then, louder than the sounds of car horns and bus engines coming from the open window in the next room. Ayda had expressed her distaste for the meaninglessness of life in the postsocialist era and had then gotten quiet. Talalyan and I could have taken this as a sign that it was time for us to leave, but something kept us there. We sat with Ayda's feelings rather than being pushed away by them. A tear streamed down Ayda's face. She wiped it away, finally saying "No, I was a chemist." She let out a quick laugh and then explained that she and her husband both worked at a chemical plant, but then when it closed in 2006, they could not find similar work. Instead, she had to take whatever jobs she could find. At that time, she told us, they were more concerned about surviving and did not often feel emptiness or sadness. But over time, she realized that the problem was not about surviving and making money. "Okay, you survive. Then what?" she asked, pointing to a problem deeper than the financial struggle. While Ayda did not deny that people had a hard time making it in the postsocialist era, she argued that the more pernicious processes had to do with something more profound than getting by.

> You see, it is about the goals [*npadaknerov*] with which one survives. You survive, then what? What goals do we, Armenians, have? We just want to survive. In this, we lose life's meaning. This is what saddens me. We don't work with meaning. We work only to survive. When I was working at the chemical plant, I was working for our people. Our Soviet people, Armenians among them. What I do now is work for one person. What many Armenians do is work for foreigners. They are the ones who own most of the factories and the other places of work. But even if the owner is Armenian—the people I work for are Armenian—what is the purpose of the work? What am I working for?

Throughout the interview Ayda repeatedly teared up. Feeling as though maybe some of her sadness was informed by loneliness, I asked her if she had friends or relatives who understood her and her commitment to her work. She did have some relatives but she had learned not to share with them her interest in art, understanding that they had no appreciation for it. She told us that she could tell that we were people who would understand—that is why she had invited us in. "Sometimes I think to myself that maybe people, because they are trying to survive, are afraid of looking around them and thinking too much, afraid that maybe they will find emptiness. But they have changed, our people. This life has changed them."

While Ayda and many other Yerevantsis might believe that employment in Armenia is largely for foreign entities, this is a misconception. Like any misconception, however, it is based in some realities. While a small proportion of Armenia's general economy, foreign direct investment (FDI) is central to many public and politicized discussions. FDI peaked in 2008, at $943 million, and dropped off substantially since then (it was at $47 million in 2020) (World Bank 2023). Much of this foreign investment has been in the mining and energy sectors, which do not provide a large number of jobs (even if they promise to). These industries, however, have been the object of much contention and public unrest. Mining, as I will discuss in chapter 6, is at the center of environmental struggle as it has led to the destruction of various mountains, villages, and water systems. Energy is the object of social anxiety, especially because Armenian access to natural gas is dependent on the Russian company Gazprom (an international energy agency) and, as a result, costs have increased (*JAMnews* 2022) or people have been repeatedly threatened with increases. In 2015, when the state attempted to raise the cost of electricity, because its privatized electricity grid was largely controlled by the Inter RAO company of which the Russian government owns 52.68 percent of shares (Sabonis-Helf 2007, 430), it was met with a large protest movement called #ElectricYerevan. Besides Russia, which is the largest foreign investor in Armenia, large FDIs also flow from Greece, Cyprus, and Germany. For these reasons, many Armenians believe that their economy is a colony or a puppet of foreign entities— either Europe or Russia, depending on whom you ask. This often gets tied to narratives of employment, although the largest employers in the Republic continue to be the agriculture and public sectors (Honorati et al. 2019, 17). Importantly, even while this is the case and the World Bank finds that the public sector pays better than private sector work (72), it refers to agriculture and the public sector as the least productive sectors in Armenia's economy and continues to advise privatization and the growth of private industry and private employment.

Ayda's sense of meaning was obviously greatly informed by Soviet-era Marxist philosophy, especially when it came to collective labor. She understood labor as a way of contributing to the body politic; in other words, not just producing goods, but producing a social world that would make use of those goods. In this framework, labor is not a commodity tied to the individual who owns it and can sell it. It is a social relation—a necessary means of belonging to and contributing to a social world. It was that very social world—the space of the collective Soviet Union, of which Armenia formed a part—that Ayda and some others felt had been lost in the postsocialist era.

Lost with this collective social relation built from labor was often also the opportunity for labor itself. As factories shut down, the possible spaces even for selling one's labor as a commodity dwindled. As people focused on the narrowing financial opportunities, they shifted their focus away from more important processes—the processes that made for human, symbolic, cultural, and ideological life-worlds. A focus on financial survival alone missed seeing that so much else had been lost. This was a topic of constant discussion between my language instructor, Knar, and me over the years that we worked together. For Knar, the biggest loss from deindustrialization was not so much that people had fewer financial opportunities, but the loss of so many other social, political, and moral sensibilities that accompanied labor as a social relation. These, for Knar, included collective feelings of belonging to, and with, others and the possibilities of having the workplace as the site from which to organize and to imagine common struggle and a common world. "People who work together think together," was Knar's motto, something she repeated multiple times as the moral of various stories she would tell.

The Gortzaranayin district was just one space of abandonment in Armenia, in just one city. Across the country, there were many other sites just like it. Vanadzor—once called Kirovakan—a smaller city in the north, for instance, was another heavily industrialized space during the Soviet era that had now become a landscape of abandonment. Gyumri—once known as Leninakan—once a vibrant space of both industrial production that drew in an internationalist working class from other Soviet Socialist Republics and cultural production where many of Armenia's artists and filmmakers worked, was largely destroyed at the end of 1988 by a catastrophic earthquake. Rather than rebuilding, Gyumri experienced heavy abandonment. In 2013, it was still recovering from the earthquake; many continued to live in makeshift housing, and the population was barely half of what it had been in 1988 (Chapple 2018). Driving on many of Armenia's roads, pitted by potholes, this feeling of (dis)organized abandonment would be palpable when, amid miles of fields of trees and shrubbery that created a sense of an uninhibited natural environment, one suddenly caught a glimpse of a socialist realist statue. Statues marked turns and milestones of the roads or bus stops, relics of a built environment that once existed, giving access to a memory of desire for a particular future—socialist realism as a genre established on desired future possibilities (Fitzpatrick 2000)—that did not quite pan out. These glimpses elicited uncanny feelings—as if one had suddenly been transported to a future, but a future that was imagined from the past, allowing one to witness life not as it was but as desire for a life as it could have been. Imaginaries of collectively building a new world, of paving the road toward a collective future, had, in time, been abandoned, as had these markers.

Spaces of abandonment—forgotten places—are not outside history (Gilmore 2008). They are also sites of ongoing practices, struggles, and relationships to and feelings about built environments and experiences of space. Chaos and disorganization were the basic characteristics that Armenians—from our interlocutors, to activists, to academics—ascribed to the space of the Republic. Spaces forced to become abandoned—like Northern Avenue or the Pak Shuka (Closed Market) discussed in chapter 3—in order to build something else that felt empty of the logics and rationalities that had once organized those spaces. The logics of these new spaces were on frequencies and in rhythms foreign to the rationalities that had organized space in the socialist era.

"It is Chaos, chaos. There is no law, no intent, no tradition that is behind all of this construction" remarked Hovhannes, a man in his fifties in the neighborhood of Yerord Mas. "It's complete chaos how they are building this city. I am an architect, so I am telling you, as an architect, that these new constructions are not part of any kind of plan. I don't see the idea in them. Who knows who is even building, for what they are building, for *whom* they are building." Hovhannes worked for the city, but he maintained that his job over the last ten years had been to uncritically approve new construction. "In the past [in the Soviet era], there was a plan. The people need something, we need to build it. And so we built it. Now all they do is build, destroy, then build. But you don't know for what and you can't even ask! This is the thing that is really interesting. You don't even know *who* to ask!"

Hovhannes's daughter Anahid, perhaps in her late twenties, also participated in a part of the interview. She interrupted him, smiling at us as if she were saving us from her father's rantings and ravings. "*Pap jan* (daddy dear), they are building *zargatsman hamar* [for development]." The term *zargatsum* connotes not only "development" in the economic and infrastructural sense, but also progress and enlightenment. *Zarganal*, often used to convey economic expansion, also brings with it notions of betterment. But, because the term was also once a part of Soviet ideology, it has—at least for some—produced contradictions. Hovhannes countered his daughter's intervention precisely through these contradictions: "Aghchi jan [dear girl, patronizingly], what are they developing? Their pockets? *Who* are they developing [*Um en zargatsnum?*] If they are developing, it is in a way that is incomprehensible to me. *Aha*," he sang, condescendingly, "they 'developed' Northern Avenue. What did that develop [*Et inch zargatsrets?*]" Hovhannes explained that in the Soviet era, development was done for the purposes of fulfilling the needs (*karikner*) of the society. People needed food, shelter, clothing, to get from one place to another, and education, and it was around these needs that centralized plans were organized. Hovhannes emphasized labor as a special need. People needed labor to feel like they had a purpose (*npadak*), but labor was also what made possible the fulfillment of other needs. Postsocialist development was not organized around needs, according to Hovhannes, but rather around private wealth.

Anahid, however, remained in disagreement. She interrupted again. "Dad, people don't just want to survive, they want to have other things in life. Life is not satisfactory with just working and surviving." Hovhannes looked at his daughter for a moment and then turned to Talalyan and me and, smiling, explained that it was he who had taught his daughter the art of debate. The comment was condescending and yet loving—paternalistic (and patriarchal). Hovhannes continued to question his daughter, adding that no one ever said that the goal of life was to work and survive, but if people were not working, they were not surviving, and if people were not surviving, nothing else could be possible. "At one time this country had poets and artists. That was work, too."

He lamented that his daughter's generation believed that life was about having things. His demeanor no longer expressed the excitement with which he had earlier condemned new development projects. It became one of genuine sadness, expressing the loss of something big.

Hovhanness and Anahid's debate reveals some of the biggest disagreements between the "new" postsocialist generation, sometimes defined by older generations as those who have no memories of Soviet life, and the older generation, often described by younger people as those who are stuck to an old way. But, what this debate also opens up is the massive space of contradiction through which everyday life is experienced by those (like Hovhannes) who, understanding the order of space vis-à-vis Soviet socialist ideologies of "alternative modernity" (Kotkin 2001), witness capitalist and neoliberal transformation as nonsensical. For them, the offbeat rhythms, the discontinuities of space, and the unevenness of landscapes made postsocialist spatial configuration feel like a disconfiguration. A kind of ugly fragmentation of an urban landscape.

In Yerevan, between 2005 and 2009, a construction boom with a 40 percent annual growth led to many new buildings appearing on the landscape, paid for by remittances from abroad as well as by private wealth. Many of these construction projects were residential buildings (like on Northern Avenue). This nonexportable production, however, soon led to a "construction bubble" followed by a massive decline in value, during which construction volumes fell by 37.4 percent in 2009. The year 2019, however, saw another construction boom—one that was also suddenly halted by the COVID-19 pandemic as well as by the "44-day war." Current tax laws incentivize construction by refunding interest paid on mortgage loans for houses or apartments purchased from a developer. While these laws were initially implemented to encourage buying, in consideration of the emptiness of many new developments, they also led to the overcrowding of the center of Yerevan with new buildings (Badalyan 2021). Construction, and especially in the city center, is also seen as critical for the beautification of the city to promote tourism, which is an important part of the country's economy, and which provides a remittance and donor-bearing diaspora a "global city" to showcase. While much of the city is made of pink and gray tufa, widely available in Armenia's geological landscape, the newly constructed city built into and on top of the old one is made of steel and glass, the "cladding of globalized redevelopment" (Miles 2014, 154).

Urban redevelopment projects act as commercial thoroughfares and cultural centers. Northern Avenue, while a housing redevelopment site, is also a part of a new city that offers consumer goods and a space for street performers, for strolling (wandering), and for socializing. The Cafesjian Cultural Center and Foundation that connects the central part of the city to the Monument neighborhood on the hillside above it via a long stone staircase, is also a part of this new city. It provides those moving from the Monument neighborhood on the hillside to the urban center below a beautiful view of Mount Ararat (in Turkey) in the distance as well as a view of statues by world-renowned artists. Indoors, the Cafesjian Center is also an art museum and a performance venue. In the city center, one can visit a number of restaurants, cafés, bars, and clubs. The new, redeveloped (and privatized) Yerevan is beautiful for tourists and has much to offer some Yerevantsis, too. This beautification, however, is unpleasant for those who not only derive no benefit from it, but who see (through their own experience of time and history) only the destruction of places of critical need—state-provided housing, sites of education, or public parks—and construction only for construction's sake. From their vantage point, the "development" of Yerevan does not appear to be developing much.

The Rhythms of Postsocialist Space

This organized disorganization of everyday life has a rhythm that is distinguishable from the wanderings of people through the space of the city. This is perhaps most true at the site of the "singing fountains" (*yergogh shatrvanner*) of Republic Square. In the evenings, when the sun goes down, the fountains light up. Music plays as the fountains spurt water into the air, in sync with the movements of music and lights. The fountains produce their own rhythm; they are also, however, in a rhythm with the movements of the city around them. On summer evenings, after a very hot day, families and tourists gather around them in front of the National Art Gallery, causing a strange slow-down in foot traffic. International tourists and Armenians—some from other neighborhoods of Yerevan, some from other towns or villages in Armenia—come to see the fountains sing and dance. But life as usual for those in Yerevan continues as well. Those who work in the city make their way home, trying to avoid the crowds building around the fountains. The restaurants, cafés, and bars fill up as the evening begins, and those socializing in such places try to work around the sound of the fountains and the people gathered on the streets to watch, making their own rhythms through laughter, an occasional argument, talk, hellos, and goodbyes.

The lives of those whose work revolves around others' leisure, those who make their ways in and through the wandering crowds, are annoyed by the leisurely strolling in and around Yerevan's central district. One evening I ran into Lillia, a waitress at Central Spot who was running late for work. As we walked together, her annoyance with the slow movement of bodies-in-wandering was palpable. "Don't you hate having to get through slow-moving cows who don't know where they're going?" she asked me as she tried to pick up the pace. Those on paths toward a destination conflicted with the aimless pathways of the wanderers. Lillia's mood became more distraught as she got caught amid a crowd gathered at the crosswalk to get to Northern Avenue—a crowd made up of people who might have been headed toward the fountains or who were just out and about making use of public wandering grounds like Northern Avenue. I remembered my conversation with Arthur (with which I began this chapter). While Arthur's characterization of the Avenue's wanderers was joyless, Lillia read the crowd as careless. Both joylessness and carelessness were applicable to the wandering crowd whose aimless rhythms lacked purpose and passion.

The fountains of Republic Square are important for Yerevan. They are a sightseeing "must" for those guiding any new visitor through the city. They are an important venue for many Yerevantsi families and even for those living outside Yerevan, who cannot afford many other forms of entertainment. The fountains, right there in the middle of Republic Square, are free. One can watch and listen without paying a dram. The fountains, along with other central destinations of Yerevan like the Cascade or Northern Avenue, are leisurely wandering grounds. But those who came of age in the Soviet era who visit the site now might feel slightly out of sync with the feelings of time and space that were once attached to those sites and perhaps especially to Republic Square. The Square, where the fountains are now located, was once the location of Lenin's statue. This was the center of the Republic, both spatially and ideologically. It was now the site of evening entertainment, free from the old ideology. Or, perhaps, free from any ideology—free from the constraints of organization, connection, and the legibility of purpose.

Lenin's statue, originally erected in 1940, was brought down in 1991 during the independence movement, leaving only its pedestal behind until that was also removed in 1996. Like other sites in Yerevan that were once a part of ideological activity, the fountains are now the site of deflection: a show of lights, water, and music in celebration of something not quite sure of itself, perhaps an attempt at drawing attention away from the nation's (moral) perversion. Like Republic Square, Liberty Square, a few blocks to the north, was once the location of the national independence movement; but now (at least on most days) it is the site of leisure-for-pay: children's toys (bikes and kid-sized electric cars) for rent, bouncy houses, coffee and ice cream shops. This is, of course, not to say that Republic Square or Liberty Square were not also sites of leisure and entertainment during the Soviet era. Instead, it is to point out that during the Soviet era, leisure and entertainment were focused around a common social cause: around a Symbol, around a Father, around a coherent ideology that provided purpose. The era of the nation's perversion had changed the Father's circumstances.

A centralized ideology that once asserted itself in the very spatiality of the city and its intentional construction has been, in the postsocialist era, rendered a simulacrum. "Now we are supposed to go to those places *not* to understand and live their histories, *not* to know about the struggles that made this Republic and this city possible, *not* to think at all. And we shouldn't forget that this [change] was intentional. Giving people something silly [*himar*] to believe in—fun, empty happiness, blind nationalism, 'look, how good it is to have a family'—is how they have tried to make something very ugly look very beautiful," Mika Danielyan, the late human rights activist, once told me, referring to Liberty Square's morphing into a playhouse. Danielyan was speaking about the memory of the state murders that took place in the streets on March 1, 2008, to squash a post-presidential election protest that had turned into the occupation of Liberty Square. These kinds of descriptions of the postsocialist city were common among progressives. Shushan Avagyan, a founding member of the Queering Yerevan collective and a feminist writer and translator, for instance, once conveyed her opinion that the government wanted to render the public childlike (*mankakanatsnel hasarakutyuny*), in order to depoliticize the people and make them unaware and unable to resist.

In 2013 there was a public discussion about how to develop Republic Square. Although the leader of the Architect's Union of Armenia, Mkrtich Minasyan, argued that the Square was complete and had been for a long time and did not need any further development, the city called for proposals of plans for a redeveloped Square. A reporter for *ArmeniaNow* wrote: "Studying the submitted projects makes it clear that the majority has focused on the vacant space left after removing the Lenin statue, each of them suggesting a solution of sorts. One of the project authors suggests a church be built in that space, others suggest a giant cross, or an arch, or a lighthouse" (Gevorgyan 2013). The absence of Lenin's statue had left a vacancy, a gap, a missing Father that many, at least the architects who participated in the project, felt needed to be filled. The removal and nonreplacement of Lenin's statue was meaningful. In its absence, it stood as a symptom of Armenia's perversions.

Lenin, as a symbol, is critical to understanding Soviet as well as post-Soviet world-making. Alexei Yurchak (2017) has shown how Lenin—turned into *Leninism*, a doctrine of Soviet Truth that provided the grounds for the sovereignty of Soviet leadership—was only partially connected to the real historical flesh-and-blood Lenin. Lenin's actual word was banished from politics in 1924, even prior to his death, and subsequently canonized only in death. It is this double banishment (first politically and then in death) that gave Lenin his power as a symbol for sovereignty: Lenin's discourse became an empty signifier, an authoritative discourse through which all other Soviet leaders would have to speak (Yurchak 2005). Yurchak (2015) argues that the preservation of Lenin's body as physical form was tied to this project of maintaining Lenin(ism) as symbolic form. In this way, the toppling of Lenin's statues across the post-Soviet landscape can be read as a symbolic gesture of toppling (the sovereignty of) the Soviet Union itself. These monuments have not always been toppled, however. There are multiple ways in which they have produced new spatial and semiotic meanings in the post-Soviet era (Adams and Lavrenova 2022). In some cases, such as in Ukraine, "Leninfall" occurred much later. Lenin statues brought down during the 2014 "Revolution of Dignity"—and later legislatively justified in "decommunization laws"—can be read, as Anastasiya Pshenychnykh (2020) does, as deliberate attempts to transform contemporary feelings and relationships to the past during a politically heightened moment. This is not so much about the aftermath of the Soviet Union but about feelings about Russia within different spatiotemporal and geopolitical landscapes. While statues of Soviet-era leaders were toppled in Russia as well, nostalgia has more recently led to the restoration and upright placement of many once more in Moscow (including those of Lenin), giving the monuments new artistic and historical significance (Boym

2001). In Armenia, political feelings about the Soviet Union in 1991 were caught up in the politics of Nagorno-Karabakh. By the end of 1990, after two years of demanding, to no avail, that the centralized government unify the Nagorno-Karabakh Autonomous Oblast and the Armenian SSR, demands transformed into calls for independence. The fall of Lenin's statue, thus, came as a demand: the end of Soviet Armenia and the birth of an independent, unified Armenia (which never materialized politically). Now, decades later, there were no contemporary political leaders with the legitimacy to be put on a pedestal. There was a lack of a centralized ideology through which to produce a Symbolic order in the present. Lenin's disappearance, in other words, had only partially solved the problem of a sovereign Armenia.

During the Soviet era, all major landmarks in the city acted as symbols of state authority and official socialist ideology. Proposals for Lenin's statue to be replaced by a church perhaps speak to a desire to fill this gap. Churches built in the post-Soviet era have been meant to provide a meaningful center of legitimate authority. This has much to do with the role of the Armenian Apostolic Church in the Republic. While the Armenian state allows alternative religious organizations, including other denominations of Christianity, to exist in the country, the Republic, since its founding, has given a special privilege to the Armenian Apostolic Church. Unlike any other organization, the Church has permanent representatives in schools, prisons, and the armed forces. Serzh Sargsyan, Armenia's former president, consistently emphasized the Church as playing a critical role not only in national identity but also in national security (Mkrtchyan 2015). As Narek Mkrtchyan (2015) has argued, state cooperation with the Church provides a two-way relation that guarantees hegemony for both the state and the Church. While the state provides legitimacy for the Church, the Church also uses its social legitimacy to support state ideology. There is some continuity between this current arrangement and the historical dynamics between the Armenian Church and state. The Church—and especially the Armenian patriarchate of Constantinople—held great institutional power since the decline of the Armenian states/kingdoms in the fourteenth century, when the Church took up much of the responsibility in forging a collective identity for Armenians within and beyond the Ottoman Empire through ideology, intellectual life, and education (Ayvazyan 2018). In these ways, the Church has had an important place within Armenian public life for many centuries.

Because of the role of the political-economic elite (popularly deemed immoral) within contemporary Church politics, the legitimacy as well as the meaning of the Church in public life has been shifting. In 2013, oligarch Gagik (Dodi Gago) Tzarukyan opened a church in the city of Abovyan, on the outskirts of Yerevan—part of an ongoing project in which he said he aimed to build at least ten more churches in Armenia in the next five years. The opening of the church was a big national event to which then President Serzh Sargsyan, Belarussian president Alexandr Lukashenko, Robert Kocharyan (the second President of Armenia, who was responsible for the implementation of state violence on March 1, 2008), and others were invited. Gathered together outside of the church on a hot day in May, the invited statesmen and members of the public stood in front of a long banquet table on which snacks and drinks were served. For the statesmen and businessmen, this event would have looked like any other social event they attended regularly, with a full service of drinks (including bottled water) and food. For those who constituted the "public," who had been invited as a gesture to Armenian society, however, this was anything but regular. For them, the banquet table was much more attractive than the church itself as well as more immanent to life. As various news networks reported that evening, the president and the other political and business officials had already gone inside for the church's consecration and did not notice the hundreds of "hungry" people crowding the banquet table and grabbing anything they could get their hands on. Reports included video footage, showing security guards hired for the event helping people grab from large bowls of radishes and other food and stuffing it into plastic bags. This scene of desperation was one discussed for weeks that spring in Yerevan. The ostentatious display of food, drinks, and water that went largely untouched by the authorities but was ravaged by the crowds was a blatant display of Yerevan's perverse economic gap and oligarchic authority. The church, in other words, had little to offer in terms of its spatial configuration of the city of Abovyan. The public found meaning, instead, in the opportunity to scavenge that which was left over from the very theft of what had once been their commons. While state symbols like Lenin's statue stood for authority, they also configured senses of meaning and ideology that ordered life, thus providing Symbolic authority. Dodi Gago's church demanded respect for authority, but it provided little in return.

This large gap between everyday existence and the oligarchy's demand for recognition of their authority is further underscored by the layers of history in Armenia's landscape. In 2015, there was another church opening. This one involved a more complex politics of destruction, construction, and renewal. Yerevan's new Saint Anna Church was built right next to the thirteenth-century church known as the Holy Mother of God Katoghikos Church, which stood at the center of Yerevan. It had survived and had been preserved through the Soviet era. Until 2008, directly next to the Holy Mother of God Katoghikos Church was Armenia's Institute of Languages (a part of the National Academy of Sciences), a building that exhibited the centralized Soviet State's ideological devotion to learning and science. Academic institutions were important locations of state ideology, exemplifying the value placed on learning. "I must say that the tasks of the youth in general, and of the Young Communist Leagues and all other organisations in particular, might be summed up in a single word: learn," said Lenin (1920). But in 2008, this building of higher learning was taken down to build instead St. Anna's, a monument to the oligarchy's "mini-empire" (in the words of blogger Mika Artyan [2008]), or what Caroline Humphrey (1991) describes as a "suzerainty." The consecration of St. Anna's four pillars, on April 30, 2015, was undertaken by Archbishop Navasard Kchoyan, a de facto pocketed official of the church of then President Sargsyan's government. Kchoyan is best known, perhaps, for his Bentley, his handgun, and his defense of the right to have both. President Sargsyan, as well as other state officials, attended the consecration, making the ceremony one among many rituals celebrating not only the new churches filling Yerevan's urban landscape and the many layers of erasure and revision of the past but also the illegitimacy of this assemblage of corrupt institutions. Since independence in 1991, there have been one hundred new churches built in Armenia and Nagorno-Karabakh at an estimated cost of $50 million in construction, paid for by the political-economic elite (Sarukhanyan 2017). The city, once centralized and organized around ideology—an ideology that interpellated citizens into a common social project—had produced a gap between the wealthy and powerful—those condemned as Armenia's perverse (*aylandakvatz*) lot—and everyone else. Postsocialist public space monumentalized this gap and the elite's private wealth.

Queer and Perverse Wanderings

Ayda, Knar, and Hovhannes's concerns regarding contemporary Armenian life—tied to what they perceived as the spatial disconfiguration of their city—are moral in nature. Their concerns do not necessarily explicitly point to political-economic realities, and if they do, those realities are only (perhaps arbitrary) contexts for other processes that have gone wrong. Rather than capitalism, privatization, or the commodification of life and labor, the objects of their critique are life's meaninglessness as a result of a focus on survival or material accumulation, a lack of collective feeling that has led to degenerate behavior, and the senseless development projects that do not provide what people need but that might make some people rich. Similarly, critiques of oligarchs using their wealth to build churches when the masses are scrounging for their means for survival do not often question the processes by which the elite came upon their wealth. Castigation focuses, instead, on the humanitarian uses for which this wealth could be used, or on the lack of care the oligarchs show for their fellow Armenians. Underneath these moral condemnations, however, are feelings of anger, disgust, and weariness. These feelings are not articulated in politicized claims, yet they exhibit clear assessments of capital leaving life and its spaces in ruins. This is crucial as activists use these profound feelings of exasperation to cultivate politicized movements, as I will show in chapter 6. These feelings are commonly oriented toward figures deemed sexually and morally perverse—the homosexual and the oligarch whose actions are seen as producing degenerate spaces and as leading to the annihilation of Armenia; ultimately, however, they reveal capitalism as the perversion of life.

While late capitalism's organization, especially for those whose lives are undone and redone by its forces, might feel like disarray everywhere, its spatial configurations as perversion become clear in the experience of wandering through a post-Soviet city. Capital relies on forms of speculation and uneven development for the purposes of dispossession/repossession, making disorder out of order to privilege private wealth and its continued accumulation. Capital wanders through landscapes looking for opportunities with only private wealth as its plan. The speculative organization overlaid onto a planned economy and planned public space produces an arrhythmia, an offbeat affective experience that might only be discernible from the position of having once experienced a rhythm. This is not to say that Soviet planning was perfectly in rhythm or that there were no moments of speculative imagining or ideological contradiction. But the objective of those plans (even in their moments and spaces of failure), of fulfilling human needs, of providing an ideology of social need and structural care, was motivated by a sense of cohesion that capital lacks not only in practice but also in theory. Capital's (dis)organization does not provide answers to the *why* that the Soviet regime provided. Sometimes there are no answers—development occurs but with seemingly no apparent rhyme or reason. Sometimes life is organized in ways that feel without purpose, without meaning. At other times, the continuity of life that moved from one space to another becomes a discontinuous wandering with little connection between places of work, life, production, reproduction, leisure, and fun, and with no centralized underpinning to explain why. Yerevan, as a post-Soviet city, thus, becomes a site of leisurely wandering transformed into wandering-as-ontology. This wandering is perverse—a purposeless movement of meanings and ideologies that have no concrete locale, no destination other than the thriving of wealth in elite hands.

Perverse wandering-as-ontology is also, however, a site that makes possible queerness: practices of desire, love, intimacy, sex, and social reproduction that deviate from the proper and that thrive in conditions abandoned by moral surveillance, by the Law of the Father. This queerness is also without plan, rhyme, or reason. (Dis)organized abandonment perverts the continuity of a proper, surviving Armenianness led by a strong, moral Father, and thus makes possible perversion's *other*—queer—side. This queer possibility cannot just be dismissed as the openness of capital to pluralism and the diversification of lifestyles (see, for instance, Muñoz's [2009] critique of this). This analysis has repercussions for how we understand the making of space in the context of neoliberalization. Spaces abandoned by the state and capital are also abandoned by moral policing and its insistence on propriety, thus leaving space for and making possible forms of life and existence outside of propriety. This visible queer life in new queer spaces is condemned as perversion because it emerges in a context of improper life conditions—as the failures of the means of reproduction. Moral panic and, along with it, sex panic, result from capitalist alienation and discontent and, thus, alongside these feelings of impropriety are also condemnations of a perverse political economy.

Perverse political economies, however, might also make possible queer new worlds—worlds of the future evincible in the present uses of abandoned spaces, like in the Botanical Gardens. Moral abandonment makes room for new, emergent, and queer potentials for unprecedented futures that complicate any formulaic demand or desire that the nation survive in its current ontological form. That some queer life dwells within these abandoned and out-of-the-way places is seen by some, like Arthur, as a sad reality that must be overcome. However, while these are not necessarily proper and respectable forms of life—including respectable lesbian, gay, bisexual, or transgender identities and lives—their untamed existence continues to produce unsettling potentials for other worlds and other kinds of life in the margins of public space. The modes of production that follow state socialism produce disorientations but also possibilities for human as well as more-than-human life. Queer wanderings in postsocialist urban space, such as the queer tour of Yerevan that Arthur gave me in the summer of 2011, move in pursuit of signs of sexual and gendered alterity and pass through abandoned spaces back into spaces-in-development and back into abandoned spaces that are differentially impacted by the signs of postsocialist development. These wanderings orient themselves around queer desire and, as they do so, they also produce new cartographies—new paths made of escape and discovery. Abandoned spaces like the Hrazdan *dzor* or the Botanical Garden become sites of emergent perversions as well as sites of emergent refuge and belonging—that is, until they are un-abandoned and become sites of capital's speculation and interrupt the possibilities of movement and the logic of life. Postsocialist spatial perversions—spaces in ruins and the queer potentialities embedded within them—also have critical temporal impacts, to which I now turn.

Put aside empty arguments,
Aimless and misplaced
I lost the pages of my mind . . .
And the right address, and the right address, for my here. . . .

RUBEN HAKHVERDYAN, FROM "MY WHITE HORSE"
("CHERMAK DZIS")

But the slumbering city was not placated; it was volatile.
Who could predict when it might rouse, bolt, and hurtle
us all into the future?

SAIDIYA HARTMAN, *LOSE YOUR MOTHER*

CHAPTER FIVE

An Improper Present

"My sweet girls, it's good that you are interested in finding out about Armenian families. It's very important. But you will not find anything. There are no families in Armenia. There are no families left. You should research something else." These were the words of Arpine, an older woman in the neighborhood of Sasuntsi David, who had invited us into her home after Lucine Talalyan, my research collaborator, and I knocked on her door one morning in March 2013. She offered us coffee. We refused, as we usually did, but she insisted, so we waited in her living room while she went to the kitchen to prepare it. When she returned with the coffee, we asked her our first question, about the role of family in Armenia. "Family is the base [*himk*] of Armenia," she said, which we had come to expect after a month of these interviews. "Family is the base of Armenia," as well as its negation, "There are no families in Armenia," or some other versions of each were repeated by a majority of those with whom we spoke. Arpine continued to explain that without the family, there could not be a nation (*azg*) because it is the family that provides the nation its strength and it is the family that has allowed Armenians to survive. I asked Arpine about the contradiction of what she had just stated and what she had said earlier, about there not being families in

Armenia. "This is the problem. The government does not let the people have families. Most people are leaving, starting families elsewhere, and those who stay are unable to create their families. Because of the economic situations they face, even when they do, the pressure destroys [*kandum e*] the family," Arpine clarified. Families were being destroyed, and the nation was on a similar path to destruction.

This chapter examines the negating articulations of Armenia in the present. "There are no Armenian families," "There is no Armenia," "There are no Armenians," "There is no Armenian government," and other such statements were repeated time and again as Talalyan and I went door to door talking to Yerevantsis about their everyday lives and experiences of family. These statements are metaphorical. They form an idiomatic style within the Armenian language, expressing the inadequacy of something by dismissing its existence altogether. But the commonality of these claims during the time I was conducting my research points to widespread sentiment that something was seriously the matter with the nation. These negations take us to the heart of the widespread feeling that Armenia's perverse realities had destroyed the nation's possibilities for proper social reproduction.

The emphasis of these statements was most often on the political-economic realities of post-Soviet life: the destruction of social welfare mechanisms, the high cost of necessary goods and services, unemployment and underemployment, the theft of the commons by the ruling elite, and high taxes levied on small businesses and on other property. These realities were part and parcel of privatization and the emergence of capitalism that had given rise to the oligarchy. However, like Ayda, Hovhannes, and Knar in the previous chapter, who felt that Yerevan's spatial disconfiguration was spurring on and spurred by lack of meaning and purpose and thus producing degenerate behavior, our interlocutors frequently discussed these systemic and structural realities of postsocialism in moral terms. While individuals complained about real conditions of precarity caused by privatization—the cutting of state welfare mechanisms, monopolies, and political violence that evidenced a Republic in political-economic ruins—these realities were expressed through the rhetoric of a nation and morality in ruins. For many of our interlocutors, these historical changes had repercussions beyond history—in other words, beyond events, structures, and systems. Under the conditions of the moral and sexual perversions within everyday life and its grave consequences for proper social reproduction, Armenia's Symbolic order, the realm in which the nation took collective moral and ideological shape, was becoming something no longer recognizable to itself.

The contradictory simultaneity of the negation, "There are no families in Armenia," and the affirmation of the family as the "base" or foundation of Armenia indicates a spatiotemporal disturbance. Armenianness was out of step with its proper temporal path. While scholars who have analyzed forms of negating statements that have existed since the 1990s point to a "before" and "after" of the Soviet Union[1]—perhaps rightfully so—the negations Talalyan and I consistently heard did not necessarily pose themselves against any particular temporal domain of a "before." While we frequently came upon discussions of how life was once better in the Soviet Union, we also heard claims about *mer papery* (our forefathers), the heroes of Armenia's longer history, and the millennia of a surviving and thriving Armenianness. There were also different post-Soviet presents: the one that existed prior to 2008 (before the state's use of the military to violently crush peaceful protest), when resistance and the making of a proper future were still possibilities on the horizon; and the one that came after 2008, when change was no longer a prospect. Armenianness, in other words, was Armenianness until a Symbolic, rather than a necessarily historical, rupture occurred. Our interlocutors most frequently longed for a proper Armenian present, that which had existed throughout the nation's history; and they felt that this, the present, was an improper time.

Even as these statements are negating in their affect toward the present, they carry potentials for futures that may not be dependent on propriety. If the *aylandakutyun* (moral perversion) of the nation places Armenianness and Armenia in crisis, these perversions also have potentials for future forms of being and becoming that might not look like or be in continuity with Armenian pasts. In the previous chapter, I focused on the radical spatiotemporal possibilities of capitalism's perversion of space—wherein both the state and capital leave spaces abandoned and thus less surveilled by the Law of the Father, opening up spaces for the experience of queer intimacy. I argued that these spaces of abandonment were not proper and dignified; they unsettled present propriety and placed the future of Armenianness in question. Here I am interested in how negations of the present, based on the transformation of political economy, make possible potentialities of radically different futures. Talalyan's and my interlocutors at times touched upon the potentials for new, unknown, and perhaps not even Armenian futures within the moral ruins of the past and present. These potential futures are not often celebrated, certainly. They were mourned, instead, as signaling the end of Armenianness. However, reading between the lines, I show how within these rhetorics of the nation's moral perversion are potentials for queer futurity.

Interrogating futurity in an anxious context, I focus on the transformations of an ontological Armenianness taking place along with political-economic shifts. Will there be a future for the nation? Will it be a future of survival—an ongoingness of Armenianness? Or will contemporary perversions transform the nation so deeply that what comes after will be something else? Descriptions of Armenia as a country that is no longer legible as a country (as Armenia) articulate "asignifying ruptures" (Deleuze and Guattari 1987, 9), carrying potentiality in a multiplicity of directions. They might become resignified and then reorder a chaotic world into a proper one again. They might, however, also refuse resignification and make way for "unruly visions" (Gopinath 2018) of an Armenia that might not look like something that has existed before— something in continuity—but something that might exist otherwise. These are forms of (potential) futures that may be queer: futures that do not resignify, domesticate, or normalize the present but deviate toward unprecedented space-times.

Families in Ruin

On the first day of our survey interviews among households in Yerevan, in February 2013, Talalyan and I were making our way down the stairs from the third floor to the second floor of a residential building in Shengavit, when we were greeted with suspicion at the landing. Mkrtich and Karen, two men who had lived in the building their entire lives, were making their way up the stairwell. "Who are you? Are you looking for someone?" asked Mkrtich. He was familiar with most residents, he told us. He even made sure to get to know the new ones. We explained that we were conducting interviews with households regarding the role of the family. Mkrtich's suspicion waned. "If you want, I can tell you everything and you won't have to conduct any more interviews," he started. "I can tell you, for instance, that there is no family in Armenia."

Mkrtich was in his thirties, married, with two children. Karen was in his late twenties and not yet married. They had known each other for Karen's whole life—both had been raised in the building, but in separate units. Talalyan and I learned that they were just returning from the airport, where they had dropped off their last remaining friend in Armenia who had, like all their other friends, finally decided to emigrate. Mkrtich was living with his parents and his wife and sons, and Karen with his mother, father, and sister. "I want to know what family you are talking about," Karen demanded, turning to Mkrtich and rhetorically muttering, "They're asking about the family." After a dismissive sidebar for a few moments, they returned to our larger conversation, determined to convince us of their perspective. There were no families in Armenia. When asked to elaborate about the family's lack of existence, Mkrtich referred to the massive depopulation of the country: "There are no Armenian *people* left. If out of four or five million people, there are one [million] left, what Armenian people? There's no one left here." Our interlocutors, who often alluded to this depopulation as the continuation of the Genocide, saw poverty, unemployment, underemployment, the lack of necessary social services, and the high cost of living due to monopolies—the results of the ruling elite's immorality as I discussed in chapter 3—as the main factors spurring emigration.

For Karen and Mkrtich, as well as for many others, the ruling elite had done more than cause emigration. They had left "families in ruin" (*qandvac dnner*) by perverting the proper roles and functions of the family's composition, especially the proper masculinity of the Father. Like many of our interlocutors, Karen and Mkrtich insisted that the institution of the Armenian family was different from that of other nations and, like other Armenians, they maintained that the family was more essential to the survival of the Armenian nation than it was for other nations. If it were not for the Armenian family, they explained, Armenians would have been wiped off the map of peoples of the world during the early twentieth-century Genocide, if not millennia before that. When Talalyan and I asked Karen and Mkrtich to discuss the differences between the Armenian family and those of other nations, Mkrtich identified the "strong father" who was, in the present, disappearing:

MKRTICH: For the Armenian man, one characteristic that makes him better is that he will do any job to take care of his family. He is the master [*der kangnogh*, which also carries a sense of responsibility] of his wife, of his children. The father. He will do anything and never complain about it. A man who loves his family, I mean someone who really loves his family, he can't live here.

This is not about some kind of patriotism or who really loves his nation and who doesn't or something like this. This is a matter of really loving your children. If a man really loves his children, he cannot stay here. It becomes a matter of time—leaving one hour or two hours earlier is a matter of how much you are going to benefit your children.

TALALYAN: But things change, of course. Roles are changing—men and women are changing.

MKRTICH: Yeah, but the negative changes are coming from the wrong places. Everything changes, of course. The country changes, the government changes, families change, new technologies emerge. But if it's a negative change, then why? Because the Armenian father makes sure that his children are raised right so that things will only progress toward the good. In our own time we didn't know what family ruin [*dun qandvel*] was, but now a three-year old child understands all of that. He sees everything and then notices what is happening. He is only a three-year old boy [talking about his own son].

Mkrtich ignored the impetus of Talalyan's question—about the assumption that men and fathers are breadwinners, a role that many women assume today. He did, however, concede that things change, although to him these changes were negative. For Mkrtich, it was not feminists who were responsible for the destruction of the patriarchal household; it was the political-economic elite. Here there seems to be an inversion of cause within rhetorics of *aylaserutyun* (sexual perversion), which is said to be founded on the figure of the homosexual, and *aylandakutyun* (moral perversion), which is said to be rooted in the figure of the oligarch. For Mkrtich, it was the oligarch who was causing the sexual and gendered perversions of the family. In Mkrtich's analysis, the slippages between sexual perversion and larger moral perversion are key because they provide insight into how political-economic processes—because of their impact on social reproduction—become concerns regarding moral propriety that then easily veer into questions of the sexual.

Throughout the interview, both Karen and Mkrtich repeated *chen toghnum, chen toghnum* (they don't let you, they don't let you) almost compulsively. At one point, Talalyan asked them, "Who doesn't let you? What don't they let you do?" Mkrtich explained:

MKRTICH: They don't let you provide for a family. The family is impossible (*anhnarin*). . . . Right now, I'm here but that doesn't mean that I am not constantly looking for opportunities to leave. I work any job I can get my hands on—construction work here, electrical work there. But there are so many like me looking for employment, so I get paid very little. If I refuse a job, someone else will be there to take it right away, for lower pay. Listen, the problem is not only economic. The problem is about dignity. The Armenian family has to have a strong father. When my son sees me constantly struggling, he doesn't see a strong father.

ME: But your son sees you struggling for the good of your family. Isn't this what you mean by strong father?

MKRTICH: Yes, of course, the Armenian father will do everything he can to do the best for his family. But what I mean by struggle is that those in the government do not allow me to have my dignity. And my son sees this. Lots of children see this. It is not just fathers. Mothers too. Everyone. I do not have any personal or familial freedoms here. If I want to start a business, for example, so that I can make a better life, they will not let me. . . . The taxes and restrictions they place on businesses—I won't even discuss the ways in which these larger chains, supermarkets, and so on already make it impossible—some oligarch or government official working for an oligarch will come stomp me out. In short, Armenian citizens are not treated like people. And our children see this. And we cannot have the family life that our forefathers [*mer papery*]—even in the Soviet times—had. Do you understand? . . . People who care for their families are leaving. And who is left? These *aylandakner* are becoming even stronger and making it more impossible for others like me to stay. We all want to leave. In this way, in a few years, there will be no more Armenia.

In Mkrtich's analysis, there was a metonymic link between fathers, like himself, and the Fathers who filled the seats of Armenia's authority. Without legitimate Fathers, fathers themselves had become illegitimate—they could no longer be the strong, dignified men who looked after their families. Without a "strong" man and father in the household, children also did not learn proper roles, and they might then themselves become immoral and undignified. For these reasons, Mkrtich insisted that any Armenian father who cared for his family would try to leave the country, leaving Armenia empty and in ruins. While financial needs mattered, these moral deviations weighed heavily on his understanding of what had gone wrong and would continue to go wrong in the nation.

Problems with the impossibility of proper masculinity also unearthed concerns around domestic violence.[2] Among the first twenty interviews Talalyan and I conducted, we realized that many of our interlocutors were often bringing up this problem themselves—usually indirectly as a lack of peace and kindness among family members. We added a question to our existing repertoire to explore this further. And going forward, most of our respondents agreed: there was domestic violence in Armenia, there was too much of it, and it was because of social and economic conditions affecting familial relations. As Violet, a woman in her late fifties, explained: "People fight a lot more now and sometimes, because life is so anxious [*anhangist*], it leads to physical violence." Violet used many comparisons between the postsocialist "now" and the Soviet "then" to describe changes to the Armenian family. She spoke of the conditions of solidarity in Soviet times, and how these had dwindled in the present. Aghavni, a woman in her forties, explained, "There are so many reasons to fight nowadays. It wasn't like this before. Husband and wife fight about money, they fight about their children and how to raise them right, they fight about whether the woman should work, how much she should work. There are too many reasons. These conditions are ruining families." Aghavni added, "Armenian men are not violent. But, they have become pathetic in these conditions and unfortunately, sometimes they resort to violence." In the conditions of perversion, what was once the (nonviolent and loving, dignified) Armenian man had become something other.

There was a contradiction between the ways our interlocutors approached the problem of domestic violence and the ways in which it was often represented in popular media. During a 2016 press conference in Yerevan, psychologist Anna Badalyan suggested that it was largely "through a woman's fault that a hand is raised against her," and that "if a woman is well-established and psychologically mature, cases of violence will be reduced" (Alina Nikoghosyan 2016). These kinds of explanations (victim blaming) of domestic violence were also articulated in popular culture—such as in serial television shows in which violence against women was common but resulted from a woman stepping out of her place and upsetting a man in her life. Within these narratives, in order to avoid violence against herself, a woman should avoid crossing a man's authority and stay in her proper, natural role as silent mother and caretaker. Our interlocutors, however, and especially the women,[3] often discussed domestic violence as a result of larger life conditions—both within the space of the familial home and within the larger space of the nation-family. Women also frequently highlighted the novelty of domestic violence as a new phenomenon that had no place among Armenian traditions and that was not properly Armenian.[4] Many of the men and women with whom we spoke, however, also insisted on the man's position as the proper master of his home. Even if violence against women was not properly Armenian, in other words, a narrative of the man as master of his home frequently established domestic violence as a natural extension of a man's proper role.

Women, while often agreeing that men were the proper masters of the home but that violence against women was improper, more frequently attributed this violence to economic tensions and particular reconstructions of gender roles in hard times. Shushan, for instance, was putting her newborn daughter down for a nap when we knocked on her door. She joined us in her living room a few minutes later. Becoming a mother, she told us, had changed her opinions on many matters.

> It's hard, you understand? Living in this country, with all of the corruption, economic concerns, people leaving. We don't know our future. Before I had the baby my husband and I were both working. I plan on returning to work soon, but we fight about this a lot. I want to work but I also want to raise my daughter. He [her husband] thinks that I should be home with her. But we cannot afford that. We both need to work. And he thinks that if he is a good father he should make enough for all of us as a family. But this is not possible. These are the kinds of things we fight about. And our situation is better, I think, than most people. I used to think that domestic violence or other such phenomena were extreme situations, but now I am thinking about these kinds of issues a lot. It's not happening in our home, but I can understand how it happens. Ours is a masculine culture. Men like to feel strong. But in these pitiful conditions it is hard for men to feel strong so they start becoming anxious.

Shushan, like many other women with whom we spoke, contextualized the common occurrence of domestic violence within that of a larger economic crisis, but she also attributed it to changes in masculinity and masculine behavior within that larger context. Some people also linked the violence within homes to the general perversion of the authorities (the Fathers) of the nation. Remember, for instance, Astghik in chapter 3, who objected to the violence of the "brutes" in power because that violence does not just stay out there; it comes home. The public (political-economic) mechanisms in the country had produced new masculinities—violent, pathetic, anxious, and aggressive—and, thus, produced new, gendered tensions between men and women in the home.

Men, however, more commonly insisted that domestic violence was wrong and left it at that. In the neighborhood of Charbakh, we spoke to Hrach and his three sons in their living room. He told us that he has taught his sons never to raise a hand against a woman "no matter what she did"; as he said this, he looked to his teenage sons for approval, and they each nodded in agreement. "A man is larger and stronger and whatever a woman has done cannot be solved with physical violence. A man who uses his strength on a woman like that is not a man," he added. Hrach, like other men who told us that domestic violence was never appropriate, qualified this claim by recentering a woman's behavior as being at the heart of the violence. In this way, men's discussion of violence within the home framed it as wrong, but without any context for how and why it happened—aside from a woman's inappropriate behavior. Men were willing to naturalize the phenomenon more so than women were.

Even as economic tensions were a part of the analytic framework that our interlocutors, especially women, used to make sense of domestic violence, and even as their narratives often refused violence as inappropriate culturally, these explanations were not necessarily politicized ones. Rather than an analysis of the relationship between capitalism and patriarchy,[5] "economy" and "financial difficulties" were put into moralistic terms. Blame was laid not on the economic structures or systems but on the moral qualities of the ruling elite. Both men and women with whom we spoke usually understood Armenianess as a "masculine culture" and rarely named capitalism as a problem. It was the kinds of men—improperly masculine men—who ran the country and their immoralities that were taken as problematic. Conceivably, then, if Armenia had more proper men to govern it—who could govern in morally appropriate ways (through patriarchy as well as through capitalism)—then these problems, which were moral in nature, would not exist.

The rhetoric of families in ruin highlights a spatiotemporal perversion of home (space) as well as the present (time). While the language of "ruin" focused in on the space of home—where fathers no longer lived in the conditions necessary to be good men and fathers, and where financial tensions led to violence, upsetting the peaceful balance that should have existed there—these senses of home included the space of the nation. Within our interlocutors' analyses, families themselves were ruined through their metonymic relation to the illegitimate Fathers of the nation-family. While these Fathers, the political-economic elite who also were in the position to govern the nation's Symbolic order, should have provided moral authority so that the nation could continue to be proper and survive, they instead upset this order by way of their excessive enjoyment (surplus jouissance), which in turn also continued to produce a larger context of a ruined nation-family in which there were no longer any proper families.

The Emptying of Tradition

While most of our interlocutors prioritized economic concerns but moralized them, there were also some who understood the destruction of Armenia as embedded purely in the disintegration of morality. They highlighted the loss of traditions and values to Westernization and Russification, both of which were seen as having had dire effects on the structures of familial care and intimacy. Very few of those with whom we spoke made mention of the homosexual. However, in highlighting the importance of tradition and of specifically Armenian values that were being destroyed by the import and influence of the West and Russia, these framings had much in common with the rhetoric of sexual perversion (aylaserutyun) in which the figure of the homosexual is located. This was especially true in the depoliticization and moralization that discussions of tradition as such advanced. Elizabeth and Hrant, whom I discuss further below, as well as a few others, with whom Talalyan and I spoke, separated morality from political economy, deflecting from questions of power in much the same way that the figure of the homosexual did. For them and a few others, the disintegration of proper Armenianness was a sui generis moral problem. These moral problems, however, were far larger than homosexuality.

Anna and her mother-in-law, Elizabeth, argued that the time of "now" was one of cultural deterioration. Following up on this claim, we asked them if the Armenian family was different from other families in other nations. They both responded with a strong, "Yes, of course," and then, when asked to expand, Elizabeth offered the following.

ELIZABETH: The Armenian family is *avandapasht* [literally, tradition-worshipping], my dear. It's in the blood, the blood.

TALALYAN: What traditions are Armenian?

ELIZABETH: Just imagine, you have to imagine . . . I had gone to an excursion *ardasahmanum* [to a foreign country, in this case a Western European country] when I was young and there, there were half naked women in bars, dancing. They invited me to come out with them to one of those nightclubs. I didn't want to go.

ANNA: Well, they're different, of course. What we call tradition differs . . .

ELIZABETH: And this was waaaay back, probably thirty years ago. Imagine what has happened to them now. But with us too, of course, a lot of things have changed. . . . For example, now young people say, "Okay, that's your opinion. Don't push it on me. Don't violate my rights. Let us grow up however we want. Live however we want. Breathe the way we want. Wake up when we want, eat what we want." How can this be allowed?! A family is a family. They have to wake up together, sit down to eat at the table together, understand each other, recognize each other, right? But now they've made it so that everyone is for themselves—when they wake up, when they eat—everything the way they want it for themselves. But see this is not good. This is not proper [*chisht chi*]. The value of the family gets lost in this way.

ANNA: Mom *jan* [dear], this has nothing to do with anything. It comes from the conditions of the country, from not having bread . . . it's all dependent on money, if people can get by.

ELIZABETH: *Jan*, listen . . . a strong family is the basis of our country. If the family is strong, where everyone is strongly connected to one another—where the big family is the public itself—when that [the public] itself connects and relates as a family, where everyone in the public relates as a family to everyone else in the public, do you understand what a big success for our country that is? After that there will be no defeating us. We have been a small people, but against that big Persia, Vardan Mamikonyan [the fifth-century military leader who led Armenians in a battle against the Persian Empire and was able to defend Armenia's rights to practice Christianity] won when he forced the opposing army to go back. Or else why would they move back? The Turks, they would have by now eaten us raw otherwise. The Armenian people are very smart. When we play chess, when I feel in a bind, I start to think more strongly. And in these cases, I always win. We always come out of difficult situations. Why am I telling you this? Man, especially the Armenian people, when he feels constrained, his mind works better. You see it all the time. Whenever we are in tight times, we start to cooperate with one another. See?

When Elizabeth connected the family unit to other families who made up a public, she was articulating a sense of the nation-family. However, according to her narrative, this nation-family was being weakened by those who learned foreign values. One of these foreign values was the liberation, based on individuality, that young people wanted from their kin. This loss was mourned by Elizabeth as well as by others as a loss of the traditional, close-knit Armenian family that lived together, ate together, and was intimately aware of the lives and experiences of each of its members. The placement of value on individuation—especially as young people saw themselves as separate from their families and wanted to make their own decisions—took away from the collective sensibilities of a strong family and a strong nation and further weakened these entities' ability to stand strong against other, foreign values.

While both Anna and Elizabeth agreed that the Armenian family, and thus Armenia's strength as a nation, was disintegrating, they disagreed on how and why. For Anna, Armenia was in a difficult situation; it was in a political and economic bind where people were finding it difficult to have access to "bread." For Elizabeth, however, the issues were entirely moral: Armenians, through their commitment to proper morality, have to gather their collective strength in times of such crises. A dominating tension was palpable between Elizabeth and Anna. Elizabeth, the mother of the man of the house, was the woman in charge, and Anna—although not really expressing any discontent about this, at least not during the time of the interview—acquiesced to Elizabeth's claims and her speech. It would also be important to note that Elizabeth had also been senior to Anna when they both worked in the same school as teachers, where Anna still worked at the time of the interview and from which Elizabeth had already retired. Later in our discussion, as I will take up below, they examined this dominating relationship through their understandings of their personalities.

There were others with whom we spoke who articulated the problem in the language of lost traditions and values. Some mourned the fact that their sons and daughters—or if not theirs then those of others—were "living separately" in nuclear households and away from their patrilocal places of residence. While there was some tolerance for young married couples moving out when there was no room, when multiple siblings and their families continued to reside in their father's home, or when there might be tension between mother and daughter-in-law, moving out for reasons of privacy was deemed untraditional. While none of our interlocutors discussed any cases in which sons or daughters had moved out prior to marriage—an act that in Yerevan at the time was seen as a betrayal of the family and the adoption of a perverse way of life—this was something that frequently came up within my own social circles and that more often than not led to fighting and discontentment in families when it was a daughter who made the choice (Shirinian 2018a).

Aside from the problem of "living separately," which some ascribed to ideas that had been improperly and immorally imported into Armenia from the West, living in Russia was also seen as destructive to Armenian traditions. As Karen said during our interview, "Armenians are now wandering (*taparum en*) around the world, with no home. Do you think they just hold on to their own values and traditions when they are there—let's say in Russia? No! They become Russian. They become Turk. They become I don't know what—Yezidi even." Karen was expressing what many others feared as well—that Armenians were emigrating in such large numbers that it did not just leave Armenia empty, it also meant that Armenianness was itself disintegrating, being emptied of its content, through movement abroad.

Hrant, a man in his sixties, told us that his two brothers had both gone to Moscow and opened businesses there. They were living fine, Hrant told us, "but they lost their patriotism. It is gone. Completely disappeared." When I asked Hrant what he meant by this, he told us a story:

> Let me bring to you an example. My brother's daughter, who is unmarried, stays out until the middle of the night, worrying the whole

family [after asking, we found out that the woman in question was twenty-six years old]. Can you imagine? Everyone is calling here and there trying to find this girl. Then when she comes home, she tells them that it is none of their business where she has been or with whom. My sister-in-law says to her, "My dear girl, you can call and let us know you are okay, you are safe," tells her how worried her father has been, and this girl doesn't even apologize! She has no sense of father, no respect for her father, none of them do, the ones raised there. This is how they will become Russian.

For Hrant, losing respect for one's father is equivalent to losing a sense of patriotism as well as Armenianness—or becoming Russian. This loss took precedence over other concerns of Armenians in Russia, who have faced discrimination as well as acts of white supremacist violence.[6] Hrant, as if on script, repeated almost verbatim words we had heard from Karen a few weeks earlier: "Like this, there will be no more Armenian people anywhere in the world in a few years."

A Present with No Future

The feeling of lacking a proper present was emotionally contagious in Yerevan. It had spread from one household to another, from one building to another. Talalyan and I sensed it in almost every interview we conducted. As a contagion, this sense that the present was improper had effects on the collectively imagined possibilities of a future. "Because here there is no future. I look for one, but I have not found one yet and I don't think there ever will be one," Karen said. "What do people have left here? What can they have? What opportunities do they have for some kind of life?" he continued. All that people had left, Mkrtich explained, was the home their family received from the Soviet system. And this often became the only thing of value that they could sell in order to leave the country. "But is there no other way? What about struggling against this system—against the oligarchs and the authorities?" Talalyan asked. Mkrtich's response situated the present (it was 2013) against the backdrop of an Armenia that had once existed (in 2008) and in which people were willing to struggle during post-presidential election protests.

Yes, of course we participated on March 1st. There were thousands of people there. If you paid attention, at those *mitings* [political rallies], and what was happening there, you would have noticed that only workers were participating. People who had a business, or a job, or something to lose. Ninety percent of them were people who had a theory about how to save this country. These are the kinds of people who struggled. So that things would be well for them. So that their families would be safe and taken care of. But now—let me tell you what is happening now. Back then—it wasn't that long ago, five years—people had a sense of how to change things to go better. But now, things are only turning toward the bad. When I think about the future, in this country, I see nothing good. This is the difference. Because when people look forward, they see nothing.

Mkrtich saw the present (of 2013) as different from the present of a time not that long past (of 2008). *That* present was a time in which the kind of people who struggled still existed in Armenia. It was a time in which there were still workers who had a stake in changes that might benefit their lives. *This* present, the one in which Mkrtich was now speaking to Talalyan and me, was one where those very workers no longer existed in Armenia.

When pressed to explain further what he meant by the "kinds of people who struggle" and what had happened to those people today (in 2013), Mkrtich offered two explanations. First, many of those who once would have struggled had now left the country. "These were my friends, these were the people who I personally knew. And I am telling you that many of them are gone today." To this he also added that the very meanings of "struggle" had also changed; if Armenians were once willing to struggle for a better life and a better country through collective efforts in Armenia (such as through the independence movement at the end of the 1980s and early 1990s), struggle now meant leaving the country entirely, because individuals' and families' well-being and survival depended on being somewhere else, on getting out. Second, those who had stayed were no longer the same people who had once been willing to struggle. The illegitimate repressive horde had transformed them into different creatures. They had nothing to gain or to lose anymore, and they no longer sensed that anything could ever be different. Following the state violence on March 1, 2008, Armenians, Karen added, knew what happened to those who struggled in Armenia:

> If you don't get killed on the street, then you will get killed in your own home at night when they come and find you. Or, if they don't find you, you will die as a victim of the revolution, starving for years

without work while you are struggling and waiting for something to change.

The present of 2008 and the present of 2013 were very different temporal realities. Seeing nothing good in this present (2013) meant being unable to project anything good into a future time (a future present). Karen explained that this realization had changed him to the core: knowing that nothing would ever change in this country and that there was no point in struggle had made him a different person. If there had been a future for Armenia in 2008, the present of 2013 no longer offered such possibilities.

Talalyan and I had begun these interviews, for better or for worse, in the time leading up to the 2013 presidential election, and we wrapped them up a little over a month following the elections. During post-election protests, the opposition leader Raffi Hovhannisyan of the Heritage Party (Jarangutyun) condemned the reelection of Serzh Sargsyan as fraudulent and insisted on his resignation. We asked our interlocutors who complained about the oligarchy if they attended the almost daily *mitings* that made up the protests. Some said that they did but that they also had no hope that anything would change. Others told us that the only reason they attended *mitings* was to make sure that they were aware of what was taking place, because they distrusted any media that would report on the developments. Yet others told us they went only because they had nothing else to do. "What else am I going to do? Sit here and watch *serialner* [serial television shows]? If I had a job, I would go to work. If I had money, I would go to a café with my friends. But I don't have anything. So I go to *mitings*," explained Hrayr, a man in his fifties. "No, I don't see it. I thought you were an intelligent researcher and you are here asking me about what changes I want to see in Armenia. What changes? Have you gone mad? Nothing. Nothing will change. This country is *aylandak* [morally perverse] and it will remain *aylandak*."

The improprieties of the present were obstacles to the unfurling of temporality: a present in continuity with the past and headed toward a future were placed into question because the present was no longer in continuity with the past and had been perverted beyond the range of possibilities of what could be called an Armenia. These notions of an improper present produce a "devastating logic" of the here and now (Muñoz 2009, 12), a sense that what is here and now is all that can ever be. While denying the present (as too improper to qualify as a spatiotemporal moment within Armenia [as expressed through negating statements]), these narratives were also hyperattentive to the present. When we reflected on our interviews each day, Talalyan and I frequently commented on this feeling of impossibility—the "politics of the present" was made up of political-economic assumptions that chained us to the present, as if what has *not yet* been tried and done is unimaginable (M. Davis 2010, 45). It felt monotonous. Throughout the interviews we conducted, we heard stories of woe—a mother of a disabled adult who could not get access to critical care needs for her son and who was also having a hard time getting food on the table and whose husband was consistently missing in action from home and his responsibilities toward his family; a young couple who had tried their luck in Russia with hopes for a better life and had returned to Yerevan, having lost everything, and were now starting over (again) with nothing; a woman whose husband had taken to gambling and, in her efforts to make ends meet, had desperately been looking for a job only to find that most employers wanted someone far younger than her. The stories and complaints differed in their situational complexities. But they shared an orientation toward impossibility. "I'm tired [of these interviews]. Is there not anyone in this city who believes that things can be different?" Talalyan once exclaimed, exasperated, as we left one building and were wondering if we should try another building or retire for the day. That day, we decided to cut the interviewing short—having done only three rather than the usual five interviews. This was only three weeks into our survey. She, as well as I, were exhausted by this extreme present. It seemed as though there was nothing but now, and this now was already at an end.

While we did not necessarily plan on it, I noticed that as time went by and the feelings of impossibility within the interviews accumulated, we began to hear and listen differently, finding small ruptures in which a future could be glimpsed from within discourses and affects of hopelessness. If our interlocutors could not see possibility, hope, and a future, we began to see it for them, in their own discourse.

Potentiality of Ruins

Our conversation with Gayane was short. We did not enter her home, but lingered in the hallway of her building for some time. When she opened the door, she sat on a chair she had in her small apartment doorway. Gayane was an older woman, in her seventies, who lived alone in an apartment in Charbakh. Her only son had left Armenia and lived in Moscow where he had settled, married, and now had a family. As we were speaking with her—her seated in her doorway, Talalyan and I standing in the hallway—a young boy came by. "Ms. Gayane, do you need anything from the store today?" he asked. Gayane gave him a bit of money that she had in her dress pocket and sent him to the store down the street to get bread. Gayane had many health concerns that required medications she could pay for only with the money her son would send back. But her poor health, especially a problem that affected the circulation in her legs, prevented her not only from being able to make it to the pharmacy to get the medications but from getting to the store to buy food. "But this young boy, he comes by every day. He goes to the store for me. He never asks for anything. He helps me. I know that our nation (*azg*) is changing, but I will tell you that they will never change the will of our people to help one another." Gayane attributed the kindness of the boy who helped her to the beauty of proper Armenian values, which she felt would not change no matter how perverse the nation became. While she lamented the material conditions that were created by the authorities and that had significantly deteriorated the quality of everyday life, there were crevices, cracks, corners within her imagination that pointed to possibilities of moving toward a time when things would be different from the present and more like the past. There was a potential in the ruins of the present. This potential, however, was the return of the proper—a return of the Armenia that was once known, ontologically sound in the past, a reclaiming of a proper present that only *seemed* to be lost in time.

When Talalyan asked Gayane why she had not moved to Moscow to be with her son, she told us that she was old and had little life left. She wanted to die in Armenia and be buried within its "sacred soil," because "however much they destroy our nation, our country, this will always be Armenia." She emphasized time and again that there was nowhere in the world like Armenia, accentuating the land's natural qualities: the soil, the water, the air, the sun. "The apricot only ripens to such sweetness in Armenia, in our sun-kissed [*arevaham*] fields," she explained; she later added, "I have only left this land a few times in my life, but each time I have noticed that the water in our country is sweeter than anywhere else. Maybe others don't feel it, but a real Armenian, who loves their country, feels this." I had heard these sorts of descriptions of Armenianness as tied to place before. Once, while I was visiting a friend in her Yerevan apartment, her mother returned from the airport after visiting her brother in Belgium for a month. Before even greeting us, as we were sitting at the kitchen table, she poured herself a large cup of water, gulping it down, and only then saying hello. "Please, excuse me. When I return from a trip the first thing I miss is the sweetness of my country's water," she said, moving on to hugging her daughter. For a few, Armenianness might be lost in time, but it remained in place.

Resignifying the present as "proper" once again, however, could not depend entirely on the essential qualities of the land. Many of those with whom we spoke stated clearly that even the land was being destroyed. While it was mining that, at the time (2013) and into today (2023), was the largest environmental threat in Armenia, those who expressed concern with the ruination of the country's natural resources focused on the moral attributes of this ruination: the lack of appreciation that those in power had toward the beauty of their native country; the development projects that replicated a European modernity rather than attuning themselves to the particularities of the Armenian style and the indigenous materials and aesthetics of the country; and the lack of investment in agriculture that had led to the importation of fruits that many deemed naturally tasty only when grown on this land (especially apricots, but also tomatoes, cucumbers, pomegranates, and figs).

For Elizabeth, and perhaps also for Anna, the resignification—the undoing and redoing—of propriety, might demand some other, perhaps improper, modes. If Armenia were to get back on a moral track in order to survive as a nation, Armenians might have to be creative about resolving the social ills of the present—even if by nontraditional means. Elizabeth and Anna, both of whom stood firm on the question of public and political work as men's domain and caregiving within the home or in schools as the proper domain of women, also maintained that the particular God-given characteristics of women might also make them better leaders, especially for a nation that had become perverse in its orientations. When we asked Elizabeth and Anna what changes they would like to see in Armenia, Elizabeth's eyes lit up and she dove right in, as if this was something she had already thought about:

> *Aziz jan* [a term of endearment], if I had been President of the Republic, I would change so much, I would make our country so beautiful. For example, me, from a young age I have been planting trees. If you came to our garden in the village [referring to a plot of land that

her family owns in a nearby village], you would see all kinds of trees with all kinds of fruit. I am the one who plants those trees, who cares for them, who harvests the fruit. See, if a person loves nature and cares for trees—plants them and cares for them—then they are tied to that land, to that soil. They love that soil, my child [bales]! From a young age, you have to get tied to that land. For my kids, for example, I gave each of them a small square of land and told them, "this is your land." ... Write this down [to me]. It's important. "You take care of this and you take care of that." From a young age a child has to be tied to their land and water.

Elizabeth had treated her two sons and daughter equally by deeding equal plots of land to each of them. For her, this act of giving care and nurturing life—which she later described as practices more in line with feminine characteristics—was critical for both men and women to learn. Giving the land, and teaching these sensibilities of care, furthermore, were also intrinsic to her sense of herself as a nurturer, whether as a mother or a teacher. She spoke to both Talalyan and me as if we were under her care as well, educating us about proper values and using diminutive forms of address ("my child").

Surprised to hear Elizabeth putting herself in the role of President of Armenia, Talalyan asked her if she would like to see a woman president in Armenia. "Well, how would that be bad? Woman takes care of (home) economy [dndesutyun] well. This [a country] is also a big economy," she stated. Anna now also chimed in by explaining that it could not be *any* woman, but a particular woman. "It depends on how she thinks and if she really has a woman's mentality." Elizabeth agreed:

> A woman's mentality is very strong. Before a man can even think through something—one, two, three—the woman has already solved the problem. Woman, she is a devil. If I was President for example—with me, the organizational skills are very high. I would organize everything very well and very strict.

While Elizabeth saw herself as a strong leader, Anna explained that she herself would not be such a strong leader. Elizabeth agreed with her, maintaining that Anna was very gentle and loving but that she needed to get behind a leader. Both agreed, however, that as they were very good at caring for children—both their own children as well as the children they educated in school—they were perfectly poised, together, to run the country. While the qualities of strength and leadership are more frequently associated with men in Armenia, Elizabeth and Anna naturalized these as feminine qualities, too, based on the notion of woman as better at attending to economics (from the Greek term *oikos*, which refers to the family and the house, expressed also in Armenian as *dndesutyun*, or attending to house). Anna, who was meeker, more caring, and nurturing, did not have this "woman's mentality" and thus would not make a good leader.

Even in Elizabeth's line of reasoning about the disintegration of Armenia as Armenians descended on a perverse path, there were "lines of flight"—markings of a multiplicity of dimensions (Deleuze and Guattari 1987)—regarding propriety, which held potential for Armenia to become Armenia once again. This was a movement "toward" something rather than a looking back. But it was also a "toward" that was oriented in continuity with the past. Elizabeth's comments on a woman's governing capabilities swerved quite far from the path of a loving mother in the home and in schools—projecting those possibilities of motherhood instead onto the nation. Even if Elizabeth reimagined a maternal Armenia instead of a paternal and patriarchal Armenia, this nontraditional implementation emerged only from the present in which everyday life had already become so improper. There was some potential in impropriety, but that potential could be seized only by improper means—such as by a woman president. "Women are good organizers, much better than men, my girls. But women are not politicians," Elizabeth replied when Talalyan complimented her on her ideas about running the country and asked her why she had not entered politics. While Elizabeth and Anna insisted that they were Republicans and that they and would be voting Republican in the upcoming election (the Republican Party was the ruling party at the time), their political affiliation might have been a result of their past and current work sites, in public schools. They were nonetheless open to possibilities of drawing from improper modes of Armenian social organization in order to put the country back on a proper path.

Unprecedented Futures

"Yeah, life is changing. And it should change. It's a good thing that families are changing. I wouldn't want to live in the Armenia that my parents lived in," said Tatev, a young woman who had married just a few months prior to the interview and who was now living in Yerord Mas with her husband. Tatev cut the present from the past. It was, in other words, not just that Armenia was changing, but that the Armenia of the past was not one that she would have wanted to live in anyway. Yet even in making this claim, Tatev recognized that there was a sense of an "Armenia" (of the past) that was lost within the changes. Rather than a cause for mourning or hopelessness, Tatev embraced this loss as opening what we might think of as unprecedented futures.

Tatev's discourse was remarkably different from that of others with whom Talalyan and I had spoken. Many of our interlocutors—like Arpine, Mkrtich, Karen, and Hrayr—mourned the end of Armenianness and confirmed the end of the nation in the improper present and, thus, the future. Gayane, Elizabeth, and Anna saw potentials in resignifying a perverse present into a legible Armenia once again—via a return of values once held to be properly Armenian and directed toward the survival of the nation in continuity with its past. For Tatev, however, the present held great possibilities for a different world that may or may not be the Armenia of the past that was known by her or those around her. These are the possibilities that I choose to hear as a "radical hope," a kind of hope that is "directed toward a future goodness that transcends the current ability to understand what it is" (Lear 2006, 103). Jonathan Lear positions radical hope beyond the "abysmal reasoning" that cannot imagine anything beyond a dead present. Radical hope that emerges from an improper present not only imagines possibilities for a future—a future yet to come—but also imagines this future as possibly and hopefully radically different from the present as well as from the past. Negation of the present, rather than a sign of impossibility, becomes a site of opportunity. An improper present, in which Armenianness had failed its expectations of Symbolic order, is a time-space from which different potentials might become apparent and be seized.

We asked Tatev what changes she would like to see in Armenia in the coming years. She told us that she would like to see people valuing humanity, something that was missing in the present.

> You know, people, without thinking, worship their traditions (*adat-*
> *ner*). They don't see that there are ways of finding good in the world
> without them. They are scared—maybe women will become more
> free, maybe children will start not listening to their parents or their
> grandparents—and that makes them want to protect themselves. But
> what are they protecting? The world is already changing. In Europe,

it already changed a long time ago. I would want a country where people value humanity and freedom even if they have to destroy those *adatner*.

Tatev's utopic imagination did not depend on a past; it was a vision willing to shed the markers of intelligibility of past notions of personhood, values, accepted practices, and senses of propriety to get beyond what seemed to be the dead end in the present, a dead end made from fear of losing ties to the past. Earlier in our conversation, while discussing men's and women's roles, Tatev had explained that she did not really believe in "roles" because that notion implied that there was only one way to do things:

> If a woman wants to work instead of stay home and become the servant of her husband and her in-laws, this is not a moral problem. It is a problem of her freedom. She wants to be free, but they want her to be their slave. They present it as a moral problem, a problem of traditions, to justify what they want. And then they say that she has become "European-minded." Okay, fine. Let's say that this is European-minded. Then is that so bad? Does Europe have a monopoly on freedom?

In this way, Tatev brought a politicized analysis to the question of family. It is important to note here that the idea of the woman as worker in the public sphere is not new to Armenia. The post-Soviet transition was a heavily gendered one, greatly affecting the presence of women in the public sphere (Gal and Kligman 2000), especially in Central Asia and the Caucasus. In the early Soviet years, gender equality was a heavily ideological project, decked out with a Women's Department (*Zhenodtel*) that focused on educating women about the "backwardness" of their traditions and practices of staying within the home. While the *Zhenodtel* was eventually disbanded, the Soviet Union continued to set up affirmative action programs dedicated to bringing women into all sectors of society (Krylova 2011). By the late 1980s, women constituted 50.9 percent of the workforce of the Soviet Union, although the work was often segregated and gendered and women also earned only 70–85 percent of the wages men earned, even though they also carried the double burden of being largely responsible for their households and performing childcare (Pilkington 1992, as cited in Ishkanian 2003). Women also had reserved seats, through quotas, in all levels of state and Party governance, although they were largely missing from the higher levels of these institutions. Kristin Ghodsee (2018b) has argued that women fared better under socialism—both in public life as well as in private life. Following the collapse of the Soviet system—which meant the loss of politicized and ideological concern for class struggle and political-economic equality within the Party—rhetorics of "tradition" and "culture" led to both disenfranchisement in political representation as well as loss of economic security for women (Ishkanian 2003). In Armenia, as Armine Ishkanian (2008) has noted, although women have been absent from the public sphere, they also constitute the majority of NGO leaders and staff members. More recently, there has been a rise in women's presence within a growing IT sector, in which women make up 33 percent of the workforce, as compared to an average of 11–24 percent in that of other countries (Martirosyan 2020). The family (with marriage at its center) and the gendered division of labor were spaces of political struggle, and Tatev insisted that we see them as such. Transformation was not moral deviance but was achieved instead through the contradictions between justice and injustice, freedom and unfreedom.

As I have discussed, most of our interlocutors merged political-economic mechanisms with questions of morality, proper values, and tradition. While seemingly political, claims that the post-Soviet oligarchy had left Armenia in ruins were often depoliticized as political-economic problems were articulated in moral terms. Tatev, however, separated out questions of morality from these political-economic problems. While Arpine, Mkrtich, Karen, and Elizabeth approached our questions about the family from the point of view of the larger nation-family, Tatev discussed the family at the nuclear or household level, refusing the language of an ontology of national intimacy and the nation-family. This was not because she and her husband were better off financially. They did do better than many, but they were still struggling. They both worked as bank tellers in the same bank and were renting their apartment. Instead, for Tatev, while the family was a site of (political [although she did not name it as such]) struggle, the public was a site of a different kind of political struggle. We asked Tatev what she thought about the wider economic context of Armenia, to which she responded politically:

> Okay, now you are asking about political issues. It's not unconnected, of course, but different. You know, many people think that Armenia

is a colony. Of Europe, of Russia. Maybe it is. In economics, we see that Armenia is not independent and cannot be. The world is globalized. No country is independent. But to solve the economic issues in Armenia, we cannot blame other countries. We have to think about what is happening here, in our country, in the political spheres. It does not help to blame other countries.

While liberal in its political-economic analysis, this explanation leaves behind notions of a trampled-upon Armenianness. If Europe or Russia was influencing Armenian everyday life, it was not at the level of culture, tradition, or the disintegration of Armenia's Symbolic order. It was, rather, within the political sphere that these effects took shape. To change the course of Armenia's political-economic well-being, changes needed to be made in that political sphere rather than on the level of morality. When Talalyan asked her what she thought about some of Armenia's "traditions"—listing among them the desire for male children over female children, or the bringing of the red apples by the women members of the husband's family the day after the wedding night—Tatev dismissed them as *debilutyun*, stupidity.

> What can I say? It seems to me that you understand already. You know, I can tell you this, that today many women are not virgins before marriage. Most of my friends are not. But some of them receive red apples. This was not something that I had to endure, but I was shocked when one of my intimate friends had to live this. She's a virgin, she's not a virgin—what difference does it make?

As Talalyan and I both let out a laugh, enjoying this answer and Tatev's demeanor, Tatev interrupted to add:

> And let me say one more thing. You know, you were asking about Armenia's economic issues. Our people really like to get mixed up in other peoples' affairs. For them, a person should live their life for others and in the way that others like. Once in a while I think if they got more mixed up in the affairs of our president or our mayor, to see what it is they are doing with our country's money, this energy can be better spent.

Tatev, like few of our other interlocutors, did not take up a rhetoric of perversion—neither that of a sexual nature nor that of a moral one—to describe Armenia. Instead, she focused on the potentials for transformation. There were "changes" in Armenia that were for the best, such as women having the freedom to decide to work rather than dedicating their time and lives entirely to those of their children or husband. These were liberatory changes, and whether they affected Armenianness and its propriety was of no import. Indeed, she was open to the possibilities of Armenia becoming "more like Europe" and swerving from its continuity with its past. Tatev did not discuss homosexuality, and Talalyan and I (as a rule within these interviews) did not ask her. However, the figure of the homosexual would likely have had no import for Tatev, as sexual identity and practice were personal and intimate concerns and thus outside of the realm of what the public should be attuned to, namely political-economic questions and perhaps especially the oligarchy. There were, however, "changes" in Armenia that were not liberatory—the emergence of the oligarchy, economic precarity, and corruption. But these were not moral concerns in Tatev's discourse. They were political and would have to be solved in a political manner. There was potential in Armenia's future—if, that is, Armenians spent their energy politically rather than getting involved with others' moral affairs. Importantly, it was not that most of our other interlocutors were *not* concerned with what the president or the mayor were up to— indeed, they were, and these figures were very often prominent within our discussions of the family (as I pointed out in chapter 3). It was instead that they were most frequently mentioned within a narrative of moral ineptness rather than a narrative of politicized interest.

While a language of perversion narrates the present as a rupture in mythological continuity between a past, present, and future held together through proper Armenianness, Tatev's rhetoric relinquished the past and took up political potential in the present, even if this present was "improper" (in the sense that it veered away from the traditions, values, and morality deemed "properly" Armenian). She sought a future that would not look like the past at all—a future that might not be the Armenia that has been known before. By refusing a disparaging and negating rhetoric of perversion, Tatev's responses to our questions about the Armenian family might be understood as the affirmation that becomes the other side of perversion—the anticipation of a world that would not be governed by Symbolic order, which limits freedoms; that would not be led by the past; and that would not displace the need for struggle with lamentations of the downfall of morality. I read this position as *queer*: as an affirming radical change, an orientation that embraces difference, welcoming of yet unknown ways of life and forms of relation. This queerness is politicized—both in the sense of the personal, seeing struggle in everyday intimate relations and within the workings of social reproduction, as well as within notions of other political-economic domains, such as in governance, in the oligarchy, in geopolitics, and in geo-economics.

This embrace of a queer Armenia opens a temporal possibility—it is an entreaty on the future. The moral transformations of Armenia are taken up as potentials toward new worlds and, perhaps, new Symbolic orderings—or, perhaps, the refusal of authoritarian ordering entirely, although this was not something at which Tatev herself necessarily hinted but that I take up in the following chapter. The future could be unexpected. It could be unprecedented. Tatev's rhetoric of a different Armenia in the future, and in the present, takes up the possibilities of rupture as *a*signifying rather than demanding a *re*signification and a *re*ordering of the proper. Perhaps there would be a new proper, a new Symbolic order, but it would not be the one that ordered the past.

When we left Tatev's apartment, we were in a different mood than when we left the homes of many of those with whom we spoke that winter and spring. *Lavn er* ("She was good") Talalyan giddily let out, as we began to make our way down the stairs of the building. "The way she was talking made me wonder how I don't know her already," she continued. I had been wondering the same thing during our discussion. Tatev spoke a particular, recognizable, language—that of many of the activists I had come to know in Yerevan. I recognized Tatev, even without ever having met her before, because of this language, in the same way that I recognized Marine who spoke in the language of right-wing nationalism (discussed in chapter 2). Talalyan and I wondered if maybe she knew some of the same people we knew. What was recognizable in Tatev's language was her liberalism—a sense of freedom founded on individuality and choice. This was an uncommon language in Yerevan. Tatev did not problematize capitalism, especially finance capitalism (from which both her and her husband made a living, even if in the lower ranks), and globalization. This liberalism, which Tatev also clearly linked to "Europe," however, should be distinguished from the history of liberalism in Europe and the settler-colonial contexts of the United States, Canada, Israel, and elsewhere. This was not a reactionary liberalism—one that speaks in the language of freedom *in order to* justify dispossession and racism through capitalist exploitation (Lowe 2015). It was also not a liberalism that attempted to smuggle in the domestic intimate expectations into the public, as in Lauren Berlant's (2000, 4) critical commentary on the question of intimacy. Tatev's and Yerevan's progressive activists' liberalism was founded, at times explicitly, on an insistence of a public that is radically separate and free from intimate expectations. It is a liberalism that desires a public made up of strangers in relation (Warner 2005), that sees the public within the nation-family as too familiar and unbearably intimate (Shirinian 2018a). This form of liberalism certainly has its blind spots, but it also has the radical potential to sever attachments to political Fatherhood and to rupture a Symbolic order that sits comfortably in a depoliticized morality.

The queer present of radical hope I chose to hear in Tatev's discourse was not expressed so forcefully by any of our other interlocutors among the household survey interviews. However, we did hear some of its tonalities in small articulations in the discourse of others. On the topic of the Red Apple tradition, for instance, women did often express distaste. Some gestured toward the ritual as a meaningless survival. Others explained that they vehemently opposed it during their own marriages or during that of their daughters or sons. This was, however, not on politicized grounds necessarily, but because of embarrassment in getting involved in a young couple's sex life. "I will never do such a thing when my son gets married. I would be too embarrassed. That is their life and their relationship," explained one woman with a son who was recently engaged. Most of the men and women with whom we spoke held a woman's virginity as an important value, even if they did not find the Red Apple ritual necessary. "Yes, of course it is important," Berchuhi insisted, continuing, "but it is important for men, too. It is not just about the body, you understand, the heart and soul must also be pure. If two people have decided to be married then they have to come to that marriage pure in every way." But Berchuhi also explained that the Red Apple ritual was unnecessary. It was not the job of the mother or the relatives to decide the "purity" of a couple's love, but the couple themselves. "They have to trust each other and if they trust each other then we trust them." While welcoming of the end of an Armenian tradition, these articulations still maintained ties to proper social reproduction that could nonetheless be possible without it.

On the valuation of boys over girls, we also glimpsed small cracks toward the otherwise—not only in the future, but sometimes in the past as well. Mariam—who lived with her unmarried son and daughter—

explained that her son could not find work but that her daughter had been working since she was still in school. It was her daughter who helped in the household. Her son, however, she told us "is a man, you understand? He cares about himself and his boys [his friends]." Her son had never been one to help. "I know that even when my daughter gets married, she will still be tied to us and still help us and care for us. But my son, *eh*," she huffed, waving her hand dismissively. This claim about her daughter significantly differed from what other interlocutors said about daughters—that they would eventually be married off and belong to someone else and thus were not really members of the family. For this reason, sons were often preferable. When Talalyan asked about this belief, that boys and men were more valuable for the family, Mariam told us that when people said that, they were lying. Indeed, we did often hear such "lies" among our other interviewees—when, for instance, they explained that they were happy that they had had a daughter because their son had been of no help to them, but then also still insisted that having a son was more important for a family. The force of propriety in ordering the possibilities of Armenianness held firm, even in contradiction with empirical reality. Tatev's insistence on undoing this very order, by insisting that what they say *should* be was not really what should be nor *what was*, unearthed these lies and these contradictions and desired a world in which they would be resolved.

The Futures of an Improper Present

I started this chapter by thinking through negating statements—"There is no Armenia," "There are no Armenian people (anymore)," and others— that Talalyan and I heard many times throughout the course of our survey. These statements negated the present as improper. The present, I have shown, was often seen as a place of impossibility, at least for proper Armenianness. Without a proper present, or a kind of dead unmoving present—a hyperpresentism—as many of those with whom we spoke also articulated, came a loss of future. The nation would not survive because the present was barren. For some—like Arpine, Karen, or Mkrtich—the nation no longer existed. Armenianness had been rendered ruins because of the impossibility of proper social reproduction. For others, the nation's future was severely threatened. Critically, it was not the homosexual who was responsible for this destruction; it was the political-economic elite. According to many Yerevantsis with whom we spoke, oligarchs' immoralities—which not only trickled down to the Armenian body politic, spreading immorality, but which also produced material conditions that made getting by very difficult—caused proper social reproduction to feel impossible.

Crises in social reproduction—such as the high cost of food, medicine, and housing; the lack of jobs that provided a decent income; the dwindling social safety nets; and the absence of critical public services—magnified the concerns of intimacy, kinship, and other social relationships that were the sites of care. These crises exacerbated anxieties about a decline in population, enhancing concerns not only around biological reproduction but about proper social reproduction, especially in a context that was already concerned with questions of ethno-national survival. These anxieties are objects of queer concern; they easily become issues of propriety and morality and thus incite feelings of perversion (both *aylaserutyun* and *aylandakutyun*) as these are all questions about the future of the body politic. Thinking seriously about (feelings regarding) political economy in this way has implications for queer theory, especially in understanding how political-economic and moral dimensions of an issue are socially and psychically displaced and condensed into one another. Feelings (sexual and intimate) and desire about past, present, and future are deeply colored by these displacements and condensations.

A queer theory that centers social reproduction, however, also looks for sites of radical spatiotemporal possibility—alternative futures that might be more just and that might make room for life and the redistribution of the means of social reproduction. Some of our interviewees found some possibilities for the future in this improper present—even if these futures were not necessarily like Armenia has ever been known to be, and even if they were not entirely within the Symbolic order of Armenianness. These were affirmations of a time yet to come, even if from an improper present and even if improper from the standpoint of the present. This may be a queer Armenia. Something—perhaps a different form of social organization (in Elizabeth's speech) or an acceptance of what already is (in Tatev's speech)—would hurtle the improper present into a future that might be an Armenia of the past or a never yet known world.

Tatev articulated a desire for this future that might be a more "human" one. It is through a conscious political struggle, with perhaps some tenuous links to liberalism, that many activists sought to make a different future for Armenia. Grassroots activist movements often negated the negation of a present disintegrating Symbolic order as well as the present hopelessness audible within the rhetoric of perversion through what I call a "politics of 'No!'" I take up this activism in the next, and last, chapter.

Sometimes a breakdown can be the beginning of a kind of breakthrough, a way of living in advance through a trauma that prepares you for a future of radical transformation.

CHERRÍE L. MORAGA

CHAPTER SIX

The Politics of "No!"

On an early Saturday morning, a group of young women walked through the central district of Yerevan, stopping traffic at each intersection they crossed. Some had loudspeakers, into which they chanted, "Serzhe mer papan chi, menk papa chunenk!" (Serzh is not our Daddy, we do not have a Daddy!), referring to then prime minister Serzh Sargsyan. Other young women, some of whom joined the first group on their march, chanted along with them. On Abovyan Street, police vans stopped near the intersection at Republic Square, which the young women had closed off; officers dragged some of the women off to the police station as others crowded around, trying to pull them back and demanding the officers let them go. Those who were pushed into the vans did not give up on their responsibilities, ensuring that they passed on any critical tools of protest—especially the loudspeakers—to those who remained on the streets. They were not stopped by cars honking, men yelling, or taxi drivers getting out of their parked cars to curse and threaten them. The young women eventually reached Mashtots Avenue, where they closed off another major four-lane intersection. Cars honked, drivers yelled, and the threat of the police lingered. But the women continued shouting, "Serzhe mer papan chi, menk papa chunenk!" They chanted and smiled proudly, linking hands, making a human chain across the crosswalk. An older woman walked along the line, kissing each of them on their foreheads.

This event occurred some years after most of the others I have discussed in this book. It was April 20, 2018. The whole country had roiled in protest in what has since been dubbed the "Velvet Revolution." Three days after these women protested that Serzh was not their Daddy, Serzh Sargsyan resigned from his position as prime minister. Nikol Pashinyan took his place. Pashinyan—popularly called Nikol—was a longtime journalist and activist who had in more recent years become a member of parliament, and who had, at the time, been "leading" the mass decentralized demonstrations across the country. While thirty women insisting that Serzh was not their Daddy was not exactly the reason for Serzh's resignation, the anti-Daddy politics that they embodied and the larger style and aesthetics of protest that they practiced had been taking shape for years within grassroots political circles. I refer to these forms, styles, and aesthetics of protest—my object of study in this chapter—as the politics of "No!"

In the previous chapters of this book, I outlined the feelings of perversion (*aylandakutyun*) that my research collaborator, Lucine Talalyan, and I found expressed during the household interviews we conducted in Yerevan. I showed the ways in which these feelings about the nation's moral perversion were embedded in political-economic realities that were moralized, making it easier for right-wing nationalists and mainstream media to affectively transform a critique of political-economic processes into anxieties regarding gender, sexuality, and traditional Armenian values. It is from this space that right-wing nationalists were able to produce a rhetoric of sexual perversion, *aylaserutyun*, which became widespread in mainstream media. In other words, the destruction wreaked by the post-Soviet oligarchy and mechanisms of privatization were sometimes displaced onto the figure of the homosexual, the feminist, or the changing social values that were seen as threatening to proper Armenianness. At times, the figure of the oligarch and the homosexual also produced an assemblage of danger posed by their shared violation of Armenianness: their surplus jouissance, or excessive enjoyment, that did not properly produce or reproduce for the nation.

In these chapters I also pointed to the ways in which the feelings of a nation moving toward its annihilation (or having already arrived there) opened radical spatiotemporal possibilities for making worlds that were not hindered by or beholden to Armenia's Symbolic order and authority. At times these queer spaces or future imaginaries were welcomed. Most of the time, however, they were mourned as the disintegration, or end, of Armenianness, producing feelings of anger and angst. These feelings might not on their own have been political, especially as they emerged from moral underpinnings; but they were critical to political struggle because they spurred the momentum of mass social movements. In this final chapter I take up the politicization of these feelings as they made up a particular style of public refusal—"No!"—within these movements. Continuing my discussion of radical spatiotemporal possibilities, I show how struggles for justice produced possibilities, even if liminal, for imagining the nation without Symbolic authority—without, in other words, a Father.

The Father is a central figure within the Symbolic order, the world of symbols and language that grounds psychic experience. The Symbolic order, or the Name-of-the-Father, gives entry into the world of language that defines—even if symbolically—what is right and wrong, what should be and what should not be, and—in the case of my use of the concept here—what Armenianness is and is not. The Father is a contested object in post-Soviet Armenia, as I have shown throughout this book. Many feel that those who hold seats of authority in Armenia do not abide by the Law of this Father and instead threaten the nation's survival with their perversion of it. The immorality of the ruling elite places this Symbolic order—and the Name-of-the-Father—in danger. In the 2010s, Armenia was ruled by men who occupied the seat of Hayk's authority but who did not fulfill the expectations of his Law. While there have been many voices in this book who clamored for the return of a proper Father so that Armenianness could be restored, this chapter will take up the political work of those who struggle for a radically different world. This world is one that might not need a Father; it is a world in which attachments to propriety are loosened and Armenianness and its moral structures are no longer the grounds for public political claims. For those open to imagining them, radically different futures, made possible by the nation's perversion (*aylaserutyun* and *aylandakutyun*), that move away from an ontology of proper Armenianness, are welcomed as sites of life-oriented world-making.

I am interested in particular political expressions: *how* public discourse expresses political demands and claims, *what* those demands and claims are, and what kinds of imaginaries are made possible as a result. I provide a speculative close reading of public performances, performatives, and gestures that made up political movements and brought the streets of Yerevan to life between 2012 and 2013 and that led up to the 2018 "Velvet Revolution"—although I am not making any claims on causation. I am interested in *movement*, by which I mean the ways in which what is seemingly static and unmoving (a dead present) comes to a boiling point and is roused—vibrates, oscillates, refuses a static position. Some of these movements were at the grassroots level; others were engendered by state actors. Among these movements, as well as *within*, one could find that many harbored tensions, disagreements, suspicions, and at times hatreds. But they still *moved*. Close attention to these acts allowed me to locate cracks within Armenia's Symbolic order.

Saying "No!"

The most direct moment of "No!" in postsocialist Armenia was perhaps the "No!" (*Voch!*) movement itself, which campaigned for a "No" vote on the 2015 constitutional referendum that would change Armenia's presidential governmental system into a parliamentary one. The referendum was proposed by the ruling Republican Party, along with support from a revamped Armenian Revolutionary Federation (that decided to align itself with the Republicans), and it was eventually passed after more than eight hundred individual counts of voting violations had been documented.[1] The opposition argued, both prior to the election as well as in its aftermath, that the referendum was a strategy to keep "Serzhik" (Serzh Sargsyan) in power as the new prime minister after his two-term presidency was set to run out in 2018. For supporters of the referendum, the constitutional change would reaffirm hope, faith, and trust in the Armenian government,[2] restructuring the government to crack down on the fraud and corruption that had become the status quo since independence. Very few believed in these claims. As one citizen expressed to President Sargsyan: "Change yourselves, not the constitution!"[3] While most Armenians would have been glad to change the realities underpinning their lack of hope over the last couple of decades, and while most would have liked to trust in the system again, these "reforms from above" (Solty and Stepanyan 2015) were largely understood as making problems worse rather than better. Some political analysts called the referendum "transnational capital's wildest dreams" (Solty and Stepanyan 2015).

On the evening of December 6, 2015, after the referendum elections, opposition leaders held a rally at Liberty Square. Behind those who spoke on the podium—above the back steps of the central Opera House—hung a large poster of the tri-color flag of the Republic of Armenia overlaid with the simple statement "No!" (*Voch!*). This "No!" was in direct response to the referendum. But "No!" had by then already become the basis of a whole form—an aesthetics, a style, a genre—of the political. "No!" had already been heard in 2012 from those demanding the resignation of Ruben "Nemets Rubo" Hayrapetyan from National Assembly, and at the Armenian Football federation for the beatings and murder at Harsnakar Hotel. In fact, "No!" had resounded loudly earlier that year, during the June 2015 #ElectricYerevan protests in opposition to the hike in electricity prices, especially in the slogan of the movement: "No to the Pillagers!" (*Voch Talanin!*).

The politics of "No!"—its orientations, tactics, and modes of action—are entangled with what many have described as "the politics of refusal." Refusal has formed a critical part of anthropological theoretical frameworks (McGranahan 2016), especially as it provides a more complex understanding of power and domination that broadens a scope beyond "oppression" (Abu-Lughod 1990) by centering agency and sovereignty (Simpson 2014). Refusal forces us to reckon with how one political direction is always the rejection of other directions and actively involves imagination, creativity, and choice (Graeber and Wengrow 2021). Similarly, what I am describing here centers agency, especially within the grass roots of the political world. The politics of "No!" attend, however, to the specificity of a political world ordered by Symbolic morality and overseen, or expected to be overseen, by a Daddy. The politics of "No!" are thus tactics that provide a direct response to, and a rejection of, the Father's No! and that make possible imagining forms of life and living that might produce a different Symbolic order—one structured not around a Daddy and perhaps not around any other singularity. These tactics and discourses refuse the status quo and demand something else, something steeped in imaginative, creative, and desiring potential—something radically different from the world of the here and now. It is not a coincidence that the statement "No!" has some reverberations of a sexual discourse of consent and dynamics of power (Kulick 2003). Saying "No!" has high stakes. It is not just an utterance, but a reclamation of a subject position in relation to power. Those saying "No!" are saying that they will no longer be the objects of power, that they are subjects who constitute a political will of their own—one to come and one that is already here.

The politics of "No!" are not a politics of the pragmatic; they demand, but do not limit and curtail possibility so as to separate that which "can actually happen" from that which is "impossible." They do not necessarily expect a quick "outcome" and are thus invested in the processes and mechanisms of struggle that will avoid a sudden disappointment. The politics of "No!" are imbued with a negating force. They reject, they dismiss, they scorn present conditions, present structures, and present imaginaries with an ongoing impetus, with a commitment to the long-haul that sees beyond the present sets of issues, structures, laws, and realities. The politics of "No!" demand the death of the present, even if that death is a slow one.

This negation is necessary to make way for a new world to come; negation rejects the world that is (right now) in order to make possible hope for something else (to come). In the context of the improper and often seemingly hopeless present that I discussed in the previous chapter, negation is an active process that makes way for the conception (creatively, imaginatively) of a future. In this sense, negations within the politics of "No!" are also affirming. The force necessary to break out of an imagination devastated by neoliberalism (Graeber 2011, 5)—or to break out of the "broken-down present" (Muñoz 2009, 30) that is fixated on the presumably pragmatic "politics of the present" (M. Davis 2010) to produce the possibility of a future that is not a continuation of the here and now—might first make necessary the rejection of the present as well as the rejection of its reproduction. In this sense, what has often been discussed as the pattern of "prefigurative" politics within contemporary social movements since perhaps the "Arab Spring" in 2011—the enactment of more desirable futures in the present through creative and imaginative practice (Kurtović and Hromadžić 2017; Razsa and Kurnik 2012)—cannot be separated from the *actual* political. Relegating these to the prototypical—a "pre"—figures imagination and everyday practice as somehow separate from the world of the political and prioritizes the state and "official" worlds as the proper sites of world-making. Nelli Sargsyan (2019), instead, offers a notion of political praxis that does not separate the act of imagining from that of world-changing, challenging any notion of the political that prioritizes ends rather than means, institutions rather than collective becoming. Like Sargsyan, I am invested here in pointing to the cultivation of political imagination as a site of meaningful social change and suggest that the acts of refusing the "No" of illegitimate Fathers with a "No!" already produce alternative future world timelines out of the present.

"No!" as negation demands the death of the present; but it is pro-future. It refuses because it believes in something else. The politics of "No!" are invested in translating negative and negating affect—hopelessness, a sense of lack, feelings of impossibility, and all those other feelings and sensibilities associated with Armenia and Armenianness at its end—into affirming action. The politics of "No!" are interested in far more than just replacing one element with another or with making change in one particular area (an "issue"). While the politics of "No!" might sometimes emerge out of movements organized around one or another set of issues—rejecting the election of a president, a constitutional referendum, a geopolitical alliance, an oligarch's or state maneuver, or a law—the "No!" as an affective impulse is rhizomatic. It travels and connects. This "No!" also refuses to reproduce the world as it is. Its objective is to *create* (something else). Failure to (re)produce the status quo with each performative act normalizes and disseminates new and different possibilities within the body politic. Each iteration of a new creation is a new possibility—a new bug in the machine of the normal. In this sense, the politics of "No!" are sneaky. They are often doing something other than what they seem to be doing. Struggling against environmentally harmful mining, against the rise in costs of necessary services, and against corruption and fraud in government, the politics of "No!" are always *also* chipping away at the Law of the Father, at attachments to the notion of a national survival dependent on moral propriety, and at a Daddy politics that emerges from this Symbolic order.

The politics of "No!" do not want a Daddy. They know that political Fatherhood is moral and is consistently a foreclosure of the political. The "No!" demands a politicization of the world freed from the constraints of the "should," from the chains of propriety. The political tactics that I describe here, thus, do not wish for a good, strong, moral leader that could replace the immoral and illegitimate horde. In this sense, the politics of "No!" affirm perversion through its other side: its queer possibility. They refuse a social reproduction of present expectations. While not necessarily about LGBT rights, recognition, or visibility— and frequently (though not always) silent on the questions of sexuality and identity—the "No!" can be regarded a queer politics. "No!" is a response to the No-of-the-Father and a negation of a Symbolic authoritarianism; and it is a call for political imaginaries that are radically democratic and based on collective decision-making and active political desiring. The "No!" demands the survival and well-being of the people and of life but not necessarily of the nation.

Grassroots Emergences

"No!" was heard loud and clear during the 2018 "Velvet Revolution." "Serzhik, heratsir!" (Serzhik, go away!) was the main rallying cry of the movement, as intense anger was directed at the illegitimate Father whose ten years in office were too many. The movement's impetus was most commonly attributed to Sargsyan's acceptance of the nomination as prime minister when the constitutional changes, voted on in 2015, went into effect. After all, Sargsyan had promised at the time of the constitutional referendum, that he would not accept a nomination as prime minister. The demand for Serzhik to go away, however, was not the whole "No!" Within the larger life and activity of this movement was a far deeper, negating force. There were those who wanted Serzhik to go away, but there were also those who wanted not to governed by a Daddy at all, such as the women who had organized the "Serzh is not our daddy!" action. There were those who wanted a "Revolution of Love and Solidarity," for a world that would not be driven by capitalist competition and militarization. These other desires also shaped the time-space of the movement and were made possible by the decentralized form that the "Velvet Revolution" took. Unlike various other movements historically in the Republic, this movement was not located in one place—such as Liberty Square, which had been the site of the movements for Karabakh's unification with the Armenian SSR, for independence from the Soviet Union, against the 2008 and 2013 presidential election outcomes, against electricity price increases during #ElectricYerevan in 2015, and against the rejection of the constitutional referendum that same year. In 2018, protest spread throughout Yerevan and throughout the country. Protesters took to the streets daily; they blocked major intersections, took over radio stations, and blocked roads connecting cities in Armenia as well as those connecting Armenia to Georgia. Those who did not come out into the streets protested from home, banging on pots and pans from their rooftops and balconies. Protest everywhere made them more difficult for the police to squash. Furthermore, protest everywhere meant that Nikol Pashinyan—the "leader"—was not necessarily aware of all the actions undertaken. There were layers of feeling, thinking, and doing to which the Father was not always privy.

There was an earlier successful precedent for such decentralized protest—the July 2013 "We Pay 100 Dram" movement in response to the increase in the cost of public transportation from 100 dram to 150 dram. Public transportation routes, while working in coordination with the city of Yerevan, were privately owned, and the owners of the routes had collectively demanded that the Yerevan government increase the fares to keep up with rising costs for maintenance and gasoline.[4] Activists took to the streets, disseminating flyers and calling for Yerevantsis to continue paying only 100 dram and to refuse the price increase. Activists hopped onto buses and minibuses traveling throughout the city and told riders to pay only 100 dram, thus decentralizing the call. This was made possible by the customary practice of payment only before deboarding rather than upon boarding a vehicle. As riders deboarded at stops throughout the city, they were greeted by more protesters who continued to advocate for their right to pay only 100 dram. Within a few days—as the protests spread citywide, moving with and along the transportation routes—some drivers began to accept the 100-dram fare and stopped demanding "full" payment, marking an already de facto success for the movement. Celebrities began offering free rides in their own vehicles to people who could not afford the price hike. New arrangements and phone apps for free rideshares emerged—such as freecar.am. In the meantime, riot police continued to arrest activists at stops across the city (Garbis 2013). On the evening of July 25, 2013, Mayor Taron Margaryan announced that the price hike was temporarily suspended. "We Pay 100 Dram," the movement's slogan and performative utterance, enacted and made real a world that refused to accept the mayor's, the city's, and the state's policy as legitimate.

By the time the "Velvet Revolution" "succeeded"[5] in 2018, performance and performativity had become critical forms that allowed grassroots activists to imagine new political horizons as well as to actively make (liminal) worlds through these imaginaries. The beginnings of these grassroots forms can be found in Yerevan's Mashtots Park in 2012, which environmental activists had occupied in response to the privatization of the space, which they demanded be kept public. Activists who formed the Mashtots Park movement had organized themselves earlier, in 2010, through the Save Teghut Civic Initiative (hereafter Save Teghut) to protest mining near the village of Teghut in the Lori region of Armenia. Save Teghut was largely unsuccessful in affecting a change in the mine's future, but it did expand the political imagination of activists who, after rejection by local courts, continued street protests and actions and took their case to higher, international courts. In this sense, the activists "circumvented the Armenian state and government, challenging the very topography of state-society relations to which many a government official in Armenia seems to subscribe" (Skedsmo 2019, 89). Save Teghut was successful in two other ways, as well. First, it brought together various and disparate actors into the grassroots organization to work together and to form a new post-Soviet environmental movement. Those active in Save Teghut included environmental nationalists, clergymen, feminists, members of parliament, and NGO actors as well as those who opposed the NGOization of politics and the movement. Second, it merged political issues and made critical connections between them. While the movement started as a fight against a mine in Teghut, it quickly turned into a fight for transparency and democratic decision-making. Because of offshore registration policies in Armenia, 80 percent of the ownership of the Armenia Copper Program (preceded by Manes and Vallex), which had been granted a license to exploit the mine in 2004, was undisclosed. Activists, thus, questioned not only the content of the decision to grant the license—which would have massive ecological consequences—but also the exclusion of the public from processes of informed decision-making.

It was through this ability to make connections between various, interlocking political-economic processes that the Mashtots Park movement emerged. Activists' main discontent was with a plan to place retail kiosks in an area designated as a public green space on Mashtots Avenue in the central district of the city. These kiosks in question had earlier been removed from Abovyan Street, a street that was lined with cafés and restaurants, when the owners of these brick-and-mortar establishments had demanded that the kiosks on their street be removed because they were "ugly" and obstructed their patrons' views. Activists argued that the proposed placement of the kiosks in the public park—which only gained its name "Mashtots Park" during this movement—was illegal because Armenian law protected public space from private interest. After protests began, demanding that the kiosks—then just shells awaiting full construction—be removed from the public park, Mayor Taron Margaryan sent the police to prevent protesters from tearing the structures down themselves. Activists organized sit-ins to prevent further construction on the kiosks. Prompted by these turns of events in a very central part of the city, President Sargsyan visited the park and issued a statement to the mayor that the kiosks were "not pretty" (*sirun chi*) and that Margaryan should have them removed. However, Sargsyan also congratulated Margaryan on his control of the situation by his use of police. This statement, "Taron jan, sirun chi" (Taron dear, it's not pretty), became a meme for various other kinds of speech that pretended to make demands but did nothing at all.

Some of those who decided to turn their attention to the park were criticized for turning away from "actual" environmental issues (such as the mining in Teghut) to something that had nothing, or very little, to do with ecology. As Liza tells it, many of the nationalists who were part of Save Teghut were interested only in "saving Armenian air, water, and soil," placing emphasis on "saving" and "Armenia." They were not concerned with political struggle. Arthur Grigoryan, a lawyer involved in both movements, echoed these sentiments when he explained that the connection of the issues between Teghut and Mashtots were clear. Privatization was an antidemocratic practice. It was privatization that left citizens out of the decision-making processes in Teghut and that stole public space from citizens in Yerevan. It was privatization that had left Armenia and the world at large with less and less green space. The protests at Mashtots Park, which had begun with the construction of privatized kiosks, eventually turned into a wider demand, made by the Menk enk dere mer kaghaki (The City Belongs to Us) initiative that broadened the parameters of protest to include refusing oligarchic social relations themselves, relations through which the oligarchy treated themselves and were treated by the state as though they existed above and beyond the law.

Liza, Grigoryan and others who worked on both Save Teghut as well as The City Belongs to Us initiative were critical of the moral and nationalist sentiments of those who did not see the privatization of Mashtots Park as just as critical a site of protest as the mine in Teghut. This criticism extended to some from Save Teghut who did join the fight for Mashtots Park. Heghine, for instance, participated in both movements but made a different connection between the two. When I interviewed her, in Mashtots Park—at her request—she told me that Armenia, like every other nation, had its own environment and that without this environment, their societies could not survive. Each environment, however, was particular to the people of that land, she argued.

In this sense, Heghine was critical of both Armenians who emigrated from Armenia and immigrants who came into Armenia and who did not belong to the natural environment of that land. *Haye bnnutyun a* (The Armenian is nature), she repeated multiple times throughout my interview with her. While transparency, a political rather than a national or spiritual concern, was important to Heghine, this was because of the immorality of those who governed. She referred to these immoral oligarchs, both in the context of Armenia as well as in the context of the global oligarchy, as "mutants," as themselves unnatural. For her, Mashtots Park was sacred, because each tree here was a part of Armenia. She wanted to save (*prkel*) every tree from destruction by these mutants. The existence of kiosks, or even another café, in the park jeopardized this small patch of green in Yerevan.

Gender and sexuality were also critical components of the Mashtots Park movement, especially as many of those—such as Heghine—who had joined in the struggle were oriented toward nation and propriety. Liza and other women involved had been consistently irritated during planning and strategy meetings because their voices were marginalized and because the main speakers and decision-makers were men. Ideas that the women had were seldom taken seriously, Liza told me. But she and some of the other women involved had been proud of some of their ideas. For instance, on March 8, 2013, International Women's Day, a group of women armed with flowers and balloons pushed through the guards (who were surrounding the kiosks to prevent activists from dismantling or occupying them). The women entered one of the glass kiosks and danced and celebrated inside as the police, annoyed but defenseless, encircled them outside while being taunted by a larger crowd cheering the women on. "You know, on March 8 men give women flowers. This is very different from the original idea of March 8, which was about the woman worker. So, we thought, if they see us as gentle and feminine, then we can use that." For Liza, the Mashtots Park movement was a feminist movement because women were also entitled to public space and public life. Hranush, however—an older woman who worked with the Heritage Party, who had been active in environmental movements since the 1980s, and who came out in support of keeping the park as a public space—felt differently about the politics of gender. "You can't mix everything up together and expect your message to remain clear. What did gender have to do with the park?" For her, sexism was a private and not public concern. What happened within families and interpersonal relationships should be worked out there. Hranush felt that the Soviet Union had solved any problems of gender equality in Armenia long ago anyway. According to her, the real political issues of Mashtots Park had been diluted by this and "other" problems.

The "other" problems were those concerning sexuality. Teghut and Mashtots had produced a new environmental front—a group of activists who had formed a network. This front, however, was also a space of some contradiction. For many of the feminist and LGBT activists who were involved in these environmental movements, a major break took place after the firebombing of DIY Pub in May 2012. "We knew there were nationalists there. They didn't hide it, you know? But when they told us to shut up about DIY and gays because it was harmful to the movement, we realized that we could not work together." While today there is a loose association between what some LGBT and feminist activists referred to as the "nationalist wing" of this new environmental front and the political wing, this division continues to be felt.

How connections were made between various concerns mattered. While these movements were inherently political, many of the activists felt they needed to be politicized in order to form demands that went beyond the moral—beyond attachment and commitment to a Symbolic order governed by propriety, the nation's survival, as well as to the realm of what I am here calling the politics of Daddy. In various internal debates, activists were honing the affective impulse of the politics of "No!"—as politics that demanded something beyond anticorruption (a cleaner capitalism), morality, the nation's beauty, and its survival. The politics of "No!" aspired toward radically different forms of social relation; ones that did *not* assume a nation-based moral order necessitating a Daddy; ones that moved toward world-making and that would have to make the connections between environments, political economy, gender, and sexuality and create a world of liberation for all. Activists learned to work through the internal as well as the external dialectics of their struggles. Social and political movements, including the "Velvet Revolution," would continue to hash out these contradictions between the political and the national, the political and the moral, the political and the patriarchal, and so on.

Performing Authority

While the insistence on politicized activity was critical to the Mashtots movement, performative demands—which worked to actualize and bring about new (ontological) worlds—were a mainstay tactic. After various confrontations with police who forcibly and violently removed protesters from the park (where many were spending cold, snowy February nights), the activists maintained that the police force's violence and removal of citizens from public space was illegal and that the state should acknowledge this by bringing forth criminal charges. When the state did not hear this demand for justice, claiming that since the activists were not the owners of the space nor of the kiosks and could thus not become the plaintiffs, the activists decided instead to hold their own trial. They brought charges against the city for illegally authorizing the construction of kiosks in a public park. They called their court the "Green Court." The verdict: "(1) Yerevan officials have until this Friday [the trial was held on Monday] to dismantle the kiosks in [the] public garden; (2) unless the city does so environmentalists will begin to dismantle the kiosks themselves."[6] And, sure enough, on that Friday the activists kept their promise, dismantling the kiosks themselves. Grigoryan, one of the organizers of the Green Court, explained the reasoning behind the decision to hold a trial:

> We tried the courts. We tried them various times and they would not take it seriously. They kept coming up with bureaucratic excuses as to why they could not carry out the charges against the city. "There is no one with a legitimate interest who can act as the plaintiff," "you cannot sue the city," they came up with millions of excuses. So we decided that we could not take them seriously and we held our own trial.[7]

The mock trial did not *really* perform the act of law. Those who organized the Green Court did not have a *real* enforcement body to back up their authority—they had no monopoly on violence. The activists who participated in dismantling the kiosks were confronted by the police and many were arrested. The kiosks were later "officially" removed.

The Green Court's legal decision did not function in a "happy"—in J. L. Austin's (1999) words—reality with the authority to enact law. It was an infelicitous performative act. We might, then, say that the Green Court's trial was a performance and not, in fact, a performative act that acted on—did things in—the world. This mock trial, however, acted *as if* it were a real trial, and the Green Court acted *as if* it had the authority to make and enforce decisions. The trial, thus, refused and ignored its infelicities: acting *as if* and attempting to legitimize the decision-making power of the activists. This, however, was being done in a political climate in which the state was also acting *as if*—*as if* they were operating based in a system of law and order. In reality, the consistent violation of law by the state actors—often in collaboration with the economic elite—had become transparent and obvious to many Armenians. While the Green Court's *as if* authority delegitimized the actual authority of Yerevan courts, the political and economic elite of Armenia had already been delegitimizing the authority of their state and government apparatuses for quite a while. The *as if* authority of the Green Court, thus, emerged out of a contradiction within the functions of post-Soviet authority itself. The split between the Name- and the No-of-the-Father—which I discussed in chapter 3—in which the political and economic elite's power is driven by threat and force but remains fragile in its dearth of the moral virtues necessary for identification, love, and continuity with proper paternal leadership of the nation—had left a gap in Symbolic authority.

This contradiction can also be seen in the oligarchy's performative realms, or between the performative and constative dimensions of its authoritative discourse (Yurchak 2005). The elite and the state apparatuses in which the elite conducted their business (courts, laws, the mayor's office, etc.) might *perform* as the state, maintaining form and ritual—issuing orders, denying requests, intervening with force, and so forth—but the constative meanings of those performative acts were questionable, marked by infelicity: lacking the conditions of care for the Armenian people and perverting Armenianness.

The Green Court's mock trial became a moment in which the Symbolic authority—the collective psychic and moral order of the nation, steeped in a need, desire, and dependence on a Daddy politics—shifted slightly. And another political imaginary became possible—one in which the people owned their city. The politics of "No!" challenged the world-as-it-was with a world-that-could-be. Even on a micro scale, this was a time and space of future possibility.

The Green Court can be said to have been inspired by similar practices during and at the ends of the socialist era, especially by the "theatricality" (Abrahamian 1990) of the late 1980s Karabakh movement in the aptly named Theater Square,[8] known today as Liberty Square. During the Karabakh movement, as Levon Abrahamian (1990) has argued, the square became a "scene" for the capturing pleasure of photography. All actions within the square became a theatrical performance. This theatricality, he points out, included a "mock trial" of the authorities— the Soviet Communist Party in Armenia as well as the centralized government of the Soviet Union in Moscow. The mock trial was held on the "stage" of Theater Square, on the back stairs of the Opera building, which have since been used as the stage for various other political scenes, such as when the funeral of a young man who had been killed came to its conclusion there, in front of a mass public audience (77). Abrahamian argues that the Karabakh movement set up a carnivalesque world of chaos in which the previous order, the cosmos of Soviet Armenia, was suspended. However, he maintains that while the festival-like atmosphere of carnival has the potential to shift reality to a different, post-carnival reality, the Karabakh movement did little to change the everyday life and political structures of Soviet Armenia.

Abrahamian wrote his reflections on the Karabakh movement in 1989, as the movement was still unfolding, although repression by the centralized state had already seemed to have squashed it. There is a sense of finality to his narrative and analysis—as if what potential there had been in these theatrical and carnivalesque moments evaporated with the return to normal conditions. By contrast, the politics of "No!" that emerged in the post-Soviet era demanded a different relationship to the liminal. The Green Court was not part of a festival that only momentarily interrupted existing structures. The Green Court made it possible to imagine in new ways, to imagine forms of protest and action that were not simply a plea against the No-of-the-Father but that instead responded to the Father with a self-aware "No!" Rather than carnivalesque, momentary interruption, then, we might see the politics of "No!" as intervention: as the precipitation of a failure in the regular and normalized workings of the "usual" through a refusal to reproduce the world as it is.

Performative and theatrical gestures as tactics of the politics of "No!" very often enacted the death of the present, sometimes taking the form of a mock burial or other funerary practices to bury it. One epic scene of such a "funeral" was organized by Zaruhi Postanjyan, a member of parliament (Heritage Party) who was also known for being loud and improper—perhaps because she was one of very few women in

Parliament or because she had a particular style of street protest, often being carted off by police while kicking and screaming. Following the 2015 constitutional referendum, Postanjyan performed a mock burning at the stake of various higher-up members of the Republican Party. She made a video that was placed on *1in.am*'s Facebook page in which she carried out three bodies—cardboard cutouts wearing suits with cardboard heads, one with Serzhik's face, one with Gagik Harutunyan's (the president of the Republic of Armenia's Constitutional Court and former prime minister) and one with Tigran Mukuchyan's (the chairman of the Central Election Commission). She laid each one out on the street—one by one. When they were all there, side-by-side, she poured gasoline over them and lit a match. As the fire started going, she exclaimed "*Kpav!* [It caught!] Just like that! Burn, you devils!" She then explained her performance: "I, as a citizen of the Republic of Armenia . . . should have gone to my polling station today and voted. But, because of the illegal conditions in which elections are carried out in this country I, instead, am fulfilling my obligations to the Republic of Armenia in this way . . . " She gestures with one hand to the growing fire behind her. "In other words, to burn the scarecrows of Serzh Sargsyan, Gagik Harutunyan, and Tigran Mukuchyan . . . the last Bolshevik, the last *chekist* (derogatory term for a member of the KGB), and the last representative of the Armenian Republican Party." With this act, Postanjyan was not only refusing to participate in the "machinery of falsification" (Abrahamian and Shagoyan 2012, 19), but was putting that whole system to rest, burning bridges to this already-past.

The performative dimensions of the politics of "No!" made use of theatricality to transform perspectival scope. This postsocialist genre borrowed from forms of parody, overidentification, and other creative tactics of political demonstration from the late socialist era (Yurchak 2005)—for instance, the burial of copies of the newspaper *Pravda* (Truth) in Leninakan (today's Gyumri) to protest the death of truth in central Soviet media during the Karabakh movement (Malkasian 1996, 118). These postsocialist gestures, however, manifest alternative timelines of present and future. The politics of "No!" mark time in ways different from the ritualized, brutal, and oppressive present in which life and survival seem impossible, imagining different presents moving toward different futures. These tactics both refuse but also open up portals through which to glimpse alternative worlds, such as ones in which the Republican Party has been buried or in which the people have executed their masters. In other words, these performances do not just protest; they also create. They do not just critique; they also inspire. They do not just maintain the performative function while adding new constative dimension (Yurchak 2005); they produce new iterative possibilities—performatives with their own ranges of desiring, feeling, imagining, and acting.

"Hello!"

The 2013 post-presidential election protests offered new opportunities to play with the politics of "No!" This movement—unlike those for Teghut, Mashtots, the 100-dram bus fares, or even those against the constitutional referendum—was not based in the grass roots. It emerged through claims to power made by a major political actor. It was, however, an important political moment that had grassroots participation. Levon Ter-Petrosyan, Armenia's first president and the opposition candidate in 2008, did not run for reelection in 2013. At the end of 2012 he explained his decision as being for the good of a "developed democratic country," that since he was sixty-eight years old he could not run for the sake of his people, who needed someone of better capacity to lead them.[9] He also added that the Armenian National Congress (HAK) would not be participating in the upcoming election since this would be the "legitimization of the illegal regime" and basically "meaningless" since the current government of Armenia was "consistently destroying any possibility of democratic and competitive elections" and "perfecting the vote-rigging machine."[10]

Ter-Petrosyan verbalized what many Armenians already knew: it was not the elections, which were consistently rigged, that mattered; it was the post-election movement that might bring about change. In early 2013, Serzh Sargsyan, speaking to journalists in the Shirak region, was asked by one reporter what he thought his chances were in the upcoming elections in that region. His response was, "My chances . . . Out of a 100, should I punch 90? 80? 70? 60? However much you want I will punch," indicating that the number of votes was dependent on what he decided, expressing his authoritative No. A video of this moment went viral,[11] but most people did not need such blatant evidence of rigged elections to be convinced of what was to come. With threats at polling stations and at workplaces, the voting of the dead, the erasure of stamps on passports to enable the submission of multiple votes, and vote buying being reported by international and local observers, Sargsyan "won" the election with 58.64 percent of the popular vote; and Raffi Hovhannisyan, the opposition candidate, received 36.75 percent. The post-election movement in 2013 began as soon as the vote results were reported, since activists and Raffi—Hovhannisyan's "nicked" name, by which he would be called for the following few months—had been prepared for these results.

This election, however, came about in an Armenia that was slightly different from what it had been in 2008: left-of-center activists, the Armenian National Congress, and other grassroots organizations interested in making systemic changes had been shifting focus, practice, and orientation. There was far less interest within the grass roots for a "leader." Activists who had been involved in the politics of "No!"—Save Teghut, the Mashtots Park occupation, advocacy around DIY Pub, and feminist interventions into domestic and militarized violence—were critical of the effects of a top-down leadership. It was not that elections were of little importance. The importance of elections, however, was not in who won and who took office but rather in the ways in which the elections were conducted and what this said about the political field in the Republic. Even the Armenian National Congress, organized around the Republic's first Daddy and the leader of the 2008 opposition, Ter-Petrosyan, was no longer working toward the election of "leaders." It was now involved in grassroots organizing in the environmental movement, the political transparency movement, and the fight against privatization and neoliberal economic policies.

When he ran for president in 2013, Raffi Hovhannisyan had been the head and founder of the Heritage Party since 2002. He had been the first foreign minister to the Republic of Armenia, appointed in 1991 by Ter-Petrosyan. Hovhannisyan as well as the Heritage Party were pro-European, seeing acceptance into the European Union as a goal for Armenia. They advocated economic liberalism, placing a competitive free market economy as the main goal of Armenia's political-economic achievements. Hovhannisyan was born in Fresno, California. He is the son of Armenian historian Richard G. Hovhannisyan, who was a professor emeritus at UCLA. Raffi was visiting Armenia in December 1988 when an earthquake devastated the city of Lenninakan (Gyumri) and neighboring villages. Shortly thereafter he decided to immigrate (or "repatriate") to Armenia with his family.

Hovhannisyan's policy on domestic issues gave him wide popularity. In 2013, he campaigned on a platform for democratic practices and transparency. During the post-election period, he called Serzh Sargsyan to open the gates of the Presidential Palace, to the offices that belong to the people. As Marilisa Lorusso (2013, 5) writes, "His work has been in total contrast to the 'normal' pattern of a country that people feel is increasingly becoming a patronal state" ruined by the "deterioration of ethics and morality." Hovhannisyan, in other words, was untimely. He disturbed the forms that had become normal, that had taken the present on a perverse detour and made impossible the nation's proper survival in the future. He was outside of the improper present that I described in the previous chapter. Hovhannisyan's mission was to bring Armenia back on a proper path, firmly positioned against the nation's *aylandakutyun*, its moral perversions. This was, according to Raffi and many other supporters of his campaign, to be a new Armenia. But, if we were to take the "new" seriously, we might question this. Hovhannisyan was, after all, the founder of the Heritage Party. He was devoted to that which came from the past. In this sense, we might read his position within the improper present not as future-oriented, but as past-oriented—as desiring the restoration of the past rather than the creation of a new future.

As a candidate who did not shy away from his pro-Western stance, Raffi was also unafraid to take unpopular positions on what right-wing nationalists referred to as the nation's *aylaserutyun*, its sexual perversion. This pro-Western position was, unsurprisingly, a problem for the right wing. Hovhannisyan had been the only party leader in the country to visit DIY Pub after its firebombing in May 2012 to show his solidarity with the pub owners and patrons. Hayk Babukhanyan, a deputy member of the National Assembly and the leader of the Constitutional Rights Union, condemned Raffi for comparing the DIY firebombers to the Young Turks of the Ottoman Empire and for calling them "Nazis" during his visit. As Babukhanyan explained in an interview,[12] "We traditional Armenians cannot live in the Yerevan that Raffi dreams about," citing a claim that Raffi made during a *miting*, a mass rally held in Liberty Square the night before, that Armenians should be willing to pay the price of life itself to get to their goal of creating the Armenia and Yerevan of which they dream. "Who are we being asked to pay this price for?" Babukhanyan asked. In early 2013, the right-wing coalition Mek Azg Miyutyun (One Nation Alliance) plastered flyers all over Yerevan declaring "No to the Levon + Raffi American-minded Force!" referring to Ter-Petrosyan and Hovhannisyan. While Hovhannisyan was generally seen as politically "clean"—legitimate, moral—he was often accused of Euro-American impropriety (upsetting to the traditional order of a proper Armenianness). In other words, while he might not have been *aylandak* (morally perverse like the corrupt oligarchy), he was *aylaservatz* (advocating for the rights of the homosexual). A few of my interlocutors also argued that because he was American, he would not be able to play the political game—the dirty maneuvering required to get anything done in (the non-liberal democratic) Armenia.

Following the February 18, 2013, elections, Hovhannisyan led an opposition movement throughout Armenia that, by March, came to be known as the *Barev*-olution. The Hello Revolution. In Hovhannisyan's words, "I walked into farms and flea markets and met hundreds of thousands of Armenians who lived in poverty, who had no jobs and who dreamed of leaving their homeland. I shook their hands and shared their glance, and I said, quite simply, 'Hello.' And they responded in kind: 'Hello.' That was our secret covenant" (Lorusso 2013, 5). The term *Barev*-olution did critical political work for Hovhannisyan. The Heritage Party had spoken of the emigration crisis for years. Hovhannisyan stated many times during his almost-daily *mitings* following the election that Armenians were leaving their homeland because they saw no hope there. But instead of leaving, he insisted, Armenians should say "Hello!" to a new Armenia and to one another.

Hello was an affirmation. It was a welcome; a gesture of openness to another and to the future. But hello was also a negation; a negation of the present and an insistence on the necessity of welcoming another world, another set of conditions. It was a negation steeped in possibility. It demanded imagination, creativity, and desire. It demanded, in other words, desiring subjectivity, which Daddy politics constitutively excluded. To say hello was to be open to an alternative world, a new Armenia, one unlike the present. Raffi's hello, however, did not necessarily address a future but the nation of the past restored in its propriety and furnished with a new rightful Daddy.

The Ends of a Political Father

A close reading of the final day of the *Barev*-olution may shed light on this ambiguity between the future and a past, between a politics of ousting Daddy and a politics of restoring him.

On April 9, 2013, two Presidential inaugurations took place. At the "official" inauguration ceremony at the Karen Demirchian Sport and Concert Complex, attended by various men of power—oligarchs, ministers, and members of Parliament—the "fraudulent" (*keghtz*) Serzh Sargsyan was sworn into his second term in office. But down in Liberty Square, thousands of discontented Armenian citizens (and I), attended another inauguration: that of Raffi Hovhannisyan, proclaimed the "rightfully elected president" of the February 18 elections—at least by us. This other inauguration was an *as if* moment. *As if* this were the real inauguration; *as if* justice could be demanded and then enacted in one performative swoop. After about half an hour during which Raffi called on the authorities to stop their own inauguration and to join his, Raffi took the oath and became president. *As if.*

Following the dual inauguration, the opposition movement marched toward Baghramyan Avenue, where the Presidential Palace is located. This march came by popular demand. Sounding much like the protest chant at the end of the 1980s—"Kha-ra-bakh!"—people chanted "Bagh-ram-yan!" until Raffi finally conceded and led them toward Baghraymyan Avenue. But the streets leading to the Presidential Palace were blocked by riot police. Leading his supporters back to Liberty Square, Raffi called a break for the day, urging all to gather later that evening to continue to demand to cleanse Armenia of its "criminal de facto" president and government.

Not everyone took a break. A group of young activists led a March through the back streets, attempting to get around the police blockade. They did not need Daddy to tell them what to do; they did not need a leader to guide them. They knew the way themselves. They were eventually confronted by police; some were arrested.

When we returned that evening, Hovhannisyan seemed tired, even after this "break." People poured back into the Square as "Sareri Qamin" ("The Wind of the Mountains"), a popular folk song, played loudly from the speakers on the back steps of the Opera. When the song ended, a cacophony of demands filled the crisp Spring evening breeze. The crowd was fractured. Some chanted "Hi-ma, Hi-ma!" (Now, Now!), others "Hay-a-sdan!"(Armenia!), and still others "Bagh-ram-yan!" When Raffi claimed, "My dear Armenian people, I cannot hear you," it was clear that he could hear them just fine. He just could not make out the various calls from the multitude. There were too many. And, on a day like April 9—a day that held promise for shifting the country away from a perverse path—what Armenia needed the most was one movement under one Father. Or maybe not? The chants finally all merged into one that had united everyone at some point or another: "Hay-a-sdan!" (Armenia!). The nation that had survived. And Raffi followed the call. "Hayasdan," he said, sternly and quietly, as if only breathing it into his microphone. And then repeated it once more.

The last couple of months of daily *mitings* were coming to a head. The people who had been attending—not always the same crowd and not always for the same reasons—wanted something to change. They wanted a country in which they felt their well-being and their voice mattered. They wanted to feel secure, taken care of. They wanted democracy, for which they had struggled in the late 1980s. Some were tired and wanted it to be over, no matter what came of all of it—they wanted to go home, drink coffee, sleep, rest. They wanted Raffi to tell them that it was okay to do that. Others were determined to struggle until they won. They did not need Raffi to tell them to continue; with or without him they wanted to struggle. The dissonance in the chants was articulating this schism within the crowd: those who had given up entirely, those who wanted a proper Daddy, and those who felt they had outgrown one. Raffi had not yet made up his mind.

"Those who went home, those who went home out of fear, went home to eat, to sleep, to drink coffee, to preach to us: you are ours!" On this day that would either be a new beginning or just an end of the *Barev*-olution Raffi's words were starting to sound a bit confused. Was he stalling? Had he already accepted defeat? He continued his speech, cursing Obama and Putin—"and all of those others who condemn us." As he continued, making little sense, he made the big mistake of uttering the word "tomorrow": "Tomorrow we will continue." The crowd—those with the Daddy issues and those without—began to boo, scream, and groan. "Hi-ma!" It would be Now!

"My dear Armenian people, you have to know, this is not about me . . . this is for all of us." As he had said in many earlier interviews, press conferences, and speeches, *Barev*-olution was not about Raffi and Serzh. It was about the Armenian people. He often called himself a "participant," explaining that he felt lucky to be included in such a movement. However, whether or not he wanted it to be true, the post-Soviet legacy of hyperpresidentialism (Astourian 2000) and a Symbolic order governed by a long line of proper Fathers had produced Raffi as a leader (and as a Daddy) nonetheless. Even in renouncing this position, he had thus far seemed able to live with it. I wondered about this position of "leader." During these *mitings* in Liberty Square, where yellow wristbands were being handed out, where students had been striking, and during other mini revolts that had been taking place throughout the country, who was leading whom? Was there any leading taking place on this final night?

"Hima!"—Now!—an idiom of "No!" that refused deferral and demanded action in the present, demanded a reshaping of the present as a time of struggle. Many in the crowd chanted, and Raffi conceded. We would be marching toward the Presidential Palace on Baghramyan Avenue. As we approached Baghramyan Avenue, we saw the riot police blocking access onto the street at the intersection with Mashtots Avenue. Some of us were determined; we would keep going toward Baghramyan Avenue, to the Palace, whatever clashes may come. Raffi, however, was more hesitant. "Toward Tsitsernakaberd!" he called out, referring to the Genocide memorial to the south rather than to the north where the Presidential Palace was located. He led some down Mashtots Avenue toward the memorial. There was a moment of chaos and confusion as the crowd parted. Some went down Mashtots Avenue with Raffi. Some stalled at the intersection contemplating a course of action. Some waited on comrades, having lost them in the confusion. Others walked up toward the Presidential Palace on Baghramyan, not only in defiance of Sargsyan's regime but also in defiance of Raffi himself, who had called for something else. For some, then, Raffi's leadership was suspended as his "No" was refused.

While Raffi led some of the protesters to the Genocide memorial to recognize the loss of those who perished in the early twentieth century under the Ottoman regime, others (including myself) stayed behind, near the Presidential Palace. We held a candlelight vigil there, placing candles along the center of the street. A memorial. To remember and to mourn, but unsure of what we were remembering and mourning. No one verbalized it. Perhaps everyone had their own object in mind. For some perhaps it was a duplication of what was happening at Tsitsernakaberd—another memorial to the Genocide. For others, however, it might have been a memorial to the Armenia that had perished under the oligarchic illegitimate leadership of the last two decades. Or maybe a memorial to life and livelihood. Our vigil, especially the candles, drew the attention of the police who had been waiting farther up the street in riot gear. As they approached, and clashes broke out between police and protesters. A row of riot police pushed toward the crowd, demanding that we get out of the street, intensifying our insistence to stay as we pushed back. Forty minutes of this back and forth pushing and making claims to the street, Raffi-the-Father returned and took the front line. As it turns out, we had led the Father on this one as he never made it to Tsitsernakaberd.

Raffi reasserted himself in the events of Baghramyan and urged protesters to be nonviolent. After all, he repeated over and over again, these were *our* streets and we had every right to walk on them and the police had to give us this right. "April 9 is the day of national union, and today we *will* walk on our street," he declared. When the police would not let the people walk their streets, protesters began to demand that police chief Vova Gasparyan show his face and explain to the people why he would not allow them that right. After a short while, Vova appeared. His appearance on Baghramyan that night (for, by this time, the sun had completely set and it was approaching 10 p.m.) was not taken as success. Rather, he had come to urge the people to shut down the madness and go home. A short private conversation took place between Raffi and Vova, and when they reemerged into the public once again, they had decided—of all things—to pray together. Videos of this prayer circulated for days afterward as a joke on social networking sites and blogs. If the decision to march to the Genocide memorial at Tsitsernakaberd instead of the Presidential Palace on Baghramyan earlier had been a mistake, this prayer was absurd and marked the end of Raffi's movement. What was a day that began with a politicized "No!" to the illegitimate inauguration with an alternative inauguration had become an empty performance of morality.

Raffi's original intentions had been to change the conditions of Armenia by providing the nation a more legitimate leader—a Father. In this political Daddy project, he failed. Turning away from this project, he now seemed to be fighting for something else: the people's right to walk in public space. In reading failure as an end, we might have missed this nuance, that the political was being redefined. The *Barev*-olution had awakened many, marking an event in the overall torpid five years since the terror of 2008. Activists had come out; but more importantly, so had many others who had not been activists. The movement had *moved* many. Furthermore, and perhaps more to the point here, not all who had come out were following a leader; some had woken to a world without a Daddy in which they could do the political even if it violated the No-of-the-Father. In the end, Raffi's "Hello!" was infelicitous because it addressed a new, bright, and proper future, a time in which Armenia was back on a proper path of survival. It was a hollow welcome, addressed to something that was not quite there. Though the Father's future failed, the future was not necessarily foreclosed. Activists would continue to learn how to say "Hello!" in new ways, addressing new futures.

Making Future without a Father

Raffi's inauguration was a failure; but, failure is a queer art (Halberstam 2011). The confusion and wavering—of the crowd that refused to follow Raffi and of Raffi himself, who no longer felt leading to be entirely appropriate—were rooted in the politics of "No!" that had been emerging in grassroots movements since 2008. The simultaneous inauguration and culmination of a Father's authority revealed cracks and fissures in the politics of Daddy. Activists involved in the struggles for Teghut, Mashtots Park, transportation fares, constitutional changes, electricity prices, and various other grassroots movements debated, created, performed, rejected, argued, split up, got back together, all the while making possible new ways of imagining collective action and social organization. Activists imagined that they could have the power and authority to make political decisions; that what was important and what mattered did not have to center the nation; that what was "proper" and good for the nation was not necessarily what was best for the future of the people within Armenia. Critically, through all these orientations toward different worlds, activists—though never quite directly, and never quite explicitly—also rejected authoritarian power. Through doing things otherwise, they opened up a portal that offered a vision of an Armenia that did not have a proper Father and that was fine anyway. There were other ways of making a present. An improper present that affirmed its impropriety.

I have shown in this book that Armenians were deeply concerned that the nation was on a perverse path and, thus, at the end of its ability to survive. The *aylandakutyun* (moral perversion) of the ruling class, that illegitimately occupied the seat of authority, meant—for many of those with whom I spoke—that the nation did not have a proper Father, which had resulted in the moral, and sometimes even sexual, perversions of everyday life (including the emergence of the figure of the homosexual through the rhetoric of sexual perversion, *aylaserutyun*) as well as in the inability of men within the households that made up the nation to be proper fathers. This, for many, was a major violation of Armenianness and meant the annihilation of the nation itself. However, those making use of the politics of "No!" made visible another path. In the politicized atmosphere that linked Armenian land, air, and water with privatization, democratization, the need to feminize public space, and the right to be queer; the creation of new courts that would find the oligarchic state authorities guilty; the insistence that International Women's Day be a day of women's disobedience; the (mock) public execution of officials representing the machinery of falsification; and attending the *other* inauguration, but only to refuse the leadership of that "rightful president" as well, activists seemed to be saying that yes, this might not be *that* Armenia anymore—the ontologically proper one—but it is time to usher in something new anyway. There might not be a Father, but there would be a future. The politics of "No!" were built on a queer negativity.[13] The demands, affects, and feelings within these movements refused the normal and habituated world as the only viable option. Driven by a queer negativity that demanded new social relations, they refused proper reproduction.[14]

Within the liminal worlds created by grassroots activists, one could hear—sometimes quietly, implicitly—that the only response to the illegitimate as well as to the more legitimate Father's No was "No!": "No!" to political Fatherhood. In 2018, when young women chanted that Serzh was not their Daddy and that they did not have a Daddy, they were not taking a position against a particular Father—not any one Name- or No-of-the-Father. Their problem was not just with Serzhik, Robik, Levon, Raffi, Nikol, Nemets Rubo, Dodi Gago, or any of those others that occupied seats of authority—whether officially or unofficially, whether legitimately or illegitimately—which had originally, symbolically and mythologically, belonged to Hayk. They were taking issue with the entire problem of a Symbolic order that necessitated that there be a Daddy to begin with, and that that Daddy be the face, Name, and No of the possibilities and limits of life. To build a new world—a future— they wanted to do away with what was too firmly grounded in the past: the survival of the nation. Those struggling earlier had been moving toward the same realization. A future for Armenians might need to be a future without a Father, whatever that might mean for the "survival of the nation." This future might be sexually perverse; it might be morally perverse—at least by the standards of a Father. And that would be all right. Because this future could be liberatory and it could be queer.

While grassroots activists who refused the No-of-the-Father could be critical of this No and the worlds attached to it, they were also deeply aware of their own cognitive, ideological, and emotional ties to those worlds. Never having lived in a world not ordered by the politics of Daddy, and not currently having access to a Symbolic order otherwise, how could they know how and with what to make a future without Father? So, dear reader, if at this point you are pained by the questions that others have posed to me—"What did they want?" "What was the blueprint for this future?"—let me confirm your suspicions that they did not—entirely, definitively, confidently—know. There was no blueprint for the world being created with the politics of "No!" Knowing what was being refused, and why, was prioritized over what was being made—with care, with patience, and with hope. Afterall, you cannot (yet) make a blueprint for things in a world to which you have not (yet) been.

Perhaps none of this was practical. Perhaps these activists were not and would not be taken seriously. But a fundamental task has already been accomplished: it has been imagined.

Futures without Daddy, or On Not Surviving

Our global present—the spatiotemporal site of climate catastrophe, with its global inequality that is literally "off the charts,"[1] its unprecedented statelessness, its continuous and entrenched racisms and sexisms, its pandemic and a host of other crises—demands massive, radical transformation. These crises are all interrelated through the structures of racial patriarchal capitalism. In this context of multifarious global crisis, it is not surprising that much current critical theoretical focus has gone to imagining futures: decolonized futures (Tuck and Yang 2012), abolition futures (Gilmore 2022; Kaba and Ritchie 2022; Spade 2015; A. Davis 2003), fugitive futures (Hartman 2007; Bey 2019), futures without nation-states and the problem of sovereignty (Massad 2018; Kauanui 2019; Simpson 2020), alternative climate futures (Haraway 2016; Wainwright and Mann 2020; J. Davis et al. 2019; Povinelli 2016), and democratic ecosocialist futures (Angus 2016; Mann and Wainwright 2018; Hunt 2017), among others. These future imaginaries call on us to shift reference points to current social, political, and economic imaginaries—to think beyond the structures, infrastructures, and horizons of the present to see in ways that might not currently be pragmatic, ordinary, or commonplace. In Mike Davis's (2010, 45) words, what the present crises demand of us is the "ability to envision alternative configurations of agents, practices and social relations, and this requires, in turn, that we suspend the political-economic assumptions that chain us to the present." There is an urgency to these imaginaries and material shifts. They are compelled by current contradictions. These are all *critical* projects, in both senses of the term: critical of the flows and destructive forces of global, militarized, racist, and heterosexist capital as well as of absolute necessity to imagining and making worlds differently.

I would like to add to these critical projects the eradication of political patriarchy—ending the reign of not only individual Fathers who dominate political worlds today but the very structure, desire, and felt *need* for the strong, brutal Name- and No-of-the-Fathers, including those who are deemed by populist movements to be legitimate. An end to both the side that is brutal and incites fear and the side that garners love and attachment (but that still necessitates propriety). An analysis based on perversion—both as a rhetoric produced out of fear and anxiety and as an *actual* material force and structure that transforms life into nonlife—allows us to understand how, at the heart of contemporary political legitimacy today, there is a status quo of crisis. Intrinsic to social, cultural, and political orders that maintain feelings of crisis globally are claims about ontological propriety: a Symbolic order produced by the figuration of a morality protected by Father—the good, right, moral way things *should* be and the terrors that threaten this.

Moving beyond the chains of the present will require grappling with this affective structure of political Fatherhood. While attention to political-economic struggle, material infrastructures, racial capitalism, and patriarchal heterosexist oppression are key facets of analysis that are geared toward imagining and making a new world, we cannot let Daddy and desire for Daddy go unnoticed. Political-economic transformations that have taken root in late-stage capitalism also have moral consequences: widespread sensibilities that the world has gone awry, that the country and countries that we once knew are not the same, and that life is not what life should be. Daddy is produced through these feelings of moral rupture, which in turn are produced by crises in global capital. Importantly, however, Daddy is the very structure that allows for the continuation of these crises: that which holds the contradiction.

Perversion beyond Armenia, or The Survival of Other Nations

I have offered perversion in this book as a theory through which we can understand anxieties about national survival in the small postsocialist Republic of Armenia. Perversion, however, is a framework that can teach us about larger worlds: about global capitalism, about the nation-state, and about survival on grander scales such as that of our planet and of our species. Transitions from small-scale agricultural, Keynesian, or socialist systems to late-stage capitalism that provide little to no social security might also feel like life transformed into nonlife, into something that feels improper and impossible that leads to no future. Worlds in which rulers destroy the livelihoods of those over whom they rule — through economic and environmental devastation — might feel like worlds that have become immoral and that, thus, have no hope for a future. In these contexts, we might understand traditionalists' grasp on particular, rigidly defined, sets of morals and institutions as anxious insistences on the continuation of proper social and biological reproduction, or as moral displacements of political-economic feelings. The popular rhetorics of perversion (*aylaserutyun* and *aylandakutyun*) as well as their intimacy with one another point to actual realities of experiencing capitalism that might be applicable to the world and life far beyond the territorial boundaries of the Republic of Armenia, the Diaspora, and the larger postsocialist world. Beyond a moral condemnation, perversion is a real, material mechanism having to do with the conditions of life under late capitalism — it is what happens to life, sociality, exchange, production, and reproduction within the violent, exploitative, and destructive forces of capital. While the figure of the homosexual who threatens the family and makes the reproduction of a future impossible is a powerful myth that right-wing nationalists have adopted in Armenia and elsewhere (including the United States), the precarity of social reproductive mechanisms that undergird this myth are material and real.

Political Fatherhood and the problems of Daddy can be evinced within populist movements throughout the world. The leaders and beneficiaries of these movements are Jair Bolsonaro in Brazil, Vladimir Putin in Russia, Donald Trump in the United States, Narendra Modi in India, and Recep Tayyip Erdoğan in Turkey, among others. These figures have developed reputations for their use of force, and all seem to enjoy these reputations in excess (whether or not they are still in executive governmental positions). There are others, of course—a long list of strong, brutal authoritarian Fathers who lead through fear: Rodrigo Duterte in the Philippines, Viktor Orban in Hungary, Abdel Fattah al-Sisi in Egypt, and many more. These political Fathers overlook violent retrenchments of "tradition" and ensure their operations. We might liken them to figures in Armenia: they show excessive enjoyment of power through regular boasting; they laugh at and mock any attempts at curbing their power, they refuse to relinquish this surplus enjoyment of authority, and are intimately associated with personal and political violence. These Fathers however, also make attempts at engendering consent to their rule by making promises to restore the nation back to the good, moral times all while furthering the very mechanisms that perverted life to begin with. In other words, they hold the No- and the Name-of-the-Father together, preventing the bifurcation that might result in their illegitimacy. And in this we might locate their ultimate (although certainly capable of wavering) power.

Although differing slightly in policy as well as in geopolitical alignment, these national leaders are the centers of popular and populist movements that desire a "return" of their country to a quasi-mythical past, sometimes with serious geopolitical consequences. Under Erdoğan, a conservative from an Islamist background, Turkey has radically transformed from a country that celebrated its secularism into one that seeks to build a Turkic Islamist empire that some have described as neo-Ottomanism (Alekseevich 2018). Putin seems to have similar aspirations for Russia's return to empire as he develops the Eurasian Economic Union to compete with the European Union and drives war in Georgia, Chechnya, and Ukraine. These are not just projects of expansion. They are projects built on mytho-histories of the good old days, the days of prosperity and might, that are (now) under threat. Within the political ideology of Russia's Eurasianism, for instance, Russia is presented as a unique civilization that has been threatened not only by the West's political-economic encroachment but also by its cultural and ideological encroachment.[2] While these forceful geopolitical instances might be seen as aggressive and on the offensive (and they certainly are), they are often presented as defensive. In other words, a major driving force of these populist movements is the *survival of the nation*.

Threats against national survival also play a role in US politics. Trump's harking back to a time when America was great and promising to return the country to those times—so that America and the American dream can survive—have propelled support for a number of violent policy moves: the 2017 "Muslim ban," attempts at overturning the Deferred Action for Childhood Arrivals (DACA), cutting of funding for "diversity" initiatives by institutions that receive federal funding, and the proposal and passing of several state-level bans on teaching Critical Race Theory and so-called divisive concepts in schools and institutions of higher education. Most recently, the rightward turn in popular discourse in the United States has led to the overturning of *Roe v. Wade*, the 1973 Supreme Court case that ensured abortion as a constitutional right. Erdoğan's Turkey has taken a rightward turn as well. Although it was the first Council of Europe (COE) country to have signed the Istanbul Convention, protecting women from violence and creating opportunities for gender equality in 2011, it also became the first COE country ever to have pulled out of an international human rights treaty when it withdrew from the Convention in 2021 (Callamard 2021). Besides rolling back the rights of women and LGBT people (who have also been further marginalized since the rise of this Father's regime), Erdoğan's rule has also had severe impacts on Turkey's ethnic minorities, and especially on Kurds and Armenians. In 2018, Erdoğan referred to Armenians as "leftovers of the sword" (Bulut 2020), sparking fear among the country's nearly seventy thousand Armenian inhabitants. His regime has waged military as well as legal warfare against Kurds in Northern Kurdistan (Eastern Turkey) and in Western Kurdistan (Northern Syria) and has also arrested members of the pro-Kurdish HDP (Halkların Demokratik Partisi, or Peoples' Democratic Party) as well as journalists and students who speak in favor of Kurdish rights. In India, Modi's BJP (Bharatiya Janata Party, or Indian People's Party) regime—connected to the ultra-right-wing Rashtriya Swayamsevak Sangh (RSS) movement—promotes the narrative of a Hindu country in which there is no room for Muslims, which has resulted in an increase in incidents of mob violence (lynching and rape) among the body politic since Modi came into power. In these instances, nation is defined by singularity and differents—religious, ethnic, and sexual minorities within the nation—become existential threats. For the nation to survive, these existential—and we might say ontological—threats must be managed. Ethnic and racial minorities, feminists, and queers undermine nationhood, or proper ontology guided by the Law of the Father.

The Surplus Jouissance of Other Names-of-the-Father

A strong reliance on the Father's No and on acts of violence are critical for contemporary political Daddies. Bolsonaro openly praised Brazil's military dictatorship (1964–85), creating suspicion as he brags about his own ties to the military and having been involved or accused of being involved in a number of violent events during his political career (Costa and Saxena 2021), including connections to the murder of Marielle Franco, a leftist politician. When allegations of these ties to the assassination were reported, Bolsonaro went on a tirade, shouting, swearing, and condemning those who would dare accuse him (McCoy, Lopes, and Armus 2019). Putin has enacted multiple policies to crack down on opposition: the "anti-protest law," the "foreign agents bill," and the well-known "anti-homosexual propaganda law." Trump bragged about being able to do anything when one is a celebrity—"You can do anything. Grab them by the pussy. You can do anything"[3]—taking pride and joy in sexual violence against women. Appointing Brett Kavanaugh, who had openly been accused of rape, to the Supreme Court, can also be seen as insurance that sexual violence would be codified, perhaps even legally, as normal. When he was elected out of office in November 2020, Trump claimed that the elections had been fraudulent and incited a movement that delegitimized the state apparatus. The riots at the Capitol building on January 6, 2021, can be directly linked to him. Perhaps the high point of Modi's criminal brutality can be found in his 2002 refusal, as chief minister of the state, to intervene in the Gujarat massacre in which nearly two thousand Muslims were killed (Setalvad 2017). During the violence, survivors claim that upon calling the police they were told "We have no orders to save you." Following the massacre, Modi justified the violence as a "natural" reaction by Hindus, and he referred to relief camps in which Muslims affected by the massacre had taken shelter as "breeding grounds for terrorism" (Human Rights Watch 2002). This is, of course, not an exhaustive list of Fathers' brutality. Besides these excessive displays of violence and hostility toward opposition, all these figures have worked actively for the political-economic elite (from which they have also benefited), furthering economic violence. This brutality, in other words, is intricately linked to projects of neoliberalization in which each of these Daddies has also furthered the privatization of state infrastructures.

Proliferating Perverse Figures

The nation's Symbolic order and feelings of threats posed against it are highly productive sites for manufacturing consent for violent action. Like the illegitimate Fathers that I have described through *Survival of a Perverse Nation*—who relied on nodes of national anxiety like the Nagorno-Karabakh conflict and the figure of the homosexual as threats to an ontological Armenianness to maintain their power—the Fathers I am describing here find their legitimacy in their ability to displace attention from their own violent actions against the body politic by fomenting fear around other kinds of figures: the Muslim and the "Naxalite" in India, the homosexual and the feminist in Russia, the Kurd and the Armenian in Turkey, leftist "outlaws" and "criminals" in Brazil (T. Phillips 2018; Cowie 2018). In other words, these figures and the fear and hatred they might popularly command among citizens in these countries allows them to cut public spending, limit fundamental freedoms, wreak environmental destruction, and widen the gap between the elite rich and the majority poor. These Fathers might be more successful than Ruben "Nemets Rubo" Hayrapetyan, Gagik "Dodi Gago" Tzarukyan, and Samvel "Lfik Samo" Aleksanyan in cultivating legitimacy, but like the Armenian illegitimate Fathers, they all work within a field of desire and attachment to a Daddy: a strong patriarchal, but also paternalistic, figure who will be the people's savior from the threats posed against the survival of the nation.

Critically, here, for these figures and figurations to have this desired effect of attracting psychic and political energy, the conversations into which they are brought must be and remain depoliticized: stripped of their real, material, actual, structural, political-economic implications. The very question of the nation's survival is a depoliticized one. Rhetorics of the nation and threats posed against it are always displacements for actual, real discussions of material survival: the survival of social safety nets, the survival of species both human and nonhuman, the survival of the planet. We find, in other words, in all these sites with Daddy issues, structural problems associated with the anti-life forces of global capital. We find a rhetoric of sexual (*aylaserutyun*) or moral perversion (*aylandakutyun*) where there are, really, the actual material perversions of life that capital necessitates for its own survival and growth.

Just as we should problematize the *desire* for Daddy—the desire for a strongman leader who will save us and make right all that has been perverted—we should also problematize the centralization and spectacularization of Daddy as the (sole) object of condemnation in liberal politics. Daddy wants to be the center; he wants to be on top, and he wants to have control over all aspects of everything. He wants others to deliver to him that power. We cannot let Daddy take up that space. We have to see Daddy for what he really is: a consequence, a part of a larger story of crisis, a symptom rather than the thing itself, a Symbolic cause rather than a real one. Through the prisms of perversion, the politics of the Father, and the critical importance of the politicization of political-economic issues—movement away from moralization—we get a glimpse of Democratic Party politics in the United States as depoliticized and moralizing. For four years, liberal political discourse in the United States revolved around Trump's evil, and after the fact, mainstream conversations continued to revolve around the Supreme Court that Trump had a hand in shaping and Trump's role in the January 6 riots—rather than focusing on actual ongoing crises, both domestic and global. These moralizing tendencies that displace attention from politicized contextualization began even before Trump took office, when his election was explained as a problem of Russian interference and the work especially of Putin, the other Daddy over there, rather than understood through actual political-economic contexts: the repopularization of white supremacist discourse, racial and racist capitalism, the violence done to the American working class since the end of the union era of the 1980s, and the rise in rhetoric about the need for men's rights to overcome changes that have humiliated the White American Man. While Trump is gone (as of this writing), these structures that brought him to power are still with us.

Political Fatherhood and the Perversion of Life

Political Fatherhood ensnares. Attachment to the affective structure of Symbolic authority within a political framework promises to solve problems but instead traps subjects in its imaginary. While liberal thinkers ascribe attachments to strong and brutal Father-like figures in the post-Soviet world to authoritarian histories (Lipman 2013), liberal politics today also—perhaps just as deeply—suffer from a desire for, and an inability to see beyond, Daddy. Barack Obama was to save the United States from the Bush era. Hillary Clinton, also a Daddy, was to save the United States from Trump's perversions. As I write this, Biden is (claiming to be) saving the United States from Trump. In regard to everyday life, however, not much has changed. Student debt continues to accumulate, Americans continue to lack access to healthcare, police continue to murder unarmed persons of color and especially Black people, ICE continues to threaten lives, climate catastrophe worsens with hundreds of record temperatures recorded in 2022 (Duff 2022) and 2023 (McGuiness and Rohloff 2023), and military and police budgets grow as resources allocated for life fall shorter and shorter. If anything has changed, life has veered even further into the crises I named at the beginning of this conclusion. The social and biological reproduction of life is becoming less and less tenable. There seems to be no effort or plan to change the structures behind these crises. The worse things get, the more promises the Fathers make, threatening even worse futures if they are not elected. In Armenia, the liberal democratic figure of Nikol Pashinyan, who led the 2018 protests that ousted Serzh "Serzhik" Sargsyan from his seat as prime minister, did not solve any of the major problems facing the Republic. Destructive mining continues to harm and threaten lives and livelihoods ("Acid drainage in Stepanavan is a catastrophe"; Mejlumyan 2022); urban development projects continue to displace people from their homes (Mejlumyan 2020); positions of power, including court positions, mayoral positions, and other critical sites of authority, continue to be dominated by the political-economic elite who continue to rule through brutality and theft; and unemployment continues to rise, at 21.2 percent in 2020 and 20 percent in 2021, the highest official rates the country has seen in the postsocialist era (World Bank 2022). The replacement of one Daddy with a kinder, gentler, more caring Daddy did not solve the problems because the problems were always structural. Daddy and a desire for as well as attachment to him have been powerful and effective tools in constantly displacing—psychically, politically, as well as temporally—the real material causes for concern onto the moral realm and obscuring any connection to these material realities.

In this context where morality, moral arguments, and logics of salvation reign, it is critical to link those moral claims directly back to the material causes that undergird them. The framework of perversion that I have laid out throughout this book helps us do exactly that. If the figures I discussed above can become cathected objects of social, political, and economic anxiety—felt to be disturbing the proper social reproduction of the nation and threatening its survival—these figures also have real links to the actual obstacles, impediments, and violations of social reproduction. The rhetorics of sexual perversion (*aylaserutyun*) and moral perversion (*aylandakutyun*) are intimately connected and both, together, are intertwined with the actual, material, perversions of everyday life in late-stage capitalism at the sites of the social reproduction of life. It is not the Muslim, the homosexual, the feminist, or the leftist who has produced unlivable conditions; it is the political-economic elite and capital as a force, supported and propped up by Father, that have produced the very real feeling that life and its reproduction have become impossible. It is the Fathers, the oligarchs, the CEOs, and the Mafia bosses who are perverse; it is they who threaten the survival of life. To queer political economy is to reimagine what threats on the body politic look like: to see the *camera obscura* of political discourse, to replace moralizing frameworks with politicizing ones, to link social reproduction to the sites of its political and economic destruction.

Queer Social Reproduction and "No!" to the No-of-the-Father

In all the contexts I have described above, including in Armenia, feminist and queer activism is at the forefront of demanding structural transformation. Despite the fact that they are most frequently targeted for violence, it has been feminists who have started a massive social movement against rape through the song and dance "The Rapist Is You!" ("Un violador en tu camino") that began in Chile and spread quickly across the world, calling out every sphere of public life for its complicity in violence against women (Hinsliff 2020). In India, it was Muslim women who planned mass protest against the 2020 Citizenship Amendment Act, which will effectively strip many Muslims in the country from citizenship while allowing fast-track citizenship for non-Muslim minorities from select countries. It was women who, for months, occupied the Shaheen Bagh neighborhood in New Delhi (Gupta, Suri, and Hollingsworth 2020; Roy 2021) to protest the act. In November 2020, when Indian farmers from all over the country began a march to the capital to protest three farm bills that would further devastate their livelihoods, it was women on the frontlines, especially women who had toiled alongside men in the fields and who were now offended when they heard the state telling them to go home as this was not their fight (Bhowmick and Sonthalia 2021). The Black Lives Matter movement in the United States has largely been led by queer Black women (Green 2019). Feminists and queers have been on the frontlines of activism against authoritarianism (Chenoweth and Marks 2022), war (RAWA 2001), apartheid (Atshan 2020), environmental destruction (Nixon 2011), the violence of religious fundamentalisms (Awad and Al Ali 2019), and mass disappearances (Associated Press 2022) around the world.

The centrality of feminists and queers in these movements is not a coincidence. Although there is nothing natural about it, women are still widely responsible for the direct social reproduction of their own children and family and, as a result, their wider social worlds (Bakker 2007), meaning that it is women who are the most effected when the means of social reproduction are inaccessible (Al-Ali 2005). It is also women who tend to be cast as depoliticized and thus are less likely to be the direct targets of politicized violence and who can sometimes use these depoliticized positions of femininity from which to mobilize (Zia 2019; Fisher 1989). But, critically, women along with queers also experience the harshest violence associated with moral economies of Symbolic authority at the heart of emergent nationalisms. While "queer" and "feminist" in and of themselves are not necessarily radical subject positions or identities, the displacement and condensation of social reproductive failures onto moral failures under capitalist regimes produces gender and sexuality—and related spaces of intimacy, family, and so on—as spaces of heightened surveillance. In this regard, we might see the centrality of feminists and queers within these mass struggles not as a result of some essentializing identity politics but as the development of an epistemology that stems from a standpoint of fighting against the moral status quo. Feminists and queers pose intimate and embodied threats to propriety and a moral order established by the Father. If the governance of political Fathers around the world depends on the Name and the No, it is the everyday, intimate, and particularly the loud "No!" of the feminist and the queer that places the Name and the No in a most perilous threat. These figures as well as their real, material subject counterparts are the loudest on the need to imagine the world morally, affectively, socially, psychically, politically, and economically otherwise—to not be bogged down by Symbolic order and its authority, but to rely on fantasy and the imagination of new worlds. While Daddy politics—desires to replace one bad Daddy with a better Daddy—continue to rely on moral narratives, the politics of "No!" insist on the politicization of issues, systems, and structures and point to the real, material, and social reproductive failures of the present world. Based on the radical spatiotemporal possibilities of perversion that I outlined in this book, we may think beyond the *centrality* of feminists and queers within mass contemporary struggles toward *potentials for new worlds* within these and other struggles. We might read within the slogans of all these global movements the language of the politics of "No!" that insist on negating the Name and the No of existing sites of power: Daddy and his Law.

I started this book asking what survival means. When reactionary movements around the world call for national survival and demand various forms of violence for that survival, what is to be done? Based on my analysis of the rhetorics of perversion and their relation to the real perversion of life in Armenia, and based on what we can witness globally in regard to the resurgence of political Fatherhood and moral authority, what *can* be done is to affirm this threat to survival and to insist that if liberation, love, and the reproduction of life threaten the survival of the nation, of moral propriety, or of capitalism then perhaps it is time for those entities to no longer survive.

Notes

Introduction

1   See, for instance, Rofel 2007; Hoad 2007; Gopinath 2005; Dave 2012; Baer 2009; Essig 1999; Rao 2020; Atshan 2020.

2   Some are about the genocide itself—such as *Survivors: An Oral History of the Armenian Genocide* (Miller and Miller 1999), *Surviving the Forgotten Armenian Genocide* (Chorbadjian 2015), and *Verapratsner [Survivors]* (Armenakyan 2015)—but some are also not necessarily about the genocide, but rather a longer history of Armenia that precedes genocide—such as *Armenia: The Survival of a Nation* (Walker 1980) and *Roman Armenia: A Study in Survival* (Boyajian 2019). *Armenia: Portraits of Survival and Hope* (Miller and Miller 2003) examines Armenia's survival in the postsocialist era—a survival that had to traverse economic collapse, war with neighboring Azerbaijan over the region of Nagorno-Karabakh, and massive loss.

3   Don Kalb (2012) calls on us to think about "actually existing neoliberalism," which would seriously account for global capitalist crisis (with attention to its local dimensions) rather than a "a reigning policy paradigm or a state calculus" that anthropologists have been naming as "neoliberalism." This tendency reduces various interconnected issues like the financialization of Western capitalism, China's new role in production, the increase in numbers of workers in the world and its consequences for urbanization, migration, and competition, all within the "eclipse of Western hegemony," to one "state calculus": neoliberalism. Instead, Kalb argues, anthropologists should be more precise about the relationship between capitalism and the capitalist world system and neoliberalism.

4   For a comprehensive critique of how postcolonial theory leaves out criticism of capitalist structures see Chibber 2013.

5   Perversion as a rhetoric, intricately linked to queer futurity, calls on us to think about the inherent relationality between queer theory's orientations toward both negativity (Edelman 2004; Bersani and Phillips 2008; Love 2009; Ahmed 2010; Cvetkovich 2012; Halberstam 2011) and affirmation (Muñoz 2009; Freeman 2010; Nash 2019; Dean 2009; Johnson 2001; Cohen 1997).

6   See the exchange between Judith Butler (1997a) and Nancy Fraser (1997).

7   Worldometer, "Armenian Population (Live)," accessed June 16, 2022, https://www.worldometers.info/world-population/armenia-population/.

8   We did not devise any rubric for a representable sample of Yerevantsis, and the door-to-door solicitation did not necessarily produce a randomized full sample either. Most of these interviews were conducted during the late morning to early afternoon on weekdays, which meant that we were largely talking to people who did not work during those hours, most of whom were unemployed or elderly. We did, however, talk to some who did work but who worked different hours (in the service industry, for instance) or whom we caught on days off, either on weekends or sometimes on weekdays. Because we were asking about the family and because we were both women, men thought it more appropriate for us to talk to women in the household. Most of our interviewees, thus, were women. However, even when we were directly engaging women in these discussions, men in the household (husbands, fathers, fathers-in-law, or sons) would often interrupt and chime in. Some of our interviews were also with men.

9   I would learn, however, that neighborhood distribution in the post-Soviet era only sometimes corresponded to how urban space was organized in the Soviet era. Some of those living in these neighborhoods continued living in the housing that was allocated to them in the Soviet era, but their social status had changed either because they were no longer working in the industry in which they worked in the Soviet era, or because the home was now being occupied by a son or daughter who was involved in another line of work. Many had also sold the homes that were originally allocated to them. Some of those with whom we spoke were renting—usually either because they had relocated to Yerevan from one of Armenia's other cities or regions or from Nagorno-Karabakh, or because they were young couples who had moved out to be on their own. The social and financial status of the inhabitants of all the neighborhoods that we surveyed was diverse.

10   In defining perversion in this way, however, Freud made room for the fact that "normal" sexuality often included within it deviant acts and fantasies that, if developed, would be construed as perversions. The kiss, for instance, which "has among the most civilized nations received a sexual value" is not "the union of the genitals in the characteristic act of copulation" or how Freud defines the "normal" adult sexual aim (1910, 14). Freud also comes close to declaring romantic love a perversion when he points out that the sexual aim rarely ever stops at the genitals but tends to place an overvaluation on the whole of the sexual object— including psychologically, leading to a weakening of judgment (15). In other words, love is for the whole of the chosen object and not just for his or her genitals, which is what defines and limits "normal sexual aim."

It is in this openness of Freud to admitting the close relationship between "normal" and deviant or perverse sexualities that we might also
find in Freud a queer theory of the body and of sexuality (Bersani 1986).

11 The perverse subject sees himself as an object of the other's jouissance
rather than a subject with desire of his own. The perverse subject, according to Lacan, has undergone alienation, meaning that his (the pervert is often a male within Lacanian case studies [Swales 2012]) psychic
processes have been split into conscious and unconscious and the father, or some Other who represents an authority over the figure of
mother, has prohibited jouissance with the mother. The subject, however, has not undergone separation, meaning that the mother has not
symbolized her desire outside of the subject allowing for the subject to
come into his own desire. Because this separation has not occurred, the
paternal function—what we might call the No-of-the-Father—has not
formed, and thus the subject comes to firmly identify himself with the
Other's jouissance, unable to desire on his own and seeing only himself
as the object of the Other's jouissance.

12 One could make sense of discussions of life, care, and sovereign
power—the assemblage of complaint against the oligarchic regime of
Armenia—through the frameworks of biopolitics, necropolitics, and a
postsocialist neoliberal state of exception. Power as shaped by life's fore-
ceful management could be evinced from the state's and the body politic's pronatalist discourse, which demanded that bodies be disciplined
into soldiers and the producers of soldiers. This management was highly
gendered, as rates of sex selective abortion—in which female fetuses are
selected out of the population—in Armenia are some of the highest in
the world (second only to China and Azerbaijan). UNFPA reports that in
2013, there were 114 boys born for every 100 girls born in Armenia. That
number is 118 in China and 116 in Azerbaijan (UNFPA 2013). This management of life is also often mismanaged; the breakdown of the pater-
nalist state by suzerainties of oligarchic power among a newly emergent
post-Soviet fraternal horde has meant that life (as it was once known, as
it was once happening) now looked like something other than life. This
not-life life was often likened to a death-in-life—such as for taxi drivers
to whom I spoke who complained about eighteen-hour workdays every
day, which meant that they never saw their families and never had time
to enjoy anything that might be likened to life.

13 I have written elsewhere (Shirinian 2018c) about the concept of *azg*,
which means both nation as well as extended family or tribe in the Armenian language (Abrahamian 2006). At the end of the nineteenth century, as Armenian nationalist political parties began to form in what
was then the Ottoman and Russian Empires, *azg* was chosen to capture
the new modern idea of the nation. In other words, for Armenians, a

sense of identity that captures the "imagined community" (Anderson 2006) that brings all members of the ethnic marker together is that of a mutuality of being (Sahlins 2013) with intimate expectations. I argue that contrary to many contemporary analyses of the nation as *metaphorized* into family, Armenia is *practiced* as one, which is made apparent from the perspective of queer and other "genealogically perverse" bodies and their experiences of intimate demands.

14   It is with consistency to Freud's theorization of the father (and father surrogates) as forming the superego that Lacan conceptualized the notion of the Other and the Names-of-the-Father. The Other, or the cause of desire, functions through the Father or the Names-of-the-Father. This Other is both an object of fear as well as identification and love (Lacan 2013). The Names- and the No-of-the-Father, in other words, establish the superego and a moral order. For Freud, the notion of the superego was largely a personal one, tied to the very relationships and personal history of a particular subject. In other words, for Freud, the social and history as categories in psychoanalysis matter only in so far as they are of the particular analysand—and as Avery Gordon (2008, 57) has pointed out, he denied the very social contexts (especially those involving women patients) in which his ideas were developed. Lacan, however, extends these understandings of the social and of history when he brings semiology into psychoanalysis, which brings the subject not only into a particular personal social history (relation to mother, to father, etc.) but to language itself as with a history.

Chapter 1. From National Survival to National Perversion

1   Arthur Meschian, "'Aha ev Verch' [That's it], Arthur Meschian (Nov. '09)," YouTube, accessed January 2, 2010, https://www.youtube.com /watch?v=qTzZa-Va7qc.

2   It is not, however, as Michel-Rolph Trouillot (1995) argues, possible for there to be a complete disconnect between what happened and what is said to have happened. The past is, as Arjun Appadurai (1981) suggests, always debatable on the grounds of authority, continuity, depth, and interconnectedness, making it a scarce resource rather than limitless.

3   As Ann Cvetkovich (2012, 4) has suggested, "feelings" have a "vernacular quality" that allows exploration of the political that we come to know through experience. An exploration of feelings, furthermore, goes deeper than political discussions that often "operate at such a high level of abstraction that [they] fail to address the lived experience of . . . systemic transformations" (12) and thus have the capacity to get at the weight of the political on the mundane and the everyday.

4   The belief that Moses Khorenatsi was writing in the fifth century is based on his own claims that he was the direct student of Mesrop Mashtots and Sahak. Mashtots is the fourth-century "father of the Armenian alphabet" and is also credited for having invented the Georgian and Caucasian Albanian alphabets. Late nineteenth-century scholars have argued that some of the texts that Moses was citing were not available until much later (Thomson 1978).

5   If Hayk was the Father of all Armenians, the Daredevils of Sassoun produce a different national "family romance" (Rank 1914), in which the patrilocal Armenians came up against the matrilocal Muslims and in which the main hero of the epic, David, had varying kinship with the antagonist Melik, whether as stepson or step-nephew but in any case related through his mother's marriage to the enemy. In other tellings David himself leaves Sassoun after his victory and becomes the legitimate King of a Muslim province (Zolyan 2014). In varying iterations of its telling, Little Mher is either also involved in the killing of women or is himself sterile. Thus, while the multiple versions of the epic reflect different ideological and surface structure according to their times and places of emergence and retelling, Suren Zolyan (2014) points out that the epic's "deep structure" uncovers the connection between life and death, patri-locality/lineage and matri-locality/lineage, and self and other. Thus, life becomes associated with a woman's proper role and the relinquishing of the woman's proper role with death, including the inability to create life toward a future. At the heart of the epic is more than just a heroic myth with ideological reverberations through various times. The epic also makes suggestions about the proper reproduction of Armenia—of the proper life within the bounds of a morally sound Armenia that will continue to multiply in the Name-of-the-Father Hayk.

6   Sergei Oushakine (2009, 85) reflects on Russian narrative "ethno-trauma" as the revision of the nation's past that frames state institutions as non-Russian in ethnicity. The nation's story, thus, is told through a series of ethnic others responsible for changes in history (115) and is dependent on the negative (114). Armenia's ethnotrauma, similarly, relies on negativity as it casts Armenia's past as always "lachrymose" (Aslanian 2018) and as constant lament. The other/enemy, however, even if changing through time, has become encapsulated in the figure of the Turk.

7   Mika Artyan, "Spokesman of Armenian Republican Party Eduard Sharmazanov and Co Should Be Denied Visa to Civilized World as Supporters of Terrorism in Their Country," *Unzipped* (blog), May 18, 2010, http://unzipped.blogspot.com/2012/05/spokesman-of-armenia-republican-party.html.

8   Cited from an interview with Tsomak Oga on *Urvagic*, broadcast on *Kentron TV* in May 2012.

9   PS+, "Diversity March," YouTube, May 22, 2012, https://www.youtube
    .com/watch?v=Od2SojD1TPk.
10 After the media onslaught died down, Tsomak felt it was once again
    safe to return to Armenia, where she now resides.

Chapter 2. The Figure of the Homosexual

1   Yeghishe Charents is considered the most important Armenian writer
    of the twentieth century. He was born in 1897 in Kars, which was at the
    time part of Eastern Armenia within the Russian Empire. In 1915, he vol-
    unteered to fight with the Russian army on the Caucasian Front, where
    the Genocide had already begun. He was sent to Van, a city within the
    Ottoman Empire, where a large Armenian population was being mas-
    sacred or deported. This witness to massive destruction of Western Ar-
    menia and Armenians would later fill Charents's poetry with an intense
    melancholy—with descriptions of Armenia's beauty and suffering. In
    1919, Charents returned to Armenia, which had by that time established
    itself as the First Republic of Armenia, an independent nation-state run
    by the Armenian Revolutionary Federation (ARF). However, within a
    few years, this Republic would become part of the USSR. During his
    years in Armenia, Charents became a socialist and advocated for the
    Bolsheviks. It was also during these years, beginning in 1934, that his
    work was deemed "nationalist" and along with various other writers in
    Armenia, Charents became an object of Soviet and Communist Party
    criticism. In this time period, various writers, such as Vahan Totovents
    and Zabel Yesayan, were executed or sent to prisons in which they died,
    precisely for expressing their nationalist (seen as anti-Socialist) senti-
    ments. Charents, one of these victims of the Stalinist Great Purge, was
    interrogated and watched by the Party. His arrest in 1937 (which led to
    his death) has been attributed to a talk he gave to the Armenian Writ-
    er's Union in Yerevan, in 1934, in which he addressed the issue of "na-
    tional language." Charents had been part of a great literary debate at the
    time regarding form and content, or the ways in which literature could
    retain its socialist content and develop a national form. The stakes of
    this debate were eventually his life (Nichanian 2002).
2   AGLA NY, "'Homoerotic Poetry and Yeghishe Charents'—AGLA NY
    Spring Lecture with James Russell," March 2, 2015, https://web.archive
    .org/web/20150704191606/http://aglany.org/2015/03/02/homoerotic
    -poetry-and-yeghishe-charents-james-russell-4-2-15/.
3   Ishkhanyan, Vahan, "Charents, miaserakan" (Charents, homosexual),
    Tert.am (blog), accessed April 19, 2022, https://web.archive.org/web
    /20120818135100/http://www.tert.am/blog/?p=417.

4 Simon Maghakyan, "Armenia: International Women's Day Action Sparks Virginity Debate," Global Voices, March 16, 2009, https://globalvoices.org/2009/03/16/armenia-international-womens-day-action-sparks-virginity-debate/.

5 Gayane Abrahamyan, "Armenia: Yerevan Police Say Emo Music Threatens Country's 'Gene Pool,'" *Eurasianet*, December 10, 2010, https://eurasianet.org/armenia-yerevan-police-say-emo-music-threatens-countrys-gene-pool. See also Maura Johnston, "Armenian Authorities Cracking Down on Emo Music: Police Chief Claims That Musical Genre Can 'Distort Our Gene Pool,'" *Rolling Stone*, December 10, 2010, https://www.rollingstone.com/culture/culture-news/armenian-authorities-cracking-down-on-emo-music-238024/.

6 Republic of Armenia, "Protection of Equal Rights and Equal Opportunities for Women and Men," *National Assembly of the Republic of Armenia*, October 13, 2011, http://www.parliament.am/drafts.php?sel=showdraft&DraftID=5113&Reading=0.

7 "Genderayin havasarutyan anvan dak AJ-n gaghdni endovnel e aylaserutyun daratzogh orenk. Sos Gimishyan" (Under the name of gender equality, NA has secretly accepted a perversion spreading law: Sos Gimishyan), *Tert.am*, July 29, 2013, http://www.tert.am/am/news/2013/07/29/parliament-bill/.

8 Nelli Sarukhanyan, "Inchu en HH ishkhanutyunnery 'susupus' kanach luys varum aylaserutyan hamar" (Why have the RA authorities given a 'quiet' green light for sexual perversion?), *Zham.am*, July 29, 2013, https://web.archive.org/web/20130802113550/http://zham.am/am/news/11070.html.

9 Sarukhanyan, "Inchu en HH ishkhanutyunnery" (Why have the RA authorities).

10 Christ Manaryan, "Genderik boykotiki heqyaty" (The Tale of Little Gender Boycott), *Asekose.am*, August 8, 2013, http://asekose.am/am/post/genderik-boykotiki-heqiateqrist-manaryan.

11 Armenia LGBT, "First interview with Tsomak after her visit to Istanbul and participation at a gay parade," YouTube, January 8, 2013, https://www.youtube.com/watch?v=-0RQv57CMm8.

12 Drucilla Cornell and Stephen D. Seely (2014) critique Edelman's assumptions that take for granted a sense of the ethical *as* "sexual liberation." "There is nothing revolutionary about a blowjob," they argue, pointing out that actual ethical intervention would require something far more than an insistence on the expansions of sexual desires and sexual practices and that not all such expansions are necessarily ethical.

Chapter 3. The Names-of-the-Fathers

1   "Armenia's Turmoil," *New York Times*, February 9, 1998, A18, as cited in Astourian 2000. While the original editorial refers to military and security officials, this sense of an unsavory band composed of political and economic elite carries beyond the military elite who came to dominate politics in Armenia after 1996, who themselves were often in close alliance with members of the oligarchy.

2   Intimate nicknames are common within political discourse in many contexts. Beloved leaders of political movements, such as Abdullah Ocalan of the Kurdish Worker's Party (PKK) who is commonly called *Apo* (meaning uncle), gain nicknames as signs of intimate respect. George W. Bush, the forty-third president of the United States, commonly referred to as "W" (often with a Southern twang, *dubya*), gained his nickname as the second George Bush (and sometimes mocked as the less intelligent of the two as well as the least intelligent of his siblings) in a Bush dynasty. V. I. Lenin was colloquially called Lenin *Papik* (Grandpa Lenin) in Soviet Armenia, especially within official propaganda, in stories published for children, and in popular songs about the first Father of the Soviet Union. Nicknames for authority are often kin-based, calling attention not only to actually existing kin ties as sites of power (as in the case of "W") but to metaphorized kin ties, thus marking power as a site of kin-relation. While I was conducting fieldwork, the common naming of Hillary Clinton as "Hillary" and Bernie Sanders as "Bernie" in the United States had not yet emerged. These "nicks" in the name are products of top-down naming practices and parts of political branding campaigns. They are meant to familiarize a candidate and make their name a household sign. These differ markedly from the "nicks" in the names of Armenian elite. Armenian nicknames for leaders (Fathers) may be more akin to nicknames for kings and emperors in the European middle-ages—for instance, the use of the name Charles the Fat for the Carolingian emperor (881–888) who was popularly considered inadequate to rule and lethargic; or William the Bastard (an alternative name for William the Conqueror, monarch of England from 1066–1087), who was the son of an unmarried Duke and his mistress. These names, more so than "Hillary" or "Bernie" call attention to personal intimate characteristics that both recognize the sovereign as sovereign but simultaneously undermine that sovereignty. More akin, however, to Armenian practices of nicking the name is "Genocide Joe," an unwanted name given to the forty-sixth president of the United States, Joe Biden.

3   "Manvel Grigoryani yeluyty AJ ardahert nisdum" (Manvel Grigoryan's speech at an extraordinary session of National Assembly), YouTube,

posted by iLur.am, June 18, 2013, https://www.youtube.com/watch?v
=paq1o28EkI8.

4   Asbarez Staff, "No Charges Brought for Beating of Air Armenia CEO,"
    Asbarez, August 25, 2015, http://asbarez.com/139104/no-charges-to-be
    -brought-for-beating-of-air-armenia-ceo/.

5   "Ruben Hayapetyany, nra vordin ev verchinis enkernere, brnutyun
    gortzadrelov, devakan jamanak azadutyunits aporini zrkel en 'Harsna-
    kar' restoranahyuranotsayin hamaliri gortzadir marmni ghekavarin,
    isk hedagayum unezrkel" (Ruben Hayrapetyan, his son and the latter's
    friends deprive Head of Executive Body of "Harsnakar" Restaurant and
    Hotel Complex of Freedom for a long duration of time by using vio-
    lence, then deprive him of property), *Investigative Committee of the Repub-
    lic of Armenia*, May 21, 2020, https://www.investigative.am/en/news/view
    /ruben-hayrapetyan.html.

6   ArmenPress Staff, "Ruben Hayrapetyann ir hrazharakani hamar himqer
    chi desnum" (Ruben Hayrapetyan does not see a basis for his resigna-
    tion), *ArmenPress*, July 13, 2013, http://armenpress.am/arm/news/722453
    /ruben-hayrapetyann-ir-.

7   This definition comes from the *Armenian Language Dialectical Dictionary*
    (Hrachya Acharyan Institute 2001–2). I would also like to acknowledge
    Nelli Sargsyan's help in locating this definition as well as providing in-
    sight into its colloquial understandings.

8   While Grzo is nicknamed, he also has a rocky past with others holding
    "nicked" names. In the 2008 presidential election, he supported op-
    position candidate Levon Ter-Petrosyan. Following the state of emer-
    gency declared after state violence on March 1, Grzo was prosecuted for
    involvement in the protests. Although these charges were eventually
    dropped, he lost his seat in National Assembly, and his candidacy was
    not registered by the authorities in the 2012 elections. Today, he is re-
    garded as one of the more civilized oligarchs of Armenia and was voted
    in as a member of National Assembly in the 2021 snap parliamentary
    elections as a part of the Civil Contract Party, the party that led Arme-
    nia into the "Velvet Revolution" to oust the oligarchy class from power.

9   Seta Mavlian, "An Interview with Ruben Hayrapetyan: 'I was born to
    a well-off family,'" *Hetq*, September 18, 2012, http://hetq.am/eng/news
    /18363/an-interview-with-ruben-hayrapetyan-i-was-born-to-a-well-off
    -family.html.

10 Ani Hovhannisyan, "Samvel Aleksanyan's 'House,'" *Hetq*, March 23,
    2013, http://hetq.am/eng/news/24764/samvel-aleksanyans-house.html.

11 Hovhannisyan, "Samvel Aleksanyan's 'House.'"

12 Emil Sanamyan, "Running for Tsar: Armenia's Gagik Tzarukyan," *open-
    Democracy*, March 28, 2017, https://www.opendemocracy.net/en/odr
    /running-for-tsar-armenia-s-gagik-tsarukyan/.

13 Vahan Ishkhanyan, "Mean Streets: A Rare Look at Armenia's Capital Clans," March 3, 2006, https://vahanishkhanyan.wordpress.com/2006 /03/03/mean-streets/.

14 Tigran Gevorgyan, "Political Heavyweight Bolsters Armenian Opposition," *Institute for War and Peace Reporting*, November 12, 2014, https:// iwpr.net/global-voices/political-heavyweight-bolsters-armenian -opposition.

15 Gevorgyan, "Political Heavyweight."

16 Levon Ter-Petrosyan, the first president of Armenia, who is commonly referred to as Levon and whose followers are often called Levonakanner (Levonites), neither of which signifies massive betrayal of the nation, is the other exception to the general rule of nicknames.

17 "PM Pashinyan: I Am Ready to Exchange My Son for all Armenian Prisoners Held in Azerbaijan," *JAMnews*, June 6, 2021, https://jam-news.net /pm-pashinyan-i-am-ready-to-exchange-my-son-for-all-armenian -prisoners-held-in-azerbaijan/.

18 I thank Nelli Sargsyan for helping me translate this term, which is based on a Russian word meaning the same.

19 Here, Serzhik clearly refers to Serzh Sargsyan. "Mishik" refers to Sargsyan's son-in-law, Mikayel Minasyan, another oligarch of the clan whose wealth is tied up in various partnerships and financial ventures but who is perhaps best known for his role in content control of Armenian media. Mikayel (Mishik) Minasyan also acted as Serzh (Serzhik) Sargsyan's deputy chief of staff and as ambassador to the Vatican (Kopalyan 2020).

20 "Ashot Pashinyane mer gerineri pokharen padand kmna Baqvum: Pashinyan" (Ashot Pashinyan will be held hostage in Baku instead of our captives), YouTube, posted by 24TV, June 8, 2021, https://www.youtube .com/watch?v=C4Ma-R1WR_I.

21 While this may seem akin to Michael Herzfeld's (1997) concept of "cultural intimacy," my use differs markedly from his. Herzfeld argues that cultural intimacy is born out of a feeling of shared attributes within a national context, but he maintains that attributes that are embarrassing or that are public secrets are kept among the members of a cultural or national world and are not shared with outsiders. My use of national intimacy here is meant to highlight a shared Armenianness that is embedded in a genealogical continuity within the nation-family. See also Shirinian 2018c.

22 At times, however, the rhetoric that establishes oligarchic figures as non-Armenian or anti-Armenian *does* position them as ethnically other. This was the case when it came to Armenia's second president Robert Kocharyan (often called Robik) and third president Serzh Sargsyan (Serzhik), both of whom trace their familial origins to Nagorno-Karabakh.

At the time I was conducting fieldwork, there was some aggrievement about this fact, which intensified markedly after the 2020 war when the dangers of the "Turk" became more intensified. While Sargsyan had been ousted from his official seat of authority during the 2018 "Velvet Revolution," the postwar period brought great political upheaval through which Kocharyan and Sargsyan vied against Nikol Pashinyan for a return to state power. Many Armenians referred to them as "Turks" and circulated rumors about the presence of Azerbaijanis in their familial genealogies (see Karine Ghazaryan, "Disinformation: Kocharyan's Father Is Azerbaijani," *Fact Check*, November 6, 2021, https://factcheck.ge/en/story/39607-disinformation-kocharyan-s-father-is-azerbaijani). Whether or not these rumors were true, they performed affective work.

23   Mkrtichyan also added, "When we say 'national government,' we don't mean that Armenia needs to be for Armenians only. No, Armenia must be for Armenian citizens. If a Yezidi, or a Russian, or a Ukrainian is an Armenian citizen, then that person should live a dignified life. Equal to all. Just because we are a nationalist organization, we do not put any difference in someone's nationality when it comes to equality. If Yezidis or Russians have issues pertaining to nationality in Armenia, it should not matter. If one has a passport or documentation that they are citizens of Armenia, then they should be able to have access to all civil rights, their rights should be equally protected in Armenia, and so on . . ."

24   See, for instance, the writings of Walter Rodney (2018), Frantz Fanon (2004), and W. E. B. Du Bois (1992), who emphasize indignities forced upon the colonized or disenfranchised and demand self-determination and autonomy as a way of emerging a more dignified life.

25   In 2002, the National Assembly approved a new legal code that decriminalized anal intercourse between men, a remnant of Section 121 of the Soviet Penal Code. In 2011, Armenia signed the United Nation's "joint statement on ending acts of violence and related human rights violations based on sexual orientation and gender identity." In 2017, the Armenian Ministry of Justice issued a statement that same-sex marriages performed in other countries would be recognized by Armenia.

26   See, for instance, Shirinian 2017, 2019, 2021b.

27   In 2013, during a Parliamentary Assembly of the Council of Europe (PACE) meeting, member of parliament from the Heritage Party, Zaruhi Postanjyan, asked the president if it was true that he had lost the money while gambling and, if so, how he planned to cover that loss. While Postanjyan later admitted that the accusation was based on rumors and she had no facts to prove it, the question constituted a political performance of speaking out against the president in the presence of European members of PACE. While the question was meant to point out the

president's and his party's corruption, journalist Raffi Elliot, writing for *Hetq*, points out that there may have been many more fruitful questions that could have been posed. See Raffi Elliot, "What Zaruhi Post-anjyan Should Have Asked . . . ," *Hetq*, October 5, 2013, https://hetq.am/en/article/29845.

28 Within psychoanalysis, this excess is also characteristic of the pervert's psychic structure: "[T]he perverse subject is he who has undergone alienation but disavowed castration, suffering from excessive jouissance, and a core belief that the law and social norms are fraudulent at worst and weak at best" (Swales 2012, xii).

29 "Haytni en Tzarukyani vordu harsaniki tzakhsere" (Tzarukyan's son's wedding costs are known), *Mamul.am*, April 11, 2021, https://mamul.am/am/news/207774.

30 Dodi Gago, "Gagik Tzarukyani hamar shun pahele amot a" (For Gagik Tzarukyan, having a dog as a pet is shameful), YouTube, March 3, 2013, https://www.youtube.com/watch?v=swAwUH5aI8k.

31 For Lacan, there is a connection between surplus enjoyment—or surplus jouissance—and surplus value, especially in his "four discourses." As Bruce Fink (1995, 131) puts it, surplus jouissance is a product of the master's discourse, the primary of the "four discourses." Surplus jouissance is produced by the other (the slave)—an excess (remainder) of what the master needs to maintain his power. The master, as in Hegel's master-slave dialectic, is unconcerned with knowledge as long as his power is maintained. But the discourse that produces his power also produces an excess—a traumatic form of pleasure that is also a form of suffering internalized by the other.

Chapter 4. Wandering Yerevan

1 Based on the ideas of journalist and economist Ebenezer Howard (see Muradyan 2017; Fehlings 2016).

2 For more on this, see Shirinian 2018b.

Chapter 5. An Improper Present

1 Stephanie Platz (2000, 122) has suggested that while until the 1990s Armenians understood themselves as "a close [*motik*] people who value[d] closeness [*motikut'yun*]," in the early years of post-Soviet independence, this sense of closeness and intimacy was coming undone, signaling a sense that life itself was at a crossroads. "There is no life," and "There is no way out," were recitations of young and old Armenians alike, she

points out (129). Levon Abrahamian (2006) takes these articulations into Armenian everyday worlds in the postsocialist era. Abrahamian shows how the Armenian sees "himself" (*sic*) at home in his "universe": the space that is at any time the land on which Armenians reside, the place that he can make his own. Abrahamian traces popular colloquialisms like the prayer of success, "Tund shen mna" (Let your house be prosperous), and the curse, "Tund k'andvi" (Let your home be ruined), to signal an inseparable connection between Armenian cosmology and the feeling of home. He suggests that the post-Soviet "documented cases of Armenians razing their houses to the ground in order to sell the components as building materials . . . should be a signal to the collapse of the Armenian 'Cosmos'" (151).

2   It is important to note here that many of those with whom we spoke did not necessarily see domestic violence as a purely gendered phenomenon—men as violent (and as the violators) and women as passive (and as the victims). Within our household interviews, many women (and a few men) also noted that domestic violence frequently involved the mother-in-law as perpetrator. At the time we were conducting these interviews, there was a high-profile case of a woman who had survived domestic violence and decided to press charges against her husband and her mother-in-law. Mariam Gevorgyan, who was twenty-one at the time, was beaten multiple times by her husband, and was regularly subjected to being burned by a hot iron wielded by her mother-in-law. Various other cases of abuse (many of which had led to murder) involved the mother-in-law. Our interlocutors—some of whom understood intimately the politics of the household through their own experiences—were aware of these cases and did not regard domestic violence as a pattern of abuse by men against women but as one that involved the patrilocal configuration of households. For this reason, many older women reasoned that although young couples living in a "separate" household was improper by way of Armenian custom—which figures patrilocality as proper—it might ultimately be a better situation that could prevent the occurrence of violence.

3   In one particularly troubling moment during these household visits, Talalyan and I knocked on a door situated at the end of a hallway on the floor of a residential building in the district of Gortzaranayin (Factory District), and moments after our knock resounded through the concrete hallway (making a presence known to the whole floor), two other doors on the same floor opened simultaneously. It was only after these two other doors opened, that Mayranush, on whose door we had been knocking, opened her door, quickly stepped outside, and shut the door behind her. "Yes, what can I help you with?" she asked. While the two neighbor women stood outside in the hallway, listening carefully to our

exchange from their own respective doorways, we asked Mayranush, who appeared to be older than she actually was (perhaps in her thirties but appearing to be in her forties), if she would be willing to answer our questions about the family in Armenia. "Please excuse me, but now is not a good time," she responded, politely. Mayranush's eyes were red, swollen. One side of her face looked like it was recovering from a major bruise—presenting a greyish tone, not quite black or blue. Just as we were about to thank Mayranush for her time and move on, the two neighbor women stepped in to come to our aid. They took Talalyan and me by the shoulders and ushered us into one of their apartments, explaining that they would be happy to speak with us. Talalyan and I were both a bit shaken at this point, not knowing what exactly was happening, not having had enough time to piece together the various details we had caught of the situation. As we sat in Haykuhi's living room with her neighbor Anahid, the women explained to us that Mayranush had been having a difficult time with her family, especially her husband. But the women assured us that there was no need to be concerned as they were taking care (hok danel, which refers both to the act of taking care and worrying) of her. Haykuhi and Anahid refrained from imparting to us any other details about Mayranush's life and circumstances and, even during our line of questioning about domestic violence, talked in the abstract. "Violence within families," they both maintained, "was to be expected when there was no work and when so many men had become alcoholics because there was nothing else for them to do with their time. Picking up on the scene to which we had just been witness, Talalyan asked them what they thought needs to be done about domestic violence, to which Haykuhi replied that sometimes neighbors needed to get involved: "We Armenians think a lot about what the neighbors will say. This means that we know, right, what is happening in our neighbors' homes and that our neighbors know what is happening in ours? If the neighbors know something is happening, then they should do something about it. We make too much of a deal about shame. There is no shame in this. Things happen within families. In all of our families."

Taking the common refrain of "Harevannere inch kasen?" (What will the neighbors say?), often cited as the rationale for remaining "proper" within the home (and most frequently used to discipline women and girls), Haykuhi pointed out that if Armenians were so aware of what the neighbors would say and think, then the neighbors certainly knew what was happening in one another's households. This propensity for judgment and shame, to which neighbors were constantly subject, should not limit action but should instead be a cause for it—that is, it should function as a mechanism through which to step in when there was vio-

lence in a neighbor's home. In this way, while Haykuhi normalized domestic violence, she also attempted to normalize forms of action that
were also quite beyond the framework of the proper. While what happened within a family was properly the concern of that family (and
should not be made public), Haykuhi insisted that it should be a concern for the neighbors who become aware of violence in a neighbor's
home. Even if domestic violence "happened," it should not be associated
with shame, and shame around intervention should not be a limit on
action.

4   Armine Ishkanian (2008) has pointed out, however, that this is not necessarily the case. Domestic violence was a recurring problem in the Soviet republic.

5   For a review of the relationship between capitalism and patriarchy in
anthropology, Marxian theory, and feminist theory, see Sacks 1989.

6   Armenians in Russia have faced a number of incidents of violence, including murder, premised on racial difference. In 2013, at the time I was
conducting my research for this book, a major incident that captured
public attention was the treatment of Hrachya Harutyunyan after his
arrest near Moscow. Harutyunyan, a truck driver for the Russian
KAMAZ chain, veered out of his lane on the highway, crashing into a bus.
The accident led to the deaths of eighteen people and wounded thirty.
Harutyunyan, who had been working in Russia, was a citizen of Armenia, which various human rights organizations in Armenia and in Russia
claimed was the cause of the subsequent violations against him. Rather
than being allowed to wear his own clothes or men's clothes issued to
him by the prison, he was made to appear in court wearing a woman's
bathrobe, which was seen as a violation of his dignity. In the summer of
2013, when this incident was being reported on in Yerevan, discussions
of Russia often turned to it. "Look how they treat our people in Russia,"
I heard many times.

   While Soviet ideology was vehemently opposed to racism (as an
ideology)—actively forming solidarity with the anti-apartheid movement in South Africa; standing against imperialism and neoimperialism
in Asia, Africa, and Latin America; and incorporating cultural difference into its official attitudes of internationalism at home—post-Soviet
Russia has veered toward white supremacy as official ideology. Nikolay Zakharov (2015) argues that this racist tendency is due to Russia's
place in a post-Second World global reality. By asserting itself as a white
nation, Russia places itself within the "civilized world," indeed out-
civilizing Europe, which is now marred in problematic discourses of political correctness.

1 Reported by Levon Barseghyan, the Chair of the Gyumri Anticorruption Center, on CivilNet Live, December 6, 2015.

2 *Armenian Weekly*, "Venice Commission Approves Opinions on Armenia's Constitutional Amendments," October 25, 2015, http://armenianweekly .com/2015/10/26/venice-commission-approves/.

3 Arpineh Simonyan, "Vichabanutyun Serzh Sarsgyani hed: 'Duk dzez pokhek, voch te sahmanadrutyune'" (Argument with Serzh Sargsyan: "Change yourselves, not the constitution), *Aravot*, November 18, 2015, http://www.aravot.am/2015/11/18/629998/.

4 It has also been suggested that the price hike was not intended to resolve the increasing costs of service provision but for the owners to turn a profit. See "Owners of Private Minibus Routes Seek Surplus Profits and Demand Municipality to Double Transport Fare," *The Free Library*, November, 11, 2013, https://www.thefreelibrary.com/Owners of private minibus routes seek surplus profits and demand . . . -a0416865328.

5 While the prime minister did resign and the movement was able to bring in opposition leader Nikol Pashinyan to replace him, the question of "success" has been muddied since the very beginning of this movement, especially for grassroots leftist activists who see Pashinyan as a neoliberal compromise (Shirinian 2020b), feminists who see him as just another Daddy (Shirinian 2022b), and many others who see him as having failed them in the 2020 "44 Day War" (Shirinian 2021b).

6 *EcoSquared*, "Occupy Mashtots Park, Update from Armenia: Police Action Underway," March 14, 2013, https://ecosquared.wordpress.com /2012/03/14/occupy-mashtots-park-update-from-armenia-police -action-underway/.

7 While I was not present at the actual occupation of the park that spring or at the "Green Court," I interviewed Grigoryan in April 2013.

8 Theater Square was called as such until 1991 because it is the square behind the central Opera House (Theater) of Yerevan.

9 *Armenia Now*, "Vote 2013: Ter-Petrosyan Rules Out Presidential Bid over His Age," December 25, 2012, https://web.archive.org/web/20121231073254 /http://www.armenianow.com/vote_2013/42284/presidential_election 2013_levon_ter_petrosyan_anc.

10 *Armenia Now*, "Vote 2013: Opposition Bloc Refuses to Take Part in Presidential Race," December 27, 2012, https://web.archive.org/web /20130105042022/http://www.armenianow.com/vote_2013/42319 /armenia_opposition_armenian_national_congress_boycot t_election.

11 Amon Ra, "Serj Sargsyan Inchqan uzes enqan xpenq," YouTube, February 9, 2013, http://www.youtube.com/watch?v=X2jg1WR909w.

12   Hayk Babukhanyan, "Raffi Hovhannisyanin dzayn dvetsin ayn mardik, voronk uzum ein, vor Hayasdanum gey klubner batsven" (Those who voted for Raffi Hovhannisyan are those who want gay clubs to open in Armenia), *Aravot.am*, February 22, 2013, https://www.aravot .am/2013/02/22/206286/.

13   But they were certainly not antisocial. While the embrace of the death drive has generated exciting discussion and debate about queer subjectivity, queer intimacy, and queer sex (Bersani and Phillips 2008; Edelman 2004; Berlant and Edelman 2014), and while it is critical in its examination of the implications of unbelonging, the negation of the politics of "No!" does not reject the social, the relation, or belonging. Rather, this political impulse responds to a foreclosure of the social, the relation, and belonging that takes place as a result of the expectation for propriety and which makes the present and future feel impossible.

14   But they did not make the case for no future. American discourse, Lee Edelman (2004) argues (although he does not necessarily specify it as American), has historically characterized the homosexual as a narcissist because of a desire that does not contribute to the project of "reproductive futurism." Edelman provides a polemical line of reasoning that demands that queers take up this position rather than reject it. Claiming all political discourse as "reproductive" because it aims to produce a world, in the future, that is for the children, Edelman argues that politics are always conservative, embedded in status quo structures and aimed at reproducing those same structures, even if slightly altered. The queer subject is the one, already positioned as against this future, who is outside of this "politics," and thus in the position of a no future anti-reproductive aim. While Edelman's premises are provocative, what I have been aiming to show here—the ways in which we can locate the lines of flight for radically different, and politicized, futures within the present—is in line with various other queer scholars who have been critical of Edelman's approach (Halberstam 2011; Cornell and Seely 2014; Muñoz 2009; Saria 2021).

Conclusion

1   See, for instance, a graph published, ironically, by the International Monetary Fund, in which the wealth gap between the global rich and poor is so wide that the wealth of the rich literally does not fit on the chart (Stanley 2022).

2   See, for instance, the work of right-wing philosopher Aleksandr Dugin 2012, 2014; see also Shirinian 2021c for an analysis of Eurasianism's grasp and flow. At times, however, these threats on mytho-historical forms

merge with real, actual, geopolitical-economic threat—when for instance loose feelings regarding cultural imperialisms (based on human rights, feminism, and other Western ideologies deemed destructive) become real feelings of threat when NATO expands farther and farther into Eastern Europe and places troops at the Russian border.

3   "Trump on Tape: I Grab Women 'By the Pu**y,'" YouTube, October 7, 2016, https://www.youtube.com/watch?v=WhsSzIS84ks.

References

Abraham, Nicolas, and Maria Torok. 1994. "Mourning or Melancholia: Introjection versus Incorporation." In *The Shell and the Kernel: Renewals of Psychoanalysis, Volume 1*, edited and translated by Nicholas T. Rand, 125–38. Chicago: University of Chicago Press.

Abrahamian, Levon. 1990. "Chaos and Cosmos in the Structure of Mass Popular Demonstrations (the Karabakh Movement in the Eyes of an Ethnographer)." *Soviet Anthropology and Archaeology* 29 (2): 70–86. https://www.tandfonline .com/doi/abs/10.2753/AAE1061-1959290270.

Abrahamian, Levon. 2006. *Armenian Identity in a Changing World*. Costa Mesa, CA: Mazda Publishers.

Abrahamian, Levon, and Gayane Shagoyan. 2012. "From Carnival Civil Society toward a Real Civil Society: Democracy Trends in Post-Soviet Armenia." *Anthropology and Archaeology of Eurasia* 50 (3): 11–50.

Abu-Lughod, Lila. 1990. "The Romance of Resistance: Tracing Transformations of Power through Bedouin Women." *American Ethnologist* 17 (1): 41–55.

Adams, Paul C., and Olga A. Lavrenova. 2022. "Monuments to Lenin in the Post-Soviet Cultural Landscape." *Social Semiotics* 32 (5): 708–27.

Aghayan, Edward. 1976. "Aylaserutyun." In *The Explanatory Dictionary of Modern Armenian [Ardi Hayereni batsatrakan bararan]*, edited by G. B. Zahukyan and A. M. Sukiasyan, 40–41. Yerevan: Hayasdan Press.

Ahmed, Sara. 2004. "Affective Economies." *Social Text* 22 (2): 117–39.

Ahmed, Sara. 2010. *The Promise of Happiness*. Durham, NC: Duke University Press.

Al-Ali, Nadje. 2005. "Reconstructing Gender: Iraqi Women between Dictatorship, War, Sanctions and Occupation." *Third World Quarterly* 26 (4–5): 739–58.

Alekseevich, Avaktov Vladimir. 2018. "Neo-Ottomanism as a Key Doctrine of Modern Turkey." *Communication and Public Diplomacy* 1 (1): 80–88.

Amar, Paul. 2013. *The Security Archipelago: Human-Security States, Sexuality Politics, and the End of Neoliberalism*. Durham, NC: Duke University Press.

Anderson, Benedict. (1983) 2006. *Imagined Communities: Reflections on the Origin and Spread of Nationalism*. New York: Verso.

Angus, Ian. 2016. *Facing the Anthropocene: Fossil Capitalism and the Crisis of the Earth System*. New York: Monthly Review Press.

Antonyan, Yulia. 2016. "Being an 'Oligarch' in the Armenian Way." In *Elites and "Elites": Transformations of Social Structures in Post-Soviet Armenia and Georgia*, edited by Yulia Antonyan, 110–71. Fribourg: Academic Swiss Caucasus Net.

Appadurai, Arjun. 1981. "The Past as a Scarce Resource." *Man* 16 (2): 201–19.

Appadurai, Arjun. 2006. *Fear of Small Numbers: An Essay on the Geography of Anger*. Durham, NC: Duke University Press.

Arendt, Hannah. 1990. *On Revolution*. London: Penguin Books.

Armenakyan, Nazik. 2015. *Verapratsner [Survivors]*. Yerevan: 4 Plus Documentary Photography Center.

Artyan, Mika. 2008. "Armenian Church: Can't Get Enough?" *Unzipped*, October 3, 2008. http://unzipped.blogspot.com/2008/10/armenian-church-cant-get -enough.html.

Aslanian, Sebouh David. 2018. "From 'Autonomous' to 'Interactive' Histories: World History's Challenge to Armenian Studies." In *An Armenian Mediterranean*, edited by Kathryn Babayan, and Michael Pifer, 81–125. London: Palgrave Macmillan.

Associated Press. 2022. "Women Protest in Mexico City over Killings, Disappearances." *AP News*, April 24, 2002. https://apnews.com/article/mexico -caribbean-city-monterrey-796f915b66fbf35d90a4a9b3aa299912.

Astourian, Stephan H. 2000. "From Ter-Petrosian to Kocharian: Leadership Change in Armenia." Berkeley Program in Soviet and Post-Soviet Studies Working Paper Series, Winter 2000.

Atshan, Sa'ed. 2020. *Queer Palestine and the Empire of Critique*. Stanford, CA: Stanford University Press.

Austin, John L. 1999. *How to Do Things with Words*. Oxford: Clarendon Press.

Awad, Nazik, and Sondos Al Ali. 2019. "Women's Stories from the Frontline of Sudan's Revolution Must Be Told." *openDemocracy*, March 20, 2019. https:// www.opendemocracy.net/en/5050/womens-stories-from-the-frontline -of-sudans-revolution-must-be-told/.

Ayvazyan, Gayane. 2018. "The Adaptation and Localization of Modern Intellectual Experience by the Armenian Patriarchate of Constantinople (Second Half of 18th and First Half of 19th Centuries)." In *Europe and the Black Sea Region: A History of Early Knowledge Exchange (1750–1850)*, edited by Karl Kaser Dominik Gutmeyr, 391–408. Zurich: LIT.

Badalyan, Peproneh. 2021. "How Long Will the Armenian Construction Segment Grow? The Future of Construction Business in Armenia." *Tower.am*, February 19, 2021. https://tower.am/the-future-of-construction-business-in-armenia/.

Baer, Brian James. 2009. *Other Russias: Homosexuality and the Crisis of Post-Soviet Identity*. New York: Palgrave MacMillan.

Bakker, Isabella. 2007. "Social Reproduction and the Constitution of a Gendered Political Economy." *New Political Economy* 12 (4): 541–56.

Barthes, Roland. 1981. *Camera Lucida: Reflections on Photography*. Translated by Richard Howard. New York: Hill and Wang.

Berlant, Lauren. 2000. "Intimacy: A Special Issue." Special issue, *Critical Inquiry* 24 (2): 281–88.

Berlant, Lauren. 2008. "Thinking about Feeling Historical." *Emotion, Space and Society* 1 (1): 4–9.

Berlant, Lauren, and Lee Edelman. 2014. *Sex, or the Unbearable*. Durham, NC: Duke University Press.

Berlant, Lauren, and Michael Warner. (1998) 2002. "Sex in Public." In *Publics and Counterpublics*, edited by Michael Warner, 187–208. New York: Zone Books.

Bersani, Leo. 1986. *The Freudian Body: Psychoanalysis and Art*. New York: Columbia University Press.

Bersani, Leo, and Adam Phillips. 2008. *Intimacies*. Chicago: Chicago University Press.

Bertsch, Gary. 1999. *Crossroads and Conflict: Security and Foreign Policy in the Caucasus and Central Asia*. London: Routledge.

Beukian, Sevan. 2018. "Queering Armenianness: *Tarorinakelov* Identities." *Armenian Review* 56 (1–2): 13–38.

Bey, Marquis. 2019. *Them Goon Rules: Fugitive Essays on Radical Black Feminism*. Tucson: University of Arizona Press.

Bhattacharya, Tithi. 2017. "Introduction: Mapping Social Reproduction Theory." In *Social Reproduction Theory: Remapping Class, Recentering Oppression*, edited by Tithi Bhattacharya, 1–20. London: Pluto Press.

Bhowmick, Nilanjana, and Kanishka Sonthalia. 2021. "'I Cannot Be Intimidated. I Cannot Be Bought.' The Women Leading India's Farmer's Protests." *Time*, March 4, 2021. https://time.com/5942125/women-india-farmers-protests/.

Bian, Yanjie. 2019. *Guanxi: How China Works*. Medford, MA: Polity Press.

Bloch, Ernst, and Theodor W. Adorno. 1988. "Something's Missing: A Discussion between Ernst Bloch and Theodor Adorno on the Contradictions of Utopian Longing." In *The Utopian Function of Art and Literature: Selected Essays*, edited by Ernst Bloch, 1–17. Cambridge, MA: MIT Press.

Bonfiglioli, Chiara, and Kristen Ghodsee. 2020. "Vanishing Act: Global Socialist Feminism as the 'Missing Other' of Transnational Feminism—a Response to Tlostanova, Thapar-Björkert and Koobak (2019)." *Feminist Review* 126 (1): 168–72.

Borneman, John. 2004. "Introduction: Theorizing Regime Ends." In *Death of the Father: An Anthropology of End in Political Authority*, edited by John Borneman, 1–31. New York: Berghahn Books.

Boyajian, Michael. 2019. *Roman Armenia: A Study in Survival*, 2nd ed. Independently Published.

Brand, David. 1988. "Soviet Union Vision of Horror." *Time*, December 26, 1988. https://content.time.com/time/subscriber/article/0,33009,956602,00.html.

Brkovic, Carna. 2017. *Managing Ambiguity: How Clientelism, Citizenship, and Power Shape Personhood in Bosnia and Herzegovina*. New York: Berghahn Books.

Buelow, Samuel. 2012. "Locating Kazakhstan: The Role of LGBT Voices in the Asia/Europe Debate." *Lambda Nordica* 17 (4): 99–125. https://lambdanordica.org/index.php/lambdanordica/article/view/362.

Bulut, Uzay. 2020. "Turkey: Erdogan Uses 'Leftovers of the Sword' Anti-Christian Hate Speech." *GenocideWatch*, May 11, 2020. https://www.genocidewatch.com/single-post/2020/05/11/turkey-erdogan-uses-leftovers-of-the-sword-anti-christian-hate-speech.

Burawoy, Michael, and Katherine Verdery. 1999. "Introduction." In *Uncertain Transitions: Ethnographies of Change in the Postsocialist World*, edited by Michael Burawoy and Katherine Verdery, 1–18. Lanham, MD: Rowman and Littlefield.

Butler, Judith. 1997a. "Merely Cultural." *Social Text* 15 (3–4): 265–77.

Butler, Judith. 1997b. *The Psychic Life of Power: Theories in Subjection*. Stanford, CA: Stanford University Press.

Butler, Judith. 2000. *Antigone's Claim: Kinship between Life and Death*. New York: Columbia University Press.

Butterfield, Nicole. 2013. "Sexual Rights as a Tool for Mapping Europe: Discourses of Human Rights and European Identity in Activists' Struggles in Croatia." In *Queer Visibility in Post-Socialist Cultures*, edited by Narcisz and Andrea P. Balogh Fejes, 13–33. Bristol, UK: Intellect.

Callamard, Agnes. 2021. "Turkey Takes Centre Stage in the Fight for Women's Rights." *Amnesty International*, July 1, 2021. https://www.amnesty.org/en/latest/news/2021/07/turkey-takes-centre-stage-in-the-fight-for-womens-rights/.

Carsten, Janet. 2004. *After Kinship: New Departures in Anthropology*. Cambridge: Cambridge University Press.

Caruth, Cathy. 2016. *Unclaimed Experience: Trauma, Narrative, and History*. 20th anniversary ed. Baltimore, MD: Johns Hopkins University Press.

Chapple, Amos. 2018. "Still Recovering: Armenia's Catastrophic Earthquake, 30 Years Later." *RadioFreeEurope/RadioLiberty*, December 6, 2018. https://www.rferl.org/a/armenias-catastrophic-earthquake-of-1988/29634413.html.

Chenoweth, Erica, and Zoe Marks. 2022. "Revenge of the Patriarchs: Why Autocrats Fear Women." *Foreign Affairs*, February 8, 2022. https://www.foreignaffairs.com/articles/china/2022-02-08/women-rights-revenge-patriarchs.

Chibber, Vivek. 2013. *Postcolonial Theory and the Specter of Capital*. London: Verso.

Chorbadjian, Smpat. 2015. *Surviving the Forgotten Armenian Genocide: A Moving Personal Story*. Edited by Patrick Sookhdeo. Chicago: Isaac Publishing LLC.

Christophers, Brett. 2023. *Our Lives in Their Portfolios: Why Asset Managers Own the World*. New York: Verso.

Cohen, Cathy. 1997. "Punks, Bulldaggers, and Welfare Queens: The Radical Potential of Queer Politics?" *GLQ: A Journal of Lesbian and Gay Studies* 3 (4): 437–65.

Collier, Stephen J. 2011. *Post-Soviet Social: Neoliberalism, Social Modernity, Biopolitics*. Princeton, NJ: Princeton University Press.

Cornell, Drucilla, and Stephen D. Seely. 2014. "There's Nothing Revolutionary about a Blowjob." *Social Text* 32 (2): 1–23.

Costa, Florencia, and Shobhan Saxena. 2021. "Brazil: Cornered, Isolated and Weakened, Bolsonaro Overplays His Military Card." *The Wire*, April 1, 2021. https://thewire.in/world/brazil-bolsonaro-military-self-coup-covid-19.

Cowie, Sam. 2018. "Bolsonaro Wants to 'Cleanse' Brazil of Left-Wing 'Criminals.'" *Al Jazeera*, October 23, 2018. https://www.aljazeera.com/news/2018/10/23/bolsonaro-wants-to-cleanse-brazil-of-left-wing-criminals.

Cvetkovich, Ann. 2012. *Depression: A Public Feeling*. Durham, NC: Duke University Press.

Dave, Naisargi. 2012. *Queer Activism in India: A Story in the Anthropology of Ethics*. Durham, NC: Duke University Press.

Davis, Angela Y. 2003. *Are Prisons Obsolete?* New York: Seven Stories Press.

Davis, Janae, Alex A. Moulton, Levi Van Sant, and Brian Williams. 2019. "Anthropocene, Capitalocene, . . . Plantationocene? A Manifesto for Ecological Justice in an Age of Global Crises." *Geography Compass* 13 (5): e12438. https://doi.org//10.1111/gec3.12438.

Davis, Mike. 2010. "Who Will Build the Ark?" *New Left Review* 61 (Jan.–Feb.): 29–46. https://newleftreview.org/issues/ii61/articles/mike-davis-who-will-build-the-ark.

Dean, Tim. 2009. *Unlimited Intimacy: Reflections on the Subculture of Barebacking*. Chicago: University of Chicago Press.

de Certeau, Michel. 2011. *The Practice of Everyday Life*, Vol. 1. Translated by Steven Rendall. 3rd ed. Berkeley: University of California Press.

Delaney, Carol. 1991. *The Seed and the Soil: Gender and Cosmology in Turkish Village Society*. Berkeley: University of California Press.

Deleuze, Gilles, and Felix Guattari. 1987. *A Thousand Plateaus: Capitalism and Schizophrenia*. Translated by Brian Massumi. Minneapolis: University of Minnesota Press.

Der Khachadourian, Ardashes. 1992a. "Aylandakutyun." In *The Armenian Language New Dictionary* [Hayots lezvi nor bararan], edited by Ardashes Der Khachadourian, 60. Beirut: G. Doniguian and Sons.

Der Khachadourian, Ardashes. 1992b. "Aylaserutyun." In *The Armenian Language New Dictionary* [Hayots lezvi nor bararan], edited by Ardashes Der Khachadourian, 60. Beirut: G. Doniguian and Sons.

de Waal, Thomas. 2013a. *Black Garden: Armenia and Azerbaijan through Peace and War*. 10th anniversary ed. New York: New York University Press.

de Waal, Thomas, ed. 2013b. *The Stalin Puzzle: Deciphering Post-Soviet Public Opinion*. Washington, DC: Carnegie Endowment for International Peace.

Dragojevic, Srdan, dir. 2011. *Parada*. Belgrade: Filmstar.

Du Bois, W. E. B. 1992. *Black Reconstruction in America 1860–1880*. Introduction by David Levering Lewis. New York: The Free Press.

Duff, Renee. 2022. "Hundreds of Record Highs Broken as Japan Bakes under Historic Heat Wave." *AccuWeather*, June 28, 2022. https://www.accuweather.com/en/weather-forecasts/hundreds-of-record-highs-broken-as-japan-bakes-under-historic-heat-wave/1209207.

Duggan, Lisa. 2002. "The New Homonormativity: The Sexual Politics of Neoliberalism." In *Materializing Democracy: Toward a Revitalized Cultural Politics*, edited by Russ Castronovo and Dana D. Nelson, 175–94. Durham, NC: Duke University Press.

Dugin, Alexander. 2012. *The Fourth Political Theory*. London: Arktos.

Dugin, Alexander. 2014. *Eurasian Mission: An Introduction to Neo-Eurasianism*. London: Arktos.

Dunlap, Charles J., Jr. 2008. "Lawfare Today: A Perspective." *Yale Journal of International Affairs* (Winter): 146–54.

Edelman, Lee. 2004. *No Future: Queer Theory and the Death Drive*. Durham, NC: Duke University Press.

Ekmekcioglu, Lerna. 2016. *Recovering Armenia: The Limits of Belonging in Post-Genocide Turkey*. Stanford, CA: Stanford University Press.

Eng, David L., Jack Halberstam, and José Esteban Muñoz. 2005. "What's Queer about Queer Studies Now?" *Social Text* 23 (3–4): 1–18.

Eng, David L., and Jasbir K. Puar. 2020. "Introduction: Left of Queer." *Social Text* 38 (4): 1–23.

Essig, Laurie. 1999. *Queer in Russia: A Story of Sex, Self, and the Other*. Durham, NC: Duke University Press.

Fanon, Frantz. 2004. *The Wretched of the Earth*. New York: Grove Press.

Fassin, Didier, and Richard Rechtman. 2009. *The Empire of Trauma: An Inquiry into the Condition of Victimhood*. Princeton, NJ: Princeton University Press.

Fehlings, Susanne. 2016. "The Ignoble Savage in Urban Yerevan." *Central Asian Survey* 35 (2): 195–217.

Fink, Bruce. 1995. *The Lacanian Subject: Between Language and Jouissance*. Princeton, NJ: Princeton University Press.

Fisher, Jo. 1989. *Mothers of the Disappeared*. London: Zed Books.

Fitzpatrick, Sheila. 2000. *Everyday Stalinism: Ordinary Life in Extraordinary Times; Soviet Russia in the 1930s*. Oxford: Oxford University Press.

Floyd, Kevin. 2009. *The Reification of Desire: Toward a Queer Marxism*. Minneapolis: University of Minnesota Press.

Fraser, Nancy. 1997. "Heterosexism, Misrecognition, and Capitalism: A Response to Judith Butler." *New Left Review* 52–53:279–89.

Fraser, Nancy. 2016. "Capitalism's Crisis of Care." *Dissent* 63 (4): 30–37.

Freeman, Elizabeth. 2010. *Time Binds: Queer Temporalities, Queer Histories*. Durham, NC: Duke University Press.

Freud, Sigmund. 1910. *Three Contributions to the Sexual Theory*. Translated by A. A. Brill. New York: The Journal of Nervous and Mental Disease Publishing Company. https://archive.org/details/freud-1910-three/page/n1/mode/2up.

Freud, Sigmund. (1930) 2010. *Civilization and Its Discontents*. Mansfield Centre: Martino Publishing.

Freud, Sigmund. 1961. *Beyond the Pleasure Principle*. Edited by James Strachey. New York: W. W. Norton.

Freud, Sigmund. 1989a. *Introductory Lectures on Psycho-Analysis*. Translated and edited by James Strachey. New York: W. W. Norton.

Freud, Sigmund. 1989b. "Totem and Taboo." In *The Freud Reader*, edited by Peter Gay, 481–513. New York: W. W. Norton.

Freud, Sigmund. 2003. "The Uncanny." In *The Uncanny*, edited by Hugh Haughton, 121–62. New York: Penguin Classics.

Gal, Susan, and Gail Kligman. 2000. *The Politics of Gender after Socialism*. Princeton, NJ: Princeton University Press.

Garbis, Christian. 2013. "Yerevan's Bus Fare Protests: A Timeline." *Armenian Weekly*, July 29, 2013. https://armenianweekly.com/2013/07/29/yerevans-bus-fare -protests-a-timeline/.

Gevorgyan, Siranush. 2013. "Union Architect: No Plan Is Best for Republic Square." *ArmeniaNow*, October 24, 2013. https://web.archive.org/web/20131027111005 /http://armenianow.com/society/49494/republic_square_yerevan_mkrtich _minasyan_lenin_statue.

Ghaplanyan, Irina. 2018. *Post-Soviet Armenia: The New National Elite and the New National Narrative*. London: Routledge.

Ghodsee, Kristen. 2018a. *Second World, Second Sex: Socialist Women's Activism and Global Solidarity during the Cold War*. Durham, NC: Duke University Press.

Ghodsee, Kristen. 2018b. *Why Women Have Better Sex under Socialism: And Other Arguments for Economic Independence*. New York: Bold Type Books.

Gilmore, Ruth Wilson. 2008. "Forgotten Places and the Seeds of Grassroots Planning." In *Engaging Contradictions: Theory, Politics, and Methods of Activist Scholarship*, edited by Charles R. Hale, 31–61. Berkeley: University of California Press.

Gilmore, Ruth Wilson. 2022. *Abolition Geography: Essays toward Liberation*. New York: Verso.

Giragosyan, Richard. 2009. "Armenia at a Strategic Crossroads." *Connections* 8 (3): 109–14.

Gopinath, Gayatri. 2005. *Impossible Desires: Queer Diasporas and South Asian Public Culture*. Durham, NC: Duke University Press.

Gopinath, Gayatri. 2018. *Unruly Visions: The Aesthetic Practices of Queer Diaspora*. Durham, NC: Duke University Press.

Gordon, Avery. 2008. *Ghostly Matters: Haunting and the Sociological Imagination*. Minneapolis: University of Minnesota Press.

Graeber, David. 2011. *Revolution in Reverse: Essays on Politics, Art, and Imagination*. Brooklyn: Minor Compositions.

Graeber, David, and David Wengrow. 2021. *The Dawn of Everything: A New History of Humanity*. New York: Farrar, Straus and Giroux.

Graff, Agnieszka, and Elzbieta Korolczuk. 2022. *Anti-gender Politics in the Populist Moment*. London and New York: Routledge.

Green, David B., Jr. 2019. "Hearing the Queer Roots of Black Lives Matter." *Medium*, February 6, 2019. https://medium.com/national-center-for-institutional -diversity/hearing-the-queer-roots-of-black-lives-matter-2e69834a65cd.

Gregor, Thomas. 1977. *Mehinaku: The Drama of Daily Life in a Brazilian Indian Village*. Chicago: University of Chicago Press.

Hakobyan, Tatul. 2010. *Karabagh Diary, Green and Black: Neither War nor Peace*. Translated by Maria Titizian, Nanig der Harutyunyan, and Heghinar Melkom Melkomian. Antelias, Lebanon: Antelias Publishing.

Halberstam, Jack. 2008. "The Anti-social Turn in Queer Studies." *Graduate Journal of Social Science* 5 (2): 140–56.

Halberstam, Jack. 2011. *The Queer Art of Failure*. Durham, NC: Duke University Press.

Haraway, Donna. 2016. *Staying with the Trouble: Making Kin in the Chthulucene*. Durham, NC: Duke University Press.

Hartman, Saidiya. 2007. *Lose Your Mother: A Journey along the Atlantic Slave Route*. New York: Farrar, Straus and Giroux.

Harvey, David. 2003. *The New Imperialism*. Oxford: Oxford University Press.

Harvey, David. 2006. *The Limits to Capital*. New York: Verso.

Healy, Dan. 2001. *Homosexual Desire in Revolutionary Russia*. Chicago: University of Chicago Press.

Hennessey, Rosemary. 2006. "Returning to Reproduction Queerly: Sex, Labor, Need." *Rethinking Marxism* 18 (3): 387–95.

Herek, Gregory M. 2004. "Beyond 'Homophobia': Thinking about Sexual Prejudice and Stigma in the Twenty-First Century." *Sexuality Research and Social Policy* 1 (2): 6–24.

Herzfeld, Michael. 1997. *Cultural Intimacy: Social Poetics in the Nation-State*. New York: Routledge.

Hinsliff, Gaby. 2020. "'The Rapist Is You!': Why a Chilean Protest Chant Is Being Sung around the World." *Guardian*, February 3, 2020. https://www.the guardian.com/society/2020/feb/03/the-rapist-is-you-chilean-protest-song -chanted-around-the-world-un-iolador-en-tu-camino.

Hoad, Neville. 2007. *African Intimacies: Race, Homosexuality, and Globalization*. Minneapolis: University of Minnesota Press.

Hoang, Kimberly Kay. 2022. *Spiderweb Capitalism: How Global Elites Exploit Frontier Markets*. Princeton, NJ: Princeton University Press.

Honorati, Maddalena, Sara Johansson de Silva, Natalia Millan, Natalia Kerschbaumer, and Florentin Philipp. 2019. *Work for a Better Future in Armenia: An Analysis of Jobs Dynamics*. Washington, DC: World Bank Group. http:// documents.worldbank.org/curated/en/387401564380250230/Work-for-a -Better-Future-in-Armenia-An-Analysis-of-Jobs-Dynamics.

Hörschelmann, Kathrin, and Alison Stenning. 2008. "Ethnographies of Postsocialist Change." *Progress in Human Geography* 32 (3): 339–61.

Hrachya Acharyan Institute. 2001–2. *Hayots lezvi barbarayin bararan* [*The Armenian Language Dialectical Dictionary*], 2792. Yerevan, Armenia: Armenian Republic National Science Academy.

Hubbert, Jennifer. 2006. "(Re)collecting Mao: Memory and Fetish in Contemporary China." *American Ethnologist* 33 (2): 145–61.

Human Rights Watch. 2002. *"We Have No Orders to Save You": State Participation and Complicity in Communal Violence in Gujarat*. Human Rights Watch, April 30,

2002. https://www.hrw.org/report/2002/04/30/we-have-no-orders-save-you /state-participation-and-complicity-communal-violence.

Humphrey, Caroline. 1991. "'Icebergs,' Barter, and the Mafia in Provincial Russia." *Anthropology Today* 7 (2): 8–13.

Hunt, Stephen E. 2017. "Prospects for Kurdish Ecology Initiatives in Syria and Turkey: Democratic Confederalism and Social Ecology." *Capitalism Nature Socialism* 19 (3): 7–26.

Imre, Anikó. 2015. "Whiteness in Post-socialist Eastern Europe: The Time of the Gypsies, the End of Race." In *Postcolonial Studies: An Anthology*, edited by Pramod K. Nayar, 297–315. Malden, MA: Wiley-Blackwell.

International Energy Agency. 2021. *Armenia Energy Profile*. https://iea.blob.core .windows.net/assets/89a4a24d-fe2b-4e04-9ec7-25d3c02dbefd/CountryPages _Armenia_FINAL.pdf.

Ishkanian, Armine. 2003. "Gendered Transitions: The Impact of Post-Soviet Transition on Women in Central Asia and the Caucasus." *Perspectives on Global Development and Technology* 2 (3–4): 475–496.

Ishkanian, Armine. 2008. *Democracy Building and Civil Society in Post-Soviet Armenia*. New York: Routledge.

Ishkanian, Armine. 2016. "From Civil Disobedience to Armed Violence: Political Developments in Armenia." *openDemocracy*, July 19, 2016. https://www .opendemocracy.net/en/odr/from-civil-disobedience-to-armed-violence -political-developments-in-armen/.

JAMnews. 2022. "Gas Price Increase—a Blow to Armenia's Weakened Economy." April 2, 2022. https://jam-news.net/gas-price-increase-a-blow-to-armenias -weakened-economy/.

Johnson, E. Patrick. 2001. "'Quare' Studies, or (Almost) Everything I Know about Queer Studies I Learned from my Grandmother." *Text and Performance Quarterly* 21 (1): 1–25.

Kaba, Mariame, and Andra J. Ritchie. 2022. *No More Police: A Case for Abolition*. New York: New Press.

Kaganovsky, Lilya. 2008. *How the Soviet Man Was Unmade: Cultural Fantasy and Male Subjectivity under Stalin*. Pittsburgh: University of Pittsburgh Press.

Kalb, Don. 2012. "Thinking about Neoliberalism as If the Crisis Was Actually Happening." *Social Anthropology* 20 (3): 318–30.

Kauanui, J. Kehaulani. 2019. "Decolonial Self-Determination and 'No-State Solutions.'" *Humanity Journal*, July 2, 2019. http://humanityjournal.org/blog /decolonial-self-determination-and-no-state-solutions/.

Kharatyan, Lusine. 2016. "Tsiklits durs galu miyak yelqy Mheri durn apakarutseln e" [The only way out of the cycle is to dismantle Mher's door]. Interview by Siranush Papyan. *Lragir*, August 16, 2016. https://www.lragir.am/2016/08/03 /137168/.

Khatchadourian, Lori. 2022. "Life Extempore: Trials of Ruination in the Twilight Zone of Soviet Industry." *Cultural Anthropology* 37 (2): 317–48.

Khorenatsi, Moses. 1978. *History of the Armenians*. Translated by Robert W. Thomson. Cambridge, MA: Harvard University Press.

Kirn, Gal. 2017. "A Critique of Transition Studies on Postsocialism, or How to Rethink and Reorient 1989? The Case of (Post)socialist (Post)Yugoslavia." In *Beyond Neoliberalism: Approaches to Social Inequality and Difference*, edited by Marian Burchardt and Gal Kirn, 43–68. London: Palgrave Macmillan.

Kopalyan, Nerses. 2020. "Thick as Thieves: Bringing Armenia's Robber Barons to Justice." *EVN Report*, June 2, 2020. https://old.evnreport.com/politics/thick -as-thieves-bringing-armenia-s-robber-barons-to-justice.

Kotkin, Stephen. 2001. "Modern Times: The Soviet Union and the Interwar Conjuncture." *Kritika: Explorations in Russian and Eurasian History* 2 (1): 111–64.

Krylova, Anna. 2011. *Soviet Women in Combat: A History of Violence on the Eastern Front*. Cambridge: Cambridge University Press.

Kulick, Don. 2003. "No." *Language and Communication* 23: 139–51.

Kurtović, Larisa, and Azra Hromadžić. 2017. "Cannibal States, Empty Bellies: Protest, History and Political Imagination in Post-Dayton Bosnia." *Critique of Anthropology* 37 (3). https://doi.org/10.1177/0308275X17719988.

Lacan, Jacques. 1997. *Seminar III: The Psychoses 1955–1956*. Translated by Russell Grigg. New York: W. W. Norton.

Lacan, Jacques. 1998. *The Seminar of Jacques Lacan*. Book 11, *The Four Fundamental Concepts of Psychoanalysis, 1959–1960*. Translated by Alan Sheridan. Edited by Jacques-Alain Miller. New York: W. W. Norton.

Lacan, Jacques. 2006. "The Subversion of the Subject and the Dialectic of Desire in the Freudian Unconscious." In *Ecrits: The First Complete Edition in English*, translated by Bruce Fink. New York: W. W. Norton.

Lacan, Jacques. 2013. *On the Names-of-the-Father*. Translated by Bruce Fink. Cambridge: Polity Press.

Laplanche, Jean, and Jean-Bertrans Pontalis. 1973. *The Language of Psychoanalysis*. New York: W. W. Norton.

Lear, Jonathan. 2006. *Radical Hope: Ethics in the Face of Cultural Devastation*. Cambridge, MA: Harvard University Press.

Ledeneva, Alena. 2009. "From Russia with *Blat*: Can Informal Networks Help Modernize Russia?" *Social Research: An International Quarterly* 76 (1): 257–88.

Lenin, Vladimir. 1920. "The Tasks of the Youth Leagues." *Pravda*, nos. 221–23 (October 5–7, 1920). https://www.marxists.org/archive/lenin/works/1920/oct/02.htm.

Levi-Strauss. 1969. *The Elementary Structures of Kinship*. Boston: Beacon Press.

Libaridian, Gerard J. 2007. *Modern Armenia: People, Nation, State*. New Brunswick: Transaction Publishers.

Lipman, Maria. 2013. "Stalin Is Not Dead: A Legacy That Holds Back Russia." In *The Stalin Puzzle: Deciphering Post-Soviet Public Opinion*, edited by Thomas de Waal, 15–26. Washington, DC: Carnegie Endowment for International Peace.

Liu, Petrus. 2012. "Queer Human Rights in and against China: Marxism and the Figuration of the Human." *Social Text* 30 (1): 71–89.

Lorusso, Marilisa. 2013. "Presidential Elections in Armenia and the Opposition's Long March." Istituto Affari Internazionali Working Papers 13–14, April 2013. https://www.jstor.org/stable/resrep09800.

Love, Heather. 2009. *Feeling Backward: Loss and the Politics of Queer History*. Cambridge, MA: Harvard University Press.

Lowe, Lisa. 2015. *The Intimacies of Four Continents*. Durham, NC: Duke University Press.

Magdoff, Fred, and John Bellamy Foster. 2023. "Grand Theft Capital: The Increasing Exploitation and Robbery of the U.S. Working Class." *Monthly Review* 75 (1): 1–22.

Malkassian, Mark. 1996. *Gha-ra-bagh! The Emergence of the National Democratic Movement in Armenia*. Detroit: Wayne State University Press.

Malyan, Henrik, dir. 1972. *Hayrik* [Father]. Soviet Armenia: Hayfilm Film Studio.

Mann, Geoff, and Joel Wainwright. 2018. *Climate Leviathan: A Political Theory of Our Planetary Future*. New York: Verso.

Martirosyan, Sona. 2020. "The Need for Gender Equality in the Labor Market: Women in Armenia's IT Sector and Beyond." *EVN Report*, January 30, 2020. https://www.evnreport.com/economy/the-need-for-gender-equality-in-the-labor-market.

Marutyan, Harutyun. 2007. "Iconography of Historical Memory and Armenian National Identity at the End of the 1980s." In *Representations on the Margins of Europe*, edited by Tsypylma Darieva and Wolfgang Kaschuba. Frankfurt: Campus Verlag.

Marx, Karl. 1976. *Capital: A Critique of Political Economy, Volume One*. Translated by Ben Fowkes. Edited by Ernest Mandel. London: Penguin Books.

Massad, Joseph. 2018. "Against Self-Determination." *Humanity Journal*, September 11, 2018. http://humanityjournal.org/issue9-2/against-self-determination/.

Mattiolo, Fabio. 2018. "Financialization without Liquidity: In-Kind Payments, Forced Credit, and Authoritarianism at the Periphery of Europe." *Journal of Royal Anthropological Institute* 24 (3): 568–88. https://doi.org/10.1111/1467-9655.12861.

Mayerchyk, Maria, and Olga Plakhotnik. 2021. "Uneventful Feminist Protest in Post-Maidan Ukraine: Nation and Colonialism Revisited." In *Postcolonial and Postsocialist Dialogues: Intersections, Opacities, Challenges in Feminist Theorizing and Practice*, edited by Madina Tlostanova, Suruchi Thapar-Bjorkert, and Redi Koobak, 121–37. New York: Routledge.

Mbembe, Achille. 1992. "The Banality of Power and the Aesthetics of Vulgarity in the Postcolony." *Public Culture* 4 (2): 1–30.

McCoy, Terrence, Marina Lopes, and Teo Armus. 2019. "'This Will Not Stick': Brazilian President Lashes Out over Alleged Links to Left-Wing Politician's Killing." *Washington Post*, October 30, 2019. https://www.washingtonpost.com/nation/2019/10/30/jair-bolsonaro-marielle-franco-murder-link/.

McGranahan, Carole. 2016. "Theorizing Refusal: An Introduction." *Cultural Anthropology* 31 (3): 319–25. https://doi.org/10.14506/ca31.3.01.

McGuiness, Jackie, and Katherine Rohloff. 2023. "NASA Clocks July 2023 as Hottest
     Month on Record Ever since 1880." *NASA*, August 14, 2023. https://www.nasa
     .gov/press-release/nasa-clocks-july-2023-as-hottest-month-on-record-ever
     -since-1880.

McKinnon, Susan, and Fenella Cannell. 2013. "The Difference Kinship Makes." In
     Vital Relations: Modernity and the Persistent Life of Kinship, edited by Susan
     McKinnon and Fenella Cannell, 3–38. Santa Fe, NM: School of Advanced Re-
     search Press.

Mejlumyan, Ani. 2020. "In Yerevan's Redevelopment, New Government Follows
     Old Script." *Eurasianet*, August 24, 2020. https://eurasianet.org/in-yerevans
     -redevelopment-new-government-follows-old-script.

Mejlumyan, Ani. 2022. "Armenia Signals Readiness to Restart Controversial Mine
     Project." *Eurasianet*, June 29, 2022. https://eurasianet.org/armenia-signals
     -readiness-to-restart-controversial-mine-project.

Mikdashi, Maya, and Jasbir K. Puar. 2016. "Queer Theory and Permanent War." *GLQ:
     A Journal of Lesbian and Gay Studies* 22 (2): 215–22.

Miles, Malcolm. 2014. "Ideological Regeneration: The Cafesjian Centre for the Arts
     and the New Yerevan." In *Consuming Architecture: On the Occupation, Appropri-
     ation and Interpretation of Buildings*, edited by Daniel Maudlin and Marcel Vell-
     inga, 154–68. London: Routledge.

Miller, Donald E., and Lorna Touryan Miller. 1999. *Survivors: An Oral History of the
     Armenian Genocide*. Berkeley: University of California Press.

Miller, Donald E., and Lorna Touryan Miller. 2003. *Armenia: Portraits of Survival and
     Hope*. Berkeley: University of California Press.

Mkrtchyan, Narek. 2015. "Gramsci in Armenia: State-Church Relations in the Post-
     Soviet Armenia." *Transformation* 32 (3): 163–76.

Moore, Henrietta. 2007. *The Subject of Anthropology: Gender, Symbolism and Psycho-
     analysis*. Cambridge: Polity.

Mulvey, Stephen. 1999. "Killers Lacked Coherent Goals." *BBC News*, October 28,
     1999. http://news.bbc.co.uk/2/hi/europe/491194.stm.

Muñoz, José Esteban. 2009. *Cruising Utopia: The Then and There of Queer Futurity*.
     New York: New York University Press.

Muradyan, Tsovinar. 2017. "City of the Sun Planned as a Garden City." *Fabrikzeitung*,
     May 1, 2018. https://www.fabrikzeitung.ch/city-of-the-sun-planned-as-a
     -garden-city/#/.

Nash, Jennifer C. 2019. "Black Maternal Aesthetics." *Theory and Event* 22 (3): 551–75.

Nichanian, Marc. 2002. *Writers of Disaster: Armenian Literature in the Twentieth Cen-
     tury*. London: Taderon Press.

Nichanian, Marc. 2003. "Catastrophic Mourning." In *Loss*, edited by David L. Eng
     and David Kazanjian, 99–124. Berkeley: University of California Press.

Nikoghosyan, Alina. 2016. "Breaking the Stereotypes: Activist Says Blaming
     Women for Violence against Them Is Wrong." *ArmeniaNow.com*, November 2,

2016. https://www.armenianow.com/news/69819/armenia_domestic
_violence_women_campaign.

Nikoghosyan, Anna. 2016. "In Armenia, Gender Is Geopolitical." *openDemocracy*,
April 19, 2016. https://www.opendemocracy.net/en/odr/in-armenia-gender
-is-geopolitical/.

Nikoghosyan, Anna. 2019. "The Gendered Shades of Regime Change in Armenia."
In *Revolutionary Sensorium: Pavilion of the Republic of Armenia*, edited by Susanna
Gyulamiryan, 41–51. Yerevan: Antenor.

Nixon, Rob. 2011. *Slow Violence and the Environmentalism of the Poor*. Cambridge, MA:
Harvard University Press.

Oganesyan, Rafael, and Nerses Kopalyan. 2021. "New Poll Casts Electorate as
Largely Pessimistic and Undecided." *EVN Report*, June 17, 2021. https://www
.evnreport.com/elections/new-poll-casts-electorate-as-largely-pessimistic
-and-undecided.

Ohanyan, Anna. 2021. "What's Next for Armenia? Authoritarian Reserves and Risks
in a Democratic State." In *Armenia's Velvet Revolution: Authoritarian Decline
and Civil Resistance in a Multipolar World*, edited by Laurence Broers and Anna
Ohanyan, 231–52. New York: I. B. Tauris.

Oswin, Natalie. 2019. *Global City Futures: Desire and Development in Singapore*. Athens:
University of Georgia Press.

Oushakine, Serguei Alex. 2009. *The Patriotism of Despair: Nation, War, and Loss in Russia*. Ithaca, NY: Cornell University Press.

Özkan, Behlül. 2008. "Who Gains from the 'No War No Peace' Situation? A Critical Analysis of the Nagorno-Karabakh Conflict." *Geopolitics* 13 (3): 572–99.

Ozyurek, Esra. 2006. *Nostalgia for the Modern: State Secularism and Everyday Politics in
Turkey*. Durham, NC: Duke University Press.

Panossian, Razmik. 2002. "The Past as Nation: Three Dimensions of Armenian
Identity." *Geopolitics* 7 (2): 121–46.

Panossian, Razmik. 2006. "Post-Soviet Armenia: Nationalism and Its (Dis)contents."
In *After Independence: Making and Protecting the Nation in Postcolonial and Postcommunist States*, edited by Lowell W. Barrington, 225–47. Ann Arbor: University of Michigan Press.

Peterson, V. Spike. 2014. "Family Matters: How Queering the Intimate Queers the
International." *International Studies Review* 16 (4): 604–8.

Petryna, Adriana. 2002. *Life Exposed: Biological Citizens after Chernobyl*. Princeton, NJ:
Princeton University Press.

Phillips, Kristin D. 2010. "Pater Rules Best: Political Kinship and Party Politics in
Tanzania's Presidential Elections." *PoLAR: Political and Legal Anthropology Review* 33 (1): 109–32.

Phillips, Tom. 2018. "Brazil's Jair Bolsonaro Threatens Purge of Leftwing 'Outlaws.'"
Guardian, October 22, 2018. https://www.theguardian.com/world/2018/oct/22
/brazils-jair-bolsonaro-says-he-would-put-army-on-streets-to-fight.

Pilkington, Hillary. 1992. "Russia and the Former Soviet Republics: Behind the Mask of Soviet Unity: Realities of Women's Lives." In *Superwoman and the Double Burden: Women's Experiences of Change in Central and Eastern Europe and the Former Soviet Union*, edited by Chris Corrin, 180–235. Toronto: Second Story Press.

Platz, Stephanie. 2000. "The Shape of National Time: Daily Life, History, and Identity during Armenia's Transition to Independence, 1991–1994." In *Altering States: Ethnographies of Transition in Eastern Europe and the Former Soviet Union*, edited by Daphne Berdahl, Matti Bunzl, and Martha Lampland, 114–38. Ann Arbor: University of Michigan Press.

Popa, Bogdan. 2021. *De-centering Queer Theory: Communist Sexuality in the Flow during and after the Cold War*. Manchester: Manchester University Press.

Povinelli, Elizabeth A. 2012. "The Will to be Otherwise/The Effort of Endurance." *South Atlantic Quarterly* 111 (3): 453–57.

Povinelli, Elizabeth A. 2016. *Geontologies: A Requiem to Late Liberalism*. Durham, NC: Duke University Press.

Pshenychnykh, Anastasiya. 2020. "Leninfall: The Spectacle of Forgetting." *European Journal of Cultural Studies* 23 (3): 393–414.

Rank, Otto. 1914. *The Myth of the Birth of a Hero: A Psychological Interpretation of Mythology*. Translated by F. Robbins and Smith Ely Jelliffe. New York: The Journal of Nervous and Mental Disease Publishing Company. https://archive.org /details/mythofbirthofher1914rank/page/n3/mode/2up.

Rao, Rahul. 2020. *Out of Time: The Queer Politics of Postcoloniality*. New York: Oxford University Press.

Razsa, Maple, and Andrej Kurnik. 2012. "The Occupy Movement in Žižek's Hometown: Direct Democracy and a Politics of Becoming." *American Ethnologist* 39 (2): 238–58.

Revolutionary Association of the Women of Afghanistan (RAWA). 2001. "Taliban Should Be Overthrown by the Uprising of Afghan Nation." RAWA.org, October 11, 2001. http://www.rawa.org/us-strikes.htm.

Rexhepi, Piro. 2016. "From Orientalism to Homonationalism: Queer Politics, Islamophobia and Europeanization in Kosovo." *Southeastern Europe* 40 (1): 32–53.

Rexhepi, Piro. 2017. "The Politics of (Post)socialist Sexuality: American Foreign Policy in Bosnia and Kosovo." In *The Cultural Life of Capitalism in Yugoslavia: (Post) socialism and Its Other*, edited by Dijana Jelaca, Masa Kolanovic, Danijela Lugaric, 243–61. Cham, Switzerland: Palgrave Macmillan.

Riley, Emily Jenan. 2019. "The Politics of Teranga: Gender, Hospitality, and Power in Senegal." *PoLAR: Political and Legal Anthropology Review* 42 (1): 110–24.

Rivkin-Fish, Michele. 2013. "Conceptualizing Feminist Strategies for Russian Reproductive Politics: Abortion, Surrogate Motherhood, and Family Support after Socialism." *Signs* 38 (3): 569–93.

Rodney, Walter. 2018. *How Europe Underdeveloped Africa*. Foreword by Angela Davis. New York: Verso.

Rofel, Lisa. 2007. *Desiring China: Experiments in Neoliberalism, Sexuality, and Public Culture*. Durham, NC: Duke University Press.

Rosenberg, Jordana, and Amy Villarejo. 2011. "Introduction: Queerness, Norms, Utopia." *GLQ: A Journal of Lesbian and Gay Studies* 18 (1): 1–18.

Roth-Alexandrowicz, Melinda. 1997. "Armenia." In *Between State and Market: Mass Privatization in Transition Economies*, edited by Ira W. Liberman, Stilpon S. Nestor, and Raj M. Desai, 181–83. Washington, DC: The International Bank for Reconstruction and Development/The World Bank.

Roy, Suddhabrata Deb. 2020. "Locating Gramsci in Delhi's *Shaheen Bagh*: Perspectives on the Iconic Women's Protest in India." *Capital and Class* 45 (2): 183–89.

Sabonis-Helf, Theresa. 2007. "The Unified Energy Systems of Russia (RAO-UES) in Central Asia and the Caucasus: Nets of Interdependence." *Demokratizatsiya* 15 (4): 429–44.

Sacks, Karen Brodkin. 1989. "Toward a Unified Theory of Class, Race, and Gender." *American Ethnologist* 16 (3): 534–50.

Sahlins, Marshall. 2013. *What Kinship Is . . . and Is Not*. Chicago: University of Chicago Press.

Sargsyan, Nelli. 2019. "Experience-Sharing as Feminist Praxis: Imagining a Future of Collective Care." *History and Anthropology* 30 (1): 67–90.

Saria, Vaibhav. 2021. *Hijras, Lovers, Brothers: Surviving Sex and Poverty in Rural India*. New York: Fordham University Press.

Sarukhanyan, Vahe. 2017. "100 Churches Built in Armenia and Artsakh since Independence; Minimum of $50 Million Spent." *Hetq*, January 11, 2017. https://hetq.am/en/article/74555.

Schneider, David M. 1984. *A Critique of the Study of Kinship*. Ann Arbor: University of Michigan Press.

Schoeberlin, John S. 2004. "Doubtful Dead Fathers and Musical Corpses: What to Do with the Dead Stalin, Lenin, and Tsar Nicholas?" In *Death of the Father: An Anthropology of the End in Political Authority*, edited by John Borneman, 201–19. New York: Berghahn Books.

Sears, Alan. 2016. "Situating Sexuality in Social Reproduction." *Historical Materialism* 24 (2): 138–63.

Setalvad, Teesta. 2017. "Teesta Setalvad on How Gujarat Violence Has Changed Our Country." Talk presented at Rajmas College, Delhi, March 2017. YouTube, posted March 3, 2017. https://www.youtube.com/watch?v=TKJDhISTtTk.

Shahnazaryan, Nona, Aygun Aslanova, and Edita Badasyan. 2016. "Under the Rainbow Flags: LGBTI Rights in the South Caucasus." *Journal of Conflict Transformation* (Caucasus Edition): 1–30. https://caucasusedition.net/under-the-rainbow-flags-lgbti-rights-in-the-south-caucasus/.

Shehadeh, Raja. 2007. *Palestinian Walks: Forays into a Vanishing Landscape*. New York: Scribner.

Shirinian, Tamar. 2017. "Sovereignty as a Structure of Feeling: The Homosexual within Post–Cold War Armenian Geopolitics." *Lambda Nordica* (2–3): 93–124.

Shirinian, Tamar. 2018a. "A Room of One's Own: Woman's Desire and Queer Domesticity in the Republic." *Armenian Review* 56 (1–2): 60–90.

Shirinian, Tamar. 2018b. "Queer Life-Worlds in Postsocialist Armenia: *Alternativ* Space and the Possibilities of In/Visibility." *QED: A Journal in GLBTQ Worldmaking* 5 (1): 1–23.

Shirinian, Tamar. 2018c. "The Nation-Family: Intimate Encounters and Genealogical Perversion in Armenia." *American Ethnologist* 45 (1): 48–59.

Shirinian, Tamar. 2019. "Gender Hysteria: The *Other* Effect of Public Policy in Armenia." In *Sexuality, Human Rights, and Public Policy*, edited by Chima Korieh, 115–30. Lanham, MD: Fairleigh Dickinson University Press.

Shirinian, Tamar. 2020a. "Intimate Sovereigns: Patriarchy, the Fraternal Horde, and the Limits of Power in Armenia." *Cultural Dynamics* 32 (3): 213–29.

Shirinian, Tamar. 2020b. "Love and the Liminality of Revolution: Interpersonal Transformations in between the April–May Events in Armenia." *Anthropology and Humanism* 45 (2): 322–38.

Shirinian, Tamar. 2021a. "Political Patriarchy: Gendered Hierarchies, Paternalism, and Public Space in Armenia's 'Velvet Revolution.'" In *Armenia's Velvet Revolution: Authoritarian Decline and Civil Resistance in a Multipolar World*, edited by Laurence Broers and Anna Ohanyan, 181–200. London: I. B. Tauris.

Shirinian, Tamar. 2021b. "Post-War Spectres: The Ghosts that Haunt Armenia in the Aftermath of the 2020 Nagorno-Karabagh War." *Caucasus Analytical Digest* 121:9–15. https://doi.org/10.3929/ethz-b-000489488.

Shirinian, Tamar. 2021c. "The Illiberal East: The Gender and Sexuality of the Imagined Geography of Eurasia in Armenia." *Gender, Place and Culture* 28 (7): 955–74.

Shirinian, Tamar. 2022a. "To Foresee the Unforeseeable: LGBT and Feminist Civil Society and the Question of Feminine Desire." In *Gender, Power, and Nongovernance: Is Female to Male as NGO Is to State?*, edited by Andria D. Timmer and Elizabeth Wirtz, 240–63. New York: Berghahn Books.

Shirinian, Tamar. 2022b. "'We Don't Have a Daddy!': Marking Armenia's 2018 'Velvet Revolution' as a Site of Contesting Patriarchy." *Feminist Formations* 34(2): 125–42.

Simpson, Audra. 2014. *Mohawk Interruptus: Political Life across the Borders of Settler States*. Durham, NC: Duke University Press.

Simpson, Audra. 2020. "The Sovereignty of Critique." *South Atlantic Quarterly* 119 (4): 685–99.

Skedsmo, Pål Wilter 2019. *Armenia and Europe: Foreign Aid and Environmental Politics in the Post-Soviet Caucasus*. London: Bloomsbury.

Solty, Ingar, and Davit Stepanyan. 2015. "Post-democracy in Armenia? How the New Constitution Will Depoliticize Armenian Society." *openDemocracy.*, November 26, 2015. https://www.opendemocracy.net/en/can-europe-make-it/post-democracy-in-armenia-how-new-constitution-will-d/.

Spade, Dean. 2015. *Normal Life: Administrative Violence, Critical Trans Politics, and the Limits of Law.* Durham, NC: Duke University Press.

Stanley, Andrew. 2022. "Global Inequalities: The Big Picture on Wealth, Income, Ecological, and Gender Inequality Looks Bad." *Finance and Development,* March 2022. https://www.imf.org/en/Publications/fandd/issues/2022/03 /Global-inequalities-Stanley#:~:text=The%20poorest%20half%20of%20the ,half%20get%20just%208.5%20percent.

Stark, David, and Laszlo Bruszt. 1998. *Postsocialist Pathways: Transforming Politics and East and Central Europe.* Cambridge: Cambridge University Press.

Stenning, Allison, Adrian Smith, Alena Rochovska, and Dariusz Swiatek. 2010. *Domesticating Neo-liberalism: Spaces of Economic Practice and Social Reproduction in Post-socialist Cities.* Malden, MA: Wiley-Blackwell.

"Stepanavanum ttvayin drenajy aghed e" [Acid drainage in Stepanavan is a catastrophe]. *Epress.am,* July 8, 2020. https://epress.am/2020/07/08/1650-2.html.

Stout, Noelle M. 2014. *After Love: Queer Intimacy and Erotic Economies in Post-Soviet Cuba.* Durham, NC: Duke University Press.

Suchland, Jennifer. 2011. "Is Postsocialism Transnational?" *Signs: Journal of Women in Culture and Society* 36 (4): 837–62.

Suchland, Jennifer. 2018. "The LGBT Specter in Russia: Refusing Queerness, Claiming 'Whiteness.'" *Gender, Place and Culture* 25 (7): 1073–88.

Suny, Ronald G. 2006. "Nationalism, Nation-Making, and the Postcolonial States of Asia, Africa, and Eurasia." In *After Independence: Making and Protecting the Nation in Postcolonial and Postcommunist States,* edited by Lowell W. Barrington, 279–95. Ann Arbor: University of Michigan Press.

Swales, Stephanie S. 2012. *Perversion: A Lacanian Psychoanalytic Approach to the Subject.* New York: Routledge.

Swati, Gupta, Manveena Suri, and Julia Hollingsworth. 2020. "'They Tried to Stifle the Voices of Our Children': Meet the Women Protesters Who Have Been Occupying a New Delhi Street for a Month." CNN, January 14, 2020. https:// www.cnn.com/2020/01/14/asia/shaheen-bagh-muslim-intl-hnk/index.html

Ter-Ghazaryan, Diana K. 2013. "'Civilizing the City Center': Symbolic Spaces and Narratives of the Nation in Yerevan's Post-Soviet Landscape." *Nationalities Papers: The Journal of Nationalism and Ethnicity* 41 (4): 570–89.

Thelen, Tatjana. 2011. "Shortage, Fuzzy Property and Other Dead Ends in the Anthropological Analysis of (Post)socialism." *Critique of Anthropology* 31 (1): 43–61.

Thomson, Robert W. 1978. "Introduction." In *History of the Armenians,* by Moses Khorenatsi. Edited and translated by Robert W. Thomson, 1–61. Cambridge, MA: Harvard University Press.

Tlostanova, Madina, Suruchi Thapar-Bjorkert, and Redi Koobak. 2019. "The Postsocialist 'Missing Other' of Transnational Feminism?" *Feminist Review* 121 (1): 81–87. https://doi.org/10.1177/0141778918816946.

Trouillot, Michel-Rolph. 1995. *Silencing the Past: Power and the Production of History*. Boston: Beacon Press.

Tuck, Eve, and K. Wayne Yang. 2012. "Decolonization Is Not a Metaphor." *Decolonization: Indigeneity, Education, and Society* 1 (1): 1–40.

UNFPA. 2013. "93,000 Women to Be Missing in Armenia by 2060, if High Pre-natal Sex Selection Rate Remains Unchanged." *UNFPA Eastern Europe and Central Asia*, May 10, 2013. https://eeca.unfpa.org/en/news/93000-women-be-missing -armenia-2060-if-high-pre-natal-sex-selection-rate-remains-unchanged.

Verdery, Katherine. 1996. *What Was Socialism, and What Comes Next?* Princeton, NJ: Princeton University Press.

Visser, Oane, and Don Kalb. 2010. "Financialised Capitalism Soviet Style? Varieties of State Capture and Crisis." *European Journal of Sociology* 51 (2): 171–94.

Vosguian, Lelag. 2018. "An 'Unfinished Symphony': Professor Richard Hovannisian on the First Republic of Armenia and Its Legacy." *Horizon Weekly*, May 3, 2018. https://horizonweekly.ca/en/an-unfinished-symphony-professor-richard-g -hovannisian-on-the-first-republic-of-armenia-and-its-legacy/.

Walker, Christopher J. 1980. *Armenia: The Survival of a Nation*. New York: St. Martin's Press.

Warner, Michael. 2005. *Publics and Counterpublics*. New York: Zone Books.

Weber, Max. 1968. *Economy and Society: An Outline of Interpretive Sociology*. Vol. 1. New York: Bedminster.

Wedel, Janine. 2001. *Collision and Collusion: The Strange Case of Western Aid to Eastern Europe*. New York: St. Martin's Griffin.

Wiegman, Robyn, and Elizabeth A. Wilson. 2015. "Introduction: Antinormativity's Queer Conventions." *Differences: A Journal of Feminist Cultural Studies* 26 (1): 1–25.

Wolf, Eric. 1982. *Europe and the People without History*. Berkeley: University of California Press.

Wood, Ellen Meiksins. 2003. *Empire of Capital*. London: Verso.

Woodcock, Shannon. 2007. "The Absence of Albanian Jokes about Socialism, or Why Some Dictatorships Are Not Funny." In *The Politics and Aesthetics of Refusal*, edited by Caroline Hamilton, Will Noonan, Michelle Kelly, and Elaine Minor, 51–66. Newcastle, UK: Cambridge Scholars Press.

Woodcock, Shannon. 2011. "A Short History of the Queer Time of 'Post-socialist' Romania, or Are We There Yet? Let's Ask Madonna!" In *De-centering Western Sexualities: Central and Eastern European Perspectives*, edited by Joanna and Robert Kulpa Mizielinska, 63–84. London: Routledge.

World Bank. 2022. "Unemployment, Total (% of Total Labor Force) (Modeled ILO Estimate)—Armenia." *World Bank: Data*, accessed June 16, 2022. https://data .worldbank.org/indicator/SL.UEM.TOTL.zs?locations=AM.

World Bank. 2023. "Foreign Direct Investment, Net Inflows (BoP, Current US$)— Armenia." *World Bank: Data*, accessed August 14, 2023. https://data.worldbank .org/indicator/BX.KLT.DINV.CD.WD?locations=AM.

Ye, Shana. 2021a. "'Paris' and 'Scar': Queer Social Reproduction, Homonormative Division of Labour and HIV/AIDS Economy in Postsocialist China." *Gender, Place and Culture* 28 (12): 1778–98.

Ye, Shana. 2021b. "Queering 'Postsocialist Coloniality': Decolonising Queer Fluidity and Postsocialist Postcolonial China." In *Postcolonial and Postsocialist Dialogues: Intersections, Opacities, Challenges in Feminist Theorizing and Practice*, edited by Madina Tlostanova, Suruchi Thapar-Bjorkert, and Redi Koobak, 53–68. New York: Routledge.

Yernjakyan, Arthur. 2013. "Companies of Oligarchs and Functionaries in the Black List of Armenia's Finance Ministry." *ArmInfo*, August 26, 2013. https://arminfo .info/index.cfm?objectid=02A14080-0E58-11E3-81B30EB7C0D21663.

Yurchak, Alexei. 2005. *Everything Was Forever, Until It Was No More: The Last Soviet Generation*. Princeton, NJ: Princeton University Press.

Yurchak, Alexei. 2015. "Bodies of Lenin: The Hidden Science of Communist Sovereignty." *Representations* 129 (1): 116–57.

Yurchak, Alexei. 2017. "The Cannon and the Mushroom: Lenin, Sacredness, and Soviet Collapse." *HAU: Journal of Ethnographic Theory* 7 (2): 165–98.

Zakharov, Nikolay. 2015. *Race and Racism in Russia: Mapping Global Racisms*. New York: Palgrave Macmillan.

Zavisca, Jane R. 2012. *Housing the New Russia*. Ithaca, NY: Cornell University Press.

Zhang, Xudong. 2008. *Postsocialism and Cultural Politics: China in the Last Decade of the Twentieth Century*. Durham, NC: Duke University Press.

Zhurzhenko, Tatiana. 2001. "Ukrainian Feminism(s): Between Nationalist Myth and Anti-nationalist Critique." IWM Working Paper No. 4.

Zia, Ather. 2019. *Resisting Disappearance: Military Occupation and Women's Activism in Kashmir*. Seattle: University of Washington Press.

Žižek, Slavoj. 1989. *The Sublime Object of Ideology*. New York: Verso.

Zolyan, Suren. 2014. "The Daredevils of Sassoun: The Deep Structure of the Plot." *Studia Metrica et Poetica* 1 (1): 55–67.

Zolyan, Suren. 2016. "The Standoff in Yerevan." *openDemocracy*, July 20, 2016. https://www.opendemocracy.net/en/odr/standoff-in-yerevan/.

Index

Page numbers in italics refer to illustrations.

Armenia (*continued*)

offshore registration policies, 204; oldest leather shoe discovered in, 113–14, 120; as oppressed, 46, 78–79; as perverse nation, 14; as *pokr azg* (small nation), 3; practiced as family, 30–31, 238n13; Stalinist experience, 66–67; "there is no Armenia," 35, 164, 192; unemployment, 4, 12, 52, 142, 164, 167. *See also* annihilation of Armenia, discourse of; elections; emigration; family; Hayk (first Armenian); militarization; oligarchs, political-economic; oligarchy, political-economic (*oligarkhnere*); Symbolic order, Armenian; "Velvet Revolution" (2018); Yerevan, Armenia

Armenia Copper Program, 204

Armenian Apostolic Church, 3, 31, 61, 63, 157–58; and Gender Equality Law, 71; pocketed officials, 159; state cooperation with, 157

Armenian Diaspora, 3, 39

Armenian Election Study (2021), 119

Armenian Football Federation, 100, 102, 199

Armenian Language New Dictionary, 26

Armenian National Congress (ANC), 106–7, 212, 213

Armenianness: betrayal of, 79, 97, 113; as burden, 80; centrality of family to, 29–31; Genocide as structuring mythohistory of, 46; land, connection to, 182–83, 247n1; mourning the end of, 46, 185, 197; ontological transformations of, 166; passed down from father to son, 47–48; proper, 6–8, 24, 27, 47–48, 60, 63, 88, 98, 113, 161, 189, 192, 196–97, 215; sacralization and familialization of, 77–81; as singularity, 46, 60, 69, 76, 78–79, 81, 199, 227; singularity of resisted, 60, 76; as tied to place, 180–83, 247n1

ArmeniaNow, 156

Armenian Pan-National Movement (APNM), 52

Armenian Revolutionary Federation (ARF), 21, 54, 114, 198, 240n1; bailout of Khapa-

zian brothers, 57; *Yerkir Media* sponsored by, 23, 56, 77, 84, 86

Armenian Soviet Socialist Republic (SSR), 157, 202

Arshak the Great (King of Persia), 42

Artsakh, Republic of. *See* Nagorno-Karabakh

Artyan, Mika, 159

asignifying ruptures, 18, 166, 190

Aslanian, Sebouh David, 46, 78

Aslikyan, Lala, 62, 78–79

Asryan, Khachik, 90

Astourian, Stephen, 106

Austin, J. L., 208

authoritarianism: characteristics of Fathers, 225–26; "entrenched," 5; rejection of, 220–22

authority: performing, 208–12; state as outside moral, 113–19; tautological, 6. *See also* Symbolic authority

Avagyan, Shushan, 155

Avetisyan, Arsen, 101

Avetyan, Vahe, 101

ayl (other than, different), 25–26

Azerbaijan, 4–5; "44-Day War," 108, 152; Armenian war with, 4, 50–51; Khojaly massacre of Azerbaijanis, 5; pogrom against Armenians, 5, 40, 51, 78

azgaynakan (nationalist), 21

Babukhanyan, Hayk, 214

Badalyan, Anna, 170

Bangladesh, 145

Barev-olution (Hello Revolution), 215–20

Barthes, Roland, 38

Beglaryan, Arpi, 78

Bel (mythical tyrant), 37–38, 41–43, 63; Hayk positioned as losing to, 38, 60; resemblances of oligarchy to, 53–55

belonging: burden of, 80; of improper differents, 17, 24; queer sites of, 162; social, 40, 149, 251n13

Berlant, Lauren, 96, 97, 191

betrayal, 12, 79, 116, 176; and nicknames for oligarchs, 109–13, 120

Customs Committee, 110

Cvetkovich, Ann, 238n3

Daddy politics, 201, 207, 209; Daddy as affective structure, 224; future without political Daddy, 17, 35–36, 220–22, 223–34; Raffi's failure at, 218–20; "Serzh is not our daddy!" action, 195–96, 202; shift in dependence on, 209; structural problems displaced by, 231. *See also* Father, figure of

Danielyan, Mika, 155

Dark Ravens, 56–57

Davis, M., 200

Davis, Mike, 224

"decommunization laws," 156

Deleuze, Gilles, 18, 166, 184

Demirchyan, Karen, 54

democracy, 91, 116–17; national security pitted against, 5, 119; privatization as anti-democratic practice, 205; as spectacle, 106

depoliticization, 14, 18, 68, 155, 173, 229–30; of women, 233

desire: affective, for oligarchy, 123–24; as dangerous to Armenia, 79–80, 123; and feminist concerns, 20; for political Father, 209, 215, 224, 229–31; queer, 35, 71, 81, 141, 162

difference, 16, 60; as dangerous, 27; figurations of, 68–69; versus *Other*, 24–25

differents, 69, 76, 227; different, as noun, 24; improper belonging of, 17, 24; internal, 78

(dis)organized abandonment, 132–33, 141, 149–50, 161–62

distraction and suppression, tactics of, 89–90

Diversity March (Yerevan), attack on, 1–2, 3, 19–20, 55, 60–62; counterprotesters, 61–62, 70; and media attention to homosexuality, 84

DIY Pub (Yerevan): firebombing of, 1, 2, 3, 19, 22, 55–61, 83, 207; Hovhannisyan's visit to, 214; as site of alternative imaginaries, 55–56; trial, 22

domestic violence, 90, 142–43, 170–72, 247–49n3, 247n2

earthquake (1988), 40, 46, 51, 150, 213

Edelman, Lee, 82, 241n12, 251n14

Ekmekçioğlu, Lerna, 30

elections: 1996, 40, 52; 2008, 54, 106, 118, 155, 158, 165, 177–79, 202, 219; 2013, 35, 106–7, 179, 202, 213–20; June 2021, 108, 119; pro-Western positions, 214; rigged, 101, 106, 211–13; two Presidential inaugurations (2013), 215–20

#ElectricYerevan, 148, 199, 202

Elliott, Raffi, 236n27

emigration, 215; as choice for fathers who care about family, 167–70; fathers as migrant laborers, 17, 27, 72, 116, 206; by workers, 177–78. *See also* wandering

emo subculture, 61, 68

employment, 148–49

Eng, David L., 15

environmental activism, 148, 182, 203–7; "nationalist wing" of, 207; Save Teghut Civic Initiative, 203–4, 205

Epress.am news site, 80, 83

Erdoğan, Recep Tayyip, 225, 226, 227

Erebuni hostage incident (1873), 43–44

ethnonationalism, 52–53

ethnotrauma, 45, 239n6

Eurasian Economic Union, 2, 226

Europe, 13; anti-European sentiment, 71, 73–77, 85, 116, 214–15; Council of Europe, Armenian ascension to, 116–17; as "Gay-ropa," 75

European Delegation, 70–71

European Union, 2, 213, 226

executive branch (presidency), 106. *See also* elections

Explanatory Dictionary of Modern Armenian, 26

Factory District (Gortzaranayin), 144–45, *145*, 149–50247n2

family: Armenia practiced as, 30–31, 238n13; authorities (Fathers) as metonymic members of, 109–10, 169, 173; as base of Armenia, 163, 166; centrality of to Armenianness, 29–31; and domestic violence, 90, 142–43, 170–72, 247n2, 247–49n3; duty of all Armenians to preserve, 86–87; familialization of Armenianness, 79–81; as ideological container for survival, 29–30; masculinity of Father, 167–69; as nonexistent, 163; politicized analysis of, 186–90; queered by global inequality, 17–18; in ruin, 166–73; ruined by oligarchs, 167–70, 173; sexual perversion in caused by oligarchs, 168; "there are no families in Armenia" rhetoric, 163–67, 192; as tribe, 86–88; two notions of, 30–31. *See also* fathers; intimacy; kinship; nation-family (*azg*)

fantasy, 28, 31, 32, 82, 233, 236n10

fascism, 58–60, 79, 90

Father, figure of, 14; ambivalent feelings toward, 118; in Armenian kin relations, 17; castration, symbolic, 28, 32, 97, 246n28; forefathers [*mer papery*], 48, 165, 169; as function of superego, 31; Hayk as, 41, 47, 50, 98; illegitimacy of nation-family figures, 34–35, 109–13, 119, 173; Law of the Father, 29, 32, 98, 117, 133–39, 201; Lenin as, 156; losing respect for as loss of patriotism, 176–77; masculinity of, 41, 167; paternal function, 28; as sovereign power, 30–31. *See also* Daddy politics; Father, political; Hayk (first Armenian); Law of the Father; Name-of-the-Father; No-of-the-Father; Symbolic authority

Father, political, 17, 34; authoritarian, characteristics of, 225–26; desire for, 209, 215, 224, 229–31; as head of nation-family (*azg*), 30–31; intentions of, 215–20; and liberalism, 190–91; making future without, 17, 35–36, 197, 220–22, 223–34; moral focus as foreclosure of the political, 201; in other nations, 225–28; and perversion of life, 230–31; and populist movements, 225–27, 234; proper, 197, 217, 220. *See also* Father, figure of; illegitimacy; nation-family (*azg*)

fathers: Armenianness passed down from father to son, 47–48; failures of, 48–50; improper, 27–28, 72, 169–70; as key to Armenian survival, 29–30, 33, 220–21; made illegitimate, 169; masculinity of,

41, 167–72; as migrant laborers, 17, 27, 72, 116, 206; national reproduction based on, 46–47; oligarchs blamed by, 168–69; proper, 17, 47–50, 220–21. *See also* family

Fehlings, Susanne, 130, 140

feminism, 232–33; Armenian, history of, 30; conflicts between liberal and left-leaning activists, 20–21; French liberal tradition, 30; global socialist, 13; postsocialist, 13; targeted in Armenia discourses, 19; transnational and postcolonial, 13; Ukrainian queer and feminist movements, 13; Western liberal political agendas, 13; women's movement post World War I, 30

feudal structures, 10, 108

FIFA World Cup, 113–14

films, 25, 47–50

Finance Ministry report, 95

forefathers [*mer papery*], 48, 165, 169

foreign direct investment (FDI), 148

Foster, John Bellamy, 126–27

Founding Parliament group, 44

Franco, Marielle, 228

fraternal hordes, 12, 32, 105, 107, 124, 237n12; and boy child, 94; Freud's, 99; illegitimate, 35, 109–13

freedom, 81–86; and anxieties about homosexuality, 66–67, 78; of homosexual, 80–86, 88, 123–124; jealousy of homosexual, 80–81, 123–24; sacralization and familialization, 77–81; tolerance, views of, 84–85; and women's roles, 186

free market systems, 126, 129–30, 132

Freud, Sigmund, 25, 28, 31, 99, 236–37n10, 238n14

future: of an improper present, 192–94; humanity, valuing of, 185–86, 193–94; imaginaries of, 197, 223–24; mourning of, 166; potentiality of ruins, 180–84; present without, 177–80; reproductive futurism, 82, 251n14; as site of discipline, surveillance, and policing, 45–46; socialist realism established on, 150; unprecedented, 184–92; without political Daddy, 17, 35–36, 220–22, 223–34

Gal, Susan, 138

Galajyan, Hovhannes, 62, 63, 85–86, 115, 124

Gasparyan, Vova, 219

Gay Pride parade (Belgrade), 3

Gazprom, 148

gender: as contested term, 3, 69–72; gender-neutral pronoun *na*, 73; *genderot* (gender-like), 71; ideological project of Soviet Union, 186–87, 207; right-wing rhetoric of, 69–77; sexuality linked with, 70–71; "The Tale of Little Gender Boycott," 25, 65, 73–77, 79, 142, 144; transgender, rhetoric of, 3, 70–72, 86, 88. *See also* homosexual, figure of

"Gender Equality Law," 3, 69–72, 74

Genocide, Armenian, 3, 235n2, 240n1; denied by Ottoman Empire, 39; depopulation as continuation of, 167; family linked with survival of, 29–30; mythological position in collective consciousness, 39, 46; Nagorno-Karabakh war as "sequel," 5, 46, 78; Tsitsernakaberd, memorial at, 218; "Turk" as perpetrator of, 55; women's movement following, 30

"genocide, economic," 112–13

German Embassy, 3

Gevorgyan, Ruben, 68

Ghaplanyan, Irina, 96

Ghazaryan, Petros, 58

Ghodsee, Kristen, 13, 187

glasnost, 5, 39–40

global capitalism, 16–17, 126–27, 224–25, 229, 235n3

gomik ("homo"), 87–88

Gorbachev, Mikhail, 5

government: accused of fomenting dissent, 89–90; feelings about, 109–10; "national," 116, 245n23; seen as waging "class war" on citizens, 116. *See also* National Assembly; oligarchy, political-economic (*oligarkhnere*)

Graff, Agniezska, 70, 91

Great Patriotic War, 119

Great Purge of 1937, 67, 240n1

"Green Court" mock trial, 208–9

Gregory the Illuminator, Grigor Lusavorich, 43, 54

Grigoryan, Arthur, 205, 208

Grigoryan, Manvel, 100, 120, 121

Grigoryan, Ruzanna, 136–37

grzod (dirty or messy), 103

Guattari, Felix, 18, 166, 184

Gyumri (Leninakan), Armenia, 149–50

Hakhverdyan, Ruben, 66, 93, 128, 163

Hakobyan, Karen, 78–79, 90

Halberstam, Jack, 15

Halkların Demokratik Partisi (HDP), 227

Harsnakar restaurant murder, 101, 102, 199

Hartman, Saidiya, 163

Harutunyan, Gagik, 211

Harutyunyan, Hrachya, 249n6

Harvey, David, 132

Hayazn (nationalist organization), 1, 62, 70, 85, 116, 245n23; mock protest against, 113–15

Hayk (first Armenian), 25, 33; as both pater and genitor, 50; as Father of Armenians, 41, 47, 50, 98–99; Meschian's retelling of, 37–38, 50, 53, 54, 64; as Mets Hayk, or Larger Hayk, 42; myth of defeat of Bel in 2492 BC, 37–38, 41, 42–43; myth of split into multiplicities, 63–65; as Name-of-the-Father, 41, 69, 118, 124; power of usurped by elites, 96, 98–99, 101, 125; retelling of as loss to Bel, 38, 60; son and grandsons of, 43; values embodied by, 39, 41

Hayots Artsivner (Armenian Eagles), 90

Hayrapetyan, Ruben, 100–102, 199; as Nemets Rubo, 83, 100

hayrenaser (patriotic), 21, 73

Hayrik [Father] (film), 25, 47–50, 63

Hello Revolution (*Barev*-olution), 215–20

Herek, Gregory, 6–7

Heritage Party, 106–7, 179, 213, 214

heroes: Charents as, 66–67; fathers as, 33; mythic, 42–44

Herzfeld, Michael, 244n21

Hetq (left-of-center online press), 104

industrial sector, 51–52, 144–50

informal exchange, 125–26

Inknagir magazine, 67

Institute of Languages (National Academy of Sciences), 159

intergenerational debates, 151–52, 174–76

International Women's Day (March 8, 2013), 206

Inter RAO company, 148

intimacy, 191, 246–47n1; boy child in, 94; and expectations of others, 96–98, 124; Law of the Father based on, 117; national, 111, 187, 244n21; and nicknames for oligarchs, 33–34, 95, 99, 109; and Symbolic order, 30–31; and yards (*bak, baker*), 93–94. *See also* family

Investigative Committee of the Republic of Armenia, 101

Iravunk (right-wing media), 56, 62, 85–86, 115

Ishkanian, Armine, 30, 44, 187

Ishkhanyan, Vahan, 67

Istanbul Convention, 227

Italian Embassy, mock protest at (2013), 113–15, 117

Kalb, Don, 235n3

"Karabakh clan," 53

Karabakh movement, 52, 209–10

Karapetyan, Hrayr, 57

Kavanaugh, Brett, 228

Kchoyan, Navasard, 159

KGB (National Security Service, NSS), 89

Khapazian, Hampig, 57

Khapazian, Mgrdich, 57

Kharatyan, Lusine, 45, 64–65

Khorenatsi, Moses, 42, 45, 239n4

kings, Armenian, 42

kinship, 17, 97–98. *See also* family

Kligman, Gail, 138

Kocharyan, Robert (Robik), 53, 119, 130, 244–45n22; implementation of violence in Liberty Square, 155, 158

Kocharyan, Tigran, 59, 62–63, 68, 72, 89

Komaygi Children's Park, 88, 128

kompenzacija (exchange in kind), 126

Koobak, Redi, 13

Korolczuk, Elzbieta, 70, 91

Kurdistan, 227

Kurghinyan, Shushanik, 20

kyartus (macho street subculture), 75, 114–15, 145–46

Lacan, Jacques, 6, 28, 237n11, 238n14, 246n31

Lake Sevan, 141

"large businessmen" (*khoshor biznesmen*), 12

law, limits of, 124–27

law and order, 32, 98, 115, 209

"lawfare," 121–22

Law No. 57, "Protection of Equal Rights and Equal Opportunities for Women and Men," 3, 69–72, 74

Law of the Father, 29, 32, 98; based on intimacy, 117; politics of "No!" as chipping away at, 201; public (private), 133–39. *See also* Symbolic authority

Ledeneva, Alena, 125–26

left-wing politics, 20–21, 71, 84, 213; distraction tactics used against, 89–90. *See also* queer possibility and potential

Lem, Stanislaw, 140

Lenin, Vladimir, 156, 159; Leninism, 156; statue of, 154–57

Leninakan (now Gyumri), 40, 211

Libaridian, Gerard, 50

liberal economic theory, 123

liberalism, 20–21; Armenian, 190–91, 194

Liberty Square (Yerevan): as former site of national independence movement, 155, 202; Hovhannisyan inaugurated in, 216; Karabakh movement mock trial, 209–10; as leisure site, 155; rally against constitutional change (2015), 198–99, 202; violence of March 1, 2008, 118, 155, 158, 165, 219

life: capitalist destruction of, 4, 14–16, 130, 133, 136–37, 144; connected to green spaces of city, 136–37; as disorder, 132–33; feeling of meaninglessness, 133, 146–48, 160; focus on financial survival alone,

Nagorno-Karabakh, 4–6, 11, 79; "44-Day War," 108, 152; 2020 resurgence of conflict, 40; privatization made possible by, 51–52; as "sequel" to Genocide, 5, 46, 78

Nagorno-Karabakh Autonomous Oblast (NKAO), 4–5, 157

Name-of-the-Father, 31–32, 34; Hayk as, 41, 69, 118, 124; split from No-of-the-Father, 97–98, 209, 226. See also Father, figure of; Names-of-the-Fathers; nicknames

Names-of-the-Fathers, 31, 93–127, 238n14; and limits of law, 124–27; Names-of-the-(Illegitimate)-Fathers, 109–13; "nicking" of by use of nicknames, 97, 99–109; state authority outside moral authority, 113–19; surplus enjoyment of, 120–24, 228. See also Name-of-the-Father; nicknames; oligarchs, political-economic

National Assembly, 3, 54–55, 103, 106; "Gender Equality Law" passed by, 3, 69–72, 74

national identity, 39–40, 53, 79, 157

national intimacy, 111, 187, 244n21

nationalism: ethnonationalism, 52–53; as form of resistance against crises, 91; forms of in Armenia, 21; as sickness, 58–59; turned inward, 78. See also right-wing nationalists

national reproduction, 33, 45–47

National Revival movement, 30

national security, 5, 57–58, 119, 157

National Security Service, 121

national state time, 63

nation-family (azg), 16, 30–31, 175, 187, 191, 237–38n13, 244n21; authorities (Fathers) as metonymic members of, 109–10, 169, 173; burden of belonging to, 80; domestic violence against women in, 171; symbolic violence against, 109–10. See also family; Father, political

negation: as affirming, 200–201, 215, 235n5; as idiomatic style in Armenian language, 164; and politics of "No!," 200; of present, 165–66, 179–80; as site of opportunity,

185; temporality of, 35; "there are no families in Armenia," 163–67, 192; "there is no Armenia," 35, 164, 192

negativity, 18, 235n5; queer, 221

Nemets Rubo. See Hayrapetyan, Ruben

neoliberalization, 11; brutality linked to, 228; gender anxieties fueled by, 70; imagination devastated by, 200; as incomplete process, 11; informal networks as result of, 126; logics of built spaces, 150–52; social reproduction under, 82; of urban development, 150–52, 160–61. See also capitalism

nicknames, 33–34, 242n2; attempts at distancing from, 103; and betrayal, 109–13, 120; bifurcation of oligarchs through, 33–34, 97–98; criminality implied by, 102–4; first names used instead of last names, 99–100; (nick)names for boy children, 94–95; Nemets Rubo, 99–102; as "nicking" of authority figure, 97, 99–109; obscene, 107; refusal of, 108–9; suffix—ik (diminutive), 96; suffix—o (intimacy or innocence), 96

nomenklatura, Soviet-era, 96

nongovernmental organizations (NGOs), 20–21, 187, 204

No-of-the-Father, 31–32, 34, 237n11, 238n14; politics of "No!" as response to, 201–2; refusal of, 199, 221–22; split from Name-of-the-Father, 97–98, 209, 226; threats as function of, 105. See also Father, figure of

"No!," politics of, 35–36, 38, 195–222; 2013 post–presidential election protests, 212–15; acting as if as refusal, 208–9, 216; agency and sovereignty of, 199; anti-Daddy politics, 196; and Barev-olution (Hello Revolution), 215–20; enactments of death of the present, 210–11; of the feminist and the queer, 233–34; grassroots emergences, 202–7; "Green Court" mock trial, 208–9; "Hima!"—Now!, 217–18; making future without a Father, 35–36, 220–22; "Mashtots Park" movement, 203–7; negation as necessary, 200, 251n13;

"No!" (*Voch!*) movement, 198–202; performing authority, 208–12; and political imagination, 200–201, 204; as queer politics, 201–2; refusal, politics of, 64, 199, 208–9, 216, 221–22; as style and aesthetics of the political, 195, 199. *See also* activism; protests

"No to the Pillagers!" (*Voch Talanin!*), 199
Nzhdeh, Garegin, 52

Obama, Barack, 230
Oganezova, Tsomak, 2, 56–60, 77
oligarchs, political-economic: as alien colonizers, 113; as brutal figures, 33–34; churches built by, 105, 157–59; as committing "economic genocide," 112–13; conflation of with figure of homosexual, 27–29, 55–56, 87–88, 125; "counter-elite," 96; criminality associated with, 100–104, 113, 117–21, 127; demand for recognition, 158–59; domestic violence blamed on, 172; failures of fatherhood blamed on, 168–69; families ruined by, 167–70, 173; freedom of, 88; *gomik* ("homo") applied to, 87–88; Hayk's power usurped by, 96, 98–99, 101, 125; homosexual figure made possible by perversions of, 143–44; homosexual figure used to displace political-economic discussions, 6, 33, 82–83; homsosexuality attributed to, 34, 87–88, 91, 95–96; lack of "culturedness" and education, 96, 103–4, 107; moral perversion (*aylandakutyun*) of, 4, 8, 23, 28–29, 55, 95–96, 143–44; as oppressors, 83; philanthropy by, 105; responsibilities of, 121–24; from rural or peasant backgrounds, 96, 103–4; sexual perversion attributed to, 34, 87–88, 91, 95–96; sexual perversion said to be caused by, 168; social reproduction ruined by, 192–93; strategic positions held by, 96; surplus jouissance of, 27–28, 120–24, 196, 228; surplus value exploited by, 121–22. *See also* Names-of-the-Fathers
oligarchy, political-economic (*oligarkhnere*):

affective desire held for, 123–24; capitalist economic violence by, 4, 7; as elite fraternal horde, 12, 32; enrichment of by war, 51–53; feudal structures formed by, 10; fragility of, 32, 209; homophobia used by to displace political-economic discussions, 6, 33, 82–83; monopolies held by, 2, 11, 12, 52, 54, 104, 110–12, 120–23, 167; moral perversion of (*aylandakutyun*), 4, 8, 23, 55, 95–96, 143–44; new class of owners, 51–52; oligarchic capitalism, 11–12; performative and constative dimensions of, 209; and "pro rata" system, 51; state capture by, 4, 10, 12, 52; theft of commons by, 164; violence by, 121–22
One Nation Union (Mek Azg Dashink), 62, 68, 214
"oppressors," 83–84
"organized abandonment," 34, 132, 140–41
Oswin, Natalie, 17
Other, 24–25, 38, 61, 237n11, 238n14
Ottoman Empire, 3, 240n1; denial of Genocide, 39; Young Turks, 214. *See also* Genocide, Armenian
Oushakine, Sergei, 239n6

Pak Shuka (Closed Market), 104–5, 150
Panossian, Razmik, 52
Parada (film, Dragojevic), 3
Parajanov, Sergei, 67
parks and public places, 34
Pashinyan, Ashot, 108–9, 119
Pashinyan, Nikol, 108, 196, 231, 245n22, 250n5; and "Velvet Revolution," 202–3
paternal function, 28, 237n11
Persian Empire, 174–75
personal networks, 125–26
perverse time, 39–40
perversion: absence of Lenin's statue as, 156–57; affirmed by politics of "No!," 201–2; analysis based on, 224; beyond Armenia, 225–27; of capitalism, 9, 16, 34; colloquial feelings about in Armenia, 26–27, 29, 53; English meanings of, 26;

perversion (*continued*)

figures of, 28–29; free market systems as, 132; homosexuality targeted by rhetoric of, 19–21; as norm, 16; in psychoanalytic thought, 28; psychoanalytic view of, 28–29, 236–37n10, 237n11; queer side of, 161; radical spatiotemporal possibilities of, 16–18, 133, 161–62, 196–97; real forms of, 9, 14; as a rhetoric, 235n5; surplus enjoyment as, 27–28, 81, 196; types of, 25–29. *See also* moral perversion (*aylandakutyun*); sexual perversion (*aylaserutyun*)

Peterson, V. Spike, 17

philanthropy, by oligarchs, 105

photography, 210

Pincet (punk band), 56

Plakhotnik, Olga, 13

Platz, Stephanie, 53–54, 246n1

police: attacks on emo subculture, 61, 68; and protesters, 195, 203–04, 208, 216, 218–19

political economy: *blat* (use of personal networks), 125–26; displaced by morality, 6, 33, 82–83, 89–90, 225, 229; domestic violence blamed on, 171–72; perverse, 161–62; queering of, 8–19; statements of negation about, 165

political parties, modern formation of, 50

populist movements, 91, 225–27, 234

Postanjyan, Zaruhi, 210–11, 245n27

postsocialism: as constant crisis, 4–8; *man gal* (searching) in, 132; perverse qualities of, 14, 16, 34; as processual worlding, 10–11; public/private binaries in contexts of, 138; rhythms of spaces, 153–59; spatiality of, 2–3, 10, 34–35, 41; and transformation, 9–10

postsocialist studies, 9–15, 125–26

Pravda (Truth), burial of copies of, 211

"prefigurative" politics, 200

present: 2008 as past, 177–78; "brokendown," 200; emptying of tradition, 173–77; enactments of death of, 210–11; families in ruin, 166–73; futures of an improper, 192–94; hyperpresentism,

106, 192, 217; impossibility, orientation toward, 179–80; improper, 163–94, 220; movement "toward," 184; negations of, 165–66, 179–80; with no future, 177–80; as perverse, 127, 185; "politics of," 200; as "proper," 182; rejection of, 200–201; resignifying of, 180–82, 185, 190; ruins, potentiality of, 180–84; as unlivable, 35; and unprecedented future, 184–92

Presidential Palace (Yerevan), 214, 216, 218

Pride March (Istanbul), 56, 60

privatization, 4; as antidemocratic practice, 205; continued forms of socialist allocation, 9–10; demolition of public spaces, 104–5; made possible by war, 51–52; political-economic issues of displaced onto homosexual, 82–83; precarity caused by, 165; public amenities decreased by, 54; of public space, 133–39. *See also* urban development

propriety (proper), 16; of Armenianness, 6–8, 24, 27, 47–48, 60, 63, 88, 98, 113, 161, 189, 192, 196–97, 215; as concept, 16; expectations of national, 23, 79–80, 88; and expectations of others, 6, 8, 18, 20, 23, 30–31, 69, 79, 96, 98–99, 117, 124–25; of fathers, 17, 47–50, 220–21; multiplicity of dimensions, 184; resignification of, 180–82, 185, 190; of social reproduction, 33–35, 81, 128; as superego, 31. *See also* impropriety (improper)

"pro rata" system, 51

Prosperous Armenia Party (Bargavach Hayasdan), 105–7

protests: 1996, 52; 2008, 54, 118, 202; by ARF, October 27, 1999, 54; earlier forms of, 52–53; #ElectricYerevan, 148, 199, 202; March 1, 2008 violence in Liberty Square, 118, 155, 158, 165, 177–78, 219; mock protest at Italian Embassy (2013), 113–15, 117; police involvement, 195, 203–4, 208, 216, 218–19; *Pravda* (Truth), burial of copies of, 211; by "troika" of parties (2014), 107; "We Pay 100 Dram" movement, 203. *See also* activism; "No!," politics of

Pshenychnykh, Anastasiya, 156
psychoanalytic theory, 28–32, 236–37n10, 238n14, 246n28
Puar, Jasbir K., 7, 15
Public Information and Need for Knowledge (PINK), 19–20, 61, 89, 90; Botanical Garden event, 140; at European Delegation event, 70–71
public space: commons, abandonment of, 138; familiarization of Armenianness, 79–80; and Law of the Father, 133–39; London, 137; privatization of, 133–39; queer refuge in, 133, 139–44; rupture of connection to life, 136–37; yards (*bak, baker*), 93–94. *See also* space; urban development
public transportation costs, 11, 54, 203, 250n4
punctum, 38
punk rockers, 78
Putin, Vladimir, 225, 226, 228, 230
Putin regime, 89–90

queer desire, 35, 71, 81, 141, 162
queering of spatiotemporality, 8–19, 133
Queering Yerevan Collective (QYC), 19, 22, 155
queerness: as antisocial position, 82; as concept and conceptual framework, 15–18; and perverse wandering-as-ontology, 161; political economy, queering of, 8–19; queer negativity, 221; queer social reproduction, 232–34; transformation, possibilities for, 18, 20–21; as unintended consequence of global inequality, 17–18
queer possibility and potential, 16–18, 32, 160–62; within abandonment, 161–62, 165; *alternativ* spaces, 128–29, 141–42; within impropriety, 189–90; need for affirmation of, 141, 144; through excess, 141–42; "woman's mentality" and leadership strengths, 183–84. *See also* left-wing politics
queer theory, 11, 92, 235n5; of political economy, 8–19; "subjectless" approach, 15
queer time, 39–40, 63–64

rabiz music, 146
racial supremacy: Armenian, 52, 87; Russian, 249n6
"The Rapist Is You!" movement, 232
Rashtriya Swayamsevak Sangh (RSS) movement, 227
Red Apple tradition, 68, 188, 191
refusal, politics of, 64, 199, 208–9, 216, 221–22
religious minorities, 61
reproduction: as decision belonging to nation, 80–81; demand to have children, 80; at heart of political economy, 8; as inseparable from material production, 14; kinship as site of, 97; national, 33, 45–46; "reproductive futurism," 82, 251n14; "scientific" stories about, 87. *See also* social reproduction
Republican Party of Armenia, 37, 53, 105–7, 115, 118, 184; constitutional referendum (2015), 198–99, 202; ousted from power (2018), 40
Republic Square (Yerevan), 153–56; Lenin's statue, 154–55, 156; public discussion about development, 155–56
"Revolution of Dignity" (2014), 156
"Revolution of Love and Solidarity," 202
right-wing nationalists, 2–3; anti-European sentiment of, 71, 73–77, 85, 116, 214–15; anti-Muslim sentiments, 73; children's lives ignored by, 81–82; conspiratorial logic, 71; defined, 21; differences between, 62–63; gender, rhetoric of, 69–77; government positioned as foreign occupiers by, 55; *hayrenaser* (patriotic), 21, 73; homosexuality as focus of, 7, 86; "human rights" seen as dangerous by, 21, 85; morality emphasized over law, 115–16; NGOs targeted by, 21; religious minorities targeted by, 61; Russia not criticized by, 63; sex panic of 2012–13, 3, 32–33, 68, 70, 89–90; skinhead movement, 89–90; survival rhetoric prompted by, 80; Western values opposed by, 63. *See also* Hayazn (nationalist organization); nationalism

ruins: families in ruin, 166–73; potentiality of, 180–84; residential buildings and homes as, 35

ruptures: asignifying, 18, 166, 190; Daddy politics produced through, 224; postsocialist period as, 10, 33; of public space, 136–37; radical possibilities of, 15–18, 133, 161–62, 196–97

Russell, James, 67

Russia: Armenians in, 249n6; colonialism, 13–14; energy company ownership, 148; Eurasianism, 2, 226; feudal structures formed in, 10; "Gayropa" discourse, 75; under Putin, 226; restoration of Soviet-era statues in, 156–57; Ukraine, invasion of, 129

sacralization of Armenianness, 77–81

Saint Anna Church (Yerevan), 159

"Same City" (Meschian), 128

Sargsyan, Alexander (Sashik), 95

Sargsyan, Alik, 68

Sargsyan, Nelli, 200

Sargsyan, Serzh, 44, 54, 95, 106–8, 245n22; burned in effigy, 211; Church, emphasis on, 157, 159; and constitutional referendum (2015), 106, 198–99, 202; legitimating names for, 117–18; nicknamed Serzhik, 106, 120, 244n19; reelection of, 179; resignation of, 196, 250n5; and rigged elections, 212; second inauguration of, 215–16; "Serzh is not our daddy!" action, 195–96, 202

Sargsyan, Vazgen, 54

Sarukhanyan, Nelli, 72–73

Sasna Tzrer (Darevevils of Sassoun) (epic poem), 25, 43–45, 64–65, 239n5

Sasna Tzrer group, 43–45

Sassoun (Armenian village), 44

Save Teghut Civic Initiative, 203–4, 205

Schneider, David, 97

Seely, Stephen D., 241n12

Sefilian, Jirair, 44

self-determination, 5, 78–79, 116, 245n24

ser, seril (to generate), 25–26

sex panic (2012–13), 3, 32–33, 68, 70; Tigran Kocharyan as epicenter of, 89–90

sexuality: activism around, 201, 206–7; discourse of intertwined with political-economic conditions, 33, 82; gender linked with, 70–71; in psychoanalytic thought, 28, 236n10; public life of, 92; as site of social and biological reproduction, 14–15, 90–92

sexual perversion (aylaserutyun), 3, 7, 9, 23, 25–29, 33; 4504 (2012) as year of, 55–63; Armenian meanings of, 26; attributed to oligarchs, 34, 87–88, 91, 95–96; aylaserel (verb form), 26; caused by oligarchs, 168; meanings of, 25–26; moral perversion of, 86–88; as new Bel, 63; overlaps with aylandakutyun, 27–29, 34, 72, 86–88, 91, 123, 225, 232; as threat of convenience, 63; translation of aylaserutyun, 25–26

Shagoyan, Gayane, 103

Sharmazanov, Eduard, 57

Shurnukh (village), 3

Singapore, 17

"singing fountains" (yergogh shatrvanner) of Republic Square, 153–54

singularity: Armenianness as, 46, 60, 69, 76, 78–79, 81, 199, 227; collective "We" as, 46

Skedsmo, Pål Wilter, 204

socialism, 10–11, 13–14, 126, 186–87, 210–11; statue of Lenin, 154–57

socialist realism, 150

social reproduction: anxieties fueled by neoliberalization, 70; Armenian feminist views, 30; generalized anxieties about, 6, 196; linked with biological reproduction, 90–92; under neoliberalization, 82; within production, 16; proper, 33–35, 81, 128; queer, 232–34; ruined by oligarchs, 192–93. See also reproduction

Society Without Violence, 19–20

Solaris (Lem), 140

sovereign time, 39–40

sovereignty: and Symbolic order, 30–31; territorialized, 50

Soviet Union: "alternative modernity," ide-

temporality, 34–35; mythic time, 63–65; national state time, 63; perverse time, 39–40; queer time, 39–40, 63–64; sovereign time, 39–40. *See also* space; spatiotemporality

Ter-Petrosyan, Levon, 40, 52, 96, 107, 212–13, 243n8, 244n16; as "Levon the Terminator," 54

Tert.am blog, 67, 72

Thapar-Bjorkert, Suruchi, 13

Theater Square. *See* Liberty Square (Yerevan)

Thelen, Tatjana, 11

"This is Yerevan" (Hakhverdyan), 93

threatening figures, 68–69

Tlostanova, Madina, 13

tradition, emptying of, 173–77

transformation, 152, 190; moral, 187, 190; political-economic, 9–11, 18, 34, 127, 165–66, 223–24; queer possibilities for, 18, 20–21

transgender, rhetoric of, 3, 70–72, 86, 88

transition, versus transformation, 9–11

"traumatic departure," history as, 39

Trdat, King, 43

tribe (*tsegh*), 86–87

trickle-down effect of elite perversions, 27

Trouillot, Michel-Rolph, 238n1

Trump, Donald, 225, 226–27, 228, 230–31

Turk, figure of, 1, 55, 113, 239n6, 245n22

Turkey, 78, 226–27

Tzarukyan, Gagik, 105–7, 110, 120–21, 158; nicknamed Dodi Gago, 105, 107, 120

Tzarukyan, Nikolay, 107

Ukraine, 129, 156

uncanny, the, 53, 54, 150

unconscious, 39, 41, 77, 91, 98

unemployment rates, 52

United States, 13; Black Lives Matter movement, 232; Capitol insurrection, 2021, 228, 230; Democratic Party politics, 230; under Trump, 226–27, 228, 230

urban development: construction booms, 152; (dis)organized, 132, 160; "image spamming," 137, 140; meaninglessness of, 150–51; neoliberal logics of, 150–52, 160–61; spaces of life cut off by, 130; *zargatsum* (development, progress, enlightenment), 151. *See also* abandonment, logics of; capitalism; privatization; public space

Urvagitz (television show), 58–59

Vagharshak, King, 42

Vanadzor (Kirovakan), Armenia, 149

"Velvet Revolution" (2018), 40, 106, 108, 245n22; decentralized form of, 202–3; Grigoryan's estate entered after, 121; illegitimacy of the Fathers as reason for, 124; resignation of Sargsyan, 196, 250n5; Sargsyan's acceptance of prime minister nomination, 202

Verdery, Katherine, 10

Victims of State Needs (NGO), 130

wandering: *man gal* (to wander, to stroll, to search), 131–32, 154; queer and perverse, 160–62; *zbosnel* (going for a walk), 131. *See also* migration

"Washington Consensus," 4

wealth inequality, 121–22, 126, 251n1; and building of churches, 158–59

"We," collective, 24, 45–46, 111

"We Pay 100 Dram" movement, 203

Western capitalist institutions, 4, 10

whiteness, nationalist, 13, 249n6

Wiegman, Robyn, 16

Wilson, Elizabeth A., 16

women: in aftermath of Genocide, 30; depoliticization of, 233; in IT sector, 187; leadership qualities of, 182–84; as NGO leaders and staff, 187; in Soviet system, 186–87; as workers, 186

Women's Department (*Zhenodtel*) (Soviet Union), 186

Women's Resource Center (WRC), 19–20, 60, 68, 90

Woodcock, Shannon, 10

World Bank, 4, 51

worlding, 10–11, 16–18, 196–97
World War I, 30
"wound culture," 47

yards (*bak, baker*), 93–94
Yerevan, Armenia: *akhberutyuns* (brotherhoods), 105; "Bangladesh" neighborhood
(Malatia-Sebastia), 145; Botanical Garden (Busabanakan Aygi), 139–41, 144, 162;
Central Spot as *alternativ* space, 128–29;
city as a park, 136–38; Erebuni hostage
incident (1873), 43–44; Factory District
(Gortzaranayin), 144–45, *145*, 149–50; free
market spaces in, 129–30; as "garden city,"
132; Hrazdan Canyon (*dzor*, Mashtots Avenue), 141, 142–44, 162; Liberty Square, 54,
107, 155, 198–99, 202, 210, 214, 216–18; Lovers' Park (Baghramyan Avenue), 133–35,
135, *136*, 138–39; Mashtots Avenue, 203;
Monument neighborhood, 153; Northern
Avenue, redevelopment of, 128–31, *131*,
152–53; Presidential Palace, 214, 216, 218;
queer city, 128, 133; queer refuge in public
parks, 133, 139–44; "real," 130–31; Republic
Square, 153–55; spatial configurations of,
34; tourism, 152–53; wandering in, 129–32,
154, 160–62; Yerord Mas neighborhood,
144–46, *145*. *See also* Armenia
Yerevan Writer's Union, 2
Yerkir Media, 23, 56, 77, 84, 86
Yesayan, Zabel, 20
Young Turks (Ottoman Empire), 214
Yurchak, Alexei, 156

Zakharov, Nikolay, 249n6
Zolyan, Suren, 239n5